THE BORGIA
CHRONICLES

THE BORGIA

CHRONICLES

Mary Hollingsworth

CONTENTS

Introduction   6

Alonso de Borja
From royal secretary to servant of Rome
1414–1455   8

Calixtus III
The first Borgia pope
1455–1458   44

The Borgia nephews
Cardinals and captain-generals
1458–1471   72

Rodrigo Borgia
New titles, new relationships, new wealth
1471–1484   110

Rodrigo Borgia
From eminence to pre-eminence
1484–1492   136

TITLE PAGE IMAGE *Scenes from the papal coronation of Emperor Frederick III in Rome, 1452 (detail), tempura on panel, painted by Giovanni di Ser Giovanni Guidi (1406–86).*

Alexander VI
The second Borgia pope and his family

1493–1497   174

Alexander VI, Cesare and Lucrezia
A pope, a warrior and a widow

1498–1500   230

Cesare and Lucrezia Borgia
Conquests in battle and in love

1501–1503   272

Cesare and Lucrezia Borgia
The duke and the duchess

1503–1519   318

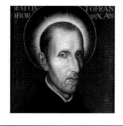

The Borgia descendants
Dukes, cardinals and saints

1520 and after   354

Maps 374 The Borgia dynasty – a family tree 376
Bibliography and Notes on the text 378 Index 380
Picture credits and Acknowledgements 384

INTRODUCTION

The Borgias – a family and its reputation

THE BORGIA LEGEND has fascinated and appalled down the centuries. Even while the family was still at the zenith of its power, the Borgia name had become a byword for cruelty and depravity. They were admired by Machiavelli for their ruthlessness and audacity, but most Renaissance Italians were outraged by the reports of their immoral behaviour that swept, colourfully, across the peninsula. Despite the fact that many of the more lurid stories were later proved to be lies, spread in anger and revenge by their enemies, the rumours had, by then, all but hardened into fact.

Thus we have our impression that the Borgia family is a Renaissance version of the Corleone clan in Mario Puzo's *The Godfather*, and we continue to be mesmerized by the elements of the tale: the unscrupulous means by which Rodrigo Borgia was elected Pope Alexander VI and then exploited his position to advance his children, notably Cesare and Lucrezia, as well as his wider family; his extortionate greed; the unparalleled corruption at the heart of Alexander's pontificate; the brutal elimination of rivals by assassination, execution and poison; the incestuous relationships between father and daughter, and between brother and sister. Not surprisingly, there was even talk of supernatural pacts with the Devil. The Borgia legend has not only spawned numerous historical accounts of the family, of varying degrees of accuracy, but also inspired writers of romantic fiction, poets, dramatists, painters and musicians – Donizetti's opera *Lucrezia Borgia* (1833) was based on a play by Victor Hugo, while Puzo's last novel, *The Family*, was based on the Borgia myth, incest and all. The legend continues to spawn offspring in modern popular culture – the more recent additions embracing films and television series, not to mention *manga* comics and even a video game, *Assassin's Creed*.

In truth, the Borgia family did not behave so very differently from those other famous Renaissance papal dynasties, such as the Medici or the Farnese, all of whom were guilty of similarly brutal strategies – and accused by their enemies of similarly lurid crimes – in their ruthless pursuit of power in the Church. All were guilty of the shameless promotion of often undeserving sons, daughters and other relations. The fact that Pope Alexander VI had children was hardly unique. Many churchmen ignored the rule of celibacy: it has been estimated that as many as a third of Rome's College of Cardinals had mistresses and children, and all would have been aware of the chapel in St Peter's that was dedicated to St Petronilla, the daughter of the first pope. Very few Renaissance popes can be seen as spiritual leaders; indeed, most preferred to behave like secular princes, playing an active and decisive role in the complex politics of the period. They also opted for splendour, displaying their power and prestige with a level of ostentation that was deeply offensive to those ordinary Christian men and women who had been reared on the biblical account of the simple life of Christ and his Apostles.

Above all, it is important to remember that the context in which the papacy operated – Renaissance society – was widely corrupt. Rome itself acted as a magnet for the greedy and ambitious, who flocked to this city where everything was for sale at the right price, from a modest post in the papal administration to a cardinal's hat. Renaissance society was also violent: petty thieves and forgers were routinely executed, their last moments watched by bloodthirsty crowds; assassins frequently ended the lives of kings and cardinals; turbulent riots were commonplace; husbands poisoned their wives on suspicion of adultery; many soldiers were killed in battle and many women died in childbirth.

So why does the Borgia family have such an *enduringly* infamous reputation? The most obvious answer is that they were foreign. After Alexander VI's death in 1503 only one other non-Italian occupied the papal throne – Adrian VI (1522–23), a Dutchman of unblemished piety and austerity – before the election of John Paul II in 1978. Unlike the home-grown papal dynasties, the Borgias had neither descendants nor compatriots to act as their protective guardians in Italy, to nurture, embellish and reinvent their historical image, and to gloss over their undeniable faults. By contrast, both the Medici and Farnese families have reputations built up carefully over the years that present them as wise rulers and cultured connoisseurs, the latter important in a country that has, for centuries, taken considerable pride in its cultural heritage.

Yet it is precisely this lack of a reinvented image that makes the story of the Borgia family so fascinating. Viewing the Renaissance through the prism of this family gives us a more accurate account of the papacy at this critical period in its history, and of life in Renaissance Italy, in all its shame and glory.

Alonso de Borja

FROM ROYAL SECRETARY TO SERVANT OF ROME

1414–1455

It was the proud boast of the Borja family of Játiva that they could trace their lineage back to the legendary rulers of the Kingdom of Aragon. History does not reveal whether this was true or not, but the family did owe its aristocratic status to King Jaime I of Aragon, known as 'the Conqueror', who had ennobled Esteban de Borja in gratitude for his role in the expulsion of the Moors from Valencia in 1240. The family seat of Játiva, the gift of Jaime I, was a hill town some 40 miles south of Valencia, which dated back to the Roman Empire. It was dominated by the Borja castle.

Alonso de Borja was born on 31 December 1378, a day that marked the end of a disastrous year in the history of the papacy.

AROUND 1375, DOMINGO DE BORJA, from a cadet branch of the family living at Torre del Canals, married Francina Martì. Their first two children were daughters: Catalina, who became betrothed to Baron Juan de Milà, and Juana, who went on to marry a cousin on her mother's side of the family.[1] Francina went on to produce two more daughters: Francisca, who became a nun, and Isabella, for whom Domingo found a prestigious husband in the shape of Jofrè de Borja, the eldest son of the main branch of the family.

Between the two sets of daughters, however, Francina gave birth to a son. Alonso de Borja was born on 31 December 1378, a day that marked the end of a disastrous year in the history of the papacy. The Great Schism, which split the Church and saw competing pontiffs struggle for supremacy, was to last for over fifty years.

In 1392, at the age of 14, Alonso was sent to the prestigious Catalan university at Lérida to study canon and civil law, subjects at which he excelled, and he was appointed a lecturer after finishing his studies. At Lérida he also came to the attention of Pedro de Luna, the Catalan noble who had succeeded the Avignon pope Clement VII in 1394 and

PREVIOUS PAGE **Alonso da Borja,** *see page 32.*

RIGHT **King Jaime I of Aragon.** *This vellum page of the Vidal Mayor manuscript (c.1290–1310) shows the king receiving the codification of his kingdom's laws from Vidal de Canellas, Bishop of Huesca. The cultured Jaime I (ruled 1213–76) substantially enlarged his state with the conquest of Barcelona, Valencia and the Balearic Islands. One of his most prestigious projects was the cathedral at Lérida, where Alonso de Borja would acquire his first benefice.*

OVERLEAF **Pope Gregory XI returns to Rome,** *as painted by Benvenuto di Giovanni (1436–1518). Gregory XI (1370–78) was determined to return the papacy to Rome, from Avignon. Political considerations delayed the move – not least the Hundred Years War between France and England, violent uprisings in the Papal States and an empty treasury. He was ultimately convinced by the personal appeal of a young Dominican, St Catherine of Siena, seen here in her black and white habit.*

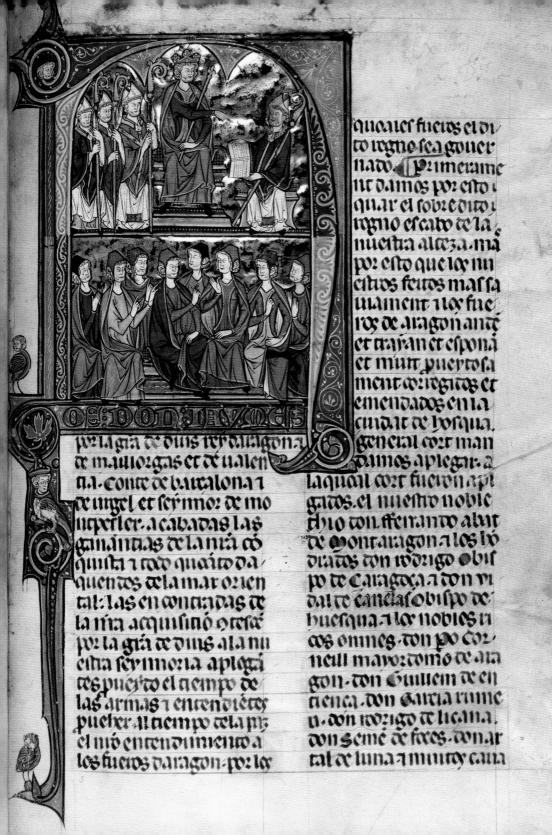

quoales fueros el di
cto regno sea gouer
nado. Primerament
damos por esto i
quar el sobredicto i
regno escado de la
nuestra alteza: ma
por esto que los nu
estros feitos mas sa
uiament los fue
ros de aragon ante
et trayan et espona
et mujt puertosa
ment corregidos et
emendados en la
ciudat de huesqua.
general cort man
damos aplegar: a
la qual cort fueron apl
gados. el nuestro noble
tho con fferando abat
de montaragon: a los hó
drados con rodrigo obis
po de caragoca. a don vi
dal te canelas obispo de
huesqua: a los nobles ri
cos ommes. con po cor
nell mayordomo de ara
gon. con Guillem de en
tienca. con garcia rume
u. don rodrigo te licana.
don seme de feces. don ar
tal de luna i mujtos cana

OS DON IAYMES
por la gra te dius rey daragon.
de mallorgas et te ualen
tia. conte te barcalona i
te ungel et seynnor te mo
nt pesler. acabadas las
ganantias de la nra con
quista i todo quanto da
uentos tela mar orien
tal: las encontradas te
la nra acquisitio otesa
por la gra te dius a la nu
estra seynnoria aplega
tes puesto el tiempo te
las armas i entendietes
puesto al tiempo tela pa
el mjo entendimiento a
los fueros daragon. por los

The Great Schism

The pope had resided in Avignon, France, ever since the French Pope Clement V had spurned Rome in 1309. But in 1377, in response to urgent calls for the successor of St Peter to return to his rightful seat, Pope Gregory XI set up his court in Rome.

The 'conclave' of cardinals assembled to elect a new pope, following Gregory's death in March 1378, witnessed unprecedented violence. The Roman mob broke into the Vatican and forced the cardinals to elect an Italian pope, Urban VI. The French cardinals declared the election invalid and elected their own pope, Clement VII, returning with him to Avignon. The supporters of these two pontiffs were openly divided into political factions – England and the German states for Rome; France, Spain, Burgundy, Scotland and Portugal for Avignon.

In 1409 the cardinals of both obediences, under pressure from Europe's secular rulers, agreed to summon a council at Pisa to end the 'Great Schism'. Neither pontiff would attend the council, so its members declared them deposed and elected a third pope, Alexander V; when he died in May 1410, John XXIII was elected in his place. There were now no less than three popes, each claiming legitimacy as the rightful heir to St Peter. The spiritual credibility of the Church was at a very low ebb.

chosen the name Benedict XIII. In 1408 Benedict appointed Alonso as assessor of the diocese of Lérida, and the efficiency with which Alonso discharged his duties brought promotion to the post of canon of the cathedral at Lérida in 1411.

Around this time, Alonso de Borja was noticed among the crowds who had gathered to listen to a Dominican preacher, Vincent Ferrer, the confessor to Benedict XIII, who prophesied a great future for the young cleric, and for himself: 'My son,' he called out, 'one day you will be the greatest jewel of your country and of your family, and receive the highest office a man can hold; you will honour me after my death, and I hope you will always live as virtuously as you do now.'

The young Alonso de Borja showed himself to be diligent, clever, trustworthy and straightforward, rare attributes in an age better known for duplicity and betrayal. His exceptional talents would soon bring him to the attention of the King of Aragon.

1414–1419

AFTER THE FAILURE OF THE Council of Pisa to end the Great Schism in the Church, the Holy Roman Emperor, Sigismund, and Europe's other rulers opened the Council of Constance in 1414, in the hope of better success.

On 20 May 1415 John XXIII, who had been elected pope by the Council of Pisa in 1410, was deposed at Constance. Gregory XII, the pope in Rome, abdicated on 4 July of his own volition, and Benedict XIII, pope in Avignon, was deposed on 26 July, though he refused to recognize the council. In 1416 Alonso de Borja was elected by the diocese of Lérida as its official delegate to the Council of Constance.

King Ferdinand I of Aragon died on 2 April and was succeeded by his son, Alfonso V. Determined to revive the old Aragonese claim to the Kingdom

14

of Naples, encompassing much of southern Italy, he decided his best chance of acquiring papal support for this plan was to oppose the Council of Constance, so he forbade Alonso to travel to Switzerland.

In 1417 Alonso de Borja was sent by the diocese of Lérida to discuss financial issues with royal officials. His abilities so impressed Alfonso V that he was taken into royal service as a secretary.

On 8 November that year, the cardinals present at Constance, along with 30 other churchmen representing the nations attending the council, assembled in the Merchant's Hall where, three days later, they elected a Roman noble,

Alfonso V of Aragon

Alfonso was born in 1395 and brought up at the Castilian court at Medina del Campo, which he left in 1412 when his father inherited the throne of Aragon. Three years later he married his cousin, Maria of Castile, and although the marriage would prove childless Alfonso had several illegitimate children.

His father died in 1416 and Alfonso, now 21 years old, succeeded to the throne of Aragon and Sicily. An ambitious ruler and a skilful soldier, Alfonso successfully went on to assert his dynastic claims to Sardinia, Corsica and Naples, where he established the capital of his state and placed its administration largely in the hands of Spanish nobles.

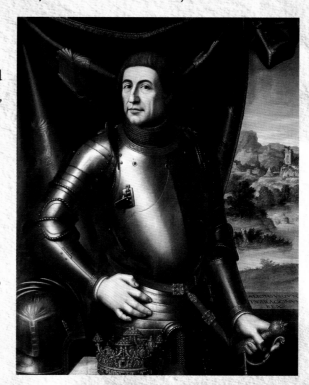

Alfonso was autocratic, and his enemies criticized his arrogance and pride; but he was also a pious man, moderate in his habits, who enjoyed hunting and tournaments and was a major patron of the arts. The magnificence of the Neapolitan court attracted many Italian humanists with their reverence for classical learning, and their propaganda promoted Alfonso as the heir to Trajan and Hadrian – two emperors of Ancient Rome who were both of Spanish birth and famous for their military prowess. He also had an excellent sense of humour and the humanist Antonio Beccadelli recorded several examples of his wit, such as 'asses are more fortunate than kings because their masters let them eat in peace' or 'a deaf husband and a blind wife make a good marriage'.[2]

Cardinal Oddo Colonna, as Pope Martin V. While the Roman and Pisan popes both abdicated, the elderly Benedict XIII, aged 89, stubbornly continued to refuse to obey the council and retreated with his cardinals to the fortress of Peñiscola, near Valencia, where he lived under the protection of Alfonso V.

In an effort to persuade the 'antipope' Benedict XIII to resign, on 17 February 1418 Cardinal Alamanno Adimari left Constance as Martin V's legate to Aragon. Alfonso V appointed Alonso de Borja to negotiate on his behalf; Alonso had persuaded the king that changing his allegiance from Benedict XIII to Martin V could be the key to gaining papal support for Alfonso's claim to the throne of Naples. Alonso was rewarded for his work with new benefices: the post of canon at the cathedral in Barcelona and the rectorship of Sant Nicolau in Valencia. On 30 April Cardinal Adimari returned to Martin V's court with the promise that the King of Aragon would do his best to persuade Benedict XIII to resign.

Also during April, on the 5th, the Dominican preacher Vincent Ferrer, who had predicted a remarkable future for Alonso de Borja, died.

Alonso was rewarded for his work with new benefices: the post of canon at the cathedral in Barcelona.

1420–1424

IN 1420 ALONSO DE BORJA was appointed vice-chancellor to the regency council that was to rule Aragon in the absence of Alfonso V, who left with a powerful fleet to assert his authority in Sardinia and Corsica, two of his Mediterranean possessions, and to negotiate with Queen Joanna of Naples.

On 30 September that year Pope Martin V made his formal entry into Rome, re-establishing the city as the home of the papacy.

Alfonso V made a triumphant entry into Naples on 5 July 1421, having persuaded the childless Queen Joanna to adopt him as her heir. However, the queen, surrounded by intriguing courtiers, fell out with Alfonso in 1423 and, with the support of Pope Martin V, adopted Louis III of Anjou as her heir instead. King Alfonso now returned to Aragon and switched his allegiance back to Benedict XIII.

Meanwhile, Christendom's borders were under threat: in 1422 Constantinople was besieged by the Turks for the first time, though they failed to capture the city. The Church itself saw one antipope replaced by another, when, on 23 May, Benedict XIII died at Peñiscola, on the Aragonese coast, and his successor, Clement VIII, was elected there on 10 June.

With King Alfonso's return to Aragon in 1423, Alonso de Borja resigned his university and cathedral posts to work full-time as Alfonso V's chief private secretary and privy councillor. The following year he was appointed Bishop of Majorca.

Vincent Ferrer

Born to an English father and a Spanish mother in 1350, the young Vincent Ferrer joined the Dominican Order, also known as the 'Black Friars', at the age of seventeen.

While suffering from a serious illness, he had a vision of Christ who commanded him to go out and convert non-believers. He celebrated his miraculous recovery by preaching to Jews and Muslims across Spain and became confessor to both Pedro de Luna (the 'antipope' Benedict XIII) and the Queen of Aragon. He led a life of apostolic poverty, fasting regularly and sleeping on the floor. He also travelled on foot through France, Savoy (straddling the modern Franco-Italian border) and northern Italy, where the miracles he wrought among plague victims fostered a popular cult. He died in Vannes, in Brittany, in 1419, and was canonized in 1455.

ABOVE **The Polyptych of St Vincent Ferrer** by Giovanni Bellini (1438–1516). This altarpiece was commissioned by the Venetian confraternity of St Vincent Ferrer for its altar in the church of Santi Giovanni e Paolo, where members of the confraternity would gather to offer communal prayers for the souls of departed members. The painting dates from around 1465, the year after the plague devastated Venice. Like St Vincent Ferrer (centre), the flanking saints – Sebastian on the right and Christopher on the left – were popularly invoked as protection against the plague.

17

1425–1429

ON 6 JANUARY 1425 Pope Martin V appointed Cardinal Pierre de Foix as papal legate to King Alfonso V. But the king published an edict threatening to kill the cardinal if he entered his kingdom. The next year, on 15 July, Martin V issued a papal brief summoning Alfonso V to Rome to explain why he continued to support the antipope Clement VIII. The king refused the invitation but, acting on the sage advice of his counsellor Alonso de Borja, he did finally agree to allow Pope Martin's legate to enter the kingdom. Cardinal de Foix arrived later that year, and King Alfonso again appointed Alonso de Borja to act as his representative in the negotiations.

The papal legate returned to Rome with only the promise that Alfonso V would do all he could to persuade Clement VIII to resign; however, thanks to Alonso de Borja's indefatigable efforts, the visit had laid the basis for future negotiations – though these were stalled in 1428 by an outbreak of the plague in Rome.

The city of Rome

Visitors to Rome in the early 15th century were shocked by the state of the city. Rome may have been the focus of the Christian world, but those who expected to find a level of magnificence appropriate to its position as the seat of the heirs to St Peter were sadly disappointed.

With a population of fewer than 17,000, Rome was much smaller than Paris, London, Milan, Naples, Venice or Florence. The huge area inside the Aurelian walls, which had once enclosed the capital of a mighty empire, was now largely empty, given over to farmland, grazing for cattle and sheep, vineyards and orchards, while gangs of brigands found refuge among the ruins of the imperial palaces and villas, waiting to rob the unwary traveller. The inhabited area of the city was clustered along the banks of the Tiber, its streets unpaved and filthy, its citizens living in poverty.

The religious buildings of this capital of Christendom were shabby: many had collapsed completely, while others had leaking roofs and weeds sprouting from cracks in their walls. The great basilicas of St Peter's and San Giovanni in Laterano were not even in the city, but out along the robber-infested roads in the countryside. The restoration of the papacy to Rome would have a major impact on the appearance of the city as successive popes, from Martin V onwards, embarked on ambitious plans of urban renewal.

In 1429 Cardinal de Foix was appointed legate to Aragon for the third time, and he arrived with the promise that Pope Martin V would look favourably on Alfonso V's claim to the throne of Naples if Clement VIII could be persuaded to abdicate. Alonso de Borja was appointed by the king to negotiate with Clement VIII in Peñiscola; on 26 July he finally convinced the antipope to abdicate and, with his cardinals, formally to elect Martin V as his successor. The Great Schism, which had split Europe for the first fifty years of Alonso's life, was now ended, thanks in no small measure to his own efforts.

Alonso de Borja now embarked on a promising career in the Church. On 31 August 1429 he was consecrated Bishop of Valencia by Cardinal de Foix, as a reward from both Alfonso V and Martin V for his loyalty and hard work.

1430–1434

ON 8 NOVEMBER 1430 placards appeared in Rome demanding that Martin V open the Council of Basle as he had promised, or be deposed. The council was to discuss Church reforms as well as other matters. On 1 February 1431 the pope nominated Cardinal Giuliano Cesarini to chair the council, but a few weeks later, on 20 February, Martin V died. He was succeeded by the Venetian Cardinal Gabriel Condulmer, who was elected as Eugenius IV on 3 March.

With a new pope in Rome, the Council of Basle opened on 23 July 1431, but five months later, on 18 December, Eugenius IV decided to close it, unwilling to be controlled by its decisions. Many delegates, however, refused to leave.

19

ABOVE **The tomb of Pope Martin V,** *in San Giovanni in Laterano, Rome. Martin V did much to restore the spiritual credibility of the papacy and its finances, both of which had been severely eroded during the Schism. He instituted necessary reforms to the curia and reorganized the government of the Papal States, which not only brought in much-needed income for the Church, but also enriched his Colonna relations. He also embarked on a major programme of restoration in Rome to repair the city's ruined churches and improve its crippled infrastructure, appointing a body of officials to maintain and clean the streets, squares, bridges, aqueducts and sewers. Their orders included sweeping the main roads every Saturday and punishing those who left their rubbish in the streets.*

ADHVC CONSPICIVNTVR
VETER. MONVMĒT RELIQVIIS
PYRRHO LIGORIO NEAP. INVENT.
ROMAE · M · D · LXX

AED · AVG. VIVARIVM

CASTRVM PRAE
TORIVM

PORTA
claudia

PORT · NVMENTANA

T · BAC
CHI ·

GESTATIO
ALEXAN. AVG.
S · Eusebÿ
S · antonÿ

AGGERES TARQI
NI

PORT · SALARIA
THERMA DIOCLETIANI
Basilica S · mariæ
magioris

PORT · PINCIANA
HIPPODROMVS
HORT · SALVSTIANI
V · de scari
DOMVS
VESPASI
S · Por leriane

S · Laurentÿ
in Palisper

S · Petri ad vincula

SPVLCHR NERONIS
VEL DOMITII
FOR · SALVSTII
V · de grima
ni
Alca
Semira
MALVM PVNICVM

T · Fortuna
CIR · FLORÆ
THER
CONSENTI
NI

TRINITATIS
QVIRI
V de Terras
Ther. Constan
tini
NA
LIS

Tor di conti
DOMVS TITI

T · pacis
T · LINI

AQVA
FORVM
Augusti
Forum
transit
orum
T · Fauntina

COLLIS HORTVLORVM
NAVMACHIÆ
SEPTA
Colanton
ino
Foru Traiani
S · Adriani
VIA SACP
VELIA
PAL

S · MARIA DE POPVLO
A · Portogalli
B · Antonini
ARA
celi
ARA
cocodia

GERMALVS
FORVM CVRIA

VIA FLAMINIA
Mausolei aug
Vsalata
S · MARC
CAPITOLIVM
Palatium
Conservatorū
forum
boari
um

S · Iacopo
CAM · MARTII
MINERVA
ARS
S · giorgi

PANTHEON
THAGRIPP
THEATER
MACELLI
IANI

M · giar
danii
CIRC · AGONALIS
PISCARIA
Scho gracū
FOR · OLI
RIVM

HORT · DOMI
TIAE
MOLES
ADRIANI
Castel s · Angel
Campus flora
VILLA · PVBLI

CIRCVS NERONIS
S · MARIA

PORT · CASTELLI
T · Severi

PORT · PALATII
PORT · S · SPIRITV
Por · S · Spiritus

ELVEDERE
Piazza di San
Pietro
BASILICA S · PERI

PORTA TORRIONIS

obeliscus aug
HIPPODROM

VATICANVS
HORT · MARIA
LAMICVS

VILLA · B · DE PESCIE

20

MEDICA.

Porta Maior

VIA PENES

VIA LABICA

MARSIANA

AQVA

Porta Maior

Aqua Cerulea et Curtia

AQVA DVCTVS.AP.

LIAE

ac. hgi

Philippi Aug.

SEVERO marcellius

CLAVDIAE

TIBERIOLIVS

COELI

S. Clementis

CARINAE

S. Quattuor

AMPHITEAT.

caput Viæ

S. Iohannis et Pauli

AQVA CLAVDIA

TEM.CLAVD.

COELIVS

SVBVRA

S. Gregory

SEPTIZONIV

PISCINA. PVBLICA

Aqua Crabra

S. priscia

AN VALI

AGR.CINC

T Veneris

S. Crucis in
Hierusalem

Lympeum
Aleandri Augu.

Porta S. Giovan

Domus Laterani

Basilica Lateranen

Amphiteatr.
Castrense

HIPPODROMVS

NOV VIA VALERIA

AQVA CRABRA

T. FAVNI

S. Stephana Rotonda

S. Mariæ
Nauicella

S. Thomas Hospital

S. Giouanni

S. Sixti

VIA LATINA

PORT
NAT

POR
S. SE
BAS

VIA APPIA

THERMÆ ANTONIANÆ

S. Balbina

CLIVVS ARALYSTRI

MAVEN

S. Sabinæ

S. Alexxy

S. Maria

T. Bonæ Deæ

INVS

BLICVS

CLIVVS PVBLICVS

EMPORIVM

HORTI D
CONSAGA

SALINA

HORREÆ DOMITIANI

VIA HOSTIENSIS

PORT S. PAVLI

S. Cai
Cestij

TESTACEVS
siue Doliolum

ENNA

GVLVM

HORT C. CAESARI

PORTA PORTVENSIS

Dietary advice for cardinals

You can eat *white bread providing you are not constipated and do not fear an obstruction, but it must be well risen, made with salt and fresh, but not warm. Otherwise you should choose bread with the proper quantity of bran and avoid eating pasta. With meat you can eat veal and pork, but this should be neither too young nor too old, domestic or wild, and with little salt. You can also eat mutton, goat and fully grown poultry, hens and capons for choice, but also pullets, pheasant, partridge and thrushes. You must apply the same criteria to fish, and choose those with solid flesh. Eggs can be fried or preserved rather than drunk fresh. You are advised to avoid ... all acidic fruits after your meal. I do not say all fruits should be avoided but especially figs and grapes should be eaten before dining. Neither do I recommend milk or cheese, though I will allow a little cheese after meals. You should eat few vegetables.*

ANONYMOUS MEDICAL MANUSCRIPT FROM THE 14TH CENTURY, QUOTED IN J. BENTINI ET AL. (EDS), *A tavola con il principe*, PP. 242–3.

In 1432 King Alfonso V summoned Alonso de Borja to Messina in Sicily, where he was equipping a powerful fleet to be used, when the opportunity arose, to seize Naples. He also appointed Alonso as his representative to the Council of Basle, hoping to force Eugenius IV to recognize the Aragonese claim to the Italian kingdom. Borja, however, refused to go, arguing that support for the council would not only lead to another schism but could also extinguish all chances of papal recognition of the king's right to the Neapolitan throne.

On 31 May 1433, the pope crowned the new Holy Roman Emperor, Sigismund, in St Peter's in Rome. The Emperor's sprawling territories stretched over much of Central Europe and parts of northern Italy.

The following year, Eugenius IV was forced to flee his own city disguised as a monk, when Romans staged a revolution against papal rule on 29 May 1434 and declared a republic. He responded by moving the papal court to Florence.

1435–1439

ON 2 FEBRUARY 1435 Queen Joanna of Naples died, at the age of sixty-four. With her heir, René of Anjou, a prisoner at the Burgundian court, Alfonso V declared himself king, taking the title Alfonso I of Naples. This did not provide resolution of the succession however, and Naples dissolved into violent civil war between the two claimants and their respective supporters.

PREVIOUS PAGE **A plan of Rome.** *Pope Martin V's entry into Rome on 28 September 1420 marked the dawn of a new age of prosperity in the long history of this famous city. The return of the papal court was a powerful stimulus to both her economy and her intellectual life. Above all it marked the beginning of the transformation of this dilapidated and impoverished centre into the magnificent capital of the Christian world. This plan dates from c.1575.*

RIGHT **King Alfonso V of Aragon in battle,** *from his Book of Hours (c.1442). Alfonso's bid to conquer Naples got off to an inauspicious start when he was decisively defeated at Ponza (1435) and taken prisoner by Filippo Maria Visconti, Duke of Milan. However, he managed to convince his jailer that a French king in Naples would be a political disaster and persuaded the duke to support his claim, thus turning his defeat into a diplomatic triumph.*

Preces pro intrantibus bellum contra paganos. a. Effunde. ps david

Deus uenerunt gentes in hereditate tuam Gloria patri. a. Effunde iram tuam in gentes que te non nouerunt et in regna que nomen tuum non inuocauerunt.

A panorama of 15th-century Naples, *as depicted in the* Tavola Strozzi, *a panel painted in 1472–3 to adorn a bed. Dominating the shoreline is the fortress of Castel Nuovo beside the pier, while the Castel Sant'Elmo stands behind on the hill of Vomera. Naples was a large city with a population of 100,000, the same size as Venice and Milan, though a long history of war and rebellion had made it far less wealthy than its rivals. Settled by the ancient Greeks, Naples had been an important centre of Hellenistic culture and became a prosperous city of the Roman Empire – the bay of Naples was a particularly popular site for the seaside villas of rich Roman*

patricians. The kingdom was later conquered by the Normans but they were ousted in 1194 by Holy Roman Emperor Henry VI. After the death of his son, Frederick II, in 1250, Naples was seized, with the aid of the pope, by Charles I of Anjou, son of the King of France. In 1282 the inhabitants of Sicily rebelled against their French ruler in a violent uprising known as the Sicilian Vespers, and proclaimed Peter of Aragon as their new king. Over the next two centuries the papacy exploited the rivalry between the Aragonese and Angevin claims to Naples in order to maintain their influence over this powerful state so close to Rome.

Alonso de Borja was sent back to Spain in 1436 to fetch Alfonso I's illegitimate son, Ferrante, and he acted as tutor to the 13-year-old prince, who was now to be formally declared heir to the Kingdom of Naples.

On 18 September 1437 Eugenius IV ordered the Council of Basle to travel to Ferrara, where it would meet members of the Greek clergy to discuss the union of the Western and Orthodox churches. This new council opened in Ferrara on 8 January 1438, but later in the month Eugenius IV transferred it to Florence.

On 18th March 1438, the Duke of Austria was elected as Albert II, Holy Roman Emperor, following the death in December 1437 of Sigismund.

Alonso de Borja arrived in Florence in 1439 at the head of a delegation from King Alfonso. Now 60 years old, Alonso was able to experience the grandeur of the papal court.

On 25 June 1439 the rump of the Council of Basle deposed Eugenius IV, but, as Alonso de Borja had predicted to his king, the wily pope averted a split in the Church with his shrewd political manoeuvring.

On 6 July the Council of Florence announced the union between the Eastern and Western Churches and on 18 December the Archbishop of Nicaea, Bessarion, was made a cardinal after he converted to the Latin obedience.

LEFT **Maiolica dish.** *Tin-glazed pottery, known in Italian as maiolica, was high fashion in Renaissance Italy. Its name probably derives from the Spanish obra de mélequa, or lustreware, which originated in Muslim Spain and was exported from Valencia to Italy in large quantities, especially to Aragonese Sicily and Naples before Italian potters began making the wares themselves in the 15th century. Expensive pieces such as this were often commissioned to commemorate births and marriages.*

ABOVE **Cosimo de' Medici and his son Piero,** *as depicted in one of Benozzo Gozzoli's frescoes of* The Procession of the Magi *(1459), commissioned by the Medici to decorate the chapel in their grandiose palace in Florence. Gozzoli included prominent portraits of this wealthy banking family in the retinue of the youngest of the Three Kings. The white-haired Cosimo, 70 years old at the time, had persuaded Eugenius IV to transfer his council from Ferrara to Florence in 1439 by offering to pay the living expenses of the pope and the delegates. But Cosimo made huge profits on the transactions of the papal court at the bank's trading counter set up outside Eugenius IV's apartments.*

Alfonso's entry into Naples

The said king wanted to make his entry by the market place next to the gate of the monastery of the Carmine, so the citizens and ministers of this place demolished a section of the wall and, when they met the king they presented him with a most magnificent chariot … covered in golden brocade with two cushions also covered in the said brocade, one for his seat and the other for his feet and the Siege Perilous. And the said king, dressed in robes of red satin lined with fur, dismounted from his horse and climbed onto the chariot and sat down under a rich canopy of golden brocade carried by the most noble men of the city and decorated with twenty-two bordons which cost 4,000 ducats. And the chariot was pulled by four most beautiful white horses in pairs … accompanied by ladies very richly dressed in satins and other silk cloths with their headdresses embroidered with pearls … and then the said princes, dukes, counts and barons came to the king and asked him if he would graciously invest Don Ferrante of Aragon as his heir to the realm of Naples and then they offered to do homage to him.

R. Filangieri, 'Rassegna critica delle fonti per la storia di Castel Nuovo', in *Archivio storico per le provincie napoletane*, 63 (1938), pp. 75–77.

ABOVE **Alfonso I's triumphal entry into Naples.**
Commemorating this key event (1442) in his reign, this is one of a series of marble reliefs depicting Alfonso's court, his family and himself that decorate the elaborately sculptured gate at the entrance to the royal palace in Naples, Castel Nuovo. A preliminary drawing for the reliefs by the artist Pisanello (c.1394–1455) suggests that Alfonso initially planned a Gothic style for the project, but the arch that was built was unmistakably classical, both in form and style, and clearly based on the triumphal arches of imperial Rome. That aspiration was clearly in accord with the tradition to which Alfonso's humanist scholars liked to promote him as its rightful heir.

1440−1444

IN FEBRUARY 1440, Frederick of Habsburg was elected as Holy Roman Emperor, following Albert II's death in 1439.

On 12 June 1442, King Alfonso finally conquered his capital of Naples, after seven years of conflict. He made his formal entry into the city on 25 February 1443 to claim his throne as King Alfonso I. He rode through the streets in a gilded chariot, decorated to resemble a mighty fortress, his orb and sceptre, the symbols of his temporal and spiritual power, in his hands. Among the elaborately decorated floats that followed the procession was one depicting the Siege Perilous, the seat at King Arthur's Round Table that was fatal to all but the knight who had achieved the Quest of the Holy Grail. It provided the motto that the king had adopted as his emblem, 'for the valiant victory which he has achieved was to signify that no other king or prince or lord was worthy of sitting on this seat, except for this king who has subjugated and won this realm'.[3]

Within weeks of the entry, the king appointed Alonso de Borja as his representative to negotiate with the papal legate, Cardinal Ludovico Trevisan. The two men met at Terracina where they drew up a treaty between Naples and Rome, which was signed on 14 June. It proved a triumph for Alonso. In return for recognizing Eugenius IV as pope, and promising to supply ships to fight the Turks in the eastern Mediterranean, Alfonso was not only invested with the Kingdom of Naples, with his son Ferrante recognized as his heir, but he was also exempted from paying all annual dues to the pope, promising instead to donate a symbolic white 'palfrey', a small horse for riding, every year on 25 January, the feast of St Peter and St Paul.

Cardinal Trevisan's cook prepares a peacock

How to dress *a peacock to make it look alive: first kill the peacock by pushing a fine knife into its head, or rather its neck, and drain the blood, as you would for a goat. Then make a cut under the bird from neck to tail, being very careful to cut only the skin, and then pull the skin off gently so that you do not break the feathers ... cut off the head but leave it attached to the skin, and do the same for the legs. Prepare the bird for roasting, with a stuffing full of good spices and stud the breast with whole cloves. Put a piece of damp cloth around the neck so that it does not dry out, and make sure you keep it damp during roasting. When the bird is cooked replace the skin and attach it carefully with wire. If you want it to spout fire from its beak, take one-quarter of an ounce of camphor, wrap it in a little cotton wool and put the bundle inside the beak and moisten it with aquavit. When you are ready to serve the peacock, light the cotton wool and it will spout fire for quite some time. You can make the bird more magnificent by decorating it with gold leaf. This recipe can also be used for pheasants, herons, geese and other birds.*

MARTINO DA COMO, *Libro de arte coquinaria*, CHAPTER I, QUOTED IN EMILIO FACCIOLI (ED.), *L'Arte della cucina in Italia*, P. 138.

29

Having devastated large areas of southern Hungary in 1441, the Turkish forces of Sultan Murat II were defeated by the army of Hungarian John (or János) Hunyadi in November 1443. A shortlived truce collapsed in 1444, after which Murat II crossed the Bosphorus into Europe to defeat an army of Hungarians and Wallachians.

On 2 May 1444 Pope Eugenius IV held a consistory at which he announced that he was raising Alonso 'Borgia' (as the Italians spelled his name) to the cardinalate as a reward for the loyal secretary's efforts in reconciling King Alfonso and the pope. At the age of 65, Alonso now resigned his royal duties and on 12 July he arrived in Rome where he formally received from the pope his red hat, signifying his new rank, and his titular church in the city, Santi Quattro Coronati.

Santi Quattro Coronati

Cardinal Alonso Borgia's titular church in Rome was dedicated to the four crowned martyrs, who were masons killed by Emperor Diocletian (ruling AD 284–305) for refusing to worship an image of Aesculapius, the Greek god of medicine.

The original church had been built in the reception hall of a great Roman palace of the Caelian Hill during the 7th century and filled with relics found in the catacombs. Largely destroyed when Norman forces sacked Rome in 1084, it had been rebuilt on a much smaller scale during the 12th century, and the exquisite cloisters date from the early 13th century.

In 1246 the chapel of St Sylvester was decorated with a fresco cycle (p. 31) recounting the story of the 'Donation of Constantine', reputedly granted by Emperor Constantine to Pope Sylvester I, giving the pope the right to exercise temporal rule over Italy. According to the story, Constantine suffered from leprosy and had been told that the only cure was to wash in the blood of innocent children, but St Peter and St Paul appeared to him in a dream and advised him to talk to the pope. Sylvester I then baptized Constantine, miraculously curing him, and the donation was the emperor's grateful present.

LEFT **Cloisters of Santi Quattro Coronati,** *Rome.* Cardinal Alonso Borgia was fortunate in that his titular church came with convent buildings attached, which provided him with a residence in Rome – and with an exceptionally beautiful set of cloisters for relaxation. Other titular churches had no such advantage and their cardinals were obliged to rent properties; only the very rich could afford to build their own palaces.

ABOVE **Fresco in the Chapel of St Silvester,** *Santi Quattro Coronati.* The highly stylized frescoes decorating this small chapel tell the story of the 'Donation of Constantine'. Below the massive central figure of Christ enthroned with his Apostles is, on the left, the Emperor struck down with leprosy. The central scene depicts the ailing Constantine, with St Peter and St Paul appearing to him in a dream to suggest that he should talk to Pope Silvester I. On the right, messengers ride off in search of the pontiff.

1445–1449

IN 1445 THE NEW CARDINAL of Valencia, as Alonso Borgia chose to be styled, settled in Rome, where he started to use his influence to gain favours for his family. He appointed his 14-year-old nephew Rodrigo Borgia, son of his sister Isabella, as sacristan at the Cathedral of Valencia.

On 10 April 1446 the new cardinal joined the confraternity of Santo Spirito, which sponsored a hospital for the poor in Rome – its statutes included the duty 'to seek out once a week through the streets and public squares sick paupers, to bring them to the houses of Santo Spirito, and to nurse them carefully'.[4]

Pope Eugenius IV died on 23 February 1447. In the evening of 4 March, 24 cardinals entered the Dominican convent of Santa Maria sopra Minerva to hold the conclave that would elect his successor. It would be the first of nine successive conclaves in which a Borgia cardinal would take part. Two days later the Cardinal of Bologna, aged 49, who had been a cardinal for less than three months, emerged as the surprising winner. One of the favourites, Cardinal Domenico Capranica, was so astonished that he had to count the voting papers himself, before the election of Tommaso Parentucelli as Pope Nicholas V was announced to the crowds in the square outside. 'Most [cardinals] would have preferred a pope of their own faction but none was actively unfriendly towards him.'[5]

LEFT **Cardinal Alonso Borgia and St Ildefonsus.** *Commissioned in 1456 by Alonso Borgia from Alfonso V's court painter Jacomart, this panel shows the cardinal wearing his ceremonial hat with its distinctive broad brim and hanging tassels; his everyday hat was a close-fitting scarlet beret. Typically, the saint is depicted on a much larger scale than the donor.*

RIGHT **The three cardinals** *in this detail from a Pinturicchio fresco are immediately identifiable by their scarlet caps, the* biretta, *marking them out as princes of the Church. Red was the cardinal's colour, for vestments and for the furnishings of their palaces.*

The College of Cardinals

Identified by their distinctive red hats that marked them out as heirs-in-waiting to the throne of St Peter, the cardinals formed a unique elite and one that operated at the apex of political power in Europe.

The college was an advisory body that, with the pope in the chair, formulated papal policy. Its regular meetings, or 'consistories', were usually private but they could be opened to the wider public if necessary. The college was an international body, with representatives of all major European states lobbying on behalf of their temporal masters. Most cardinals had been appointed as favours for these rulers; few gained red hats merely for their piety or spirituality.

Whatever their background, cardinals enjoyed the status of princes. Some were indeed born aristocrats; but others came from professional or bourgeois backgrounds, even from the labouring classes, and for them the red hat marked a massive increase in social prestige. Some had spent their youth learning how to hunt and joust; others were highly educated, with degrees in law or theology. They also varied widely in age: Alonso Borgia, at the age of 66, joined a college where the youngest member, Cardinal Pietro Barbo, nephew of Eugenius IV, was just 27 years old – the widespread practice of nepotism reflecting a pope's need for people he could trust absolutely in the key positions at his court.

Appointed for life, all cardinals had the opportunity to become immensely wealthy, though their success in acquiring rich benefices and promotion in the Church depended largely on papal favour. For the ambitious, it was essential to identify and support a future pope in the college – and, of course, each cardinal had the chance of election to the supreme power of the papacy itself.

Pope Nicholas V

Nicholas V was one of the great papal patrons of the 15th century, with ambitious plans for transforming the scruffy city of Rome into a magnificent setting for the display of papal prestige.

His most significant act was to establish the Vatican as the official residence of the papacy, moving out of the palace at San Giovanni in Laterano, the seat of the pope as Bishop of Rome. His decision to live at St Peter's emphasized his spiritual role as successor to the first pope. He enlarged the palace at the Vatican, adding an extra wing to contain his apartments, a private chapel, space for offices, a room to hold his library of precious manuscripts, and a private chapel. The chapel was frescoed by Fra Angelico with scenes from the lives of St Lawrence and St Stephen underlining his belief that papal wealth should be used for the Church, not for personal gain. He repaired Rome's water supply, restored many of the city's dilapidated churches, and planned extensive renovations to St Peter's, which were, though, never realized.

The bookseller Vespasiano described the pope's character:

His merit was apparent in everything he did and, despite the prestige of his position, his behaviour towards others was most friendly. He was witty, had a kind word for everybody, and all who had conversations with him were impressed by his fine manners and his obvious talent ... he was generous to all, never believing that his possessions were his own. He had no concept of avarice; indeed, the only possessions he had were things that no one had requested. He overspent liberally, employing a vast body of the best men he could find, never thinking about how he could afford to pay them. He trusted his own ability to provide for himself and often said that there were two things he would buy if he had the money: books and buildings.

W.G. AND EMILY WATERS (EDS), *The Vespasiano Memoirs*, P. 37.

During 1448 Cardinal Alonso's nephew Rodrigo Borgia became a canon of the cathedral chapters of Valencia, Barcelona and Segorbe, thanks to his uncle's influence in Rome. In 1449, as a particular favour to Cardinal Alonso, the pope granted Rodrigo Borgia the right to receive the income from his benefices *in absentia*, 'whether living in Rome or studying at university', to allow the 18-year-old to leave Spain and join his uncle in Italy.[6] The cardinal now sent his nephew to a school at the Vatican, where, together with several relatives of Church dignitaries, he was given a classical education by the humanist, Gaspare da Verona. 'He is very handsome, always smiling, good-natured, suave and eloquent,' judged the tutor, adding that 'it is quite remarkable how beautiful women are attracted to him, more powerfully even than a magnet attracts iron.'[7]

The year 1448 also witnessed a serious defeat for the Hungarian forces of John Hunyadi at the hands of Sultan Murat II at the Battle of Kosovo. Turkish control in the Balkans appeared to be established.

On Christmas Day 1449, Nicholas V formally opened the Jubilee, to be celebrated in Rome for the Holy Year to come.

LEFT **St Lawrence appointed deacon by Pope Sixtus II.** *In 1447–8 Nicholas V commissioned the Dominican friar Fra Angelico (c.1395–1455) to decorate his private chapel in the Vatican with scenes from the lives of St Lawrence and St Stephen. The pope wished to give visual expression to his belief that large scale expenditure on artistic projects should be for the Church's glory, not the pope's.*

The Jubilee in Rome

The first Holy Year was celebrated in Rome in 1300 by Pope Boniface VIII. The concept was based on Old Testament accounts of the Jubilee that took place every 50 years and required Jews to free their slaves and to restore land purchased since the previous Jubilee to the original owners. Translating these acts of restitution into a Christian context, Boniface VIII granted a full pardon for their sins to all those people who visited the major churches of the city.

For the pilgrims it was an opportunity to experience the spiritual centre of their faith and to view sites and relics of Christian legend. For example, the crib where Christ was supposedly born could be seen at Santa Maria Maggiore; the towel with which St Veronica was reputed to have wiped Christ's face before the Crucifixion was shown to the faithful at St Peter's. Rome was where St Peter and St Paul had both preached and died for their faith, along with armies of nameless believers who had been butchered in the circuses for the entertainment of pagan emperors.

As many as a million pilgrims would visit Rome during a Holy Year, placing a great strain on the city's resources, but bringing welcome funds for the papal coffers.

35

1450–1455

Pilgrims flocked to Rome in their thousands for the Jubilee year of 1450.

PILGRIMS FLOCKED TO ROME in their thousands for the Jubilee year of 1450. It was a busy year for the cardinals who accompanied the pope as he took part in the celebrations.

On 24 May 1450, Whit Sunday, Cardinal Alonso Borgia attended the magnificent ceremonies in St Peter's to mark the canonization of the popular Franciscan preacher Bernardino of Siena. The cost of his new vestments, as well as those worn by Nicholas V and the other cardinals, came to 7,000 ducats, and were paid for by the cities of Siena and Aquila.[8]

Rome's population was swelling rapidly under the influx of pilgrims. One chronicler recorded that:

There were so many people in Rome that there was not enough accommodation for them all, even though every house became an inn. The pilgrims offered to pay generously and pleaded, for the love of God, to be taken in, but in vain, and they had to sleep outside where many died of the cold. It was terrible to witness. And so many came that the city itself

starved ... you could not get to St Peter's because of the enormous crowds on the streets, and San Paolo fuori le mura, San Giovanni in Laterano and Santa Maria Maggiore were full of people praying. Rome was so full that it was impossible to get around. When the pope gave his benediction at St Peter's the whole area was densely packed with pilgrims, and they even filled the orchards from where it was possible to see the benediction loggia.[9]

In the middle of May 1450 the city was hit by an epidemic of plague. By 15 July the situation was serious enough that most cardinals and the pope himself left Rome. The crowds of pilgrims also declined, only to rise again with the onset of colder weather in the autumn.

As the Jubilee neared its end, on 19 December, another disaster struck when the Ponte Sant'Angelo was blocked by some

LEFT **Pilgrims at St Peter's.** *Special arrangements were made in the towns and cities of the Papal States to feed and house the hordes of pilgrims travelling to Rome during a Jubilee year; in Rome itself stocks of foodstuffs rarely proved sufficient. These crowds of people testified to the piety of ordinary men and women in Renaissance Europe. The drawing is 16th-century.*

Relics and curiosities at San Giovanni in Laterano, Rome, in 1450

Item *Outside the main church up on a platform is a lovely little chapel decorated with marbles, porphyry and mosaics which is called the holy of holies because there are an enormous number of relics of the saints there ... on the altar of the said chapel is the image of our Lord Jesus Christ painted by the hand of St Luke himself ...*

Item *Next to the said chapel of the holy of holies is a staircase that goes down to the piazza San Giovanni which is six braccia* wide with some large marble steps, and this was the staircase from Pilate's palace in Jerusalem where Christ stood when Pilate pronounced his death sentence, and it came from Jerusalem, and those who come for the Jubilee, especially those from over the Alps, show particular devotion by climbing up on their knees.*

Item *By the said holy of holies in one of the corridors are two porphyry seats on which the pope is put after he is elected and, through a hole in the seat of the chair, it is decided whether he is male or female...*

Item *In a chapel in the church is the rod of Aaron in a bronze casket on the altar, and the laws that God gave Moses.*

Item *In the said place, above the said box, is the wooden table where Christ ate with his Apostles, about three braccia square.*

Item *In the said church on the main altar are the heads of St Peter and St Paul, decorated with gold and silver and many precious stones, encased behind an iron grille which is locked with many chains and keys so that they will not be stolen ...*

Item *By the said San Giovanni is the baptistery where St Sylvester the pope baptized Emperor Constantine when he was cured of leprosy.*

* The length of the old Italian unit *braccia* varied from city to city, but may be thought of as approximating an 'arm's length'.
A. PEROSA (ED.), *Giovanni Rucellai ed il suo Zibaldone*, PP. 70–2.

37

Many who escaped had their clothes ripped off.

runaway horses, probably frightened by the dense crowds of pilgrims hurrying across the bridge after the papal benediction at St Peter's had been cancelled. Those behind were completely unaware of what was happening on the bridge and continued to surge forward. The resulting crush forced hundreds of people into the River Tiber, leaving many dead and many more injured. An eye-witness, Giovanni Inghirami, described how:

That evening in the church of San Celso there were 176 corpses, men and women, but mostly women … they say many more have fallen into the Tiber, including those who climbed on to the parapets to escape and those who were thrown in. Many who escaped had their clothes ripped off their backs and they

were running about, some in their hose, others in shirts, some even naked, and the women all dishevelled, looking for their companions who they feared had died. By midnight San Celso was full of the dead; some found a father, others a mother, a brother, or a son, and their cries deafened the city ... even those who fought in the Turkish wars had not seen such a terrible sight. [10]

In 1451, Rome was wracked again by an epidemic of the plague during the summer months: 'it is appallingly hot here, worse than anyone can remember,' wrote the Milanese ambassador on 29 July, continuing, 'men of every nation are leaving the city, and justly so, because, in truth, it is a sepulchre for brave men'.[11]

On 9 March 1452 the cardinals gathered at St Peter's to welcome Emperor Frederick III, who had come to Rome to be married to Eleanor of Portugal and to be solemnly crowned Emperor by the pope.

Early in January 1453 a group of political agitators, resentful of what they saw as the tyrannical rule of the papacy, were discovered to be plotting against the pope. On 7 January their leader, Stefano Porcari, was arrested and taken to the fortress of Castel Sant'Angelo where, under torture, he confessed. Their plan had been to set fire to the Vatican on 6 January while the pope and the College of Cardinals were celebrating high mass in St Peter's, to take Nicholas V and his cardinals prisoners, killing any who resisted, and then to proclaim a republican government in Rome.

The coronation of Emperor Frederick III

The Emperor wore the sacred robes of Charlemagne, something which no Emperor had done for hundreds of years and this was judged a very great honour, by the grace of God.

After the reading of the Gospel the Emperor and empress were conducted by the pope to the altar of St Peter, where they knelt while the pope spoke some words in Latin and put the crown of Charlemagne on the Emperor's head. Then the pope gave him Charlemagne's sword and he brandished it before putting it back in the scabbard. And then the pope put the holy sceptre in his right hand and the royal orb into his left and when the prayers were over he kissed the pope's foot and went back to his seat.

THE MEMORIES OF THE IMPERIAL COUNSELLOR (L. VON PASTOR, *History of the Popes*, VOL. II, PP.155–6).

LEFT **The 'Seven Churches' of Rome,** *from Antonio Lafréry's Speculum Magnificentiae Romanae (1575). Five of the ancient basilicas of Rome date back to the reign of Emperor Constantine, who adopted Christianity as the official religion of the Roman Empire in 313 and embarked on a campaign of church building to provide visual evidence of the power of the new faith: San Sebastiano, built over the catacombs of the once persecuted Christians; San Giovanni in Laterano, built over the site of his cavalry barracks; Santa Croce in Gerusalemme, erected by his mother Helena, who endowed the church with a relic of the True Cross; San Lorenzo fuori le mura, the huge basilica with a nave 98 metres long, which he built over the supposed tomb of St Lawrence; and St Peter's, built over the shrine dedicated to the first pope. The immense structure of San Paolo fuori le mura was built to commemorate St Paul, while Santa Maria Maggiore was the first Roman church dedicated to the Virgin, after the Council of Ephesus (431) officially declared Mary to be the Mother of God.*

ABOVE **The Betrothal of Emperor Frederick III and Eleanor of Portugal.** *The decision of Frederick III to travel to Rome for his marriage and coronation caused much consternation across Italy, where many feared the arrival of an Imperial army, and Nicholas V tried in vain to dissuade the Emperor. In the end, Frederick III's entourage contained only 2,000 men, and he was royally entertained on his progress from Venice to Rome. His bride, meanwhile, travelled by sea to Livorno and then on to Siena, where the betrothed couple met for the first time; it was reported that the groom, aged 37, was much impressed with the beauty of his lovely 16-year-old bride. They were married by the pope in St Peter's on 16 March 1452 and Frederick III was crowned three days later in a magnificent ceremony, the last Imperial coronation to take place in Rome. The scene is from Pinturicchio's cycle of the life of Pius II (1502–9) in the cathedral at Siena.*

Six months later, on 8 July, there was more dramatic news in Rome, of significance to all of Christendom. The beleaguered city of Constantinople had fallen to the Turkish forces of the new young Sultan Mehmet II. The bombardment, which had begun on 6 April, had destroyed many of the city's churches, and the conquest of this eastern Christian bulwark on 29 May was a calamity. The Byzantine Emperor Constantine XI was killed in the onslaught. According to the Milanese ambassador, 'the Holy Father and the cardinals are very frightened and embarrassed about what has happened at Constantinople and they say that they want to send legates to all the powers in Italy'.[12] On 30 September 1453 Nicholas V responded to events by announcing a crusade against Mehmet II, granting an indulgence to all who would take part.

In November 1453, Cardinal Isidore of Kiev, who had been the papal legate in Constantinople, finally returned to Rome with first-hand stories of the Turkish atrocities. He had only managed to survive the massacre through disguise, and by dressing a corpse in his ecclesiastical garb, but he had been captured nonetheless and sold as a slave before escaping to Venice. His reported descriptions made for sobering reading:

RIGHT **The Siege of Constantinople (1453),** *from the illuminated French manuscript* Le Voyage d'Outre Mer *(c.1455). European unease at the growing Ottoman power in the eastern Mediterranean turned to real alarm in 1452 when Mehmet II started building a massive fortress on the Bosphorus. The castle, which gave Mehmet II control of the straits, provided a launchpad for his conquest of Constantinople. The city's army of just 7,000 men was powerless in the face of the Sultan's 80,000 soldiers.*

It is clear that the sultan is more powerful than either Caesar or Alexander, or indeed any other prince who has ever wished to conquer the world. Amongst other things that the cardinal said was that the sultan has more gold than perhaps any other prince has ever minted. He said there were 230 ships in the water but that the sultan could have easily built as many as he wanted; there are 30,000 cavalry at the moment and many more infantry but he could get as many men as he wanted so that his army will be all-powerful at sea and on land. The sultan is planning to move against Italy immediately ... the cardinal also said that they are praying to God seven times a day from the highest places on all the major buildings in all the cities to bring war, schism and discord among Christians.[13]

At the beginning of 1454, the pope's personal fortunes declined sharply. By 29 January 1454 he was so ill with gout that the cardinals had to attend a secret consistory in his bedroom. He remained largely incapacitated in this way as the months wore on, and during late March of 1455 he grew steadily worse. Late in the evening of 24 March 1455, Alonso Borgia was summoned with the other cardinals to the pope's bedroom, where they gathered around his sickbed to listen to his final speech. Early the following morning, the Feast of the Annunciation, Pope Nicholas V died.

Alonso Borgia had long since established a reputation as a shrewd, dry lawyer and diplomat, highly respected for his legal knowledge and his administrative skills. He was also a kindly man and deeply religious, and as Cardinal of Valencia he had rapidly acquired a reputation for honesty and incorruptibility at the papal court. The books found in his study after his death were almost all religious and legal works.[14] 'An old man who has lived an honourable and virtuous life' was the judgement of one contemporary.[15] In common with most of his colleagues, he had used his position as cardinal to advance the careers of his family and compatriots, and his household was staffed almost entirely by Catalans. But, living modestly in the small palace attached to Santi Quattro Coronati, behind the Colosseum, he had dutifully attended consistories and carried out his obligations, playing little part in the politics and intrigue of the papal court. Now that a new papal election was imminent, he would have to become involved.

> Alonso Borgia was summoned with the other cardinals to the pope's bedroom, where they gathered around his sickbed.

LEFT **Sultan Mehmet II.** *Known as 'the Conqueror', Mehmet II took Constantinople at the age of 21 and expanded his empire into Asia Minor and the Balkans. He chose to make Constantinople the capital of his powerful state and ornamented it with buildings that proclaimed the nature of his power. He converted the 6th-century church of Hagia Sophia into a mosque by plastering over the Christian imagery and adding minarets, and he built the impressive Topkapi Palace as his residence. This portrait, painted by the Venetian artist, Gentile Bellini, who was invited to Mehmet II's court at Constantinople, depicted the sultan shortly before his death in 1481 at the age of 49.*

Calixtus III

THE FIRST BORGIA POPE

1455–1458

None of the ambassadors reporting on the chances of the individual cardinals in the coming conclave, nor the touts who would have been taking large numbers of bets in Rome on its outcome, considered that the elderly and pious Cardinal Alonso Borgia had the remotest chance of election to the papacy. At the age of 77 he was too old to offer stability; moreover, apart from his connections with Naples, he had no political power, nor had he made any effort to ally himself with the political factions within the College of Cardinals. But the prophecy about Alonso's fortunes made by St Vincent Ferrer some forty years earlier was about to be realized.

1455

ON 3 APRIL, Maundy Thursday, Alonso Borgia assembled with his fellow cardinals in St Peter's to hear the mass of the Holy Ghost and to listen to a sermon exhorting them to chose a worthy pope. On Good Friday they followed the papal cross in procession from St Peter's to the Vatican palace, where the doors were sealed behind them. There were twenty cardinals in total in the College of Cardinals, but five of them were unable to reach the city in time. Of the fifteen potential candidates present, only seven were Italian; there were also four Spaniards, two Frenchmen and two Greeks. All were divided by various loyalties to the rival Colonna and Orsini factions, who dominated the politics of Rome.

46

PREVIOUS PAGE **Calixtus III,** *see page 65.*
LEFT **Cardinal Bessarion,** *painted by Joos van Ghent (fl. 1460–75). Born c.1403 in Trebizond, on the Black Sea, he adopted the name Bessarion when joining the Order of St Basil. A powerful intellectual, he was a delegate to the Council of Florence in 1438 and shocked many of his fellow Orthodox Christians by converting to the Roman faith.*
RIGHT **Francesco Sforza, Duke of Milan (1401–66),** *painted c.1460 by Bonifacio Bembo. This condottiere successfully exploited his military talents and political guile to succeed his father-in-law as ruler of Milan in 1450.*

The rituals of papal elections

On the death of a pope, an army of workmen moved into the Vatican in order to isolate a section of the palace from the outside world, bricking up doors and covering all the windows with thick black cloth.

The entrance to the 'conclave' was guarded by armed soldiers as well as bishops and ambassadors. Each cardinal had his food prepared at home and it was brought every day to the entrance of the conclave packed in a special basket, which was carefully inspected by the bishops. Working two-hourly shifts, they opened pies and roasted birds to make sure nothing had been secreted within, and sniffed the wine, before the baskets were placed on a set of revolving shelves, specially constructed by workmen to allow the food to pass unaided into the conclave hall.

Inside the hall, wooden cubicles were built for each of the cardinals: measuring 10 feet by 15 feet, they were draped with hangings – purple for those cardinals who had been created by the dead pope, and green for the rest. Each cubicle was assigned by lot a few days before the conclave opened and clearly identified by its owner's coat-of-arms. It was a cramped space, furnished with charcoal braziers for reheating food and candles for light; here, the cardinal, together with his courtier or secretary and their menial servant, would sleep, wash, eat and use the commode. In the summer the heat and stench would have been intolerable.

The cardinals assembled, without attendants, every morning, and sometimes twice a day, in an adjoining hall for the lengthy voting process known as a 'scrutiny'. They went in turn to the voting table, where they wrote the names of up to three candidates on a piece of paper before placing it in an urn. The votes were then counted by the official in charge, who announced the result and burned the papers. It was also possible to elect a pope by 'accession', whereby one cardinal verbally nominated a candidate and asked the others to vote directly. In each case the winning candidate needed to acquire the votes of two-thirds of the electorate. The long hours between the scrutinies were spent plotting and negotiating, and much use was made of tactical voting, especially in the early stages, to get support from non-favourites and build up a faction powerful enough to swing the election.

ABOVE RIGHT **The Benediction Loggia at Old St Peter's and the Vatican Palace, Rome.** *This drawing, made in 1539 by the Dutch artist Marten van Heemskerck, shows how Renaissance popes embellished this focal point of their power and prestige: the massive three-storey arcades (facing front) of the Benediction Loggia started by Pius II in 1461; the pitched roof of the Sistine Chapel, built by Sixtus IV (begun 1477) just visible behind the ornamented entrance to the palace; and the imposing extension to the palace itself, on the right, started by Leo X in the 1520s.*

On 8 April, the Milanese ambassador reported to his master, Duke Francesco Sforza, that:

> ... up to this hour no one has been elected to the papacy despite the fact that there have already been three scrutinies ... it is to be hoped that the fourth, which they are holding at this moment, will produce a result because the cardinals are particularly worried about the people of Rome, who are beginning to complain about the delay and we, who are part of the guard at the palace, keep trying to reassure them ... If God allows them to agree on someone we will add a note to this letter and send it at speed with the courier we are holding in readiness here in case there is any news ... we are in danger of having everything stolen by the angry mob which has gathered here to see the pope when he is elected. We will let your Lordship know in what way and when this election will happen, that is to say, who is elected and how.[1]

On the previous day, the scholarly Cardinal Bessarion had emerged as the favourite, to the horror of the French: 'Shall we elect a Greek to lead the Latin Church?', one argued, adding for good measure that 'Bessarion has not even shaved off his beard yet.'[2] By the following morning it was clear that they needed to choose a compromise candidate, and so, on 8 April, the conclave elected Alonso Borgia as pope.

At 77 years old, Alonso Borgia was the oldest cardinal in the college. 'The cardinals have agreed on the Cardinal of Valencia,' wrote the Milanese ambassador, 'because he is old and they each hope that they can get their own candidate elected at the next election', which, given Alonso's age, was expected to be soon.[3] 'He is a man of great piety and scholarship, a friend and ally of King Alfonso, whom he served,' reported the Sienese envoy, while the bishop of Florence praised his good nature, his shrewd mind and his lack of bias.[4]

At 77 years old, Alonso Borgia was the oldest cardinal in the college.

49

A prophecy realized

When they held the next scrutiny they tried the method known as 'accession' and two-thirds of the cardinals gave their votes to the man who had been judged the most improbable candidate at the outset: Alfonso, Cardinal of Valencia. He was a famous lawyer with much experience, but now old and very frail because he was over seventy. It is said that he predicted his election a few years ago, before the last conclave, telling everyone he met that he would be pope but they all thought he was senile and disbelieved him but now his prophecy has come true. He said it had been predicted by St Vincent, another Spaniard whom he later made a saint. Alfonso then sat on the throne and chose the name Calixtus III and swore a solemn oath to focus all his energy against the Turks.

F.A. GRAGG AND L.C. GABEL (EDS), *The Secret Memoirs of a Renaissance Pope*, P. 65.

The new Borgia pope chose as his papal title 'Calixtus III', and he made a solemn vow: 'I, Pope Calixtus III, do promise and swear to the Holy Trinity, Father, Son and Holy Ghost, to the Virgin Mary and to the Apostles Peter and Paul, and to all the heavenly host, that I will do all in my power, even sacrifice my life if need be, to reconquer Constantinople, which has been captured and destroyed by Mehmet II in punishment for our sins.'[5]

Even before his coronation, Calixtus III began to take stock of the financial state of the Church. Nicholas V had left debts of 70,432 florins,[6] and the new pope ordered a special audit of the account books. He also initiated an inventory of the valuable manuscripts bought by Nicholas V for his library, with the intention of removing their costly silver bindings to sell for the crusade.

50

LEFT **Medal of Sultan Mehmet II.** *This traditional image of a warrior astride his warhorse displays the sultan's military prowess.*

RIGHT **St Lawrence distributing alms** *in one of Fra Angelico's Vatican frescoes (1447–8). When Roman soldiers ordered St Lawrence to give them the fabled wealth of the Christians, he pointed to a crowd of paupers and the sick, saying: 'Here is the treasure of the Church.'*

An era of austerity

Immediately after his election, Calixtus III, who preferred a plain, austere lifestyle, made radical cuts to papal expenditure.

At the Vatican he reduced household costs by 40 per cent, sold all his predecessor's expensively carved furniture, buying plain chairs and tables instead, replaced the valuable silver candlesticks in the papal chapel with ones made of lead, and removed the costly velvet and silver bindings from Nicholas V's manuscripts (though he kept the texts, which are still in the Vatican library).[7] He stopped work on Nicholas V's ambitious programme of urban renewal and sold off jewels and valuables from the papal treasury. King Alfonso of Naples bought several gilded vases and cups, a silver wine cooler, sweetmeat platters and silver chapel items.[8] When gilded plates were placed on the pope's dining-table, he is reported to have told his steward to take them away to raise money for the crusaders, adding: 'Terracotta is good enough for me.'[9]

Nevertheless, malicious tales soon spread that the pope was a philistine, unaware of the real value of these treasures:

When Pope Calixtus III saw the five hundred wonderful books in rich bindings with silver clasps which had belonged to his predecessor, he was amazed, for this old lawyer had only used books bound in cheap cloth before. On entering the library, instead of praising the dead pope's learning, he exclaimed: 'Look where the treasure of the Church has gone!' and then started to break up the collection, giving many to Cardinal Isidore of Kiev, but he had become senile with age, and the volumes, which had cost many gold florins, were sold by the cardinal's servants for a few silver coins.

W.G. AND EMILY WATERS (EDS), *The Vespasiano Memoirs*, PP. 186–7.

On 15 May, Calixtus III published a papal bull proclaiming his crusade against the Turks.

The new pope celebrated mass in St Peter's on the morning of 20 April before coming out onto the steps of the ancient basilica to be crowned with the papal tiara by the senior cardinal-deacon, Prospero Colonna. Then, in a huge procession of cardinals, prelates, Roman barons and magistrates, he embarked on his *possesso*, riding across the city on a white horse to San Giovanni in Laterano where he was consecrated as the Bishop of Rome. At Montegiordano, by the great Orsini palace, he was met by a group of Jewish rabbis who offered him a copy of the Torah, which he rejected with the customary words: 'We ratify your law but we denounce your interpretation.' In the Campo dei Fiori there was a violent confrontation between supporters of the Orsini and Colonna families.

On 15 May, Calixtus III published a papal bull proclaiming his crusade against the Turks. It contained measures for raising money to equip the fleet and an offer of indulgences to all those who would fight. It was decided that the fleet would leave on 1 March the following year. 'The pope thinks and talks of nothing else but the crusade,' wrote Gabriele da Verona, adding that 'he deals with other matters with a single word but speaks about this subject continually.'[10]

Calixtus III's second priority, after the crusade, was the canonization of St Vincent Ferrer, who had predicted his election to the papacy some forty years earlier. This was planned for 23 May, but the process had not been completed in time, so it was postponed to 29 June.

Meanwhile Calixtus began to promote the Church careers of two of his nephews. Rodrigo Borgia was made Dean of Santa Maria in Játiva on 3 June, and a month later the pope appointed Luis Juan de Milà, the son of another of his sisters, as Governor of Bologna.

During the summer of 1455 Calixtus III appointed legates to be sent to all the rulers of Christendom to ask for their help in financing the crusade. On 8 September he gave the legate's cross – the symbol of his authority – to Cardinal Alain Coëtivy, who left for France, and to Cardinal Juan Carvajal, who was travelling to the territories of Germany, Hungary and Poland. He also appointed Pedro de Urrea, the Archbishop of Tarragona, to lead a small fleet into the Aegean to face the Turks. The next day it was reported that the pope 'performed the ceremony with much devotion and with tears in his eyes, because he is so passionate in his determination to go to war against the Turks, and anybody who gets in his way is guilty of a great sin'.[11]

Work started on building and equipping the new fleet in the autumn, and the port of Rome soon resembled a naval dockyard. Calixtus III appointed cardinals Ludovico Trevisan, Pietro Barbo, Domenico Capranica, Latino Orsini, Bessarion, and Guillaume d'Estouteville to a commission that would take charge of the work. The quantities of iron and timber to build the galleys, arms, armour, banners

The new Borgia cardinals

After a long debate in consistory, the pope created three cardinals: two were his nephews, Luis of Santi Quattro Coronati and Rodrigo of San Niccolò, and the third was a prince of Portugal, Jaime of Sant'Eustachio. They all showed promise despite their youth – indeed, it was said that the ages of all three cardinals added together still did not make enough years for one. It was clear that these men had not been made cardinals for what they could give the Church, but rather for what the Church could give them, and it is a mistake, often made, to choose an office for a man rather than find a man for the office. The creation of these cardinals was not made public immediately ... and the other cardinals hoped to deceive the pope, who they thought would die soon, but in the end it was the pope who deceived the cardinals for, that summer, when there was only one cardinal left in Rome, he made the creation public.

F.A. GRAGG AND L.C. GABEL (EDS), *The Secret Memoirs of a Renaissance Pope*, PP. 66–7.

and tents for the soldiers, and even the biscuits baked for the expedition, were recorded in the papal account books.

Late in September news reached Rome that Pedro de Urrea, far from setting sail for the Aegean to defend Christendom, had in fact joined forces with King Alfonso of Naples to launch an attack on Genoa. This treachery would lead to seriously deteriorating relations between Calixtus III and his old patron. There was more unwelcome news from Naples on 4 October, when the pope was informed by King Alfonso's ambassadors that the new alliance between the powerful states of Naples and Milan would be celebrated with the marriage of Don Alfonso, the grandson of the king, and Ippolita, the daughter of Francesco Sforza, Duke of Milan.

On 17 December in a magnificent ceremony in St Peter's, Calixtus III appointed Cardinal Trevisan as Admiral of the Fleet and legate with papal authority to govern Sicily, Dalmatia, Macedonia and Greece, as well as Cyprus, Crete, Rhodes and other islands in the Aegean.

There was more unwelcome news from Naples on 4 October.

OVERLEAF **Ponte Sant'Angelo, Rome,** *as depicted in a fresco. This bridge was built by Emperor Hadrian (117–38) to provide access for the processions to his magnificent tomb on the bank of the Tiber opposite the city. During the Middle Ages, Hadrian's mausoleum was converted into the massive and forbidding fortress of Castel Sant'Angelo, which guarded the approaches to the Vatican and St Peter's. The structure of the bridge, dangerously weakened by centuries of torrential floods, was substantially repaired under the pontificate of Nicholas V. One of the few ancient bridges to survive, it was widely admired during the Renaissance as a great wonder of Ancient Roman engineering.*

1456

WITH PREPARATIONS FOR THE CRUSADE well under way, Calixtus III now turned his attention to his nephews. On 5 February Pedro Luis Borgia, elder brother of Rodrigo, was given the prestigious post of Captain-General of the Church and the governorship of the great papal fortress in Rome, Castel Sant'Angelo. On 20 February Calixtus III held a secret consistory in the Vatican at which he persuaded the twelve cardinals present to sign the document creating three new cardinals – his nephews Luis Juan de Milà (aged 26) and Rodrigo Borgia (aged 25), and Prince Jaime of Portugal (aged 43). The names were not to be published immediately but, in a highly unusual step, Calixtus forced the cardinals, on pain of excommunication, to agree that in the event of the pope's death Rodrigo's title was to be considered published and he was to be allowed to take part in the conclave.

On 15 March, after Calixtus III had threatened Giorgio de Saluzzo, the Bishop of Lausanne, with excommunication, the latter finally surrendered the keys of Castel Sant'Angelo to Pedro Luis Borgia.

A week before, all Rome had been amazed when it was reported on 8 March that a Turkish prince had been baptized in San Lorenzo in Damaso.

In April Calixtus III issued a papal bull depriving the errant naval commander Pedro de Urrea of his post, and authorized Cardinal Trevisan to appoint someone else in his place. Meanwhile, the pope remained busily engaged with building and equipping the ships for the crusade, an expensive task: a year after his election, Calixtus III had spent over 70,000 ducats on the fleet.[12] This ambitious project had taken longer than expected. The original date for the fleet's departure, 1 March, had been highly optimistic; the project had already been delayed by a month, but it was only at the end of April that work was nearing completion.

On 4 May Calixtus III requested the head of the Augustinians to order all his preachers to concentrate exclusively on preaching the crusade, or risk excommunication. Finally, on 31 May, he formally invested Cardinal Trevisan with the legate's cross. 'Fasten on your sword, beloved son,' wrote Calixtus III to his

On 20 February Calixtus III held a secret consistory in the Vatican.

RIGHT **A Turkish scribe painted by Gentile Bellini** *during his service at the Ottoman capital. The fall of Constantinople in 1453 was a spiritual calamity for Rome and Christendom; but for the Venetians it was an economic issue and their decision to negotiate a diplomatic settlement with the Turks, whereby the sultan promised to recognize the city's commercial interests, was a pragmatic response, a typical example of how effectively the commercial mentality could adapt to change. Although many Venetians had fought in the defence of Constantinople, and many had been killed in the Turkish assault, they soon returned to trade at the sultan's religiously-tolerant court; and when the sultan asked for a good painter in 1479, the Venetian government sent their best in the shape of Bellini. He stayed there for two years.*

57

It was feared
by many as
a portent of
some great
disaster.

legate, 'keep your promise, for God will be with you, and neither money nor any other necessity will be lacking.'[13] Trevisan left Rome at the head of a fleet of 27 galleys carrying over 1,000 sailors, 5,000 soldiers and 300 cannon,[14] sailing down the Tiber to Ostia and then on to Naples, where he was expecting to join forces with 15 ships that King Alfonso had finally promised to provide.

In the middle of June a comet appeared, its fiery tail clearly visible in the night sky; it was feared by many as a portent of some great disaster.

Halley's comet causes consternation

Then there appeared for many days a fiery comet with a great hairy tail. The astrologers predicted a terrible plague, a great rise in the price of food or another enormous disaster and, so to avoid God's wrath, Calixtus ordered several days of public prayer in order to inflict any such calamity directly on the Turks.

PLATINA, Vitae Pontificum, P. 342.

The pope berates King Alfonso

It is a pity *that no Christian ships were near Ragusa because they would have given much encouragement to the Hungarians, who complain bitterly that our fleet has not yet arrived. Your ships could have frustrated the Turks, inspired the Christians in the East and rescued Hungary from danger. But instead you traitorously used our money to betray us. God and the Holy See will bring retribution down on you! Alfonso, King of Aragon, aid Pope Calixtus because if you do not God will surely punish you.*

CALIXTUS III TO ALFONSO I OF NAPLES, UNDATED 1456 (L. VON PASTOR, *History of the Popes*, VOL. II, PP. 365–6).

On 29 June Calixtus III sought to galvanize Christendom further by publishing a papal bull ordering all priests to preach a sermon against the Turks, *Oratio contra paganos*. He also required the bells in churches across Europe to be rung between noon and vespers in order to remind Christians to say their prayers for success.[15]

At the beginning of August the papal fleet was still anchored off Naples, waiting for the ships that King Alfonso had promised but now seemed reluctant to supply. The cost of the paying and supplying the men on board was mounting daily; moreover there were reports from Greece that the Turks had conquered Athens, and others from Hungary that the Turks were poised to invade. Calixtus III urged Cardinal Trevisan to depart and wrote a strongly worded reproof to King Alfonso. That evening, together with some of the promised Neapolitan galleys, Cardinal Trevisan finally sailed from Naples. On 6 August news arrived in Rome that the Hungarians, led by John Hunyadi, had managed to defeat the Turkish armies besieging Belgrade.

On 24 August, Jacopo Calcaterra reported the pope's reaction concerning the repulsing of the Turks to Francesco Sforza, Duke of Milan:

Having arrived back in Rome yesterday, I went to see the pope and found him in bed with some pain in his knee which I took to be gout. His Holiness received me with much affection, even though I had not been long absent ... He said again and again what a magnificent and glorious victory it was and praised Hunyadi to the stars, saying that he was the greatest man that the world has seen for three centuries ... and he said that God had granted us this triumph in order to shame all those who had denounced the crusade and had criticized his own actions by saying he had thrown away 15,000, 20,000 even 40,000 ducats, money which past popes had collected and safeguarded with the treasure of the Church. He clearly told me that he had been accused of this by King Alfonso.[16]

I went to see the pope and found him in bed with some pain.

59

ABOVE **Emperor Constantine offers the imperial tiara to Pope Silvester I.** *This late 13th-century fresco from Santi Quattro Coronati in Rome shows the pope wearing a mitre, the head-dress that symbolized his spiritual power, and receiving from the emperor the tiara, the conical hat that was the symbol of temporal imperial power – the so-called 'Donation of Constantine'. The tiara was an emblem of secular authority widely used in the pre-Christian world. Interestingly, the symbol migrated east where it became a typical head-dress of Hindu and Buddhist deities – and the umbrella or parasol being held over the emperor, another traditional imperial symbol, would later become one of the emblems of the Buddha himself.*

With the crusade now underway, Calixtus III turned his attention to the restoration of authority in the Papal States. A few days earlier, on 21 August, he had appointed Pedro Luis Borgia as his governor in Amelia, Assisi, Civita Castellana, Foligno, Narni, Nepi, Nocera, Orvieto, Rieti, Spoleto, Terni and Todi.

In September Rome was hit by an outbreak of the plague. Most of the cardinals left Rome, but Calixtus III, together with Cardinal Domenico Capranica, remained in the city. On 17 September the pope seized the opportunity to publish the creation of his two nephews and the Prince of Portugal as cardinals. By 2 October it was reported that Calixtus III was seriously ill: 'his condition is such that he might die at any moment,' the

The Papal States

When Emperor Constantine moved his capital from Rome to Constantinople (modern-day Istanbul, in Turkey) in AD 330, he made a clear distinction between his own secular power and the spiritual authority of the pope, who remained in Rome.

The collapse of the Roman Empire in the West in the fifth century, however, left Rome unprotected. Determined to retain its independence, the papacy 'discovered' the Donation of Constantine, a document purporting to give Rome the right to rule territory in Italy. The papacy and the Holy Roman Empire (embracing much of Central Europe) waged a long struggle for control of the peninsula, which came to an end in the decades around 1100. While many prosperous mercantile cities, such as Florence and Siena, won their independence, the papacy established its authority over much of Central Italy.

The Papal States were bordered to the north by the papal fief of Ferrara and the imperial fief of Milan, and to the south by the Kingdom of Naples, another papal fief. The states themselves varied from prosperous cities, such as Bologna and Perugia, to tiny hilltop fortresses in the Apennines, such as Narni. Some were ruled directly from Rome by governors appointed by the pope; others were quasi-autonomous, ruled by vicars who were granted the states as papal fiefs.

61

The pope persuaded the College of Cardinals to allow him to create six more cardinals.

Milanese ambassador informed his master.[17] But the pope recovered by the following month.

On 17 November, in a public consistory, Calixtus III gave red hats bestowing cardinalships on his nephews and investing them with their titular churches – his own title of Santi Quattro Coronati to Luis Juan de Milà, and San Nicola in Carcere to Rodrigo Borgia. The pope persuaded the College of Cardinals to allow him to create six more cardinals on 17 December. As one of them, Enea Silvio Piccolomini, punningly remarked: 'Never before had it been so hard for a cardinal to enter the Sacred College; the door hinges [*cardines*] were so rusty they would not move and the pope had to employ a battering ram and other sorts of war machines to break down the door.'[18] Piccolomini's creation had been requested by Emperor Frederick III, and there were candidates proposed by the Duke of Milan and Charles VII the King of France.

In an attempt to improve his relationship with Alfonso of Naples, Calixtus III also gave a red hat to the uncle of Alfonso's beloved mistress Lucrezia d'Alagno. When Lucrezia was in Rome during December, reputedly with 'a retinue that was as grand as if she were indeed queen', Calixtus deliberately honoured his old patron by receiving her publicly in consistory, to the distaste of many in the college of Cardinals.[19]

A profusion of cardinals

It was Advent, which some call the election season for cardinals and there was a bitter argument in consistory because the pope wanted to create cardinals but he was opposed by the college. First they argued that there were too many cardinals already and then poured scorn on the men he nominated, arguing vociferously against all of them. Calixtus, however, got the better of the college, especially thanks to the vigorous assistance of those three cardinals he had already created, and made it clear to the College that he was in charge, as was fitting.

F.A. GRAGG AND L.C. GABEL (EDS), *The Secret Memoirs of a Renaissance Pope*, P. 71.

RIGHT **Calixtus III gives the red hat to Cardinal Piccolomini.** *The receiving of the red hat was the first of a series of rituals that took place over several days or weeks to mark a cardinal's official appointment. After receiving his hat, the new cardinal formally visited all the other members of the college before attending a ceremony at which his 'mouth was closed' (clausura oris). At his next meeting with the pope his 'mouth was opened' (aperitio oris) and he was given a ring and the name of his titular church in Rome. It was only after all these ceremonies had been completed that he could finally take part in the government of the Church. The painting is one of Pinturicchio's ten scenes depicting the life of Pius II (Enea Silvio Piccolomini), which were commissioned in 1502.*

1457

ON 7 JANUARY the new Cardinal Luis Juan de Milà left Rome as legate to Bologna. A fortnight later, on 19 January, Cardinal Rodrigo Borgia departed to take up the post of legate to Ancona, his first important mission being to restore order in this city which had revolted against papal rule.

Calixtus III, meanwhile, was preoccupied with the crusade. News arrived that Cardinal Trevisan had successfully established his headquarters at Rhodes and had succeeded in fighting off a Turkish fleet sent to attack Lesbos. However, the pope's attempts to raise much-needed funds from Europe's rulers were proving futile. On 16 February he urged his legate in France, Cardinal Coëtivy, to press Charles VII to send the money he had promised and, in particular, the offerings which had been collected in churches throughout the country but which the king was refusing to forward. On 27 March Calixtus III announced his intention to bestow the prestigious papal award of the Golden Rose on the king in a vain attempt to make him change his mind. 'The pope asks for help but nobody takes any notice,' wrote Cardinal Piccolomini, adding that 'he issues threats but no one is afraid.'[20]

On 1 May, soon after Cardinal Rodrigo had returned from his successful mission to Ancona, Calixtus III appointed his nephew as Vice-Chancellor of the Church: aged just 26, Rodrigo now held one of the most prestigious posts in Rome, worth 6,000 ducats a year as well as a lucrative income from backhanders and bribes.[21] 'Rodrigo Borgia is now head of the Chancellery,' wrote Cardinal Piccolomini, noting that 'he is certainly young, but he is old in judgement.'[22]

The Golden Rose

The Golden Rose, a spray of fake roses covered with gold leaf and ornamented with sapphires and diamonds, was given out by the pope every year on the fourth Sunday in Lent, as a present for services to the Church.

It was dispensed with the words: 'Receive this rose from our hands, we who take the place of God on earth, although we are not worthy. The rose is the symbol of the Church, of Jerusalem triumphant and of Jerusalem militant. For all faithful Christians, this flower, the most beautiful of all flowers, is a symbol of joy and the crown of saints.'[23]

RIGHT **Pope Calixtus III as patron of Siena.** *Commissioned from Sano di Pietro (c.1456) by the Sienese government in gratitude for the pope's support of its policies, this votive altarpiece contains delightful detail, so typical of medieval Sienese painting, of pack horses being driven into the city. Siena's cathedral is clearly identifiable by the distinctive black-and-white inlaid marble cladding on the exterior of its bell-tower.*

PASTOR ǢENIO ALMIO POPOL XPIANO
A TE dI SIENA ORMAI LAVRA RENdo
FA ·CH ALLEI VOLCA OǢNI TVO SENSO HVMANO

VERǢINE MAdRE ·A·IO ǢARA CONSORTE
SEL TVO CALISTO E ǢENIO ATANTO dONO
ASIENA NÕ TORAMI ALTRO CHE ·IORTE

✠CALISTVS ·IIIᵒ· SANIVS PETRI ǢESENI·PIXIT

During this year the fragile relations between Calixtus III and his erstwhile master, Alfonso I of Naples, deteriorated further. In June the pope refused to agree to the nomination of the king's candidate to a Neapolitan bishopric, and he excommunicated Alfonso's ambassador who had threatened the pope with the summoning of a council. According to Biagio Ghilino, writing to Duke Francesco Sforza of Milan on 23 June, Calixtus III starkly informed Alfonso: 'Know, Your Majesty, that the pope can depose kings.' The king reportedly replied: 'Know, Your Holiness that a king, if he wants, can depose the pope.'[24]

At the same time rumours were circulating in Rome that the pope intended to marry his handsome nephew, Pedro Luis, into the Colonna family. This would not only further damage his relationship with King Alfonso, who supported the Orsini, but would also inflame the traditional Colonna–Orsini rivalry in Rome itself. The situation was exacerbated when Calixtus III sent Pedro Luis, his captain-general, to seize several Orsini strongholds that the pope claimed belonged to the Church. War between the two factions broke out in Rome, and in the middle of July Cardinal Latino Orsini fled the city.

On 19 August the Prefect of Rome, Gianantonio Orsini, died and that same day – with a majority of Borgia allies in the college, including cardinals d'Estouteville, Barbo and Piccolomini – Calixtus III appointed his nephew Pedro Luis in Orsini's place. But two weeks later, on 1 September, the Milanese ambassador reported that the plans to marry the new prefect to a Colonna had cooled.

Pedro Luis fell seriously ill in late October, and on 11 December the pope appointed Cardinal Rodrigo to replace him as Captain-General of the Church.

LEFT **King Charles VII France,** *painted c.1445–50 by Jean Fouquet. Crowned at Rheims in 1429, Charles VII ended the Hundred Years War with England and reduced English possessions in France to just Calais. Using his struggle with England as an excuse, he made no contribution to Calixtus III's crusade, going so far as to ban soldiers en route to the crusade from travelling through his realm.*

The unpopular Catalans

Preoccupied with preparations for the crusade, Calixtus III left the day-to-day business of governing the states of the Church and the city of Rome to his relatives and fellow countrymen.

'There were murders every day and street fights and nothing but Catalans everywhere,' complained one chronicler.[25] Many of the key fortresses in the Papal States were in the hands of members of the Borgia family. A majority of the galley captains were Catalans, as were Calixtus's secretaries, doctors, treasurers and even his cooks. The Romans ridiculed Borgia claims to nobility: the pope's father, they said, was no aristocratic landowner but rather a peasant labouring in the fields. The meteoric rise to power of the two handsome Borgia brothers – Pedro Luis, arrogant and energetic, and Rodrigo, the shrewd politician with a silver tongue – made them particularly unpopular. 'The pope is blinded by love for his family,' it was said.[26] There was even a rumour, reported by the Milanese ambassador, that 'the pope has made his nephew Pedro Luis the Emperor in Constantinople'. 'This is not a joke,' he added, in case Francesco Sforza might misunderstand.[27]

> There were murders every day and street fights and nothing but Catalans everywhere.

1458

MUCH TO THE RELIEF of Calixtus III, and of Cardinal Rodrigo, Pedro Luis began to recover in January and he resumed his former position as Captain-General of the Church.

The seriousness of the papal breach with Naples was evident by the beginning of the year. In January, Cardinal Rodrigo offered to negotiate between Calixtus III and King Alfonso, and there were rumours in March that the cardinal would be sent to Naples to talk with the king. By June, however, it was clear that relations had broken down completely. The Duke of Milan was told that Calixtus said that 'the holy Church has had no peace since the king [Alfonso] acquired the realm and that he has been a continual thorn in the side to Martin V and Eugenius IV and himself. He intends, when the king dies, to free the papacy from this servitude by disallowing the succession of the king's [illegitimate] son.'[28]

Early June brought more immediate concerns when plague broke out in Rome. All who could do so now left the city: Cardinal Rodrigo Borgia went to his villa at Tivoli, while Cardinal Piccolomini, who had gout, went to the baths at Viterbo. Calixtus III, however, remained in Rome, pondering the news that King Alfonso was seriously ill with fever.

During the summer, Calixtus's fundraising for the crusade continued apace. He sold the old mint to Rodrigo Borgia for 2,000 ducats.[29] On 24 June gravediggers discovered an ancient marble sarcophagus containing two wooden coffins, one for an adult and a smaller one for a child. Calixtus removed the silver linings from the coffins, as well as the gold thread which had been used to embroider the rich fabrics in which the two bodies had been buried, and sold the precious metals, raising a further 1,000 ducats.[30]

On 27 June Alfonso I of Naples died, aged 62. He left his Kingdom of Aragon to his brother, Juan II, and that of Naples to his illegitimate son, Ferrante. The news reached Rome two days later and the pope, according to Cardinal Piccolomini, 'held back

ABOVE **Book of Hours belonging to Alfonso V of Aragon (1442).** *He was known as 'the Magnanimous', and Alfonso's reign marked a new period of Aragonese expansion in the Mediterranean, notably the hard-fought conquest of the great Kingdom of Naples, which would later be absorbed into the Spanish Empire. Leaving his wife, Maria of Castile, as regent in Aragon, he spent half his reign in Naples, where his government was manned by Catalans and he made Catalan the official language of his court. The kneeling figure of the king, dressed in robes and a crown rather than armour, and the bed in the background emphasise his dynastic ambitions rather than his considerable military achievements.*

neither his tears nor his laughter, weeping with sadness for the fragility of life and with joy for the removal of his enemy'.[31] On 30 June he ordered all the cardinals to the Vatican for a consistory at which he distributed the dead king's Aragonese benefices. He gave the lucrative see of Valencia to Cardinal Rodrigo. Later that day he made plans to send Pedro Luis Borgia at the head of an army to conquer Naples, and the price of wheat rose abruptly in anticipation of war.

On 12 July Calixtus III signed a papal bull claiming Naples as a lapsed fief of the Church and repudiating Ferrante's succession. He ordered all claimants to the Neapolitan throne to come to Rome; it was widely believed that the pope intended to make his nephew Pedro Luis the new king.

The pope was reminded of his own mortality on 21 July when he suffered a violent attack of gout. His condition was serious enough for Cardinal Rodrigo to return from Tivoli on 25 July and pray in St Peter's for his uncle's life. A week later, the Mantuan ambassador reported that the pope had now been ill for eight days, 'very weak with fever, and deposits in his urine; he cannot digest anything, food goes in and comes out unchanged'.[32]

By 30 July rumours were spreading through Rome that Calixtus III had died. Mobs of citizens vented their anger on any Catalan they could find, while rich merchants, apprehensive of rioting on a larger scale, locked up their goods in

He made plans to send Pedro Luis Borgia at the head of an army to conquer Naples.

Calixtus III and the death of a king

The pope shows signs of being pleased at the death of the king [Alfonso] and of being resentful of his behaviour while he lived. For, the moment the news arrived, he sent a soldier to the house of the king's ambassador with orders to arrest him and take him to Castel Sant'Angelo. But the said ambassador, who had had news of the death of the king earlier and fortunately been informed of the pope's intentions, had left immediately, leaving most of his possessions which Calixtus III then seized.

ANTONIO DA PISTOIA TO FRANCESCO SFORZA, 4 JULY 1458 (L. VON PASTOR, *History of the Popes*, VOL. II, PP. 559–61, DOC. 52).

Calixtus III, like so many who forget the favours they have received, failed to remember that he had been born in Alfonso's realm and had been much favoured by the king, who had appointed him as royal councillor and, moreover, that he owed his career in the Church to King Alfonso, even his election to the papacy.

FRANCESCO GUICCIARDINI, *Storia d'Italia*, BOOK I,3.

69

The frail and elderly pope's condition deteriorated dramatically.

padlocked chests. On 31 July the College of Cardinals met in emergency session and appointed a commission of four cardinals – Bessarion, d'Estouteville, Coëtivy and Barbo – to gather the necessary troops to control the violence that was growing in the city. 'His Holiness the pope is gravely ill, and has already been pronounced dead three times,' reported the Milanese ambassador on 1 August, adding that 'since yesterday he has been a little better, but nothing to give any real hope of recovery.'[33] Calixtus III, however, still had the strength to grant the cities of Terracina and Benevento to Pedro Luis, and to announce his intention of creating five new cardinals.

On 4 August the frail and elderly pope's condition deteriorated dramatically. Determined to retain the power he had acquired during his uncle's papacy, Pedro Luis Borgia planned to hold on to his castles and to use his troops to force the election of a pope favourable to his interests. His brother, however, counselled caution: Rodrigo knew that their future depended on agreement with the cardinals rather than armed opposition. Pedro Luis, therefore, surrendered all his fortresses, including Castel Sant'Angelo, in return for a payment of 22,000 ducats, and his troops swore their obedience to the college.

The following day, the Milanese ambassador reported that 'His Holiness is gravely ill; yesterday evening he received the last rites and there is no more hope for his life, indeed it is only the medicine that is keeping him alive.'[34]

In the dark hours early in the morning of 6 August, Pedro Luis thought it wise to flee Rome, with the assistance of his brother and their ally Cardinal Pietro Barbo. At Ostia there was no sign of the galley he was expecting, and instead he took refuge in the fortress at Civitavecchia. That evening Calixtus III, the first Borgia pope, finally died. The Milanese ambassador informed Francesco Sforza that 'the pope died today at nightfall; the Catalans have all fled and those who are harbouring them are so detested that it will go badly for them if they are found out before the election of a new pope'.[35]

During his short papacy, Calixtus III had shown little enthusiasm for the patronage of art and architecture that appealed to so many other popes, instead devoting his energies – and the wealth of the Church – to the crusade against the Turks and the aim of reconquering Constantinople. Despite his advanced age and poor health, he left to posterity 38 bulky volumes of papal bulls, a testament to the vigour and zeal with which he pursued his goal. He also succeeded in significantly broadening and deepening the influence of the wider Borgia family.

71

LEFT **The Tiber flowing past the fortress at Ostia.** *During the 15th century the Tiber was navigable upstream as far as the port of Rome, where galleys offloaded their cargoes of foodstuffs and luxury wines. The fortress, which guarded the entrance to the river, was originally erected by Martin V and rebuilt in the 1480s.*

ABOVE **Woodcut of Calixtus III.** *History has been unkind to the first Borgia pope, who is frequently criticized for his lack of interest in art and architecture and, above all, for his promotion of his Borgia relatives. By contrast, the zeal and determination with which he protected Christendom from the Turkish threat is often forgotten.*

THE BORGIA NEPHEWS

CARDINALS AND CAPTAIN-GENERALS

1458–1471

The pontificate of Calixtus III had dramatically changed the course of the lives of his Borgia nephews. Luis Juan de Milà and Rodrigo Borgia had held only minor benefices in Spain in 1455 but now, just three years later, they were both cardinals: appointed for life, they were princes of the Church operating at the centre of the European political arena, with the chance of great wealth and power, so long as they played their cards right. However, the death of their uncle had left Rodrigo's important position as Vice-Chancellor of the Church and that of his brother Pedro Luis, the papal army's captain-general, both highly vulnerable to the policies of the new pontiff. Neither cardinal had any chance of election themselves – Luis Juan was 28 years old, while Rodrigo was 27, both far too young for the papal tiara. The family's fortunes depended on securing the election of a pope favourable to their cause.

1458

I am the senior cardinal, I can boast royal blood.

MOST CARDINALS WERE absent from Rome, escaping the summer heat and the plague, when they heard of the death of Calixtus III, and they hurried back to the city. Cardinal Enea Silvio Piccolomini rode down from Viterbo, and Cardinal Luis Juan de Milà arrived in Rome on 11 August, having covered the 190 miles from Bologna in three days.

PREVIOUS PAGE: **Pius II convokes the Council of Mantua,** *in one of the frescoes commemorating the pope's life commissioned (1502) from Pinturicchio by his nephew Cardinal Francesco Piccolomini to decorate the cathedral library in Siena.*

RIGHT **Cardinal Guillaume d'Estouteville.** *This portrait bust by the Florentine sculptor Mino da Fiesole provides a true likeness of the powerful cardinal, who played a leading role at the papal court from his appointment in 1439 to his death in 1483. A major patron of the arts, he amassed an impressive library of classical texts, built the church of Sant'Agostino with its adjoining convent in central Rome and his own palace nearby, possibly the grandest cardinal's residence in 15th-century Rome.*

On 14 August, to the shock of all the college, Cardinal Domenico Capranica, one of the leading candidates for the papal tiara, died after a short illness. On 16 August eighteen cardinals went into the Vatican palace to take part in the conclave: eight Italians, five Spaniards, one Portuguese, two Frenchmen and two Greeks.

At the first 'scrutiny' on 18 August, the voting revealed cardinals Filippo Calandrini and Piccolomini as the leading contenders, each with five votes, but this was a long way off the necessary twelve needed for election. There had been no votes for the wealthy and ambitious Frenchman, Guillaume d'Estouteville, who now opened his campaign by criticizing both favourites. Piccolomini, he argued, was poor and lame from gout: 'How will a penniless pope revive a penniless Church, or a sick pope a sick Church?', while Calandrini was 'stubborn and will not listen to advice'. 'I am the senior cardinal,' he continued, 'I can boast royal blood and I have excellent connections and resources,' adding, significantly, to appeal to the pockets of his poorer colleagues, 'I have many benefices which I will have to distribute among you when I resign them after the election.'[1] D'Estouteville's support grew as the day progressed, as 'many met in the privacy and quiet of the lavatories, and agreed on how they might elect d'Estouteville'.[2] Rodrigo Borgia, lured by the promise of retaining his vice-chancellorship, was one of those who offered their support to the French cardinal.

During the night, however, Calandrini and Piccolomini rallied the opposition. In conversation with Rodrigo, Piccolomini cast doubt on d'Estouteville's promise of the vice-chancellorship: 'Will a Frenchman favour a Frenchman or a Catalan?' he queried.[3] At the scrutiny the following morning, it was clear that d'Estouteville's bid had failed. Cardinal Rodrigo then got to his feet and announced 'I accede to Cardinal Piccolomini'; another ten cardinals followed him and finally Cardinal Prospero Colonna gave the twelfth vote to enable the election of Cardinal Piccolomini as Pope Pius II.

At the scrutiny the following morning, it was clear that d'Estouteville's bid had failed.

75

On 20 August, the day after his election, the new pope held a consistory to announce his intentions. The first priority was the restoration of his authority in the Papal States. Despite opposition from the French cardinals, he recognized Ferrante's claim to the throne of Naples, ordering the Neapolitan ambassadors to be given royal status.

Cardinal Rodrigo was rewarded for his support in the conclave by the confirmation of his post as vice-chancellor and a second titular church, Santa Maria in Via Lata, which had belonged to Domenico Capranica, as well as the abbey of Valdigne, a lucrative benefice in Spain. Pius II also began to negotiate with Pedro Luis Borgia, who was still technically Captain-General of the Church and safe in the stronghold of Civitavecchia. On 3 September, the day of the papal coronation, the pope reached agreement with Pedro Luis, but three weeks later, on 26 September, the young Borgia, still in his twenties, died of fever at Civitavecchia.

At a public consistory on 12 October, in front of the cardinals, the papal court and foreign ambassadors, Pius II gave a lengthy speech in which he announced that he would hold a congress at Mantua, at which all Christian princes would be represented, to discuss the details of a crusade against the Turks.

LEFT **Cardinal Piccolomini submits to Eugenius IV** *in the name of Emperor Frederick III, in another of Pinturicchio's frescoes. The election of Pius II brought a highly experienced diplomat to the papal throne. He had been involved in negotiations between France and England to end the Hundred Years War, travelling to Burgundy and the Low Countries; he had also sailed to Scotland and ridden south to London. As secretary to Frederick III, he had also travelled extensively through Germany, Austria and Hungary.*

The politics of the conclave

At daybreak *Cardinal Piccolomini went to visit Rodrigo, the vice-chancellor, to ask whether he had been persuaded to support Cardinal d'Estouteville. 'What do you expect,' he replied, 'the election has been decided … I am putting my own interests first and am joining the majority. D'Estouteville has sent me a note assuring me I will retain the vice-chancellorship. He will be elected whatever, and if I do not cast my vote for him I shall lose my post.' Piccolomini retorted, 'you are an idiot … you might have the note but Cardinal Coetivy will have the vice-chancellorship; it may have been promised to you but it is also promised to him. Will d'Estouteville be true to you or to him? Will a Frenchman favour a Frenchman or a Catalan? Will he favour a foreigner or one of his own nation? Be careful, you innocent child … because you will find yourself at the back of the queue if a Frenchman is elected pope.'*

F. A. GRAGG AND L. C. GABEL (EDS), *The Secret Memoirs of a Renaissance Pope*, P. 77.

77

1459

ON 22 JANUARY CARDINAL RODRIGO BORGIA and his household left Rome, along with the rest of the papal court, to escort Pius II on the long journey north to Mantua, where the planned congress would open in June. The journey was slow, not least because of the pope's ill-health. By 1 February they had reached Perugia, where they stayed three weeks. On 24 February they entered Siena, Pius II's home city, where they celebrated Easter on 25 March.

ABOVE **Courtyard of the Palazzo Piccolomini,** *Pienza. Pius II's restoration of his birthplace, Corsignano, which he renamed Pienza in honour of himself, was an ambitious project, which involved not only measures to improve the economy of Pienza, but also the reconstruction of its centre. He transformed this modest border fortress into an imposing and modern city,* *creating a landmark in the history of town planning. Pius II himself financed the new cathedral and this elegant Renaissance palace on the main piazza, built (as were many other buildings here) by Bernardo Rossellino (1409–64). Several members of the pope's court also built residences here, including Cardinal Rodrigo Borgia, who paid for the Bishop's Palace (Palazzo Vescovile).*

On 25 April the papal cavalcade arrived in Florence, where the weather was unpleasantly wet. This wealthy city entertained the papal party in magnificent style, with processions, banquets and other festivities which cost the republican government over 22,500 florins. There was jousting on 29 April and a ball the following day, and the annual May Day feast was celebrated with a lion hunt in the main piazza. A lawyer, Ser Giusto, described the spectacle:

> Pius II entered Florence in great honour; with him were 12 cardinals and many horses and courtiers. Because he was ill with gout, he was carried into Florence on his pontifical chair, which was supported on the shoulders of various lords ... The weather was frightful, with heavy rain, and the festivities were not as good as they should have been. The pope lodged at Santa Maria Novella ... On Tuesday 1 May they closed off the Piazza della Signoria and held a lion hunt there. They brought in bulls, cows, buffaloes, horses and wild boar and then they let in about twelve lions but these lions made no effort to attack the animals, indeed they tried to run away and were terrified. There was also a huge ball made of wood, built in such a way that the man inside could drive it wherever he wanted, and he rolled all over the piazza chasing the lions and the other animals, and that was a wonderful device.[4]

Pope Pius II

Enea Silvio Piccolomini was born into a noble but poor Sienese family. As pope he rebuilt the village of Corsignano, where he had been born, transforming this insignificant settlement into a bishopric and renaming it Pienza, after himself. He was clever, well-educated and ambitious, and he worked as a secretary for several cardinals before becoming a diplomat for Holy Roman Emperor Frederick III. A leading supporter of the Council of Basle, he switched his allegiance to Eugenius IV once it became obvious that the pope had the upper hand. He was made a cardinal by Alonso Borgia, Pope Calixtus III, in 1456.

A writer and historian, Piccolomini was crowned poet laureate by Frederick III and is justly claimed as the first humanist pope. His works include a play, *A Tale of Two Lovers (Lucretia and Euralius)*, biographies of the famous men of his day, a treatise on the education of young boys, texts describing the topography of various parts of Europe and Asia and, most famous of all, his own autobiography, the *Commentaries*. Written in the third person, this book records his experiences travelling around Europe, his admiration for Joan of Arc, the beauties of the Tuscan landscape and his shock at experiencing the harsh severity of a Scottish winter. Above all, the work provides a unique insight into the political machinations at the papal court of Renaissance Rome.

The papal entourage enters Mantua

Pius II entered the city in a procession which was ordered as follows. First came the servants of the curia and the households of the cardinals, followed by the less important officials of the curia. Then came twelve horses without riders, each with gilded saddles and harness, after which three banners were carried by nobles wearing armour and riding horses dressed in costly caparisons: the first banner showed a cross, the second the keys of St Peter and the third the five crescents of the Piccolomini coat-of-arms. Then came a red and yellow canopy followed by the holy relics carried by priests dressed in sumptuous vestments. After the relics came a great gilded cross, followed by all the ambassadors and deacons, along with the auditors, scribes and lawyers of the curia. Next came the Eucharist surrounded by tapers, and the sacred Host of our Saviour was in a golden tabernacle mounted on a white horse under a silken canopy. Next came Galeazzo Maria Sforza, son of the Duke of Milan, and Ludovico Gonzaga, Marquis of Mantua. These two were followed by the cardinals and finally Pius II himself on his throne, dressed in his papal robes and his mitre shining with precious jewels.

F. A. Gragg and L. C. Gabel (eds), *The Secret Memoirs of a Renaissance Pope*, pp. 110–11.

The next day they entered Ferrara, where Pius II was received by seven princes.

Leaving Florence on 5 May, the papal cavalcade entered Bologna four days later, and stayed until 16 May when they departed to travel by boat along the waterways of the Po plain to Ferrara. The next day they entered Ferrara, where Pius II was received by seven princes of the ruling Este family, not one of whom could claim legitimate birth. 'Most of the Italian princes ruling today were illegitimate', Pius II wrote in his memoirs, but few could claim such loose morals as Niccolò III d'Este, the father of the current ruler, Borso, who had sixteen siblings, all but four illegitimate. Niccolò III was known by his subjects as the 'Cock of Ferrara'.

On 27 May the papal court finally arrived in Mantua, where the pope and his cardinals would remain for over seven months.

On 1 June Pius II opened the congress with a celebratory mass, despite the lack of delegates as few European rulers had yet sent envoys. The cardinals began

PREVIOUS PAGES **A tournament,** *by the Ferrarese artist Battista Dossi (1490–1548). These entertainments were staged to celebrate marriages, feast days or visits, and they presented an opportunity for the host to display his status. Diplomats reported the pageantry in detail – the gilded emblems glittering in the sun, the magnificent outfits, superb horses from the best studs in Europe and the elegance of the ladies seated in the stands. Competitive and highly dangerous, jousting – part of the education of all young aristocrats – challenged the skills and bravery of both horse and rider, encouraging the strength and dexterity that cavalrymen needed in battle.*

RIGHT **Ludovico Gonzaga, Marquis of Mantua** *(seated). Part of the cycle, painted in 1465–74 by Andrea Mantegna, in the Camera degli Sposi of the Palazzo Ducale, this intimate portrait shows the marquis with a letter in his hand and conferring with his secretary, surrounded by his family and courtiers, with his favourite dog, Rubino, lying quietly under his chair.*

to criticize Pius II 'for being so stubborn and rash … and foolish to come to Mantua where so few envoys had arrived, and even fewer were expected to make the journey. The city sat in the middle of a swamp and was unhealthy, they said; it was far too hot and they did not like the heavy wine or any of the food; many were ill and some had fever; and all they could hear was the croaking of the frogs.'[5]

With little business to do, the cardinals turned to enjoying the entertainments on offer. In July Pius II had to reprimand several of them, including Rodrigo Borgia, for their unseemly behaviour at a boating party on the lake.[6] Delegates finally started to arrive in late summer: envoys from Burgundy arrived in August, and Francesco Sforza, the Duke of Milan, entered Mantua the following month.

ABOVE **The Palazzo Ducale, Mantua.** *The Gonzaga family seized power in Mantua in 1328, when they expelled their rivals, the Bonacolsi (the event commemorated in this 1494 painting by Domenico Morone), and established control of the city, where they would rule until 1627. Skilled diplomats, and linked by marriage to several important ruling dynasties in Europe, they fostered the image of a cultured and illustrious court. This view shows the main square in Mantua with the old cathedral flanked by the bishop's palace on the left and the ducal palace on the right. The ducal palace was once the town hall until the Gonzaga took it over and embellished it after they had seized power. It was distinctive for the open loggias on its façade, which make a telling contrast with the heavily fortified strongholds preferred by many other Italian rulers.*

The first round of talks began on 26 September, but political issues divided the delegates and the congress was inconclusive.

1460

PIUS II CLOSED THE CONGRESS of Mantua on 14 January and, five days later, set out with the papal court on the return journey to Rome.

At a consistory on 5 March, the pope created five new cardinals, including his own nephew Francesco Piccolomini. He also took the opportunity to harangue the College of Cardinals on what he considered inappropriate behaviour: 'you refuse to give up hunting, gambling or the company of women; you host unsuitably grand banquets and wear vestments that are far too rich, you amass expensive gold and silver plate and keep an excess of horses and servants'.[7]

On 8 June cardinals Rodrigo Borgia and Guillaume d'Estouteville, having been asked to be godparents to the daughter of a Sienese noble, attended a private party to celebrate the christening in the nobleman's garden. Pius II, who was at nearby Bagni taking the waters, was given a highly coloured account of what had taken place, and strongly rebuked Rodrigo, though not d'Estouteville, for taking part in what he had been told was an orgy. He wrote to the cardinal on 11 June:

> We have heard that three days ago several Sienese ladies were assembled in Giovanni Bichi's garden and that you, with little care for your position, were with them for five hours during the afternoon, and that you had one cardinal with you who, if not for the sake of the apostolic throne at least for his advanced age, should have reminded you of your rank. From what has been said, there was much dancing and flirting and that you behaved as if you were one of the worldly boys. Decency forbids a complete account of what is said to have taken place, things of which the names alone are unsuitable to your position: husbands, fathers, brothers and other relatives who accompanied the young girls were forbidden to enter so that you could be free to enjoy yourself, and that you yourself, along with a few servants, organized and directed the dancing. They say that in Siena at the moment no one is talking of anything else and everyone is ridiculing your frivolity; it is certain that here at Bagni, where there are many visitors, both ecclesiastical and lay, you have become a laughing-stock.[8]

A present from the Duke of Milan

After Francesco Sforza had returned to Milan, he sent Pius II three plump young oxen, which had been reared on turnips, washed and combed every day and bedded in clean straw. The pope gave one to Sigismund, Duke of Tyrol, and divided the second between the ambassadors, keeping the last one for himself and the cardinals, who said they had never tasted better meat before. But this had been an expensive present because Pius II had had to tip the men who brought the oxen with 10 ducats.

F. A. GRAGG AND L. C. GABEL (EDS), *The Secret Memoirs of a Renaissance Pope*, P. 137.

85

Rodrigo apologized profusely but added that the party had not been at all unseemly, and the pope agreed he may have been hasty in believing the gossip:

> We have received your letter and take note of the explanations which you give. What you have done, beloved son, is not without blame, however it is less disreputable than it first appeared. You are forgiven but you are warned to behave more discreetly in future and be assured that as long as you mend your ways and live modestly, you will have a father and protector.[9]

Pius II now drew up plans to reform the College of Cardinals: 'all cardinals must be legitimately born, over thirty years of age, with doctorates in theology or canon law, of blameless morals and experienced in administration; for the so-called crown cardinals, the relatives and nominees of princes, an ordinary education is enough'.[10] He also banned jugglers and musicians, hunting, and banquets, except when required to entertain visiting dignitaries.

1461

TOWARDS THE END of this year, on 18 December, Pius II created six new cardinals, including Francesco Gonzaga, the son of the Marquis of Mantua who had been his host for the Congress of Mantua two years previously. In the light of Pius II's attempts to reform the College of Cardinals, this appointment was a particular favour, as Francesco was just 17 years old.

At Christendom's eastern edge, the last vestige of the Byzantine Empire, Trebizond, fell to the Turks.

1462

AT THE END OF MARCH, at his new palace in Rome, Rodrigo Borgia received the young Cardinal Francesco Gonzaga, who was making his customary rounds of his new colleagues after receiving his hat: 'The vice-chancellor's palace is not yet finished,' reported Francesco, 'but what has been done is more beautiful than I can say.'[11]

LEFT **Titian's *The Andrians*.** *This picture (from the early 1520s), based on Ovid's account of the island of Andros, where the fountain in the Temple of Bacchus freely spouted wine during the ides of January, belongs to the genre of bacchanals that was hugely popular in Renaissance Italy. Renaissance banquets were often bawdy affairs, where guests indulged themselves with elaborate dishes of food and substantial quantities of drink – the word 'banquet' did not mean a formal feast where guests were individually seated around a great table but a party where they were free to roam and chat – and indulge in those staples of courtly life: gossip and flirtation.*

Piazza Santa Maria del Popolo, Rome. *This piazza played an important role in the ceremonial life of Rome. Entering through the adjacent city gate, the Porta del Popolo (not shown), it was here that important visitors from the north travelling down the Via Flaminia were formally greeted by the cardinals and the papal court, before beginning their ceremonial entry into the city. (The obelisk, brought from Egypt by Emperor Augustus, was erected here by Pope Sixtus V in 1589.)*

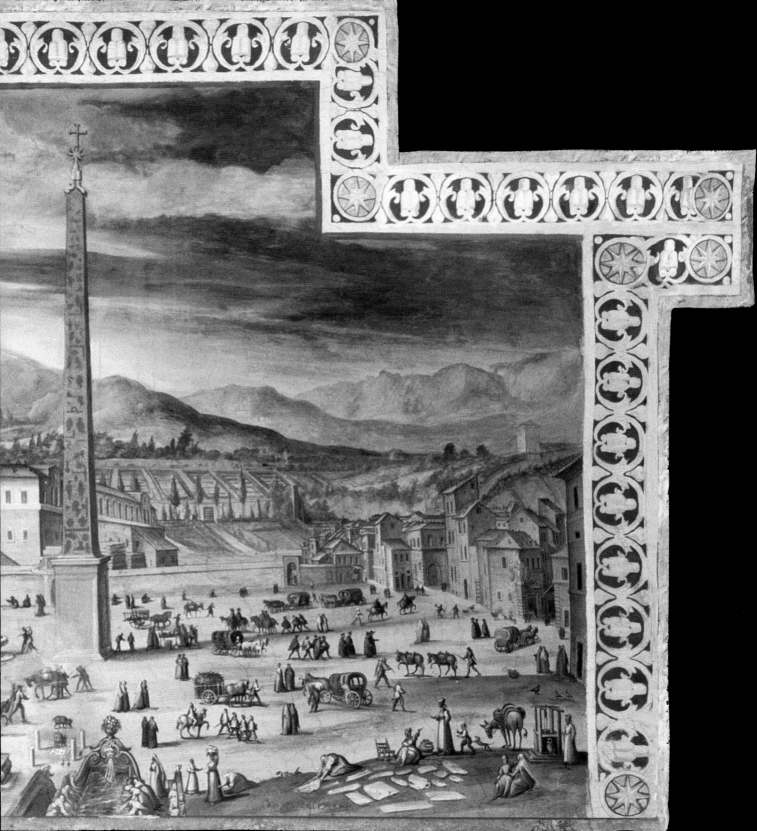

On 11 April, the Tuesday before Easter, the cardinals assembled at the Porta del Popolo to escort the treasured relic of the head of St Andrew, the brother of St Peter, which had been saved from the Turks invading Greece. Although it had rained ferociously all night, the weather had miraculously cleared up for this solemn event. The cardinals walked through the city to St Peter's, an occasion remembered by Pius II, who noted Rodrigo Borgia's talents:

> It was quite a sight to see so many old men walking through the thick mud with palm fronds in their hands and mitres on their greying hair ... those who had been born to luxury and had always travelled on horseback covered two miles that day even though they wore heavy vestments ... Guillaume d'Estouteville, of royal blood, also had his own weight to carry, for he was old and fat; Alain Coëtivy, a tall figure with a large belly also had difficulty with his weight, but both managed joyfully; Juan Carvajal, a Spanish lawyer who had just returned from Hungary, was particularly admired because, although he was old and ill, he walked the whole way courageously and cheerfully, praying as he went ... Alessandro Oliva and Jacopo Tebaldi had a hard time, one in poor health and the other sixty-six years old ... the rest were young and energetic, like Pietro Barbo, the nephew of Eugenius IV; Luis Juan de Milà, nephew of Calixtus III ... Rodrigo Borgia, the vice-chancellor, nephew of Calixtus III and an exceptionally capable man ... the cardinals walked in procession with exceptional dignity so that the crowds along the streets were moved to prayer.[12]

In early May, with the plague raging in Rome, Cardinal Rodrigo was one of seven cardinals accompanying Pius II on his journey to Viterbo. They left early in the morning, stopping for lunch by a spring in the woods, and dozed afterwards under the trees.[13] 'Everything was green that May,' wrote Pius II, 'the meadows and woods alive and the birds singing joyfully.'[14]

On 27 May the papal court celebrated the feast of Corpus Christi in Viterbo, the cardinals competing with each other for the splendour of their pageants. The Dominican Juan Torquemada underlined the spiritual importance of this feast with a representation of the Last Supper and the Institution of the Eucharist. Juan Carvajal portrayed the Fall of the Rebel Angels, with a hideous dragon, whose head was cut off by a soldier playing the part of St Michael. Rodrigo Borgia's display emphasized the supreme power of the pope. After the ceremonies were over, Cardinal Luis Juan de Milà hosted a splendid lunch in the papal palace, 'with gold and silver plates spread with the most delicious dishes'.[15]

RIGHT **Fresco of silver dishes and cups.** *The credenza, or sideboard, as painted here was an important feature of Renaissance dining. It was here that a host would display his wealth and taste and, at a more practical level, it was where his cooks prepared and served the cold hors d'oeuvres and sweet dishes that formed such a distinctive part of the grand Italian feast.*

Rodrigo Borgia's Corpus Christi entertainments

The vice-chancellor's display took up 74 feet along the street. Behind a costly purple curtain ... was a lavishly decorated room with a sumptuous bed and a fountain which spouted water and the finest wine. When Pius II approached the curtain he found boys singing like angels who genuflected before the Eucharist and welcomed the pope before retiring behind the curtain, chanting 'Raise your gates, O princes, and King Pius, will enter.' Inside the room were five kings dressed magnificently and guards who pretended to stop the pope entering but when they heard the angels they asked 'Who is this King Pius' and the angels replied ... 'The lord of all the world'. So the curtain was raised to the sound of trumpets and other instruments and the five kings knelt before the pope and recited verses praising him ... there was a tapestry canopy making a roof above the fountain in the square and banners which showed the coats-of-arms of Calixtus III and Cardinal Rodrigo.

F. A. GRAGG AND L. C. GABEL (EDS), *The Secret Memoirs of a Renaissance Pope*, PP. 257–8.

It was during this year that Rodrigo Borgia's mistress gave birth to a son.

In early June, the peace was broken when plague broke out in Viterbo and the cardinals moved away with Pius II, first to the Farnese castle at Capodimonte. There the papal court was entertained to a boat race on the Lake of Bolsena, while Pius II discussed politics with the cardinals away from the shore, though they did watch the race with 'pleasure and amusement'.[16] By the end of November the cardinals were at Lake Trasimeno, near Perugia, after an exhausting autumn moving from place to place in the papal cavalcade. The strain was proving difficult for several cardinals, not to mention their households. Francesco Gonzaga's majordomo, the head of his household, complained: 'I know it is important for a cardinal who wants to get on to follow the pope, but if the cardinal left his household in a safe place and took only the essential servants with him, that would make about twelve persons; this is what the other cardinals do, such as d'Estouteville and Borgia.'[17]

It was during this year that Rodrigo Borgia's mistress, whose name has not been recorded – he was 'living discreetly' as the pope had advised him – gave birth to a son. Rodrigo named him Pedro Luis, in memory of his older brother who had died so tragically four years earlier. The cardinal would send him at a young age back Spain, to be brought up in the Borgia circle at Játiva.

1463

IN MAY PIUS II accepted the invitation of Guillaume d'Estouteville, Cardinal-Bishop of Ostia, to visit the ruins of that Ancient Roman port in the company of several cardinals, including Rodrigo Borgia. While they were looking around, a dispute developed between Cardinal Rodrigo and the pope's private secretary, Gregorio Lolli, about the location of a palace, and they agreed that the loser must pay the winner a forfeit of a large sturgeon, an expensive fish. Rodrigo lost the bet. That night a dangerously violent storm hit the tents where his household was camped.

That night a dangerously violent storm hit the tents.

ABOVE **Cope of Pius II.** *The cope – a wide ceremonial cloak, fastened at the front with a clasp – was used for benedictions and processions. Designed to give visual expression to the power and wealth of the Church, it was usually elaborately decorated with religious imagery and often embroidered with expensive gold and silver thread. This cope was made in England during the 14th century and given to Pius II by Tomaso Paleologo, the ruler of Morea; it was one of a series of rich vestments that the pope donated to Pienza cathedral, in his home town.*

Cardinal Rodrigo survives a storm

When Pius II *got back to Ostia he saw that the fishermen had caught a huge dolphin ... said to be the portent of a terrible storm. That night, 15 May a violent tempest broke out ... the winds tore down trees and everything in their way, the sky flashed, there were loud claps of thunder and great bolts of lightning shot out of the clouds ... and so much rain fell that it seemed as if God had decided again to flood the earth ... Rodrigo Borgia's household was lodged outside the walls of the town in two tents and they were destroyed in a violent gust of wind, which snapped the ropes, broke the poles and ripped the canvas to pieces ... everyone fled but the night was too dark for them to see where they were going and they ended up in a bed of thistles which badly lacerated them. Finally, bloodstained and exhausted, they found the vice-chancellor in his rooms in the palace, frightened by the ferocity of the storm. When he saw his staff, he was less concerned for their well-being than for the safety of his gilded plate.*

F. A. GRAGG AND L. C. GABEL (EDS), *The Secret Memoirs of a Renaissance Pope*, PP. 300–2.

On 23 September Pius II held a secret consistory in which he subjected the cardinals to yet another long lecture about their lifestyles:

> The priesthood is derided by many. They say we live too comfortably, acquire undeserved wealth, pursue ambitions before all else, ride the fattest mules and the best horses, decorate our robes with trailing fringes, wear our red hats over plump cheeks, breed hunting dogs and spend too much on actors and parasites, but spend nothing on defending Christendom. They are not wrong; many of the cardinals do just this and, it seems to me, that the extravagance and arrogance of our court is excessive. It makes people hate us and nobody will listen when we speak the truth.[18]

The speech was Pius's prelude to announcing his plans for the crusade, which, to their astonishment, he intended to lead in person. Machiavelli would later comment that this was 'an old man trying to do a young man's job'.[19] The pope also encouraged the richer cardinals to support the venture by financing the building and equipping of individual galleys. Cardinal Rodrigo was one of the few to do the pope's bidding, mortgaging his palace and contributing his income from his see of Valencia.[20]

In November Pius II decided to raise funds for the crusade by appointing more 'abbreviators' – the men, many of whom were Latin scholars, who drafted all the papal briefs – on the basis that they would pay for their prestigious posts in the chancellery. Furthermore, he decided to organize them into a formal college. As head of the chancellery, Cardinal Rodrigo objected to the plan, which substantially curbed his powers; but the priorities of the crusade came first.

1464

ON 18 JUNE Pius II left Rome for Ancona on Italy's eastern coast, where he expected to meet the Venetian fleet and board one of the galleys to lead the crusade. The journey was very slow in the summer heat as the pope was suffering from the side-effects of his troublesome gout. The Milanese ambassador reported they were only making six or seven miles a day.[21] Rodrigo Borgia, riding with cardinals d'Estouteville and Eroli, joined the papal cavalcade at Terni in late June.

By 3 July they had only reached Assisi, and it was another ten days before they arrived at Loreto. Here Pius II donated a golden chalice to the Casa Santa, the revered relic of the House of the Virgin, which had been miraculously transported from the Holy Land in 1294. The chalice was inscribed with the pope's earnest prayer for his recovery: 'I, a miserable sinner, turn to you and beg you with all my heart to cure me of this terrible fever and cough, and to restore power to my failing limbs.'[22]

By the time they reached Ancona on 19 July Pius II was seriously ill. Many cardinals had also sickened. Cardinal Jacopo Ammanati had developed a high fever in Spoleto, Cardinal Nicholas of Cusa fell ill with the plague in Todi, while Cardinal Pietro Barbo was suddenly struck down with the plague in Loreto. Ancona was in

chaos, with thousands of crusaders jamming the streets, many with no money; there was not enough accommodation or water and the plague that broke out there in late July killed many of them.

On 10 August the Mantuan ambassador reported that Cardinal Rodrigo Borgia 'is ill with the plague, and this is true,

> By the time they reached Ancona on 19 July Pius II was seriously ill. Many cardinals had also sickened.

95

ABOVE **Palazzo Venezia,** Rome, shown in a later drawing. Begun in 1455 by Cardinal Pietro Barbo as a modest palace attached to his titular church of San Marco, the building was dramatically enlarged after his election as Pope Paul II in 1464, with the addition of a full set of papal reception halls, robing rooms and private apartments, all lavishly decorated with coffered wooden ceilings. The foundation diggers were ordered to hand over all gold coins, jewels, stones and metals they found on the site, which was close to the Ancient Roman Capitol.

he has pain in one ear and under the arm on that side,' and that 'the doctor who first saw him said he had little hope,' especially, the envoy added enigmatically in Latin, 'as he has not been alone in his bed'.[23]

The Venetian fleet finally arrived on 12 August, but the pope was too ill to welcome it in person. On 14 August the cardinals gathered around his sickbed in the bishop's palace, where they listened to what were his parting words. Pope Pius II died the following day and, three days later, the cardinals left Ancona to accompany his body on its last journey, back to Rome.

The conclave to elect the next pope opened in Rome on 28 August, its members comprising ten Italians, four Spaniards, four Frenchmen and the Greek Cardinal Bessarion, the favourite. Thanks to Pius II's policy of creating Italian cardinals, they had an over-all majority for the first time in centuries. After the opening ceremonies were complete, the cardinals settled into the cubicles that had been prepared for them in the Great Chapel. Pietro Barbo had recovered, a result he believed of his prayers to the Virgin of Loreto; but the elderly Nicholas of Cusa was dead. Cardinal Trevisan was still ill but did go into the conclave, as did Rodrigo Borgia, who arrived at the Vatican with his head swathed in bandages; Cardinal Torquemada arrived in a litter early in the morning of 29 August.

The first scrutiny was on the morning of 30 August and when the votes were counted, Pietro Barbo had achieved a two-thirds majority with 14 votes, one of which was from his friend Cardinal Rodrigo.

On 4 September the Mantuan ambassador reported that Rodrigo Borgia was 'in high standing' with the new Pope Paul II.[24] However, he was not present at the papal

LEFT **Pius II arrives at Ancona to launch the crusade,** *in another of Pinturicchio's 1502 commissions on the pope's life. As he left Rome on 18 June 1464, the pope was heard to say goodbye to the city that would never see him again. Despite the extreme pain and fever brought on by gout and kidney stones, the threats from his cardinals that they would be forced to forbid his embarkation, and the warnings from his doctors that he would not live beyond two days at sea, he remained stubbornly determined to lead the crusade in person.*

Pope Paul II

Pietro Barbo, who, aged 23 had been created a cardinal by his uncle Pope Eugenius IV in 1440, was now just 47 years old and in excellent health.

Unlike his predecessor, who had hectored the cardinals on their worldly way of life, Paul II wholeheartedly adopted the role of a secular prince. He staged elaborate celebrations for visiting dignitaries and for Carnival, and shortened the interval between Jubilees to 25 years. Most symbolically, he moved out of the Vatican, preferring the palace he had built at his titular church of San Marco, known as the Palazzo Venezia. He now enlarged this palace into a papal residence, with its own papal benediction loggia, justifying his actions with the argument that St Mark had been a disciple of St Peter. At the palace he amassed one of the greatest collections of antiquities and other valuable objects of the period: antique marbles, bronzes, cameos and coins, vases of semi-precious stones, early Christian ivories, precious reliquaries encrusted with pearls and sapphires, Byzantine icons and costly Flemish tapestries.

97

LA·PORT·IMBREE·IEO.

zhon̄· regis

panthasileē

Verꞇigunt̃ troiā̄ euā panthasilea · Bellatrices ūille ħderate ·
Ut biᵗorium inuadiēt galea · Hos priamꝰ fauit ordinate ·

Pħilimenes et eneas
Diomedes reɣna rii

coronation on 16 September; as the senior cardinal-deacon in the College of Cardinals he should have had the prestige of placing the papal tiara on the head of the new pope, but he was too ill to attend.

That autumn plague broke out again in Rome; one envoy reported that 'almost all the cardinals' palaces are hospitals'.[25]

It was not until early October that Cardinal Rodrigo was well enough to leave his palace.

It was not until early October that Cardinal Rodrigo was well enough to leave his palace. According to Giacomo d'Arezzo, the Mantuan ambassador, writing on 9 October, 'the vice-chancellor has been ill with the plague, however yesterday he was seen out, even though the scar left by the plague is not yet healed'.[26] The cardinal, the envoy continued, was also happy with the news that the new pope intended to restore his powers over the abbreviators in the papal chancellery, which Pius II had removed. Giacomo d'Arezzo himself was less happy: 'This restitution has impoverished many of those who bought their post, and I am one of them.' Bartolomeo Sacchi, the humanist better known as Platina, was another of the recent appointees, and furious: 'As soon as Paul II was elected he sacked all the abbreviators who had been appointed by Pius II, arguing that they were incompetent or uneducated … he stripped those men of their positions without hearing their own stories. These were men he ought to have been encouraging and rewarding, because they were clever and learned.'[27] On 3 December Paul II issued the decree formalizing his cancellation of Pius II's reforms to the College of Abbreviators, thus rewarding Cardinal Rodrigo for his support in the conclave.

1465

ON 22 MARCH the wealthy Cardinal Ludovico Trevisan died at the age of 64, leaving 400,000 ducats to his nephews. The pope, however, intervened and gave the entire estate to charity.[28]

It appeared to many that the pope was also devoting considerable charity towards himself. On Easter Sunday, 14 April, Paul II astonished observers by appearing at mass in St Peter's wearing a new papal tiara, which the Milanese ambassador estimated had cost over 60,000 ducats.[29]

PREVIOUS PAGE **Tapestry depicting the War of Troy,** *one of a 15th-century series made in France. Very expensive to make, tapestries were considered the most luxurious furnishings in Renaissance Europe. An average set could be bought for just 500 scudi, the equivalent of ten years' work for a successful master builder; a magnificent set would cost much more – those who could not afford the real thing might have fake tapestries frescoed on their walls, at a fraction of the cost. For the rich and powerful, frequently on the move between their palaces and villas, or travelling further afield, portability was an important aspect of display. Tapestries were easily rolled up and relatively light to transport, and they could be used to convert bare walls into rooms of sumptuous grandeur.*

1466

CARNIVAL IN ROME was particularly splendid this year, the celebrations considerably increased by a decree of Paul II who added new processions, public banquets and races, notably a horse race along Rome's principal thoroughfare, the Corso, starting at the Arch of Marcus Aurelius by the church of San Lorenzo in Lucina and ending at the papal palace, Palazzo Venezia.

On 8 March Francesco Sforza, Duke of Milan, died very suddenly after an illness of just two days; he was succeeded by his son Galeazzo Maria.

At Christmas Paul II appeared in a new litter, which was said to have cost as much as a palace.

Carnival in Rome was particularly splendid this year,

ABOVE **San Giovanni in Laterano,** *drawn by Marten van Heemskerck (1498–1574). The magnificent basilica with its adjoining palace, begun in 313 by Emperor Constantine, was the prime focus of papal power in Rome until the pope took up residence at St Peter's in the 15th century. The equestrian statue of Emperor Marcus Aurelius was widely believed to represent Constantine himself. The imperial sculpture at the Lateran underlined the links between the papacy and the emperors of Ancient Rome.*

OVERLEAF **Galeazzo Maria Sforza, Duke of Milan,** *painted c.1471 by Antonio and Piero Pollaiuolo. Having succeeded his father at the age of 21, he developed expensive tastes. He established Milan as an important centre of music, and amassed an impressive collection of valuables, including jewels, lavishly illustrated manuscripts, relics and an item that particularly impressed one visitor: a unicorn's horn.*

Carnival in Rome

Rome's Carnival lasted from 26 December to Shrove Tuesday. It was the season of feasting, parties and entertainments, characterized by uninhibited behaviour and misrule.

People wore masks or costumes, often dressing up as the opposite sex, and roamed the streets and squares in gangs pelting the unwary with water and eggs. Bakers sold special biscuits and fried pastries to the crowds watching races, mock battles, bullfights and processions of elaborately decorated floats. One of the more exciting events took place at Monte Testaccio by the Tiber wharves. This artificial hill, which had been created during Ancient Roman times with piles of discarded crockery pots and jars, provided a slope down which cartloads of pigs were thrown, tumbling down to the people jostling below to catch a prize and take it home for the kitchen.

Platina evoked the novelties introduced by Paul II in 1466:

Paul II instituted most magnificent entertainments and sumptuous banquets in imitation of the games of the Ancient Romans, proposing eight races to be run for prizes of bolts of cloth during Carnival: old men, youths and boys, even Jews all tried their chances in the races as too did horses, mares, asses and buffaloes, and the spectators watched them all with immense pleasure. The race track was from the Arch of Domitian [i.e. the Arch of Marcus Aurelius] to the Church of San Marco, where the pope himself enjoyed the spectacle. After the boys' race he gave a coin to each entrant, even though they were all covered in mud.

PLATINA, *Vitae Pontificum*, p. 380.

1467

THIS YEAR SAW THE BIRTH of a second child to Cardinal Rodrigo Borgia and his anonymous mistress; he named this daughter Isabella, after his mother.

On 18 September, after a three-year struggle with the College of Cardinals, Paul II was able to create eight new cardinals. They included the Archbishop of Naples, Oliviero Carafa, aged 37, an eminent lawyer and the candidate of King Ferrante I; Francesco della Rovere, aged 53, a Franciscan from a very humble background who had worked his way up to become minister-general of his Order; and Marco Barbo, aged 47, the pious and respected nephew of the pope.

103

1468

DURING CARNIVAL in late February, it was discovered that a group of humanists, who had lost their livelihoods as a result of Paul II's reforms to the College of Abbreviators, were plotting to assassinate the pope. Three of the four leaders escaped, but Platina was arrested and taken to Castel Sant'Angelo with other suspects. 'People are being arrested every night and we are beginning to understand the extent of the plot,' reported Giovanni Bianchi, the Milanese ambassador, on 28 February; he explained that there had been 'a very real danger that it might have succeeded if the pope had not been protected by God'.[30] With the plot uncovered, Paul II vented his anger against humanist learning and astrology. The following day Bianchi described his audience with the pope:

> His Holiness started to condemn these humanist studies, saying that if God preserves his life then he will do two things. First he will make it illegal to study these useless histories and poems because they are full of heresies and slanders, and then he will make it illegal either to teach or practise astrology ... children of barely ten years of age go to school already knowing a thousand vulgarities, and think how they will learn a thousand more when they read Juvenal, Terence, Plautus, Ovid and the others. Juvenal, said the pope, does show some inclination to criticize these vices but by writing about them he teaches his readers what they are.[31]

In the middle of March it was reported that, true to his word, 'the pope has prohibited all schoolmasters from reading the ancient poets because of the heretical beliefs found therein'.[32]

In April the first cases of a new outbreak of plague were confirmed in Rome, and the situation soon worsened, aggravated by the warming weather. On 21 May it was reported that Paul II was unwell and had cancelled all audiences.[33] He was still in bed on 15 June but had recovered sufficiently by 8 July to leave Rome, where now up to 50 people were dying every day.

Returning to Rome in the autumn, the pope created new cardinals on 21 November, giving red hats to two more of his nephews, Giovanni Battista Zen and Giovanni Michiel.

On Christmas Eve the Holy Roman Emperor, Frederick III, arrived in Rome, visiting the city in fulfilment of a vow he had made while in prison in Vienna. Cardinal Rodrigo gathered with the rest of the College of Cardinals at the Porta del Popolo, where they were kept waiting several hours after sunset for the imperial party, delayed, many people thought, by the Emperor's astrologer. The sombre cavalcade of 700 horsemen, all dressed in black to mark the recent death of the empress, rode through the city escorted by the cardinals and by 3,000 torches. It took them two hours to reach St Peter's, where Frederick III was received by Paul II. On Christmas Day the two rulers celebrated mass together in St Peter's, again with the cardinals in attendance. Imperial–papal relations required some careful etiquette:

> [The Emperor] arrived at St Peter's and was greeted by the pope at the high altar, where he knelt down and kissed the pope's foot and then his hand before rising to kiss his face and then going to his seat, which was separated by the width of two men from the papal throne. It was two feet lower than the throne but slightly higher than the seats of the cardinals. After some speeches and ceremonial the two men went to the palace. His Holiness had the Emperor beside him and held his hand and in this way they went to the papal apartments, from where the cardinals accompanied the Emperor to his rooms in the palace on the floor below ... [the next day] the pope met the Emperor, whose head was bare which is a sign of great respect and His Holiness made him put his hat back on ... .[34]

LEFT **Castel Sant'Angelo, Rome.** *Dark and damp, and infested with spiders, snakes and rats, the underground dungeons at this papal castle were notoriously unpleasant for the criminals and enemies of the state incarcerated there. Above, by contrast, were luxurious papal apartments, which provided the pope with a secure refuge in times of war or civic violence. This 18th-century drawing by Piranesi successfully conveys the imposing nature of the edifice.*

Humanists and humanism

The term 'humanism' was invented in the 19th century and imbued with post-Enlightenment idealism. But in a Renaissance context, the term had very different connotations.

Renaissance humanists were neither humanitarians nor were they agnostics; rather, they were intellectuals who studied the literary culture of the ancient world. They revived the rules of classical Latin, which, in their view, had degenerated since the fall of the Roman Empire, and they used that ancient language to write their own literary, historical and ethical works in imitation of their Roman forbears. In Rome, many humanists were employed in the curia as secretaries and administrators, and they used their keen intellects to promote the supremacy of papal power, likening the pope and the College of Cardinals to the emperor and senators of Ancient Rome.

1469

Later that year, Rodrigo's unnamed mistress gave birth.

ON 9 JANUARY Cardinal Rodrigo Borgia was chosen, along with Cardinal Angelo Capranica, to escort Emperor Frederick III along the road from Rome to Viterbo, according to the courtesy granted to important visiting dignitaries.

Later that year, Rodrigo's unnamed mistress gave birth to the cardinal's third child, another daughter, whom they named Girolama.

On 19 October the Archbishop of Toledo, Alonso Carillo, secretly solemnized a marriage between Ferdinand, heir to the throne of Aragon, and Isabella, heiress of Castile. The bride and groom were cousins and had a papal dispensation for their union, but the document was a forgery, drawn up by Ferdinand and his father King Juan II with the assistance of the archbishop.

On 6 December Cardinal Juan Carvajal died, in Rome. He was elderly – 70 years old – and frail, and his teeth were so loose that he could only chew his food with the aid of a mechanical contraption.[35]

1470

ON 12 JULY the Turks captured the large island of Negroponte (later called Euboea or Evvoia), just off the eastern coast of mainland Greece. With most of Greece now under the rule of Sultan Mehmet II, Venetian power in the Aegean appeared crushed. At the year's end, on 22 December, Paul II announced an alliance of the Italian states against the infidel, which was celebrated with bonfires across Rome.

1471

AT THE BEGINNING of April the Marquis of Ferrara, Borso d'Este, arrived in Rome accompanied by a large cavalcade including 500 nobles, hundreds of servants and several strings of pack mules. After mass on Palm Sunday, on 7 April, Cardinal Rodrigo Borgia gathered with his colleagues for a consistory at which they gave their approval to Paul II's intention to invest Borso as Duke of Ferrara. The ceremony, held in St Peter's on Easter Day, 14 April, was a splendid affair, and the Ferrarese ambassador was particularly impressed by 'the most excellent singers of the papal choir'.[36] Borso was treated with exceptional honour and given a 'large, regal and imposing palace not far from the Vatican'[37] as his residence while he was in Rome, while the rest of his entourage was accommodated in various inns in the city. The bill for the hospitality, paid by the pope, came to 7,938 florins, half the total cost of the visit.[38]

On 15 April Paul II awarded Borso the Golden Rose in a ceremony at St Peter's, which the new duke then carried in procession from the Vatican to Palazzo Venezia for a banquet. A few days later, he went hunting with the cardinals in the countryside outside Rome.

On the morning of 26 July the pope held his usual consistory with the cardinals, a long one lasting for six hours. Afterwards he decided to dine

> On 22 December, Paul II announced an alliance of the Italian states against the infidel.

LEFT **Borso d'Este and his court.** *These frescoes, commissioned from the painter Francesco Cossa for the Palazzo Schifanoia, one of Borso's residences in Ferrara, show the magnificently dressed duke surrounded by his courtiers, mounted on horses from the stables for which Ferrara was particularly famous. An astute politician, with a taste for the extravagant, Borso (1413–71) managed to upgrade his status by persuading Emperor Frederick III to raise the imperial fief of Modena into a dukedom and Pius II to convert the papal fief of Ferrara in a similar manner. He was responsible for commissioning one of the most expensive books in 15th-century Italy – a Bible lavishly decorated with hand-painted miniatures which cost over 2,000 ducats.*

The pope's dining-table

He loved to have a large number of dishes on his table, though he generally chose the worst, and complained if what he wanted was not provided. He drank much and often but his wine was weak and diluted with water. He loved melons, crabs, sweets, fish and pork, and I believe it was this peculiar diet which caused the apoplexy of which he died, for the day before his death he had eaten two very large melons.

PLATINA, *Vitae Pontificum*, P. 397.

The wax candles at his funeral cost 1,852 florins.

al fresco in the gardens of the Vatican – some reported that he had not worn a hat, despite the hot sun, and had eaten a lot of melons, widely thought to be particularly indigestible. He did not feel well enough to hold his usual audiences that evening. An hour later he suffered a severe stroke and died. The Milanese ambassador, Nicodemo Pontremoli, described the events to Galeazzo Maria Sforza in a letter of 2 August:

... he had attended consistory on Friday 26 July which had lasted all morning, six hours, and he seemed in excellent spirits. He dined late in the afternoon and ate three melons, not very large ones, and some other light dishes of the sort that are usually eaten at this time of year. Afterwards he told his manservant that he did not feel very well and they cancelled his evening audiences. He went to lie down ... an hour later the manservant heard a noise and hurried to the pope's room and found him foaming at the mouth and close to death ... so from the beginning to the end it lasted no more than an hour.[39]

He was only 54 years old. 'It is an incredible shock,' wrote the Archbishop of Milan, 'especially as he has been so healthy for so long.'[40] The wax candles at his funeral cost 1,852 florins, and over 6,000 florins were spent on gold brocade and other materials.[41]

The unexpected death of Paul II inevitably heralded another conclave. The astute Cardinal Rodrigo Borgia had played a significant role in the election of the previous two popes, who had both confirmed his position as vice-chancellor and rewarded him with other honours, establishing his prestige in the College of Cardinals. These achievements now hung in the balance.

RIGHT **Tomb of Paul II in Rome.** *In sharp contrast to his predecessors, Paul II showed little crusading zeal – indeed, he went back on the agreement signed by all the cardinals before the election to continue the crusade and, instead, he directed papal funds to the building of the Palazzo Venezia. He also showed little care for Rome's heritage. He quarried marble from the Colosseum and pillaged other ancient monuments for travertine and other materials for the building of his palace. Much criticized for his attack on humanist learning and for the suppression of the College of Abbreviators where many humanists were employed, Paul II was not wholly opposed to the culture of classical antiquity – his collection included many valuable antiques and he did finance repairs to several Roman triumphal arches.*

RODRIGO BORGIA

NEW TITLES,
NEW RELATIONSHIPS,
NEW WEALTH

1471–1484

Rodrigo Borgia, Cardinal of Valencia, was no pious churchman. He had effortlessly combined his career at the top of the Church hierarchy with a secular lifestyle of princely magnificence. Anonymous mistresses had already borne him three children, all of whom he had acknowledged. In itself, this fact did not disqualify him from a credible bid for the papal tiara on the death of Paul II. More challenging for the Spanish-born cardinal was the fact that the conclave was now overwhelmingly Italian. He would need to call upon all his political skills to ensure his survival in the longer term.

1471

Cardinal Rodrigo had just one supporter, Francesco Gonzaga,

THE CONCLAVE TO ELECT Paul II's successor opened in the heat of summer on 6 August, attended by eighteen cardinals, only three of whom – Bessarion, d'Estouteville and Rodrigo Borgia – were not Italian. Eager to serve his master, the Milanese ambassador managed to get hold of a list that recorded exactly how everyone had voted. Cardinal Rodrigo had just one supporter, Francesco Gonzaga, and he convinced the young man to join him in an alliance to secure the election of Francesco della Rovere. The unblemished piety of this Franciscan cardinal, combined with his lack of connections in the wider political arena, enabled Cardinal Rodrigo to gather the necessary two-thirds of the votes in the conclave.

On 9 August the election of Francesco della Rovere was announced to the crowds gathered outside the Vatican, and he chose the name Sixtus IV, in honour of Pope Sixtus II, the martyr of the early Christian Church whose feast day was 6 August, the day on which the conclave had opened.

PREVIOUS PAGE **Cardinal Rodrigo Borgia,** *by an anonymous Spanish painter. Nobody could have described Rodrigo Borgia as conventionally handsome, but he had other qualities in his favour. He was urbane and stylish, he knew how to make friends and how to amuse his guests, and, above all, women found him irresistible.*

RIGHT **Pope Sixtus IV,** *painted (c.1475) by Joos van Ghent. This powerful intellectual had made his name defending the Franciscan stance on Church controversies such as the divinity of the Blood of Christ and the Immaculate Conception of the Virgin. As pope, he considerably increased the privileges awarded to the Franciscans and did much to enhance the cult of the Virgin, spending hours in prayer to her, his Franciscan habit concealed beneath his papal robes.*

Pope Sixtus IV

Francesco della Rovere, who was 57 at his election, was the son of a modest trader from Savona on the Ligurian coast of northwestern Italy.

He had become a Franciscan at an early age, climbing rapidly through the hierarchy of the Order thanks to his intellectual ability and zeal for reform. As the Order's minister-general he had tried to root out laxity and corruption in Franciscan convents, and his appointment as a cardinal by Pope Paul II had been welcomed by all in favour of Church reform.

As pope he forcefully promoted traditional Christian views. He appointed the scholar Platina as Vatican librarian, and Platina used his humanistic talents in support of the Church by writing a history of the papacy from St Peter to Sixtus IV.

Above all, the pope testified to his belief in the supremacy of the Christian tradition through a programme of building and decorating in Rome, the scale of which was unprecedented and made him arguably the most prolific patron of art in 15th-century Italy. By the time of his death, Rome had been transformed: he improved the water supplies, paved the streets with bricks, built new bridges and hospitals, repaired old churches and erected new ones; he also tore down the crumbling stadium of Domitian to create the modern Piazza Navona, which became the site of Rome's market. His best-known projects were at the Vatican, where he created the Vatican library and built the Sistine Chapel.

BELOW **Sixtus IV founds the Vatican Library,** *one of the scenes from the life of the pope commissioned to decorate wards in the Ospedale Santo Spirito, rebuilt by Sixtus IV. They are accompanied with events from the life of the hospital's founder, Pope Innocent III (1198–1216).*

On 13 August Sixtus IV hosted a lunch party for the cardinals at Castel Sant'Angelo. After the meal they examined the treasure collected by Paul II, which, before the election, all the cardinals had agreed to devote to the crusade. They were amazed by the quantities of gold, pearls and other jewels in the coffers: two papal tiaras valued at 300,000 ducats, a superb diamond, which Paul II had used as collateral to secure a loan from Cardinal d'Estouteville, and much more, all worth a total of nearly 900,000 ducats.

Sixtus IV was crowned on 25 August on a platform erected on the steps of St Peter's, high enough to be visible to the crowds massed in the piazza. There they watched as Rodrigo Borgia, the senior cardinal-deacon in the College of Cardinals, placed the tiara of St Gregory the Great on the new pope's head.

Five days later, on 30 August, Sixtus IV held a consistory in which he rewarded those cardinals who had supported him in the conclave. Rodrigo was promoted to a cardinal-bishop, one of the six top posts in the college, and given the lucrative abbey of Subiaco, with its castles east of Rome. On 30 October he was ordained a priest before his consecration as Cardinal-Bishop of Albano.

The papal coronation and possesso

The ceremonies of the papal coronation were ancient and arcane. During mass inside St Peter's the new pope was consecrated by the senior cardinal-bishops of Ostia, Albano and Porto, while the master-of-ceremonies ritually scorched a bundle of flax rags in front of the pontiff with the words 'Holy Father, see how quickly the glory of the world passes away.'

The coronation proper took place on the steps of the basilica, where the pope was crowned with the tiara by the most senior cardinal-deacon in the college. This was followed by a huge procession through the heart of Rome, known as the *possesso*, in which the pope, his cardinals and other dignitaries of the Church, government officials and foreign diplomats all took part. They rode across the Ponte Sant'Angelo and along the Via Papalis (now the Via di Banco di Santo Spirito and the Via del Governo Vecchio) to the Capitol and on, past the Colosseum and San Clemente, to San Giovanni in Laterano.

At some stage during the *possesso*, the pope would be greeted by the chief rabbi of Rome and offered a copy of the Torah, to which he would reply: 'we ratify your law but denounce your interpretation of it', thus allowing the Jews the right to live in Rome without explicitly approving their faith. At San Giovanni in Laterano the new pope took possession of this ancient basilica, his seat as Bishop of Rome. There the pope also sat on the so-called 'throne of filth' the *sella stercoraria*, before being raised to his feet by the cardinals, an act that symbolized the Biblical words: 'He raiseth up the poor out of the dust and lifteth up the beggar from the dunghill, to set them among princes, and to make them inherit the throne of glory.'

115

Rodrigo Borgia, Cardinal-Bishop of Albano

Sixtus IV *in a secret consistory discharged Cardinal Filippo Calandrini, Bishop of Albano, who held the church of Albano and transferred him to the church of Porto, vacant after the recent death of Cardinal Juan Carvajal, or rather of Cardinal Richard Olivier, and the church of Albano now vacant was given to Cardinal Rodrigo Borgia, known as the Vice-Chancellor, at this time deacon of San Niccolò in Carcere, who is to take authority in this church as bishop and shepherd. He was afterwards accompanied by all the cardinals to his residence, as is the custom.*

VATICAN ARCHIVES (EUBEL, *Hierarchia*, II, 37 N. 307).

On 15 December Sixtus IV gave red hats to two of his young nephews, both Franciscans: Pietro Riario, aged 26, and Giuliano della Rovere, two years older.

In a secret consistory on 23 December Sixtus IV announced the appointment of five legates to negotiate with 'kings, princes and other Christian rulers in defence of the Christian faith against the most impious Turks'. Cardinal Rodrigo was to be sent as legate to Spain.

> ## Cardinal Rodrigo was to be sent as legate to Spain.

1472

ON 8 JANUARY Cardinal Rodrigo Borgia was appointed Chamberlain of the College of Cardinals and assigned the seal by the outgoing chamberlain, 'and this was agreed by all the most reverend cardinals'.[1]

On the 22nd of the same month, the head of the Roman branch of the Medici bank, which had charge of the lucrative papal account, informed his master in Florence, Lorenzo de' Medici, that the new pope was living beyond his means.[2] During the year 1471–2 the pope spent 144,000 ducats building and equipping 24 new galleys for the crusade.

Cardinal Rodrigo received 2,800 florins from the papal treasury on 12 February to cover the expenses of arranging his trip to Spain.[3] Early in May he had a private audience with Sixtus IV in which the pope gave him orders for his coming mission. In addition to soliciting help for the crusade, Rodrigo was also charged with negotiating peace between the rulers of Aragon and Castile, ending the civil wars that plagued both countries, and encouraging the union of the two kingdoms. He was to use his own judgement about the marriage of Ferdinand of Aragon and Isabella of Castile and, if he thought it was appropriate, give them the papal dispensation that Sixtus IV had drawn up to replace the forged dispensation with which they had been married.

The cardinal received his legate's cross from the pope on 15 May and 'resigned his post of chamberlain with the unanimous consent of the cardinals and consigned the seal to Guillaume d'Estouteville, Bishop of Ostia who will serve as chamberlain for the rest of this year'; that same day he left Rome with his large and splendidly clad retinue to ride to Ostia, 'from where he travelled by sea to Catalonia and Spain'. [4] The party included three bishops and two painters.[5]

In late May, under the command of Cardinal Oliviero Carafa, the galleys paid for by the pope set sail for the eastern Mediterranean, carrying 4,700 soldiers; in the autumn Carafa captured the Turkish town of Izmir.

A month after setting sail, on 17 June – and earlier than expected, after an unusually easy voyage across the Mediterranean – Cardinal Rodrigo's two galleys anchored off Valencia, where preparations for his arrival were still incomplete. However, it was not until 21 June that he made his formal entry into his bishopric. On that day 'all the councillors, the governor and 12 important nobles were waiting on the road with a splendid canopy which was lifted above the cardinal and his horse, and carried by men on foot to the walls of the city, and the gate was ornamented with rich red hangings.

Florins and ducats

Money was a complicated business in Renaissance Italy. Each of the many states of the peninsula had its own silver-based currency as well as its own system of weights and measures. There were also internationally recognized gold coins, such as the ducats minted in Venice and Rome and the Florentine florin – they were broadly similar in value.

A labourer earned about half a ducat a week, or 25 ducats a year, while a skilled builder or painter could make twice that amount, or roughly a ducat a week. A chef in a cardinal's household was also paid around 25 ducats a year, but this was supplemented by free board and lodging.

A ducat would buy 10 capons, 270 fresh eggs, 50 kilograms (110 lbs) of flour or a pair of good hand-made leather boots. The rich could pay as much as 20 ducats for an antique bust, 30 ducats for a large decorated silver platter and 50 ducats for a good horse.

Translating Renaissance money and buying power into a modern context is difficult. Nowadays, both chefs and builders can earn £500 ($800) a week with ease, suggesting an equivalence of £500 to the ducat; but the same formula does not work for flour, 50 kilograms of which now costs only £30.

ABOVE **Gold ducat.** *Minted in Naples during the reign of Ferrante I, this type of coin typically displayed a profile portrait of the ruler, in this case the crowned head of the king.*

117

1471–1484 ✦ RODRIGO BORGIA

Then loud trumpets and drums sounded as he made his entrance into the city.'[6] And Cardinal Rodrigo, riding under his *baldacchino* – his canopy – progressed through the city streets to the cathedral.

On 24 June he invited the civic dignitaries of Valencia to a lavish banquet. At some stage during late June or July, Rodrigo was also reunited with his family in Játiva and his son Pedro Luis, who was now ten years old. His mother, however, had died in 1468.

On 31 July Cardinal Rodrigo left Valencia for his first meeting with King Juan II of Aragon and his son Ferdinand. Impressed by the prince, who was now 20 years old, the legate decided in favour of his marriage to Isabella of Castile and presented the couple with the papal dispensation he had brought with him from Sixtus IV, thus legalizing the marriage. By December, Rodrigo was in Castile negotiating with Enrique IV, Isabella's brother, who finally gave his agreement to a marriage that would prove of major significance to Spain's future.

1473

EARLY IN THE YEAR Rodrigo returned to the Aragonese court, where he successfully negotiated the end of the civil wars that had divided the kingdom. The excellent relations he now established with Ferdinand would soon result in royal favours for the cardinal's son Pedro Luis.

On 11 September Cardinal Rodrigo made his will, an understandable precaution given the danger of his impending return voyage, and with his party boarded two Venetian galleys bound for Ostia. Off the Italian coast, near Pisa, the ships ran into a terrible storm. Rodrigo's own galley just avoided disaster, but the cardinal watched as the other ship sank, drowning over 200 men of his household including all three bishops, and destroying cargo worth 30,000 florins. Rodrigo finally landed at Pisa and made his way over land back to Rome.

Rodrigo's own galley just avoided disaster, but the cardinal watched as the other ship sank.

RIGHT **The Virgin of the Catholic Kings.** *This anonymous altarpiece of the Adoration of the Virgin with St Dominic and St Thomas Aquinas was commissioned by Ferdinand of Aragon and Isabella of Castille. In keeping with the custom of the times, they commemorated their role in donor portraits of themselves kneeling in prayer before the Virgin's throne. The inclusion of two Dominican saints reflects the powerful role played by the Order in the Spanish Inquisition, which enforced Christian belief in their kingdom. Also included in the altarpiece are portraits of their two children, Juan and Isabella, designed to emphasize their dynastic ambitions for the newly united Spain.*

The Ligurian pope and his nephews

Sixtus IV had many relatives who were eager to benefit from his power and influence and keen to find lucrative employment in Rome.

Having given red hats to Pietro Riario and Giuliano della Rovere, Sixtus IV invested their brothers with fiefs in the Papal States and found illustrious wives for them. For Girolamo Riario, younger brother of Pietro, who until 1471 had run a grocery business in Savona, the pope arranged a marriage with Caterina Sforza, the illegitimate daughter of Galeazzo Maria, the Duke of Milan, and made him Lord of Imola, a title he bought for his nephew for 40,000 ducats. The pope had had to borrow the money from the Pazzi bank, because his usual Medici bankers had refused the loan, distrusting the growing power of the papal nephews in Italy. For Cardinal Giuliano's brother, Giovanni della Rovere, Sixtus IV arranged a marriage with Giovanna, the daughter of Federigo da Montefeltro, Duke of Urbino, and the title of Lord of Senigallia and Mondavio.

On 24 October Rodrigo was met at the gates of Rome by his fellow cardinals and escorted back to his palace. The following morning he was received by the pope in a public consistory: he may have failed to gain much more than promises from the Spanish monarchs for the crusade, but in political terms the legation had been a triumph.

Much had changed in the 17 months Rodrigo had been away. Above all, there was the growing influence of two papal nephews – Cardinal Pietro Riario, his uncle's favourite, and Cardinal Giuliano della Rovere. The Ligurians, who had arrived in large numbers in Rome following the accession of Sixtus IV, in the hope of jobs from their compatriots, were detested by the Romans almost as much as the Catalans had been during the pontificate of Rodrigo's uncle, Calixtus III.

During the autumn Cardinal Rodrigo, now aged 42, embarked on a romantic affair with Vanozza de' Cataneis. From a modest, probably artisan, background, she was only 11 years younger than him, and beautiful.

1474

EARLY IN THE YEAR, on 5 January, Cardinal Pietro Riario died after two weeks of fever and stomach trouble: there were rumours of poison, but his death was more probably due to overindulgence – it was said that he had managed to spend over 300,000 ducats since he acquired his red hat, and he left debts of 60,000 ducats on his death.[7]

In June Sixtus IV dispatched his nephew Cardinal Giuliano della Rovere at the head of troops to restore order

RIGHT **Neptune calming the storm,** *from engravings in an early 15th-century edition of Virgil's* Aeniad. *Sea travel was a hazardous business. Although galleys kept close to the coast, they could still be caught in the violent storms that regularly erupted in the Mediterranean, and they also ran the risk of attack by pirates, in particular the corsairs operating off the coast of Algeria. However, it was unquestionably quicker to sail – a galley could travel over 50 miles in a day, while overland travellers would average less than half that distance. It was also substantially cheaper and the preferred method for transporting bulky cargoes around Europe.*

in the papal fiefs of Todi, Spoleto and Città di Castello; 'well-used to the severity of monastic life, he did not flinch at the harshness of a soldier's lot,' recorded Platina.[8]

On 10 October Sixtus IV announced the betrothal of Giovanni della Rovere, younger brother of Cardinal Giuliano, and Giovanna, daughter of Federigo da Montefeltro, Duke of Urbino (and thus ruler of the largest fief in the Papal States). Two days later the pope invested his son as ruler of the papal fiefs of Senigallia and Mondavio.

In Spain, Enrique IV of Castile died on 11 December, leaving his kingdom to his daughter Isabella.

Also this year, in order to give Vanozza the status of a married woman, perhaps because she was pregnant, Cardinal Rodrigo married off his mistress to Domenico da Rignano, an elderly lawyer who was no doubt paid well for his agreement.

Ruler of the largest fief in the Papal States.

TEMPLA DOMVM EXPOSITIS·VICOS·FORA·MOENIA PONTES·
VIRGINEAM TRIVII QVOD REPARARIS AQVAM·
PRISCA LICET NAVTIS STATVAS DARE COMMODA PORTVS·
ET VATICANVM CINGERE SIXTE IVGVM·
PLVS TAMEN VRBS DEBET·NAM QVAE SQVALORE LATEBAT·
CERNITVR IN CELEBRI BIBLIOTHECA LOCO·

1475

THIS WAS A JUBILEE YEAR in Rome, the first since 1450 and the first since the intervals between jubilees had been reduced to 25 years.

On 14 January, as a mark of his special favour, Sixtus IV appointed Cardinal Rodrigo to travel with Cardinal Giuliano della Rovere to Terracina, where they were to welcome King Ferrante I of Naples on his entry into the Papal States. The king made his formal entry into Rome on 28 January at Porta San Giovanni, bringing so many falcons in his train that the large population of owls in the city was completely wiped out.[9] The two cardinals also accompanied Ferrante I when he left Rome after his pilgrimage on 1 February to return home.

The crowds of pilgrims in Rome by Ascension Day, 4 May, were huge: 'large numbers of people have gathered here for the Jubilee,' wrote the Milanese ambassador on 5 May, 'more than have ever been seen before'.[10]

In the middle of September Vanozza de' Cataneis gave birth to a boy, named Cesare; as Rodrigo Borgia's second son, he was destined for a career in Church.

Misfortune struck Rome on 8 November when the Tiber flooded, leaving the streets covered with stinking mud. Plague soon broke out in the low-lying areas that had been inundated.

1476

IN MAY ANOTHER OUTBREAK of the plague engulfed Rome. The law courts closed and cases were heard instead on the steps outside.[11] On 10 June 'the pope left Rome because of fear of the plague ... with six cardinals he appointed to accompany him: Guillaume d'Estouteville, Rodrigo Borgia, Oliviero Carafa, Stefano Nardini, Francesco Gonzaga and Giovanni Michiel'.[12] The cardinals and the ambassadors headed for Viterbo, but the plague had preceded them there, and they were forced to move on. By 8 July they were in Amelia, where the pope had a bad attack of gout.

By 8 July they were in Amelia, where the pope had a bad attack of gout.

LEFT **Sixtus IV appoints Platina.** *While the central kneeling figure in this fresco is Platina, pointing down to the inscription he himself has written to commemorate his appointment to take charge of the pope's new Vatican library, it is the other figures that interest us. Sixtus IV, seated on his chair, is surrounded by his family. On the right are two nephews destined for careers in the Church: Raffaello Riario and the imposing figure of Giuliano della Rovere in his cardinal's robes. On the left are Girolamo Riario and Giovanni della Rovere, their secular achievements visible in their gold collars of office.*

Rodrigo Borgia, Cardinal-Bishop of Porto

Sixtus IV in consistory at Narni, by his own wish, has discharged Rodrigo the Vice-Chancellor who held the church of Albano and transferred him to the church of Porto which became vacant after the death of Cardinal Filippo Calandrini, the last bishop of this church.

VATICAN ARCHIVES (EUBEL, *Hierarchia*, II, 37 N. 307).

On 24 July at a consistory held in Narni, Sixtus IV promoted Rodrigo to the cardinal-bishopric of Porto, which had become vacant two days earlier.

By 26 September the papal court was in Foligno where news arrived that the plague was abating and that it was safe to return: they left Foligno ten days later and arrived in Rome on 23 October.

Two months later, on 26 December, the Duke of Milan – Galeazzo Maria Sforza – was assassinated, leaving his seven-year-old son Giangaleazzo as duke under the regency of his mother, Bona of Savoy. Sixtus IV feared the worst, writing 'the peace of Italy is at an end'.[13]

Towards the end of this year, Rodrigo Borgia's mistress bore him another son, whom Rodrigo named Juan.

> Rodrigo Borgia's mistress bore him another son, whom Rodrigo named Juan.

1477

ON 2 FEBRUARY SIXTUS IV celebrated Candlemas (the Feast of the Purification of the Virgin) in the Great Chapel in the Vatican. It was the last known occasion on which the building was used before it was demolished to make way for the Sistine Chapel.[14]

On 25 June Cardinal Rodrigo was made papal legate to Naples by Sixtus IV. King Ferrante had specifically asked for this appointment to solemnize his marriage to his first cousin, Joanna of Aragon, the sister of Don Ferdinand of Aragon. The groom was fifty-three years old, the bride just twenty-two.

RIGHT **Triumph of Death.** *In this 14th-century fresco decorating the Camposanto ('field of the dead', i.e. burial ground) in Pisa Cathedral demons swoop down to snatch souls from the pile of corpses growing on the ground as the plague claims its victims, while cherubs hold inscriptions aloft to warn of the vanity of life. The image provides a stark visual expression of the universal terror provoked by the plague – the suddenness with which it struck and the inexorability of death. Rich or poor, male or female, cleric or lay, none was spared and it was widely believed that plague was a punishment from God for the sins of society.*

The Sistine Chapel

Sixtus IV began the construction of the Sistine Chapel in 1477 to replace the dilapidated Great Chapel, erected by Pope Nicholas III in 1268. Using the old foundations, work proceeded quickly: by 1481 the interior decoration was underway and the chapel was inaugurated on 15 August 1483.

Rising high above the roofs of the Vatican palace, the massive brick structure and its severe crenellated parapet was intended to be clearly visible from the piazza in front of St Peter's. It was an important focus of papal ceremony, not solely the pope's chapel but also the place where God spoke directly to Man in the conclaves to elect a successor to St Peter.

Sixtus IV's choice of form and decoration deliberately underlined the importance he attached to Christian tradition. The proportions of the chapel match the Biblical account of the Holy of Holies that housed the Ark of the Covenant in Solomon's great temple at Jerusalem. The expensive inlaid marble floor and the parallel scenes from the Old and New Testaments on the walls were both features of the great early Christian basilicas in Rome. The ceiling, before Michelangelo's frescoes masked it in 1508–12, was painted a rich azure blue studded with gold stars, just like the vaults in the church of St Francis at Assisi. The scenes from the lives of Moses and Christ, chosen specifically to promote papal primacy, were painted by Sandro Botticelli, Pietro Perugino, Luca Signorelli, Cosimo Rosselli, Domenico Ghirlandaio and Bernardo Pinturrichio, some of the most renowned artists of the Renaissance.

Cardinal Rodrigo left Rome on 22 August for Naples where he performed not only the marriage service but also the coronation of the young Joanna as queen, and returned to Rome on 4 October.

On 10 December Sixtus IV created seven new cardinals. One was Giovanni, the son of King Ferrante, and three others were papal relatives, including the 16-year-old Raffaello Riario.

1478

ON 26 APRIL an attempt was made to assassinate Lorenzo de' Medici while he was at mass in the cathedral at Florence. Lorenzo survived, but his brother Giuliano was stabbed to death. The perpetrators, members of the Pazzi family, were intent on crushing both the Medici bank and the Medici regime in the city. Sixtus IV's nephews played a key role supporting the Pazzi and, although the pope insisted he knew nothing about the plot, the event sparked off war between Florence and Rome. The pope acquired the powerful support of the armies of Ferrante of Naples, who was keen to extend his authority into Tuscany.

An attempt was made to assassinate Lorenzo de' Medici.

On 28 June Ferdinand of Aragon and Isabella of Castile had their first son, Juan, Prince of Asturias. Cardinal Rodrigo Borgia was named as godfather.

By July, the plague that had broken out in May had become serious enough for the pope to leave Rome. Cardinal Rodrigo was one of the cardinals who left with Sixtus IV on 11 July for Bracciano, the stronghold of the Orsini family, returning to Rome in the autumn.

LEFT **The Sistine Chapel in the 15th century.** *This modern reconstruction is designed to show how the chapel appeared before Michelangelo's additions early in the 16th century. This lavishly decorated chapel was used on a regular basis for papal masses, which were attended by the cardinals, members of the papal court and specially invited visitors. The fictive hangings frescoed on the walls below the Biblical scenes would have been covered by costly tapestries for important events.*

ABOVE **Medal commemorating the Pazzi Conspiracy.** *Commissioned (1478) from Bertoldo di Giovanni by Lorenzo de' Medici, whose profile ornaments it, the medal marked Lorenzo's escape from the Pazzi assassins in 1478. The event itself marked the point at which power in Florence became concentrated in the hands of the Medici family and their inner circle.*

1479

ON 19 JANUARY King Juan II of Aragon died. He was succeeded by Ferdinand II. By virtue of the marriage of Isabella of Castile and Ferdinand, the two Spanish kingdoms were now united under this dual monarchy.

On 7 September, King Ferrante I's army, led by his son Alfonso, Duke of Calabria, defeated the Florentine forces at Poggio Imperiale, forcing Lorenzo de' Medici to go to Naples to sue for peace.

Later that month, there were developments in Milan. Ludovico Sforza, brother of the late Duke Galeazzo Maria, seized control of the regency council and reigned as duke in the name of his ten-year-old nephew, Giangaleazzo.

1480

IN APRIL VANOZZA de' Cataneis gave birth to a third child in Cardinal Rodrigo's castle at Subiaco, this time a daughter. They named her Lucrezia. Rodrigo also arranged for Vanozza, following the death of her first husband, to marry the Milanese Giorgio de Croce, a secretary in the curia.

At an early age, Lucrezia was sent to join her brothers at Palazzo Montegiordano, the Orsini palace in Rome. There she would be brought up by Cardinal Rodrigo's cousin Adriana de Milà, for whom the cardinal had arranged a marriage with Ludovico Orsini, Lord of Bassanello.

LEFT **The Hanging of Baroncelli,** *by Leonardo da Vinci. The hanging of murderers and other criminals was a popular sight in Renaissance Europe. In Rome criminals were regularly executed in the Campo dei Fiori, the site of the city's daily market and of many of its taverns. Contemporary diaries are full of accounts of criminals, their crimes and their last moments. This drawing by Leonardo shows the corpse of Bernardo Bandini Baroncelli, who was executed after the failure of the Pazzi Conspiracy in Florence (1478): the town hall became a hideous gibbet, its walls festooned with the dangling cadavers of the plotters who had been hung alive out of the windows.*

Around this time Rodrigo acquired a post in Rome for his nephew Juan, son of his sister Juana and a canon of Valencia Cathedral. At the age of 35, Juan now became a corrector of apostolic briefs in the curia.

On 15 May the pope gave red hats to five new cardinals: this meant that sixty per cent of the College of Cardinals had now been created by Sixtus IV.

During the summer came welcome news that the Knights of St John, under their heroic leader Pierre d'Aubusson, had successfully fought off an attack on Rhodes by the Turks. On 11 August the Turks retaliated with an audacious assault on mainland Italy, seizing the southern port of Otranto. The attack was particularly brutal: the Turks killed half the inhabitants and captured many others to sell as slaves. 'The terror in Rome was so great, it was as though the Turks were already at the gates of the city itself,' wrote the historian Sigismondo de' Conti, adding that 'even the pope considered leaving.'[15] At a consistory on 14 August, the cardinals unanimously agreed that expelling the Turks from Otranto must be a priority, and legates were sent to rulers across Europe to ask for their assistance. In the view of Sixtus IV:

> If the Italians desire to safeguard their estates, their homes, their wives, their children, their freedom and their lives, and if they desire to remain in the faith to which we have all been baptized and through which we shall be reborn, they must trust us and they must prepare to go to war.[16]

Louis XI of France offered 100,000 scudi a year for the crusade on 28 August, and other powers soon joined him with offers of assistance.

ABOVE **Carved wooden cradle.** *This elegantly made cradle, created some time during the 16th century, would have been commissioned by a wealthy family for the eagerly anticipated arrival of a new child. But for all mothers, in this era before the development of modern obstetrics, childbirth was notoriously dangerous. Many women died in labour, others succumbed to puerperal fever after giving birth, and the mortality rate among babies was also high.*

On 1 October, as a special favour to Cardinal Rodrigo, Sixtus IV legitimized his son Cesare so that the five-year-old boy could pursue a career in the Church. The document explained that Cesare was 'the son of a cardinal and a married woman'. The cardinal's older son Pedro Luis had been legitimized by the pope a few years earlier.

During this year Sixtus IV advanced his own family interests too by investing his nephew Girolamo Riario, Lord of Imola, with the papal fief of Forlì.

1481

Otranto was retaken from the Turks to much rejoicing.

ON 23 MARCH SIXTUS IV sent a letter to all Italian rulers proclaiming an alliance for the crusade between Rome, France, the Holy Roman Empire and the Italian states – with the exception of Venice, whose commercial priorities had forced her to make peace with Sultan Mehmet II through the Treaty of Constantinople. Sixtus IV was to supply 25 galleys; Ferrante I of Naples promised 40 galleys; Milan offered 30,000 ducats, and Florence contributed another 40,000 ducats.[17]

In late May Rome was buzzing with rumours that the sultan had died, and they were confirmed as true by the Venetian ambassador on 2 June. Rome celebrated by ringing the church bells, firing the cannon at Castel Sant'Angelo and starting bonfires that lit up the city all evening.

On 30 June Cardinal Rodrigo and his colleagues went with the pope to the ancient church of San Paolo fuori le Mura to bless the departing fleet. Sixtus IV then held a public consistory, which was attended by the captains of all the galleys, who ceremonially kissed the pope's foot. The cardinals then escorted Sixtus IV down to the Tiber, where they were greeted with cheers, salutes and salvoes of artillery 'that delighted both eyes and ears', as one chronicler reported.[18]

On 10 September, Otranto was retaken from the Turks, to much rejoicing.

RIGHT **View of the Borgo.** *Protected by heavily fortified walls and the Tiber, the area between Castel Sant'Angelo and St Peter's, known as the Borgo, was effectively a separate unit in the 15th century, distinct from the rest of Rome both in terms of geography and function. At that time it was not a major residential district, though many employees of the curia lived here, as well as some prelates, although most cardinals lived in the city proper. The bulk of the Borgo's inhabitants were traders cashing in on the lucrative pilgrim market, such as owners of lodging houses and money changers, while its streets were lined with shops and stalls selling icons, holy oil, candles and other religious souvenirs. The Ponte Sant'Angelo is visible to the right of the castle, while the Borgo is dominated by the great central piazza in front of St Peter's.*

1482

WITH THE THREAT of the Turks receding, the old animosity between Sixtus IV and Ferrante resurfaced, exacerbated by the traditional rivalry in Rome between the Colonna and Orsini clans, as the former declared for Naples and the latter for the pope. Milan and Florence supported King Ferrante, while Venice took sides with Sixtus IV, from whom she hoped to acquire the prize of Ferrara. Soon, most of Italy was engulfed in war. In the middle of April, Ferrante I's armies, under the leadership of Alfonso, Duke of Calabria, and Lorenzo Colonna, marched north into the Papal States. On 30 May the Neapolitan army entered Rome, but was quickly expelled by the troops of Girolamo Riario and the Orsini.

The public consistory held on 2 June in the Vatican turned into a brawl, with both sides accusing the other of treason. Sixtus IV had cardinals Giovanni Colonna and Giovanni Battista Savelli locked up in Castel Sant'Angelo as hostages for the good behaviour of the Neapolitan troops camped around the city walls.

Some months before, in March, Cardinal Rodrigo's six-year-old son Cesare was made an apostolic 'protonotary' – a sinecure in the curia with several privileges – by Sixtus IV. When the boy turned seven during the year, he was given benefices in Játiva and other cities in Spain.

On 8 July, Rodrigo Borgia added the see of Cartagena to his own increasingly impressive list of benefices. His brood continued to expand, too. During the year Vanozza de' Cataneis gave birth to her fourth child, named Jofrè after Cardinal Rodrigo's father.

On 23 July the captain-general of the Venetian armies, Roberto Malatesta, arrived in Rome with his troops and, on 23 August, achieved a resounding victory over the Neapolitan army at Campo Morto (the 'Field of Death'), so named for the malaria that was endemic in this marshy area west of Rome. The disease claimed the life of Malatesta on 10 September.

The drawbacks of Christianity

The Christian religion *teaches all men to suffer and this has weakened the world and made it the lure of scoundrels. The ancients erected their altars only to those who had acquired fame on earth, such as ruling princes or triumphant generals. The Christian religion, however, praises humility and a contemplative existence, the highest achievements being submission, temperance, and disdain for worldly honour. The ancients only prized great brains, physical strength and the other characteristics which make men powerful.*

NICCOLÒ MACHIAVELLI, *Discorsi*, II, 2.

During September news arrived in Rome that Federigo da Montefeltro had died of malaria while fighting in Ferrara; he was succeeded as Duke of Urbino by his ten-year-old son Guidobaldo.

Sixtus IV and Duke Alfonso of Calabria finally agreed a truce on 28 November, and on 12 December the pope signed a peace treaty with Naples, Florence and Milan.

1483

ON 7 JANUARY the Mantuan ambassador reported that he had been unable to have an audience with Sixtus IV because the pope had been ill with a chest infection and swollen glands for the past three or four days, 'but it is not a serious illness, indeed he is as lively as if he were only forty years old'.[19]

The death of Cardinal Guillaume d'Estouteville on 22 January at the age of 71 left Rodrigo Borgia the richest cardinal in the College of Cardinals, where he now took over d'Estouteville's post as Dean of the College. During this year, Rodrigo also accrued the prestigious post of Archpriest of Santa Maria Maggiore in Rome.

Cardinal Rodrigo continued to exert his influence assiduously on behalf of his family. His nephew Juan became Archbishop of Monreale, and the cardinal found husbands among the Roman nobility for his two eldest daughters: during the summer the 16-year-old Isabella was married to Pietro Matuzzi, an important figure in the Roman government, while her sister Girolama, two years younger, married Gianandrea Cesarini. But tragedy later struck when Girolama and her husband both died soon after their wedding. Isabella and Pietro moved into a house provided by Cardinal Rodrigo close to his palace.[20]

On 9 August, the anniversary of his election, Sixtus IV used the now completed Sistine Chapel for the first time.

At the end of the month, on 29 August, Louis XI of France died. He was succeeded by his 13-year-old son Charles VIII.

133

ABOVE **The founding of Santa Maria Maggiore.**
One of the panels of an altarpiece by the Florentine painter Masolino, this was commissioned by Pope Martin V for the basilica. It depicts the legend of how Pope Liberius (352–366) was inspired to build Santa Maria Maggiore after a miraculous fall of snow in August delineated the ground plan of the church.

1484

Rodrigo had gained significant favours from Sixtus IV.

IN JANUARY the Colonna–Orsini rivalry erupted into rioting in Rome. 'Everyone in the city was frightened for his life and his property', the Ferrarese ambassador informed his master.[21] At the end of May the riots escalated dramatically. One inhabitant had 'two wheelbarrows filled with stones placed by the door, which I had barricaded, and had larger stones set by the windows and loggia upstairs.[22]

On 17 March Pope Sixtus IV gave a cardinal's hat to Ascanio, brother of Ludovico Sforza. This act effectively legitimized Ludovico's seizure of power in Milan, so that he was recognized as *de facto* ruler.

In the middle of June Sixtus IV took to his bed with a fever, though he recovered quickly. But on 3 August the pope had a violent attack of gout. A week later, on 11 August, he had to dismiss the cardinals who had gathered at the Vatican for a consistory because he had had a bad night. He felt better that evening, well enough to give audiences to several ambassadors after vespers. However, that night his condition deteriorated rapidly. The pope died on the evening of 12 August.

Sixtus IV's long pontificate had seen Rodrigo Borgia established as one of the most influential cardinals in the college, alongside the pope's nephew Giuliano della Rovere. Thanks once again to his shrewd dealings in the conclave that had enabled this pontiff's election, Rodrigo had gained significant favours from Sixtus IV. He had been promoted within the college from cardinal-deacon to cardinal-bishop, an advance that required his ordination as a priest; he had gained several lucrative benefices; he had been given the prestigious appointment of legate to Spain, enabling him to return home for the first time since he was eighteen. His position at the top of the hierarchy in the College of Cardinals had enabled him to develop strong political ties with Naples and Spain, and to deepen and extend the prospects of his nephews, and of his own children, of which there were now four more from his relationship with Vanozza de' Cataneis. He was surely at the apex of his power.

RIGHT **Tomb of Pope Sixtus IV.** *The long pontificate of Sixtus IV was celebrated by his nephew, Cardinal Giuliano della Rovere, in an exceptionally magnificent bronze tomb by Antonio del Pollaiuolo for the chapel that the pope had built in Old St Peter's. It was decorated with panels depicting the Liberal Arts and the papal coat-of-arms ornamented with an oak tree (in Latin: robur). The statue of the pope is stunningly lifelike, its face based on his death mask and the vestments faithfully modelled. The realism seen in this portrait is one of the hallmarks of Renaissance art, and illustrates how far fashions had changed from the idealized portraiture and stiff drapery folds that were typical of the Middle Ages.*

Rodrigo borgia

from eminence to
pre-eminence

1484–1492

In August 1484, for the first time since he had been created a cardinal at the age of 25, Cardinal Rodrigo Borgia was one of the favourites entering the conclave for election to the ultimate office. He had been a central figure at the papal court for nearly 30 years. Thanks to his astute support of the winning candidates in the last three conclaves, he was also now the richest cardinal in the college and one of the most influential, wielding enormous power in Rome. But there were other serious challengers too, and there was a formidable obstacle in the shape of a college populated by the appointees of Sixtus IV, not least Rodrigo Borgia's rival Giuliano della Rovere.

1484

Few cardinals attended the funeral.

THE DEATH OF POPE SIXTUS IV was followed by rioting in Rome on a major scale, directed in particular against his family and supporters. Cardinal Rodrigo hired armed troops to guard his magnificent residence from the mob, bringing in substantial quantities of artillery for their use; many other cardinals did the same. Few cardinals attended the funeral services for the dead pope on 17 August – even Sixtus IV's nephew, Cardinal Giuliano della Rovere, was too frightened to venture outside the security of his palace and do honour to his uncle. The tension eased, however, in the next few days, especially after Cardinal Giuliano persuaded Caterina Sforza, who had seized Castel Sant'Angelo in the name of her husband Girolamo Riario, to surrender the fortress to the college in return for 8,000 ducats.

PREVIOUS PAGE **Rodrigo Borgia** *(see also page 164). By 1484 the papacy had survived the crisis of the early 15th century, reasserting its spiritual supremacy in the Christian world and its temporal authority in Italy, while refilling its coffers after the depredations of the Great Schism. But criticism of the increasingly secular nature of papal and clerical power was growing more vociferous.*

RIGHT **Caterina Sforza,** *painted by Marco Palmezzano (1460–1539). A formidable figure in any age, Caterina Sforza showed more warlike spirit than her father Galeazzo Maria, supporting the interests of her husband Girolamo Riario and their six children. After the death of her first husband, she married into the Medici family and her descendants became grand dukes of Florence until the line died out in 1743.*

Meanwhile factions were emerging for the coming conclave, and Cardinal Rodrigo was widely reported to be busy gathering votes. On 15 August the Mantuan ambassador reported that Cardinal Marco Barbo was one of the front-runners, but dismissed his chances because he would favour Venetian interests. On 18 August the Florentine envoy reported the rumour that Cardinal Rodrigo was 'trying to corrupt the world, some with money, some with jobs, others with benefices. I know he has offered his office and palace to Giovanni of Aragon and 25,000 ducats as well as the abbey of Subiaco to Cardinal Colonna, and made a similar offer to Cardinal Savelli.'[1] These two cardinals were both members of the rival faction that was emerging under the leadership of Giuliano della Rovere. On 21 August the Ferrarese ambassador wrote that 'Rodrigo Borgia is certainly one of the candidates, and working hard for support' but then quoted the old Roman proverb predicting that the favourite rarely won: 'He who enters the conclave a pope will leave it as a cardinal.'[2]

The conclave opened on 26 August, and 25 cardinals processed into the Vatican to take up residence in their cramped cells, erected for the first time in the new Sistine Chapel. At the first scrutiny on 28 August, Marco Barbo received ten votes, well short of the seventeen he needed for election. Cardinal Rodrigo had the support of the cardinals of the league signed by Naples, Florence and Milan, including Giovanni of Aragon, Giovanni Battista Orsini and Ascanio Sforza, but without the votes of the absent Spanish cardinals he had little hope of election himself. Giuliano della Rovere now promoted his ally Giovanni Battista Cibò, a weak character who owed his red hat to Giuliano's influence and whom Giuliano would be able to manipulate for his own

Rodrigo Borgia's character and wealth

He has many talents and is very adaptable, a fluent speaker and, though he is not among the greatest literary figures, he can write well. He is shrewd by nature and applies immense energy to all his projects. He is thought to be extremely wealthy and has enormous influence through his many connections with kings and princes.

He has built himself a magnificent and roomy palace between Ponte Sant'Angelo and the Campo dei Fiori. The revenues he receives from his numerous benefices and abbeys, both in Italy and Spain, as well as his three bishoprics of Valencia, Cartagena and Porto are huge, and the post of vice-chancellor is said to bring in 8,000 ducats a year. He owns large quantities of silver plate, pearls, hangings, vestments embroidered in gold and silk, and a library full of scholarly books, all of such superb quality they might belong to a king or a pope. I will not describe his splendid litters and the caparisons for his horses, or his gold, silver and silks, or his magnificent clothes and collections of valuables.

JACOPO GHERARDI, *Diarium Romanum,* IN *Rerum Italicarum Scriptores,* XXIII, P. 130.

ends. The plotting and scheming went on all afternoon, and well in to the night. According to the master-of-ceremonies, Johannes Burchard, who was one of the officials in charge of the conclave, Cibò sat up into the early hours of the morning signing notes promising favours to Rodrigo Borgia and all his party. 'It is all the wrong way round,' joked Cardinal Piccolomini, 'the pope is writing notes on his knees and we, who are asking for them, are standing upright.'[3]

At 9 o'clock on the morning of 29 August it was announced to the crowds outside St Peter's that Cardinal Cibò had been elected. He took the name Pope Innocent VIII.

For Cardinal Rodrigo and the college, the new pontificate was essentially a continuation of the rule of the della Rovere family. 'This Pope is directed by others', wrote the Florentine ambassador on 29 August; 'Giuliano della Rovere had little influence with his uncle,' wrote the envoy of Ferrara, 'but he gets exactly what he wants from the new pope.'[4]

On 12 September Innocent VIII's coronation took place, followed by the customary ride across Rome to San Giovanni Laterano. Wearing his gilded tiara and riding a white horse, the splendid procession passed off peacefully enough, though fear of violence against the Jews persuaded the organizers to stage the traditional ceremony with the rabbis inside the safety of Castel Sant'Angelo.

On 20 October Alfonso, Duke of Calabria, arrived in Rome to do homage to the new pope on behalf of his father Ferrante I of Naples, and to congratulate him on his election. On 22 October Cardinal Rodrigo hosted a splendid banquet for Duke Alfonso at his palace. Among the other guests were Cardinal Giovanni of Aragon, Alfonso's younger brother, Cardinal Giuliano della Rovere and Cardinal Ascanio Sforza, who sent a long description of the palace to his brother Ludovico.

On 26 November Innocent VIII held a consistory to appoint a new Captain-General of the Church. Cardinal Giuliano della Rovere's influence over the new pope was apparent when Innocent VIII nominated the cardinal's brother, Giovanni della Rovere, who already held the post of Prefect of Rome.

A portrait of Innocent VIII

These are the qualities of His Holiness: he is a man of over average height, of ordinary learning, pleasant and humane while he was a cardinal ...he has an illegitimate son, aged over 20 years old and currently in Naples, and married daughters who have sons; he has a brother and many nephews, one of whom, Lorenzo, is a priest and canon of St Peter's, and I would guess that he will be amongst the first cardinals ... [Innocent VIII] is by nature heavily-built and is 53 to 54 years old ... God keep him so that he does things which are pleasing to God and worthy of the papacy and will preserve the peace in Italy.

GUIDANTONIO VESPUCCI TO LORENZO DE' MEDICI, 29 AUGUST 1484 (LA TORRE, P. 4).

141

ABOVE **Tomb of Innocent VIII.** This grandiose wall monument in St Peter's, commissioned from Antonio and Piero Pollaiuolo by his nephew, Cardinal Lorenzo Cibò, displayed the pope with his right arm lifted in the traditional gesture of papal benediction. Innocent VIII had been born the son of a Roman senator and educated at the Aragonese court in Naples. He had worked in the curia, where he was involved in setting prices for the sale of posts in the papal administration, before acquiring his cardinal's hat. As pope, he preferred to emphasize the secular nature of his power rather than its spirituality, and the level of opulence at the court he established at the Vatican was set to rival those of his fellow princes.

1485

ON 12 MARCH Innocent VIII was taken ill with a high fever and stayed in bed for the next three months. On 16 March the college refused to allow him to create any new cardinals, arguing that they had all agreed before the election to reduce their numbers to twenty-four from the current contingent of twenty-eight.

On 20 May Cardinal Rodrigo's son Pedro Luis, now fighting in the army of Ferdinand and Isabella to extend their authority over the last Muslim-governed parts of southern Spain, took part in the conquest of the 'impregnable' fortress of Ronda, which guarded the borders of Granada.

At the beginning of July plague broke out in Rome, and spread rapidly. During the summer disturbing news began to arrive from Naples. Ferrante I, acting, it was said, on the advice of his son Alfonso, had decided to assert his authority over his unruly barons. Of Alfonso one contemporary remarked: 'No man is crueller than him nor worse, nor more vicious, nor so greedy for his food as him.'⁵ The barons now began a revolt against the king and appealed for aid to Innocent VIII, who, in their support, began preparations for war with Naples.

Innocent VIII nominated Cardinal Rodrigo as Archbishop of Seville on 26 August, against the wishes of Ferdinand II who wanted the post for his own illegitimate son. On hearing the news, Ferdinand's angry response was to seize the Borgia estates in Spain and imprison Rodrigo's son Pedro Luis. The quarrel was quickly healed however, for Rodrigo declined the appointment just days after it had been offered, and Pedro Luis was released.

Rodrigo Borgia entertains

Many of the cardinals visited the Duke of Calabria today who spent an hour with Innocent VIII ... I went with Cardinal Sclafenati to visit His Holiness who was with the Cardinal Giovanni of Aragon; shortly afterwards Cardinal Rodrigo Borgia and Cardinal Giuliano della Rovere arrived and we all went to the palace of the vice-chancellor who gave us a dinner, which was admirable, well-planned and sumptuous. The palace is superbly furnished. The main hall is hung with sets of tapestries and there is a small room next door which is also hung with beautiful tapestries, with matching carpets on the floor, and a bed hung with red satin and a sideboard completely covered in silver and gold plate, beautifully worked, as well as other platters, dishes and other things in vast numbers and very lovely to behold. Next to this are two more rooms, one hung with the grandest tapestries with carpets on the floor and another bed hung with Alexandrian velvet, and the second more ornate than the others with another bed hung with gold brocade and overlaid with a cover lined with sables and trimmed with gold fringe, all as elaborate as could be with a table in the middle covered in Alexandrian velvet and beautiful chairs.

CARDINAL ASCANIO SFORZA TO LUDOVICO SFORZA, 22 OCTOBER 1484 (L. VON PASTOR, *History of the Popes*, VOL. V, PP. 528–9, DOC. 2).

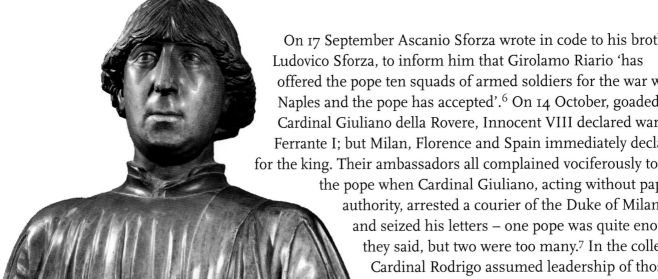

On 17 September Ascanio Sforza wrote in code to his brother, Ludovico Sforza, to inform him that Girolamo Riario 'has offered the pope ten squads of armed soldiers for the war with Naples and the pope has accepted'.[6] On 14 October, goaded by Cardinal Giuliano della Rovere, Innocent VIII declared war on Ferrante I; but Milan, Florence and Spain immediately declared for the king. Their ambassadors all complained vociferously to the pope when Cardinal Giuliano, acting without papal authority, arrested a courier of the Duke of Milan and seized his letters – one pope was quite enough, they said, but two were too many.[7] In the college, Cardinal Rodrigo assumed leadership of those cardinals who opposed the war. Later that year Ferdinand II rewarded Cardinal Rodrigo by investing Pedro Luis as Duke of Gandia, and arranging a marriage between Pedro Luis and his own first cousin, the nine-year-old Maria Enriquez.

Earlier in October, Cardinal Giovanni of Aragon had arrived in Rome to negotiate with the pope, but on 7 October the Ferrarese ambassador reported that two of the cardinal's household had died of the plague and that the cardinal himself was in bed.[8] Ten days later Cardinal Giovanni died from the pestilence.

Vanozza was now a wealthy woman, owning three inns.

1486

ALTHOUGH CARDINAL RODRIGO'S relationship with his mistress Vanozza de' Cataneis had been over for some years, he now arranged a new marriage for her following the death of her second husband. It was to be with Carlo Canale, a Mantuan who worked in the curia and had been in the household of Cardinal Francesco Gonzaga. The document showed that Vanozza was now a wealthy woman, owning three inns in central Rome – the 'Serpent, the 'Cow' and the 'Sun'.

On 23 March Innocent VIII sent Cardinal Giuliano della Rovere as legate to France to propose an alliance with King Charles VIII. In response, a French royal embassy arrived in Rome on 31 May to negotiate the details of the alliance. But Cardinal Rodrigo and Ferdinand II's ambassadors tried to obstruct the negotiations and, at a public consistory a few days later, Cardinal Rodrigo had a heated exchange of views with the French Cardinal Jean Balue.

LEFT **Portrait bust of Ferrante I of Naples.** *As King of Naples for almost 40 years after succeeding his father Alfonso, Ferrante I (1423–94) played a major role in Italian politics and arranged alliances with other rulers in the peninsula, choosing Ippolita Sforza, daughter of the Duke of Milan, as a bride for his heir Alfonso of Calabria. He also arranged politically useful marriages for his daughters: the Duke of Ferrara for Eleonora, the nephew of Sixtus IV for Giovanna and the King of Hungary for Beatrice.*

ABOVE **Ceramic tiles from the ducal palace, Gandia.** *Little remains of the original castle at Gandia, the residence of the Borgia dukes, which was rebuilt at the beginning of the 17th century. These elaborate floor tiles, in the Spanish style, suggest that the family preferred to emphasize their Catalan origins, rather than the Italian connections that brought them to power and influence.*

By the end of July Ferrante I's army, led by his son Alfonso of Calabria, was camped outside the gates of Rome, and on 10 August Innocent VIII was forced to capitulate and sign a peace treaty.

Towards the end of the year Cardinal Rodrigo's son Pedro Luis arrived in Rome. The cardinal hoped to keep him out of mischief until his intended bride was old enough to wed.[9]

1487

IN THIS YEAR POPE INNOCENT VIII made an alliance with Florence, sealing the relationship with the marriage of his own son Franceschetto Cibò, a dissolute man in his late thirties, with the 16-year-old Maddalena, daughter of the rich banker Lorenzo de' Medici. The bride entered Rome on 13 November, and on 18 November the couple were guests of honour at a banquet hosted by the pope in the Vatican.

1488

ON 14 APRIL A GROUP of citizens from the papal fief of Forlì assassinated their lord, Girolamo Riario. His widow Caterina Sforza managed to hold the castle long enough for troops to arrive from her uncle, Ludovico Sforza of Milan.

In August, tragedy struck Cardinal Rodrigo's family when his eldest son Pedro Luis died, aged just twenty-four. He

LEFT **Cameo of Ludovico Sforza.** *On the assassination of Galeazzo Maria, Duke of Milan (1476), his wife Bona of Savoy took over as regent for their young son Giangaleazzo. But real power lay in the hands of Giangaleazzo's uncle, Ludovico, who seized control of the regency council to rule in his nephew's name.*

State entries into Rome

The etiquette of a formal entry into the city of Rome followed a distinctive pattern. Visitors were met outside the gates of the city, and the grander the guest the further away from the city he or she was met.

They were then accommodated in a villa or palace outside the walls for the night and entertained to lunch the next day. The formal entry was normally held in the late afternoon, and the visiting party was briefed by the papal master-of-ceremonies. As the visitors arrived at the gate, usually the Porta del Popolo if they were travelling from the north, they would be formally received by the cardinals and members of the curia, as well as their households, and escorted along the streets to the Vatican or St Peter's, where they were received by the pope.

had left a will naming his half-brother, the nine-year-old Juan, as his heir to the Duchy of Gandia, and he also left 10,000 ducats to be used as a dowry for his half-sister Lucrezia.

1489

A NEW ALLIANCE between Milan and Naples was cemented in February with the marriage of Giangaleazzo Sforza, the Duke of Milan, and Isabella of Aragon, daughter of Alfonso, Duke of Calabria. Meanwhile relations between King Ferrante of Naples and Pope Innocent VIII steadily deteriorated.

In the spring a group of officials employed in the curia were found to be forging papal bulls and making a good income with them. The documents were mainly dispensations allowing remarriage, though one gave the Norwegians permission to celebrate mass without using wine.[10] The forgers were all hanged and then burnt in the Campo dei Fiori.

On 9 March the College of Cardinals finally gave in to Innocent VIII's demands to be allowed to create his own cardinals. Among the recipients of the red hats were his illegitimate nephew Lorenzo Cibò and Giovanni de' Medici, the 13-year-old son of the banker Lorenzo de' Medici, whose appointment was to be kept secret for the present.

From Rhodes, on 13 March, the Turkish Prince Djem – son of Mehmet II – arrived in Rome, after fleeing to the island on the accession of his brother and

> The forgers were all hanged and then burnt in the Campo dei Fiori.

147

rival Bazajet as sultan. From there he had travelled on to France with Pierre d'Aubusson, the Grand Master of the Knights of St John, who had achieved renown by fighting off the Turkish siege of Rhodes in 1480.

On 21 May Cardinal Rodrigo hosted the festivities for the marriage of the sixteen-year-old Orsino Orsini, the son of Ludovico Orsini and his cousin Adriana de Milà, and Giulia Farnese, aged just fifteen. Within months of the wedding the beautiful Giulia had become the mistress of the cardinal, who was now 58 years old.

Meanwhile relations between Ferrante I and Innocent VIII were deteriorating further. On 27 June Niccolò Orsini was named Captain-General of the Church and, three days later, the pope threatened King Ferrante with excommunication if he failed to pay the tribute he had promised (according to their 1486 treaty) within 60 days. On 11 September the pope held a public consistory, inviting all ambassadors in Rome to discuss the problem of Naples. The pope explained how Ferrante had not conformed with the treaty terms and declared him to be deprived of his crown, returning Naples to the states of the Church.

1490

IN AUGUST POPE INNOCENT VIII became so ill that he received the last sacraments, and he was still in bed on 26 September when rumours spread that he had actually died. The College of Cardinals managed to stop his son Franceschetto Cibò from seizing valuables

> ## The 'unusually eloquent' Rodrigo Borgia
>
> *He is tall with a medium complexion, neither dark nor fair. He has dark eyes and a full mouth. His health is excellent and he has enormous energy. He is unusually eloquent and blessed with innate good manners, which never leave him.*
>
> L. VON PASTOR, *History of the Popes*, VOL. V, P. 388.

LEFT **Raphael, detail from *Girl with a Unicorn*.** *Traditionally assumed to be a portrait of Rodrigo Borgia's mistress Giulia Farnese, this portrait (c.1505) is usually attributed to Raphael, a master of the genre. The unicorn was a widely recognized symbol of virginity.*

RIGHT **Late 15th-century chalice.** *Made in L'Aquila, this silver-gilt chalice is ornamented with bosses carrying with busts of saints, once enamelled, and a base with lobes decorated with figures of Christ, the Virgin and other saints, which have also lost most of their original enamelled colour.*

from the papal treasury, taking charge of it themselves. By 28 September it was clear that the pope was not dying but had suffered a stroke, from which he was slowly recovering.

On 9 October Cardinal Rodrigo added the bishopric of the island of Majorca to his now immense list of benefices. That autumn he sent his teenage son Cesare to study at the University of Perugia.

The 16-year-old Cesare left Perugia to study law

1491

CARDINAL RODRIGO exploited his Spanish connections further this year to negotiate a marriage between his daughter Lucrezia, now 11 years old, with the Spanish nobleman Juan de Centelles.

On 23 August 1491, 'work was begun on Santa Maria in Via Lata, that is to say the destruction of this church and the building of another as well as the demolition of the triumphal arch [of Diocletian] above which the church will be built. To fund the cost of this church the pope has contributed 4,000 ducats, the vice-chancellor 3,000 ducats and the chamberlain 2,000 ducats.' [11]

During the year Cardinal Rodrigo added the Hungarian see of Eger, worth 10,000 ducats a year, to his collection of lucrative benefices, and he continued to use his considerable influence on behalf of his family.

On 12 September he managed to get his son Cesare nominated as Bishop of Pamplona.

That autumn the 16-year-old Cesare left Perugia to study law at the University of Pisa, where his Catalan courtiers did not impress: 'the men in his entourage are little, they do not care for good manners,' wrote one of Giovanni de'

A self-confident Italy

Italy had never known such peace and prosperity as it did in the years around 1490. There were crops growing in the mountains and arid places, as well as on the lush fertile plains. No other foreign power held sway in the peninsula and Italy had a great abundance of people, of commercial activity and wealth, which was evident above all in the magnificence of her many princes, in the splendour of her many great and noble cities and the excellence of her governments.

FRANCESCO GUICCIARDINI, *Storia d'Italia*, I.

150

RIGHT **Cesare Borgia.** *This portrait, presumed to be of Rodrigo Borgia's second son, shows a young noble expensively attired in an elegant black velvet doublet. The embroidered cuffs of his white shirt show below the sleeves, one of which is fashionably slashed. The tight-fitting clothes of the period, designed to show off a fine masculine physique, were a marked contrast to the long shapeless robes and coats worn by men of the Church.*

Macchiavelli's 'new prince'

There is nothing *that makes a prince more respected than great achievements and unique deeds. We have in our own times Ferdinand of Aragon, the present King of Spain. We can almost call him a new prince, because from being a weak king he became, through renown and glory, the First King of Christendom; and if you think about his deeds, you will find that they were all very great and some were extraordinary. At the beginning of his reign he conquered Granada and this victory formed the foundations of his state.*

NICCOLÒ MACCHIAVELLI, *The Prince*, CHAPTER 21 (*Tutte l'opere*, I, P. 374).

Medici's courtiers, also studying at Pisa, adding insultingly that 'they look like *marrani* [louts]'.[12] By contrast, the Ferrarese ambassador described the young Cesare Borgia himself as having 'great talents and a noble bearing, like the son of a prince. He is invariably carefree and cheerful, and always seems in high spirits.' He added, presciently, that 'he shows no propensity to be a churchman'.[13]

On 25 November, the Feast of St Catherine of Alexandria, the last portion of the Iberian peninsula under Muslim rule – Granada – capitulated to the armies of Ferdinand and Isabella of Spain. The terms of surrender obliged the Moors to vacate Granada within 60 days.[14]

1492

THE YEAR WOULD BE a momentous one, inaugurating a revolution in Europe's understanding of the world, a new era in the politics and peace of Italy, and a transformation in the fortunes of Rodrigo Borgia, his family and his compatriots.

On 2 January Spanish troops entered Granada and, four days later, King Ferdinand and Queen Isabella made their ceremonial entry into the city to celebrate the expulsion of the Moors from their kingdom. To proclaim this Christian victory, the papal banner embroidered with a silver cross – which had been donated to the Spanish monarchs by Sixtus IV, and carried by the troops throughout their long campaign – was hoisted over the Alhambra palace.

The news arrived in Rome on 1 February, in a letter written by the king himself, 'confirming the truth that the King of Spain has entered Granada with the greatest triumph', and was announced to the city by the pealing of

RIGHT **Isabella of Castile, Queen of Spain,** *enters Granada, accompanied by members of her court and her ladies-in-waiting. This is one of a pair of panels that commemorate the conquest of Granada from the Moors in 1492; the other panel shows King Ferdinand making his entry into the city surrounded by his entourage. They form part of the decoration of the Royal Chapel in the cathedral at Granada, which was built by the Catholic Kings, in celebration of this landmark in the history of Spain, as a burial chapel for themselves and their descendants. The chapel also contains Isabella's crown and Ferdinand's sword, as well as the tombs of many of their descendants.*

Lent was marked by reports of the pope's increasing ill-health.

the great bell on the Capitol.[15] On 5 February Innocent VIII led a procession of cardinals and prelates to San Giacomo degli Spagnoli, the national church of Spain in Rome, where he celebrated a special mass to give thanks for the victory. The cardinals hosted more secular celebrations too. Cardinal Rodrigo staged a bullfight in the courtyard of his palace, a novel entertainment for Rome, at which the guests saw five bulls killed. The Spanish ambassadors were guests of honour at a banquet held at Cardinal Raffaello Riario's palace, where they watched a theatrical performance of the conquest, culminating in the royal entry into Granada. Indeed, the Christian victory was celebrated throughout Carnival that year.

Lent, which started on 7 March, was marked by reports of the pope's increasing ill-health. On 19 March the Mantuan ambassador reported that he was suffering from abdominal pains.

On 23 March Cardinal Rodrigo joined his colleagues in consistory to witness the ceremonies conferring a red hat on Giovanni de' Medici, who had been created a cardinal in secret three years earlier and, now that he was 16 years old, his status could be made public.

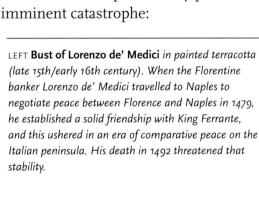

On 31 March Ferdinand and Isabella published an edict requiring all Jews to convert to Christianity or to leave Spain; most went to Portugal, although many moved to Rome, which was known for its tolerance. As a reward for expelling both the Moors and the Jews from Spain, Innocent VIII gave them the title 'Catholic Kings'.

During April news arrived from Florence of the death of its *de facto* ruler Lorenzo de' Medici on the 8th of that month: he was just 43 years old and died from the complications of gout. The succession of his inexperienced son Piero heralded an end to the uneasy balance of power shared by Milan, Florence and Naples. The death of Lorenzo was preceded by portents of imminent catastrophe:

LEFT **Bust of Lorenzo de' Medici** *in painted terracotta (late 15th/early 16th century). When the Florentine banker Lorenzo de' Medici travelled to Naples to negotiate peace between Florence and Naples in 1479, he established a solid friendship with King Ferrante, and this ushered in an era of comparative peace on the Italian peninsula. His death in 1492 threatened that stability.*

154

A comet had been seen a short time before and wolves had been heard howling. A mad woman had been heard at Santa Maria Novella shouting that a bull with horns of fire had set light to Florence. The city's lions began fighting among themselves, and the best one was killed. And, a day or two before he died a bolt of lightning struck the lantern on top of the dome of the cathedral, and several great stones fell down in the direction of the Palazzo Medici.[16]

Politically, the death of such a major figure was a blow to the fragile peace of Italy. To the historian Francesco Guicciardini:

> His death was most unfortunate for all Italy, partly because the struggle to maintain peace was no longer in his hands but also because he had proved useful in restraining the outbreaks of animosity and suspicion that often surfaced between Ferrante of Naples and Ludovico Sforza, two princes of similar status and ambition.[17]

Cardinal Rodrigo's support for King Ferrante I of Naples throughout the wars following the revolt of his barons, and his efforts to reconcile the king with Rome, now bore fruit. On 27 May Alfonso of Calabria's son, named Ferrante after his grandfather, arrived in Rome to secure the Aragonese succession to the throne of Naples. He was received with much honour, and Cardinal Ascanio Sforza hosted a lunch party for the prince that lasted all day.

Charles VIII's ambassadors were also in Rome at this time, seeking a dispensation from the pope to allow the French king to marry Anne, the wealthy heiress of Brittany; at the time she was betrothed to Maximilian, the eldest son of Emperor Frederick III. With Charles VIII now planning to revive the Anjou claim to Naples, of which he was the heir, the envoys tried to persuade the pope not to agree to Ferrante I's request. But it was to no avail. On 4 June Innocent VIII held a secret consistory in which he confirmed the Aragonese succession to Naples,

RIGHT **Bust of Charles VIII of France.** *Inheriting the French throne in 1483 at the age of just 13, Charles VIII had grandiose ambitions. He planned first to enforce his claim to Naples, and then to use the kingdom to launch a crusade that would see him enthroned as King of Jerusalem. His invasion of Italy (1494) would mark the end of a long era of Italian independence.*

Cardinal Ascanio Sforza hosted a lunch party for the prince that lasted all day.

and when the French ambassador tried to attend the consistory to lodge a formal complaint, he was barred from entering.

On 23 June Innocent VIII was reported to be in better health: 'the pope, thank God, is much improved,' wrote the Mantuan ambassador, 'and he wants to travel to some places outside Rome in order to take a little pleasure in the hope that this will improve the state of his health'.[18] However, a day or two later, it was reported that the pope had fallen ill again, this time with a suppurating ulcer on his leg and a high fever.

On 9 July Cardinal Rodrigo received the welcome news that, as a favour to King Ferdinand of Spain, Innocent VIII had elevated Valencia to the status of archdiocese, making Rodrigo now Archbishop of Valencia.

The pope, meanwhile, having rallied somewhat in late June, was now visibly deteriorating. On 17 July he summoned all the cardinals to his bedroom in the Vatican, where they gathered around his sickbed to hear him apologize for his failure to live up to the onerous job of supreme pontiff and listen to his hope that they would choose a more worthy successor. On 19 July the Florentine ambassador wrote that 'there is no hope for his life' and 'his strength is entirely gone,' but that 'he remains fully conscious'.[19] In the evening of 25 July, Pope Innocent VIII died.

The violence that always threatened to erupt in Rome at the death of a pope did not materialize this time: 'It is true that several people have been murdered, and that some others were badly wounded when it became known that the pope was dying,' wrote the Mantuan ambassador, 'but after his death the situation improved.'[20]

On 3 August, far from Rome in southwestern Spain, the Genoese adventurer Christopher Columbus set sail from the port of Palos in the ambitious hope of discovering a new and shorter route to the Indies.

In Rome the rumour mills were hard at work, as were the bookmakers, predicting who would be elected the next pope. The College of Cardinals was split between the supporters of Giuliano della Rovere and those of Ascanio Sforza; moreover, Cardinal Giuliano knew he had made too many enemies during the pontificate of Innocent VIII to have any hope of the tiara himself,

> It is true that several people have been murdered, and that some others were badly wounded.

PREVIOUS PAGE **The Confirmation of the Rule of St Francis.** *Part of a cycle on the life of St Francis painted in 1483–6 by Domenico Ghirlandaio for Francesco Sassetti to decorate his chapel in Santa Trinita, Florence, this scene includes a portrait of Sassetti (the balding figure, dressed in red, on the right), who was employed by the Medici bank. Included, next to him, with dark hair, is Lorenzo de' Medici, an unusual and deliberately flattering gesture underlining Lorenzo's position.*

RIGHT **Christopher Columbus.** *Born in the busy Mediterranean port of Genoa in 1451, where his father worked as a weaver, Columbus was apprenticed to an agent for whom he travelled widely, sailing to England, Ireland and the west coast of Africa. Too poor for a proper education, he taught himself Latin so that he could read the texts on astronomy and geography that so fascinated him.*

Columbus and the Americas

In 1474 a Florentine astrologer, Paolo Toscanelli, wrote to the King of Portugal to suggest a new route to the spice islands of the Indies, and moreover one that he thought would be shorter than the trip being made regularly by Portuguese merchant ships to Guinea on the African coast.

A decade later Christopher Columbus used the same letter in an attempt to convince the Portuguese king to finance a voyage across the Atlantic, claiming that the distance from the Canary Islands to Japan was only 2,400 nautical miles, half that from Lisbon to the mouth of the River Congo, which had recently been found by Portuguese explorers. After many years of negotiations, not helped by the return of Bartolomeo Diaz from his epic trip around the Cape of Good Hope, which did indeed open up a sea route to the Indies, Columbus turned to Ferdinand and Isabella of Spain, with whom he signed a contract in April 1492. Sailing from Palos with three galleys – the *Santa Maria*, the *Pinta* and the *Santa Clara*, the last nicknamed 'Niña' after its owner – he did find land but, far from being the Indies or Japan, he had encountered many of the major islands of the Caribbean, including Hispaniola (modern-day Haiti and Dominican Republic). Three more expeditions followed over the next decade.

Columbus's epic journeys marked the point at which Europe became aware that there was an enormous mass of land between Europe and Asia. The Americas would prove a huge source of wealth for the Spanish crown, particularly after the *conquistador* Francisco Pizarro's defeat of the Inca Empire in Peru during the 1530s.

The new continent also vastly increased the size of the Christian world as the Spanish imposed the Catholic religion upon their American subjects. New foodstuffs had a major impact on the European diet – turkeys and maize were instantly popular, though it took Europeans longer to adapt to tomatoes, chocolate and the potato. Above all, Columbus's voyage radically altered the European view of the world.

The papal candidates assessed

There are many candidates for this conclave and first I would put Cardinal Ardicino della Porta who is of Cardinal Ascanio Sforza's party and certainly widely popular as a good man. Then Cardinal Oliviero Carafa but the King of France is said to be against him ... Yesterday it was said in public that Ascanio himself wants to be pope ... and the city is alive with this rumour, though more serious minds do not think it an option, however, it should not be discredited. Cardinal Rodrigo, the vice-chancellor, is next because of the importance of his connections and he can reward his supporters with many worthy things: first there is the chancellery, which is almost a second papacy, then the temporal power of his two cities, Civita Castellana and Nepi with Rocca Soriano, which is an eagle among the states of the Church; then there is the abbey at Aquila which is worth 1,000 ducats, and the bishopric of Albano near Rome which is worth the same, and two large benefices in the Kingdom of Naples, the bishopric of Porto, worth 1,200 ducats, and the abbey of Subiaco with its 22 fortresses and worth 2,000 ducats a year. They also say he has 16 of the best and most valuable bishoprics in Spain, quite apart from many abbeys and other benefices: the bishopric of Valencia is worth 16,000 ducats, that of Cartagena 7,000 ducats, Majorca 6,000 ducats and the abbey of Valdigne near Valencia with many vassals 2,000 ducats.

THE FERRARESE AMBASSADOR G.A. BOCCACCIO TO ELEONORA OF ARAGON, DUCHESS OF FERRARA, 4 AUGUST 1492 (L. VON PASTOR, *History of the Popes*, VOL. V, PP. 533–4, DOC. 9).

so he was planning, as in the last conclave, to have his own candidate elected. The Ferrarese ambassador, however, thought that the winner would be one of four members of Sforza's party: the front-runners were Sforza himself, aged only 37, together with Oliviero Carafa, the Archbishop of Naples, and Ardicino della Porta, from Milan, both 58 years old and both decent and pious men. The ambassador also thought that Rodrigo Borgia, now aged 61, was a good outside bet, not least because of the enormously wealthy list of benefices, including the coveted post of vice-chancellor, that he would be obliged to distribute among the college members in the event of his election. The Florentine envoy knew that the real business was still to be done: 'I won't go into detail about all these rumours, because they would only confuse you as there are so many of them, and they change every hour.'[21]

The conclave opened on Monday 6 August and 23 cardinals, 14 of whom had been given their red hats by Sixtus IV, moved into their cramped wooden cubicles in the Sistine Chapel.

The first scrutiny was held on the Wednesday, with each cardinal voting for up to three candidates. When the papers were read out, it was found that Oliviero Carafa had the most votes (nine), followed by three cardinals with seven votes each: Giovanni Michiel and Jorge da Costa, both in Giuliano della Rovere's camp, and Rodrigo Borgia. The second scrutiny, which took place in the morning of 9 August, was equally inconclusive, as was the third, held the next day. But now Carafa had ten votes, as did Michiel, while Rodrigo had eight votes with Giuliano della Rovere on seven. Still no one was anywhere near the 16 votes required for election.

That afternoon, Friday 10 August, the Florentine ambassador – who was one of the

guardians of the conclave – reported despairingly that as there had still not been an election, the cardinals were to be restricted to one meal a day, and to just bread, wine and water from Monday onwards.

During the evening and night of 10 August Ascanio Sforza worked hard to persuade the rest of his party to back Cardinal Rodrigo, for whom he had voted in all three scrutinies. On 11 August, just before dawn, it was announced that Rodrigo Borgia had been elected, taking the name Alexander VI. In the end the vote had been almost unanimous; the single vote against Rodrigo had been his own, which he had given in favour of Carafa.

In the eyes of the Florentine Ambassador Filippo Valori, 'The election of the vice-chancellor is something that is difficult to believe, and if it has really happened it has to be said that it is the work of the Holy Ghost.' [22] For Milanese interests, however, the election appeared to be something of a triumph. Ambrogio Mirabilia, reporting to the ducal secretary Bartolomeo Calchi, felt that 'Cardinal Ascanio was himself responsible for the election of Alexander VI ... and for this reason His Lordship [Ludovico Sforza] and Cardinal Ascanio have acquired much more credit and renown than I can describe in words, so that it is said that Cardinal Ascanio is not only the first next to the pope but is almost pope himself.'[23]

ABOVE **The interior of Old St Peter's.** *This fresco from the church of San Martino ai Monti, Rome, shows the interior of St Peter's as it was in the 15th century, before the building was destroyed by Julius II in 1505 to make way for his new church. Built by Emperor Constantine, the great basilica of St Peter's was the largest church in Rome and one of the most venerated churches in the whole of Christendom. The long nave, with its architraves supported on columns pillaged from ancient pagan structures, was flanked with doubled-side aisles. Between the* nave and the apse is the hexagonal baldacchino, *which Constantine erected over the cult centre established by early Christians for the worship of the first pope; it is supported by six twisted marble columns, which were long thought, erroneously, to have come from Solomon's Temple in Jerusalem. It was this unique combination of nave and apse with a transept in between – required to provide adequate space for the* baldacchino *– that established the template for church design across medieval Europe.*

Christ Giving the Keys of the Church to St Peter. *Painted in 1481–2 by Pietro Perugino on the walls of the Sistine Chapel, this fresco depicts the moment when Christ told the leader of the Apostles: 'Thou art Peter, and upon this rock (Latin: petrus) I will build my church ... and I will give unto thee the keys of the kingdom of heaven'. The scene underlined the fact that the authority of the pope derived directly from Christ himself.*

Diverse opinions of Alexander VI

He has been a cardinal for 37 years and all that time he never failed to attend consistories unless ill, which was very rare. He was an important figure throughout the pontificates of Pius II, Paul II, Sixtus IV and Innocent VIII, and had served as legate in both Italy and Spain. Few men understood the rules of proper behaviour as well as he did. He also knew how to appear at his best, making great efforts to converse elegantly and behave impeccably, in which he had the advantage of majestic height. Moreover, he was about 60 years old at his election, exactly that age at which, according to Aristotle, men are wisest. Physically strong and with a lively intellect, he was wonderfully suited to his new position.

SIGISMONDO DE' CONTI, *Le storie de' suoi tempi*, VOL. II, 53.

For Alexander VI was extremely shrewd and wise, a good judge of character, immensely persuasive, and a skilled master at the political game. But these virtues were utterly surpassed by his vices: obscene habits, lack of sincerity, audacity, mendacity, disloyalty, impiety, great greed, untrammelled ambition, barbarous cruelty and a deep desire to glorify his children.

FRANCESCO GUICCIARDINI, *Storia d'Italia*, I, 2.

Alexander VI's election was generally greeted with delight in Rome, where he was well known as a generous, easy-going and competent figure. His enemies reacted angrily however, claiming that he could not have won the election without buying votes in the conclave. The Venetian government was furious that one of its cardinals had voted for Cardinal Rodrigo, acting directly against its wishes. A young German cleric, Sigismund Sänftl, canon of Freisingen, scathingly referred to 'Alexander VI ... with his 17 children and his other *marrani*,' adding that 'it is thought that Emperor Maximilian will refuse to do him obedience because in the past he has always been against him'.[24]

The following evening, 12 August, a huge cavalcade of 800 men, including members of Rome's leading families and government officials, all carrying torches, rode through the city, which was alight with celebratory bonfires, to greet the new pope at the Vatican palace.

The Venetian government was furious that one of their cardinals had voted for Cardinal Rodrigo.

165

LEFT **Pope Alexander VI.** *Part of the decorations for Alexander VI's apartments in the Vatican, painted by Pinturicchio, this detail is from a scene that shows the Borgia pope kneeling as donor to witness the miracle of the Resurrection. He is magnificently dressed in a superb cope, ornamented with pearls and other gems and embroidered gold and silver thread; on the ground beside him glitters the priceless papal tiara.*

The contrast between the poverty of the lives of Christ and his Apostles, as described in the Bible, and the opulent lifestyles of the 15th-century popes and their courts was offensive to many. These reformists roundly condemned the extravagance with which the papacy displayed its power and prestige and, above all, the corruption that inevitably followed in the wake of this materialism.

The coronation of Alexander VI

His Holiness was crowned last Sunday with more splendour and rejoicing than any other pontiff of our times. The streets along which the pope passed, the best part of two miles, were all covered with cloth and silk hangings. They were ornamented with many splendid triumphal arches and there was also beautiful singing and music. The Roman barons all attended the coronation, as did the Lord of Camerino and members of the Baglione family of Perugia. The pope said mass early at St Peter's and then proceeded to his coronation, as is the custom, and then spent the day amid singing, music and other festivities. His Holiness distributed many coins as usual. He returned to the Vatican late in the evening accompanied by almost all the cardinals and thousands of torches, which marked the end of the ceremony. But I also wanted to tell Your Excellency that the whole court was almost dead with exhaustion, having spent the whole day on the dusty streets under the sun.

FLORAMONTE BROGNOLO TO FRANCESCO GONZAGA, 31 AUGUST 1492 (L. VON PASTOR, *History of the Popes*, VOL. V, PP. 541–2, DOC. 18).

Alexander VI was crowned on 26 August with great pomp. The new pope reputedly spent 12,000 ducats on the costly materials for the outfits of his officials.[25] The streets along his route to San Giovanni in Laterano were particularly splendid, decorated with garlands of flowers and greenery, tapestries and statuary. Much was made of his emblem, the Borgia bull: there was a fountain in the form of a bull that spewed water and wine, and a gilded bull on a pedestal with an inscription that told how Romulus, one of the legendary founders of Rome, had traced the boundaries of the city with an ox-drawn plough.[26] It was so hot, however, that Alexander VI fainted at San Giovanni in Laterano and had to be revived with a handful of cold water.

On 31 August Alexander VI held his first consistory and, as was the custom, handed out his old benefices to those whose votes had assisted his election, notably cardinals Sforza, Savelli, Colonna and Orsini. The bishopric of Majorca went to Cardinal Savelli, who also became Archpriest of Santa Maria Maggiore, while the new Bishop of Cartagena was Cardinal Orsini. The prize of the vice-chancellorship went to Ascanio Sforza, the mastermind behind his election, who also received the lucrative bishopric of Eger. The new pope now sold his palace to Cardinal Ascanio, 'because you have no proper residence in this city and because of your singular devotion to our person'.[27]

Alexander VI also distributed favours to his family. His nephew Juan Borgia, the Archbishop of Monreale, now received his cardinal's hat at the age of forty-six. His son Cesare, now aged 17, was made Archbishop of Valencia. Even Jofrè, the pope's youngest child, received a benefice in Spain – the papal brief designated the boy as twelve years old, though he was more like ten.

Within days of the election Cardinal Ascanio suggested cementing the alliance between Rome and Milan with a marriage between the pope's 12-year-old daughter Lucrezia and a member of the Sforza family. The previous year's marriage negotiations with Juan de Centelles had already been broken off in favour of Lucrezia's betrothal to a grander aristocrat, Don Gasparo, Count of Aversa.

ABOVE LEFT **The Borgia bull.** *These gilded bulls, set against a blue background, appear extensively in the decoration of Alexander VI's apartments in the Vatican. The use of dynastic emblems such as these to fill up small spaces in a decorative scheme was typical of grand Renaissance projects; but these were also ostentatiously expensive. Gold was a costly medium but so too was the lapis lazuli used as a pigment to make the blue paint.*

Rewards for Pope Alexander VI's backers

Immediately after his election to the papacy, he distributed his goods to the poor ... he named Cardinal Ascanio Sforza as vice-chancellor. He gave the abbey of Subiaco with all its castles to Cardinal Giovanni Colonna, giving him and his house the rights of patronage over the abbey in perpetuity. He gave the bishopric of Porto with its tower and all its wealth, which included a cellar full of wine, to Cardinal Giovanni Michiel. Cardinal Sclafenati got the city of Nepi and Cardinal Fregoso was given the titular church of Santa Maria in Via Lata. He gave Civita Castellana to Cardinal Savelli, who also became Archpriest of Santa Maria Maggiore. It was said that he gave others many thousands of ducats, including 5,000 ducats to the Camaldolese Cardinal Maffei Gherardi for his vote. When they heard this in Venice they stopped the revenues of his benefices, arguing that he did not need any more money. Only five cardinals received nothing: Oliviero Carafa, Francesco Piccolomini, Jorge da Costa, Giuliano della Rovere and Giovanni Battista Zen. They alone refused the tip saying that the votes for the papacy ought to be given freely and not bought with presents. It is said also that before they went into the conclave, the vice-chancellor had sent four mules laden with silver to the house of Cardinal Ascanio Sforza in order to have his vote and those of his supporters.

JOHANNES BURCHARD, *Liber notarum*, PP. 41–3.

167

The young Lucrezia Borgia

She is of *average height and gracefully built with rather a long face but a fine nose and blonde hair, pale eyes and a full mouth, with dazzling white teeth; her neck is elegant, her bosom well-proportioned, and she has a cheerful, happy manner.*

NICCOLÒ CAGNOLO DA PARMA (L. VON PASTOR, *History of the Popes*, VOL. V, P. 400).

But with Rodrigo now pope, Lucrezia's stock had risen yet higher

Rumours of the proposed match quickly circulated, to the fury of Ferrante I of Naples. On 3 September the king and Cardinal Giuliano della Rovere used their influence to enable Franceschetto Cibò to sell his papal fiefs of Cerveteri and Anguillara to Virginio Orsini, captain-general of Ferrante's armies. At a consistory a few days later, Alexander VI reprimanded Cardinal Giuliano for his part in this illegal transaction, and the cardinal retorted angrily that anything was better than letting the fiefs become the property of a Sforza. The Sforza responded by offering money and men to the pope to regain the fiefs.

Alexander VI also set about reorganizing the government of Rome. According to the record of Johannes Burchard, he 'set up a commission to inspect the prisons, appointing four men to hear the complaints in Rome, and reorganized the role of the governor of Rome and his officers. He also decided to hold audiences every Tuesday for all Romans, men and women alike, and he listened to their complaints in person; he administered justice excellently'.[28]

On 12 October, thousands of miles to the west and after more than a month at sea, Christopher Columbus and his expedition encountered an island unknown to Europeans, which they named San Salvador.

LEFT **Portrait presumed to be Lucrezia Borgia.** *In this detail from her father's Vatican apartments, Lucrezia is portrayed as the early 4th-century St Catherine of Alexandria, disputing with the philosophers sent by Emperor Maxentius to persuade her to abandon her Christian faith and marry him. The philosophers were burned at the stake for failing, while Catherine was lashed to spiked wheels: but God destroyed the contraption before she was hurt. The legacy of the instrument of torture is the Catherine-wheel firework.*

ABOVE **Columbus arrives on Hispaniola and other islands.** *These woodcuts are some of the illustrations that accompany the letter Columbus wrote describing his first voyage to the 'Indies', which he sent to King Ferdinand and Queen Isabella of Spain from the Canary Islands on his way home in February 1493 and which was published in Rome in May of that year. In the letter he recounts how he named the islands he found: San Salvador and Santa Maria de Concepcion for the Christian religion, Fernandina in honour of the king, Isabella after the queen, Juana after their son and heir, and finally Hispaniola after their kingdom. There is some debate about the exact identities of these islands, but they include parts of the modern Bahamas, Cuba, Haiti and the Dominican Republic.*

A mitre studded with precious pearls.

Embassies to congratulate the new Borgia pope were now arriving in Rome. On 5 December the envoys sent by the Duke of Milan were received in the Vatican by Alexander VI, who was 'dressed in a red cape with a mitre studded with precious pearls'.[29] On 14 December the pope received two ambassadors from King Henry VII of England in a public consistory, where they offered their obedience. It was recorded that 'the Bishop of Durham [John Sherwood] gave an elegant speech but it was not pleasant to listen to because his accent was so bad'.[30]

Just before Christmas, Federigo of Aragon, the second son of King Ferrante of Naples, arrived in Rome 'with a huge retinue and he was received with great honour by Cardinal Giuliano della Rovere'.[31] His mission, in addition to offering congratulations, was to persuade Alexander VI to abandon his alliance with Milan, but the pope refused, preferring to play off Milan and Naples against each

The Borgia power base

At the time of his election as pope, Rodrigo Borgia had five living children: his daughter Isabella, who resided with her husband in the house provided by her father, and his four children by Vanozza de' Cataneis – Cesare (aged 17), Juan (aged 16), Lucrezia (aged 12) and Jofrè (aged 10). His eldest son Pedro Luis and his daughter Girolama had both died before his election.

Rodrigo Borgia had a great many relations too, some of whom had already benefitted from his position as cardinal; all hoped to profit now that he was pope. His cousin Cardinal Luis Juan de Milà (aged 62) seems to have preferred a quiet life in Spain, but three other cousins came over to Italy: Juan Castellar (aged 51), Jaime Serra (aged 64), who was appointed as the pope's domestic prelate in the Vatican, and Francisco Borgia (aged 51), a canon at Valencia who now moved to Rome as treasurer to Alexander VI's household. The pope's nephew Juan Borgia (aged 46), the Archbishop of Monreale, moved into the Vatican and Juan's illegitimate son was given

a place in Jofrè's household. Alexander VI's great-nephew Francisco Loriz, who had acted as Rodrigo's treasurer while he was a cardinal, now took over as the papal treasurer. Another great-nephew, also named Rodrigo Borgia, was given the post of captain of the papal guard, while his two younger brothers, Juan and Pedro Luis, remained in Spain, moving to Rome later in Alexander's pontificate.

Alexander VI also appointed many Catalans to his new papal household, including his head of household Pedro de Aranda, five valets, two of the three men in charge of his household finances, his private secretary, several doctors – and even his fool.[32]

other. A few weeks later Giuliano della Rovere left Rome for his castle at Ostia and the protection of King Ferrante and Virginio Orsini.

On 25 December Christopher Columbus landed on the northern part of the large island of Hispaniola.

Before the end of the year Alexander VI had started to plan the decoration of his new papal apartments in the Vatican. In honour of the great victory he had celebrated at the beginning of this momentous year in his life, he chose to decorate the main room with scenes from the life of St Catherine of Alexandria, whose feast day marked the defeat of the Moors at Granada.

𝕿𝖍𝖊 𝖞𝖊𝖆𝖗𝖘 1484–92 had seen Rodrigo Borgia consolidate his position in Rome. Despite being outmanoeuvred by his rival Cardinal Giuliano della Rovere, who engineered the election of Innocent VIII, and despite his support for the King of Naples in opposition to papal policy, Rodrigo's status was such that he had continued to prosper. Not only did he add more lucrative benefices to his already impressive income, but he also exploited his position to the benefit of the Borgia clan, which continued to grow in size and prestige. He had used his influence to acquire a duchy for his eldest son, gain appointments in the Church for his other sons, secure husbands for his daughters, as well as accumulate benefices for his many nephews living in Spain.

The year 1492 witnessed a dramatic transformation in the fortunes of the Borgia family after the election of Rodrigo as pope. Above all, this year marked a watershed in world affairs. For Europeans, Christopher Columbus's voyage across the Atlantic redrew the map of their world and inaugurated a new age of overseas conquest, empire and trade. In Italy, an era of comparative peace, prosperity and independence from foreign influence was about to end: the conquest of Moorish Granada now set the scene for Spain to flex her muscles as a major power to rival France on the European stage.

The threat that these two superpowers posed to the uneasy balance of power in Italy had had an important impact on the election of Alexander VI. Now was not the time for a devout churchman to wear the papal tiara. The conclave decided that an astute and worldly politician would be best suited to deal with the current dilemmas and elected the experienced and urbane Vice-Chancellor of the Church. Rodrigo Borgia's moment had come.

PREVIOUS PAGE **'Arithmetic'.** *The Borgia Apartments in the Vatican consisted of a series of seven rooms, starting with a grand reception room (now the Sala dei Pontefici) and followed by smaller and increasingly intimate chambers, ending with Alexander VI's bedroom. This image belongs to the series of decorations celebrating the Liberal Arts, which ornamented the study where the pope kept his treasured possessions and books.*

RIGHT **The life of Osiris,** *in the vault of the Sala dei Santi. In the bottom scene Osiris is killed by a demon, an allusion to the threat that Muslims posed to the survival of Christendom; the top scene shows Osiris reborn as a bull, a clear reference – by way of the Borgia emblem – to the restoration of the Church under the Borgia pope.*

The Borgia Apartments

Alexander VI's private apartments were decorated with frescoes by Pinturicchio (c.1454–1513) and his assistants that expressed essentially Christian themes, including a large portrait of the pope himself kneeling in his pontifical robes before the Christ of the Resurrection.

Many of the scenes include portraits of Pope Alexander's family, such as that of Lucrezia as St Catherine of Alexandria. The choice of scenes reflected the history of the Borgia family. The Visitation in the Sala dei Santi records the fact that this feast had been instituted during the Great Schism as part of an attempt to promote unity within the Church, which had finally been brought about by the diplomacy of Alexander VI's uncle, Calixtus III, and the programme as a whole celebrated the Christian victory of Ferdinand and Isabella against the Muslim Emirate of Granada.[33]

The rooms were ostentatiously lavish, with gilded stuccoes shining on the walls and vaults, and elaborate ceramic tiles, many decorated with the Borgia bull, on the floors – these had been ordered in Valencia and were shipped, at considerable expense, from Spain. The stuccoes themselves were an innovation, inspired by the recent discovery in Rome of the buried ruins of the Golden House of Nero by the Colosseum. Most striking, however, was the ceiling of the Sala dei Santi, with its depiction of the Ancient Egyptian deities Isis and Osiris. Osiris's emblem was also a bull, which enabled one of the pope's propagandists to argue that Alexander VI himself was descended from Osiris, giving the room, with its family portraits, a more imposing dynastic resonance.

Alexander VI

THE SECOND BORGIA POPE
AND HIS FAMILY

1493–1497

In 1492, the Cardinal of Valencia's transformation into Pope Alexander VI placed the leading Borgia at the apex of the Church hierarchy. It also propelled Rodrigo Borgia into a pivotal role in European and Italian affairs at a time when complex rivalries – between Milan and Naples, between France and the emerging, unified Spain – would demand all his political instincts and shrewdness if he were to maintain Rome's independence and its authority over the Papal States. And of course the papacy brought vast opportunities for Alexander VI to improve the worldly prospects of his remaining children, a project he pursued with much zeal and openness.

1493

The expected announcement of the betrothal of Lucrezia Borgia and Giovanni Sforza, Lord of Pesaro, was made on 2 February.

ON 10 JANUARY FEDERIGO OF ARAGON – King Ferrante's second son – left Rome without any reassurance from Alexander VI that the pope would enter into an alliance with Naples. A week later the Milanese ambassador reported that Virginio Orsini was with Cardinal Giuliano della Rovere at Ostia, 'and he has told the cardinal to trust that he will protect the cardinal's fortress as well as his life, and so will the Colonna; King Ferrante is behind him too, and the castle is well fortified and provisioned'.[1]

The expected announcement of the betrothal of Lucrezia Borgia and Giovanni Sforza, Lord of Pesaro, was made on 2 February. The groom was 26, already a widower, and cousin to Milan's ruler Ludovico Sforza and Cardinal Ascanio Sforza.

PREVIOUS PAGE **Pope Alexander VI,** *see page 227.*

RIGHT **The Pesaro altarpiece.** *This votive altarpiece was commissioned from Titian by Jacopo Pesaro to decorate his palace. It celebrated Pesaro's appointment as admiral of the papal fleet in 1502, depicting the donor, in the robes of a Knight of Malta, being presented to St Peter by Pope Alexander VI. In the background are the galleys under his command, afloat on the Adriatic Sea.*

RITRATTO DI VEO DI C̄ PESARO
IN VENETIA CHE FV FATTO
GENERALE DI S CHIESA
TITIANO

Alexander VI as patriarch

Alexander VI could be moved by anger and other passions but principally by his excessive desire to magnify his children, whom he loved to distraction. Many popes had had children before but had usually hidden this sin by describing them as nephews; he was the first to present them openly to the world.

FRANCESCO GUICCIARDINI, *Storia d'Italia*, I, 3.

On 8 February the pope's nephew Cardinal Juan Borgia was made Bishop of Olomouc and, a few days later, Alexander VI gave his son Cesare three lucrative abbeys; also, around this time, he legitimized his youngest son Jofrè.

On 27 February, the second Wednesday in Lent, Alexander VI heard mass in his room and discussed his vestments for the day with his master-of-ceremonies Johannes Burchard. He held a short consistory in the Sala del Pappagallo – so-called because of the parrots painted on the walls – before mounting his horse to ride in procession to the ancient basilica of Santa Maria Maggiore, where he inspected progress on the expensively gilded coffered ceiling he had commissioned for the church.

During March King Ferrante I sent an envoy to Rome with an offer to settle the disputed acquisition of the papal fiefs of Cerveteri and Anguillara, and also to propose the marriages of two Aragon princesses: one for Cesare and one for Jofrè. But Alexander VI refused this attempt to woo him away from his alliance with Milan.

On 15 March Christopher Columbus returned from his transatlantic voyage, sailing into the harbour at Palos, on Spain's Atlantic coast. He brought back parrots, gold and several of the indigenous people from the lands he visited.

On 25 March the pope celebrated mass for the Feast of the Annunciation at Santa Maria sopra Minerva where, following tradition, he gave pouches containing 75 florins to 16 poor girls for their dowries.

One month later, on 25 April, Alexander VI announced the formation of a Holy League with Milan, Venice, Siena, Ferrara and Mantua against Naples and Virginio Orsini. In King Ferrante's view:

> The pope has no respect for the chair he now occupies ... all he wants is war with me, and he has been victimizing me ever since he was elected. There are more armed men than clergy in Rome, and he thinks of nothing but war and devastation. His cousins the Sforzas agree with him; what they really want is to run the papacy so that when he dies they can have it for themselves; Rome will end up as a Milanese army camp.[2]

On 4 May Alexander VI issued a papal bull of lasting significance. *Inter Caetera* divided the New World between Spain and Portugal; the bull, which favoured Ferdinand and Isabella, would alter the balance of power in the Iberian peninsula massively to Spain's advantage.

In the evening of 5th May, towards the hour of vespers:

> His Holiness rode out of the Vatican with his red cape over his surplice and his crimson hat, preceded by the cross, which was carried by the subdeacon. In front of the cross rode

---

LEFT **Bronze medal of Giovanni Sforza,** *who would marry Lucrezia Borgia in 1493. Portrait medals struck to commemorate an individual or an event were a distinctive genre of Italian Renaissance art. Based on the antique coins that were stamped with the profile heads of the emperors of Ancient Rome, they typified the revival of classical culture to provide images of power and prestige for a new generation of rulers. As statements of absolute authority, they were high fashion at the aristocratic courts of Italy, though less popular with mercantile patrons in Venice and Florence.*

Inter Caetera

Columbus's triumphant return in March 1493 from the West Indies, which he had claimed for Spain, led to a bitter dispute between the Spanish and Portuguese. The latter argued, on the basis of an earlier papal bull granting Portugal the right to new-found lands on the African coast, that these transatlantic territories also belonged to them.

King Ferdinand of Spain acted promptly, ordering Cardinal Bernardino Carvajal to discuss the issue with the pope, who agreed to the king's demands. Spain was given exclusive rights to the lands found by Columbus, and the pope also defined the Spanish sphere of influence over everything west of a line drawn 100 Spanish leagues beyond the Azores (this line was pushed 270 leagues further west in 1494 in the Treaty of Tordesillas). The papal bull *Inter Caetera* makes it clear that Alexander VI was rewarding Ferdinand for what the king had achieved 'in your reconquest of the realm of Granada from the yoke of the Moors and we therefore consider it our duty to grant you ... to continue your holy and exemplary action so pleasing to Almighty God ... that you may convert the inhabitants of islands and mainlands distant and unknown to the worship of Our Saviour and the Catholic faith'.

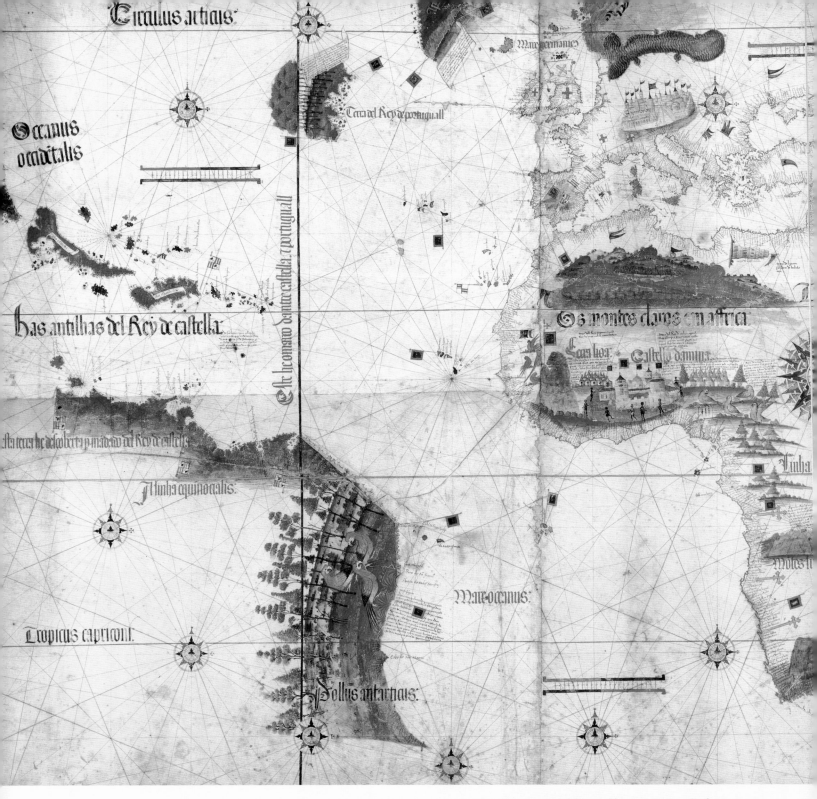

Circulus articus

Occanus occidatalis

Terra del Rey de portugual

Mare germanicū

Has antilhas del Rey de castella

Este he omaro antre castella. z portugual

Os montes claros em affrica

Lisboa Castello damina

Sta terra he descoberta p madado del Rey de castella

Linha equinocialis:

Mar occanus:

Linha

Tropicus capricorni

Polus antarticus

ABOVE **The Cantino map of the world (1502).** *This is the first map to show the Americas that can be securely dated. Acquired by Alberto Cantino in Lisbon, possibly illegally, it was sent to his master, Ercole d'Este, Duke of Ferrara who, like many other Italian rulers, was intrigued by the news of Columbus's discoveries. One should not be surprised by the level of detail with which the coastlines of Western Europe, the Mediterranean, the Black Sea, the Red Sea and the Persian Gulf are delineated – all*

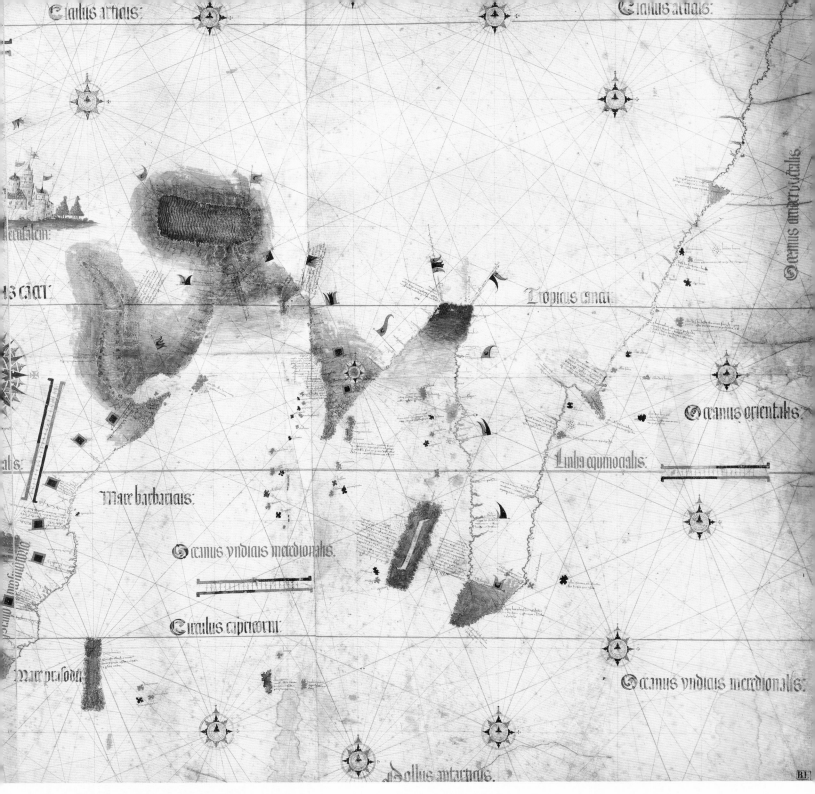

Circulus articus:

Circulus articus:

Oceanus amberoctalis

Ierusalem:

Tropicus cancri

Oceanus orientalis

Linha equinocialis:

Mare barbaricus:

Oceanus yndicus meridionalis.

Circulus capricorni:

Mare prasodu:

Oceanus yndicus meridionalis:

Circulus antarticus:

were well known to mariners and traders of the period. What is significant is that the map shows the line of demarcation as defined in the Treaty of Tordesillas (1494), by which Pope Alexander VI divided the New World between Spanish and Portuguese interests. Drawn up by the Portuguese, this map gives extensive details of their knowledge of the coastline of Brazil, as well as their journeys of exploration along the coasts of West Africa and the Indian subcontinent.

Djem, brother of Sultan Bazajet who is a prisoner of the pope, with Juan Borgia, Duke of Gandia and son of His Holiness, on the left, dressed in Turkish costume. Behind the pope came cardinals Domenico della Rovere, Antoniotto Pallavicini and Juan Borgia, followed by Ascanio Sforza and Federigo Sanseverino ... At San Giovanni in Laterano the pope dismounted and inspected the ceiling. The Turk and the pope's son also dismounted and walked around the basilica stopping here and there, notably in front of the tomb of Pope Martin V.[3]

On 5 June the Feast of Corpus Christi took place. It was traditionally celebrated with a huge procession through the streets of Rome, with the pope, his cardinals and the clergy, the notaries, abbreviators, scriptors and other employees of the curia, the papal choir, the papal household and the ambassadors with their own retinues all taking part. This year, however, it was raining heavily and several older cardinals suggested holding it in the courtyard of the Vatican but Alexander VI, seated on his chair under a canopy, insisted on going out as far as Castel Sant'Angelo before turning back to St Peter's. 'I heard from one of the cardinals that His Holiness had not wanted to shorten the procession as the cardinals had advised,' recorded Johannes Burchard, 'because the ambassador of the King and Queen of Spain arrived secretly yesterday and had been lodged at the palace of Cardinal Domenico della Rovere, from where

he wanted to see the procession but,' added Burchard, 'the pope was also thinking of his mistress Giulia [Farnese], and of his daughter Lucrezia, who were both living at the palace of Cardinal Zen and he wanted them to see him, and to see them as well'.[4]

On 12 June the marriage of Giovanni Sforza and Lucrezia Borgia was celebrated in the Vatican, and the 13-year-old bride was given away by her brother Juan, Duke of Gandia. The master-of-ceremonies Johannes Burchard described the scene:

> ... The great hall and the other rooms were covered abundantly with tapestry and velvet hangings, decorated and a throne was set up for the pope ... On the pope's orders, Don Juan Borgia, Duke of Gandia, son of the pope and brother of the bride, escorted his sister from

LEFT **St Ursula meeting the Pope in Rome.** *This is a detail from one of a series of paintings of the life of St Ursula by the Venetian artist Vittore Carpaccio (c.1465–1525), for the confraternity in Venice dedicated to the saint. Carpaccio took care to ensure his audience would recognize the city of St Peter in his detailed depiction of the crowds of mitred bishops, the cardinals in their red hats and robes, the pope in his tiara and – towering over the scene – the imposing fortress of Castel Sant'Angelo, which dominated the Roman skyline.*

ABOVE **Lovers in a landscape.** *A chivalric ideal of courtly love, this scene by Marco dell'Avogadro from Borso d'Este's Bible shows two lovers set against a backdrop of verdant pastures and a gently flowing river. Few marriages in the ruling classes of Europe were love matches; on the contrary, they were invariably arranged for political and dynastic gain.*

the palace of Cardinal Zen, where she lived with her aunt, Giulia Farnese. They processed through the rooms, Don Juan on the left of his sister, whose robe had a long train carried by a young negro girl. She was followed by Battistina, the daughter of Teodorina, the daughter of Innocent VIII. The train of Battistina's dress was also carried by a young negro girl. After her came Giulia Farnese, mistress of the pope, followed by some hundred and fifty Roman ladies ... despite my scolding none of the ladies genuflected when they passed the pope on his throne except for his daughter and one or two others who were near her ... when all the ladies had kissed the pope's foot, the Lord of Pesaro, the groom, and Lady Lucrezia, the bride, knelt on two cushions while Camillo Beninbene, citizen of Rome, asked in Italian, 'Illustrious Lord! You have, I think, seen the contract drawn up between the Lady Lucrezia here present and Master Nicola, your agent, acting in your name. You understand the details of the marriage contract, the dowry and other clauses, so it is not necessary to repeat them here. Do you consent to accept this contract, and promise to observe the terms of the contract, and to undertake your obligations as defined therein?' The groom responded,' I understand the terms, and hereby promise to observe and undertake the obligations defined therein.'[5]

184

Lucrezia's bridal feast and banquet

When they were all seated four of Cardinal Giovanni Colonna's squires entered, dressed in animal skins like savages and recited some verses about love. Then two sons of Master Andrea, the schoolmaster, came in with some of his companions, also dressed as savages, and performed a comedy so excellently that they were loudly applauded by all the guests. Then the banquet was served by the valets and squires who brought around 200 dishes of sweets, marzipan, candied fruits and various sorts of wines ... at the end the guests threw large quantities of the sweets to the people outside ... afterwards, the bride and groom left the room with the Duke of Gandia and the ladies to return to the palace of Cardinal Zen, which was the bride's residence. After their departure, the pope and the cardinals returned to their own apartments.

JOHANNES BURCHARD, *Liber notarum*, p. 82.

That evening, the pope hosted a banquet for his daughter, which raised comment from one witness, Stefano Infessura:

... some of the cardinals remained to dine and helped serve at the bridal table. The pope was in the premier seat, then the cardinal, the bridegroom and some other guests among whom there were ladies, the pope's daughter and his mistress, Giulia Farnese. At the third rank were Battistina Cibò, the granddaughter of Innocent VIII and the wife of Niccolò Orsini, Count of Pitigliano, as well as the daughter of Gabriele Cesarini and some others. As I said, all the guests were at the same table and each cardinal had a young lady next to him. The meal went on until long after midnight, with bawdy comedies and tragedies which made everyone laugh. When it was over, the pope, in person so it was said, accompanied his daughter to the palace of Cardinal Zen by the steps of St Peter's, and there the marriage was consummated. Many other things are being said, but I am not reporting them because they are not true, and if they were true they would, in any case, be unbelievable.

JOHANNES BURCHARD, *Liber notarum*, p. 96.

After the legal formalities were complete, and a ring placed on Lucrezia's ring finger under a naked sword held by Niccolò Orsini, Captain-General of the Church, the guests settled down to enjoy the food and entertainment offered by the pope.

On 19 June Alexander VI held a public consistory in which he received the Spanish ambassador sent expressly by Ferdinand and Isabella to reproach the pope for the war he was waging in Italy, and for allowing the Jews they had expelled from Spain to settle in Rome. In late July Alexander VI and Ferrante I finally settled their disagreement over Cerveteri and Anguillara, and the pope

ABOVE **Squires serving dishes at a feast,** *from a fresco in Castello Malpago, Bergamo. Renaissance feasts were superb affairs, held in the great halls of aristocratic palaces at tables that were laid with layers of spotless white linen tablecloths, splendid silver candelabra, salts, plates, dishes, cups and cutlery. Figures sculpted in sugar lent a theme to the event – devices from the coats-of-arms of a bride and groom, for example, or figures from classical mythology. Meals consisted of three basic components – a selection of cold hors d'oeuvres, the main meat or fish courses – served hot from the kitchen, as many as seven or eight for a grand banquet – and finally a cold dessert. At the end of a course, a tablecloth would be removed and the guests entertained by musicians, theatrical performances or dancing, before the trumpeters announced the arrival of the squires, led by the chief steward, bringing in the next course.*

hosted a banquet at the Vatican on 24 July, where the principal guests were Ferrante's allies Virginio Orsini and Cardinal Giuliano della Rovere.

On 2 August Alexander VI's son Juan, Duke of Gandia, left Rome for Barcelona where, with the permission of Ferdinand and Isabella, he was to marry Maria Enriquez – who had been betrothed to his dead brother Pedro Luis, the first Duke of Gandia. He sailed for Spain with four large galleys filled with silver, jewels, rich textiles and other valuables, as befitting his ducal status.

One week later, an ambassador arrived from Charles VIII to request Alexander VI to invest the French king with the throne of Naples. In a private audience with the envoy, the pope was deliberately vague. Ferrante I, however, was jubilant: 'when the envoy returns to France,' he informed his representative at the French court, 'several plans will have to be abandoned and several dreams shattered; I hope you are content that the pope and I are in

ABOVE **Juan Borgia, 2nd Duke of Gandia.** *This presumed portrait of Alexander VI's third son is in the Sala dei Santi, the great reception hall of the papal apartments in the Vatican, where he appears among the crowds witnessing St Catherine of Alexandria disputing with the philosophers. Traditionally thought to have been his father's favourite, he cuts a distinctive figure on the far right of the larger scene (see pages 304–5). The painter Pinturicchio portrayed him in profile, riding a richly caparisoned grey charger, wearing the dress of a Turkish warrior in a turban with a cloth-of-gold cloak, gilded spurs and a scimitar at his side – it is not difficult to see why his critics accused him of arrogance and pride.*

perfect agreement'.[6] Four days later Alexander VI cemented his new alliance with Ferrante by agreeing to the marriage of Sancia of Aragon, the king's illegitimate granddaughter, to his youngest son Jofrè, who was now to give up his career in the Church to become Prince of Squillace. The engagement was not to be made public until Christmas, but rumours spread quickly.

It was an indication of the authority Alexander VI enjoyed in the College of Cardinals that on 20 September he managed not only to persuade its members to create new cardinals so early in his pontificate but also to give out 12 red hats – an unprecedentedly large number; none of his predecessors had managed more than eight. One of the hats went to the pope's son Cesare, now 18 years old; another went to Alessandro Farnese, aged 25 and the brother of the beautiful papal mistress Giulia. The rest were candidates for the rulers of Europe and the Italian states, with the marked exception of King Ferrante. The Milanese were jubilant at this signal mark of favour towards their interests and ostensibly against those of Naples and its allies in the college:

> They say that Cardinal Giuliano della Rovere was playing cards at Marino when he heard the news of the new cardinals and was furious. He tried to continue with the game but after a few minutes he got up and went to his room where he was heard ranting and roaring. Then he was overcome with a fever which improved a little but has now returned. Cardinal Carafa was also furious but hid his feelings more effectively. Cardinal Michiel is still gravely ill and has not been told ... truly, I have not words to describe the honour and glory that this victory has brought to Your Excellency and to Cardinal Ascanio.[7]

In late summer the plague broke out in the camp set up outside the walls to provide temporary accommodation for the Jews who had arrived from Spain. By October it had spread into the city and Alexander VI left Rome with the papal court – first for Viterbo, where he celebrated the feast of All Saints on 1 November, and then on to Pitigliano, the castle of his captain-general Niccolò Orsini, and to Orvieto, where he installed Cesare as governor. He returned to Rome on 18 December, and

Alexander VI, the politician

Many people *think that the pope has lost his political acumen since he was elected but I think, to the contrary, that this has substantially improved. He has managed to negotiate an alliance which has made the King of Naples sigh in disbelief. He has managed to marry his daughter to a Sforza, a man who has an income of 12,000 ducats a year, in addition to the allowance paid to him by the Duke of Milan. He has managed to draw 35,000 ducats out of Virginio Orsini and make him an ally and he has managed, thanks to this alliance, to connect himself to the King of Naples, obtaining a wife and a state for his son. I don't think these are the achievements of a man with no brains. He wants to enjoy his papacy in peace and quiet.*

ANONYMOUS LETTER TO LUDOVICO SFORZA, 13 AUGUST 1493 (L. VON PASTOR, *History of the Popes*, VOL. V, P. 415 N).

OVERLEAF **Borgia altar,** *Santa Maria del Popolo (now in the sacristy), Rome. Cardinal Rodrigo Borgia had taken over patronage of the main chapel around 1473. The altar was exquisitely sculpted by Andrea Bregno; when his son died accidentally, while working on the project, Rodrigo gave him permission to record this in the upper cornice. Bregno noted there his son's age.*

AVE MARIA
GRATIA PLENA

his master-of-ceremonies Burchard again recorded some concern with etiquette:

> ... he was carried to the church of Santa Maria del Popolo, preceded by the
> cardinals and the Eucharist ... after the blessing [in the church] I said to His
> Holiness that it was not right that the cardinals should ride in front of him and
> that they should follow him ... and His Holiness authorized me to correct the
> order but, when we came out of the church, he decided to have the cardinals
> riding in front of him, and so this was done.[8]

1494

ON 27 JANUARY news arrived in Rome of the sudden and unexpected death of King
Ferrante: 'he died without the cross and without God', recorded Johannes Burchard.[9]
A Ferrarese chronicler ventured that 'it is said he died of a broken heart after hearing
that King Charles of France was bringing an enormous army into Italy to seize his
realm'.[10] For nearly 50 years King Ferrante had been a major figure in the complex
politics of Italy and a regular thorn in the flesh of the
papacy, and his death now forced Alexander VI to make
public his position regarding the House of Aragon on the
one hand, and France and Milan on the other.

In the middle of March, as expected, Charles VIII
announced his intention to invade Italy and seize the
throne of Naples, with the support of Ludovico Sforza
in Milan. But on 22 March Alexander VI responded
by issuing a papal bull confirming the legality of the
succession of Ferrante's son Alfonso of Calabria as
King Alfonso II, and he sent a brief to Charles VIII
condemning his plans for war.

On 1 April Alexander VI went to Santa Maria sopra
Minerva to hear mass, which was celebrated by Leonello Chierigato, Bishop of
Concordia. Cardinal Ascanio Sforza was heard to say: 'when the pope enters into
concord with the king of Naples, he has mass celebrated by the bishop of Concordia'.
The pope retorted wittily that 'when there is peace between His Holiness and Ludovico
Sforza, he will have mass celebrated by the Bishop of Pace' – *pace* being both the
Italian word for 'peace' and the Latin name of the Spanish bishopric of Badajoz.[11]

In a stormy consistory on 18 April, which lasted eight hours, the College of
Cardinals finally agreed to Alexander VI's request to appoint a legate to Naples for the
coronation of Alfonso II. Both Charles VIII and Ludovico Sforza were furious, but the

'A terrible year'

The year 1494, *which began in political
confusion, would prove to be a terrible year
for Italy, and the first of many disastrous
years, because it saw the start of a catalogue
of catastrophes in which the whole of
Europe became involved.*

FRANCESCO GUICCIARDINI, *Storia d'Italia*, I, 6.

189

Milanese ambassador suggested a devious solution: 'if we can persuade Cardinal Giuliano della Rovere to change sides and support France', he wrote, 'we will have created a powerful weapon against Pope Alexander'.[12] The ruse worked and on 23 April Giuliano della Rovere left his castle at Ostia, under cover of night, and set sail for France, leaving the fortress well-guarded with soldiers and stocked with provisions to last two years.

The next day, 24 April, Cardinal Juan Borgia was appointed legate to Naples, receiving the cross from his uncle before leaving Rome. On 7 May he presided over the betrothal of Jofrè Borgia and Sancia of Aragon, and the following day he crowned the new king in Naples cathedral. Alfonso II invested Jofrè as Prince of Squillace, with an income of 40,000 ducats a year, and Alexander VI gave a red hat to Luigi of Aragon, the king's illegitimate brother. On 11 May Alfonso II and Cardinal Juan escorted Sancia to her marriage ceremony, which took place in the chapel of Castel Nuovo; the bride was sixteen years old, the groom just fourteen.

Later in May, Jofrè's sister Lucrezia left Rome to travel to her husband's palace at Pesaro.

With reports arriving almost daily describing the French army massing on the frontier, to enforce Charles VIII's claim to Naples, Alexander VI

ABOVE **Alfonso II of Naples.** *Depicted in this relief from the church of San Giovanni Carbonara, Naples, Alfonso was the eldest son of King Ferrante I of Naples. He was born in 1448, and he had a successful military career, leading his father's armies to victory against the Florentines (1478–9) and against the Turks at Otranto (1481). Presiding over a court that was one of the most magnificent in Renaissance Italy, he was a major patron of the arts, building two superb villas, which he decorated with scenes of the part he played in crushing the Barons' Revolt.*

RIGHT **Jofrè Borgia and Sancia of Aragon.** *This drawing of the couple in procession is from the Codice Ferraiolo, a chronicle of Naples written by a partisan of the Aragonese dynasty. It charts the history of the city from Alfonso I's first visit to Naples up to 1498, the presumed date of the unknown author's death. Written in the local Neapolitan dialect, it is remarkable for the detailed illustrations to events that the author clearly witnessed.*

Li s barune — La maista del s re alfonso — lo pencipe de squillace — la fiolo de madama trusia — li imbasciature

Li xxi de iugnio 1494 ditto anno xii indicione dala citade napole
se partio La maista del s re alfonso per andare incanpo dala de romagno
Contra Lo s lodouico demilana per che erano nimice Calouele ua
Caciare damilana per non fare le signioriale piu milana per che isso
laueua signioriata dala morte detto iennaro per sino aquisto tienpo Loquale
sediceua caisso posedeua Lostato demilana fino attanto chelo fioliolo detto
ducade milana era deitate ello s lodouico sforza chiamato moro sentermo
Calamaista dere alfonso separte dariamo per andare Contra dettui subito appe
abisso dainimice de sua maistato chedeuesse prouedere Lo s lodouico inuerso ma
nza Loquale intennimo chere de franza epartuto dafranza per uenire intalia
Contra riamo et subito chelo s lodouico aspe auiso Como Lamaista del s re al
fonso chaieua animuso et forte et gagliardo Consforzo assoi dagiente darimo
fantaria et arteglioria senza numaro essubito Lo s lodouico sentermo que
stanoua seafronto conre defranza et ordinaro et fecino granne male Contro
de sua maistate ella maista del s re alfonso inprimis portaua innante cien
to caluppe tutte gintiliomine denapole et tutte iuuene de xx anne luno
che leuano uistute deuna diuisa con ippune de siti uerde Coniurneie de domo
schino Lionato et cauze alla diuisa et coppole de scarlata de tutto questa
diuisa ne erano quatto squatre Letre squatre erano deuna diuisa ella una
squatra portauano ippune de siti paonazo et iurneie deseta bianca Collati di
uita alle cauze tutte accauate kioiere — ello s lodouico uedenno uenire
rede franza Appressimare Inlo stato de milana subito Le dette Lo passo et
fecito possore senza darmo nissciuno et in quisto muodo Lemostrao Lidiente et se
Cillo tornore inderéto et accossi rede franza senne uenne passo passo piglia moterre
senza Conbattere per tutta Latalia ello riamo et fino dintro napole et perche non
Cibattaglio perche tutte leterre Citate et Castelle tanto defore riamo quanto di
ntro riamo Leerano Contra allua maista dere alfonso perche tutta italia sera
Contra per lo grande male uolere che ipso seaueua fatto ella ditta accalcione
perzi cheiera che uoleua Lo s lodouico che caluoccasse re deriamo Lonipote
donferconte de ragona ditto fioliolo dere alfonso prencipe decapoa che laueuo

Consummation of a Borgia alliance

At the end *of the banquet the bride [Sancia of Aragon] was conducted by the legate [Cardinal Juan Borgia] and King Alfonso to the palace just outside the castle gate, where the groom [Jofrè Borgia] and his attendants had already retired. The bride and groom now entered their private chamber, where their bed had been prepared, while the legate and the king waited outside. Once the bride and groom had been undressed by the ladies-in-waiting, and had taken their places together in the bed, the groom to the right and both nude under the bedcovers, the legate and the king entered the room. The ladies-in-waiting now drew back the bedcovers as far as their navels and the groom embraced his bride without embarrassment. The legate and the king remained chatting there for about half an hour.*

JOHANNES BURCHARD, *Liber notarum*, PP. 119–20.

left Rome on 14 July to meet Alfonso II at Vicovaro to discuss their plans for the defence of the kingdom.

As summer progressed, plague broke out in Rome, forcing Alexander VI to cancel not only the mass whereby he was expected to mark the anniversary of the death of Innocent VIII but also the festivities for the anniversary of his own election on 11 August.

On 3 September Charles VIII crossed into Savoy, at Italy's northwestern frontier, choosing 'the pass of Montgenèvre which was less arduous than Mont Cenis, which Hannibal had marched through in ancient times with such terrible hardship'.[13] Two days later, at the head of an army of 30,000 men, he entered the capital, Turin. On 9 September he arrived at Asti, where he was greeted by Ludovico Sforza and Ercole d'Este, Duke of Ferrara, together with the ambassadors of their other allies. One Milanese courtier was shocked by the appearance of the young king, who was 24 years old but 'the most repulsive man I have ever seen in all my born days, stunted and deformed with the ugliest face of any man'.[14] By 18 October Charles VIII had reached Piacenza, where he refused to meet the envoy sent by Alexander VI to negotiate peace, insisting that he would meet the pope in person in Rome.

Three days later, on 21 October, Giangaleazzo Sforza, Duke of Milan, died. This enabled his uncle Ludovico Sforza, already effective ruler of the duchy, to become the legitimate duke in his own right.

On 26 October, with the French armies on the

RIGHT **Charles VIII of France,** *painted by Jean Perréal in 1498. This king may have been notoriously unattractive – this portrait was famously flattering – but he certainly understood the scale of the logistics involved in planning his campaign to conquer Naples. He needed to raise large numbers of cavalrymen, troopers, archers and crossbowmen, as well as huge sums of money needed to pay their wages. It is often forgotten that an army does not march alone – in the wake of the soldiers came an enormous backup force, often more men than the army itself, of skilled craftsmen and labour: armourers to make weapons and helmets, and blacksmiths to shoe the chargers, as well as saddlers and harness-makers, and thousands of stable boys to care for the horses and mules. Charles VIII crossed into Italy with over 50,000 men – and both the men and the animals required feeding every day, with supplies he intended to seize with force as he travelled south.*

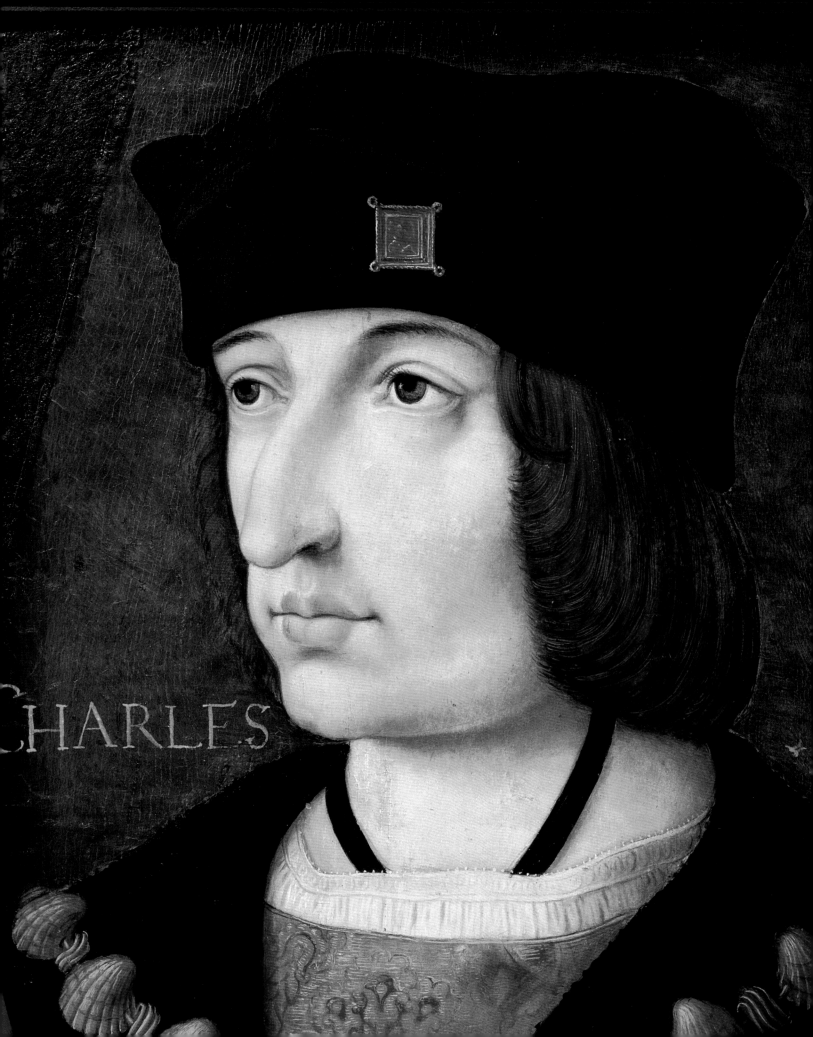
CHARLES

borders of Florence, Piero de' Medici met Charles VIII and surrendered all Florentine cities to the French without consulting the government of his city. But on 9 November the Medici were expelled from Florence and a new theocratic republic was set up under the leadership of the charismatic Dominican preacher Fra Girolamo Savonarola who, just a week before, had thundered from the cathedral: 'The sword is here, the prophecies are about to be fulfilled, it is the start of retribution!'[15]

Charles VIII and his army were moving ever closer to Rome. On 2 November Alexander VI had a private audience with his old Milanese ally, Vice-Chancellor Ascanio Sforza, who tried again to convince the pope to abandon Naples and stay neutral in the conflict that threatened, without success. On 27 November troops in the vanguard of the French army, which was now south of Viterbo, came across Pope Alexander's mistress Giulia Farnese and Adriana de Milà travelling with their attendants on the road between Viterbo and Capodimonte. The ladies 'were taken by them to Montefiascone with all their attendants, perhaps 25 or 30 horses. The pope, immediately he heard the news, sent a trustworthy valet to Marino to complain about this to Cardinal Ascanio ... and today [29 November] we have heard that all are well and have not been molested in any way.'[16] Alexander VI quickly paid the 3,000 ducats demanded in ransom by the French soldiers.

On 9 December envoys arrived in Rome from Charles VIII to request freedom of passage for his army through the Papal States on their way to Naples, which Alexander VI refused. The pope now arrested all the pro-French cardinals who were still in Rome, including even Cardinal Ascanio Sforza, though he was lodged in comfortable rooms in the Vatican palace, albeit under guard. On 14 December the cardinal assisted Alexander VI at mass in the Sistine Chapel, 'and the pope

> ## Portents of disaster
>
> **Those who profess** to tell the future, either by science or by divination, all claimed that the omens foretold that great changes and terrible events were about to happen. Strange things happened in all parts of Italy, giving rise to rumours. Three suns were seen one night in Puglia, surrounded by clouds and loud thunder and lightning. Near Arezzo soldiers on horseback were seen in the sky, accompanied by loud drumming and trumpeting. Sacred statues started to sweat in many places and monstrous births took place, filling the people with fear and dread.
>
> FRANCESCO GUICCIARDINI, *Storia d'Italia*, I, 9.

LEFT **The Four Horsemen of the Apocalypse.** *Albrecht Dürer's famous woodcuts (c.1497–8) of the Revelation of St John, foretelling the second coming that would follow the destruction of a sinful world, carried a powerful message in late 15th-century Italy. It was a theme fully exploited by the preacher Girolamo Savonarola to play on the fear of many that the invasion of Charles VIII was the first sign of the end of their world. The 'four horsemen' were the harbingers of this destruction: first came the 'Conqueror' with his bow and angel, then 'War' armed with his sword, who was followed by 'Famine' with his weighing scales, and finally 'Death', on his emaciated horse.*

chatted amicably to his vice-chancellor throughout the service'. [17]

The pope now began preparations for the defence of Rome. On 18 December all his goods were packed and sent to Castel Sant'Angelo, where work started on demolishing nearby houses to dig a deep ditch around the citadel. On 19 December the first French troops could be seen outside the walls in the fields beyond Castel Sant'Angelo.

On 24 December Alexander VI heard vespers as usual in the Sistine Chapel. The next day, Christmas Day, Cardinal Juan Borgia had expected to celebrate high mass in the presence of the pope, but a letter arrived from Charles VIII and the cardinal was sent to the Orsini stronghold of Bracciano to negotiate with the king, who was now just 25 miles north of Rome. On 26 December envoys arrived from the French camp to finalize details of Charles VIII's visit to Rome: they entered the Sistine Chapel just as mass started, leaving the master-of-ceremonies Johannes Burchard with the tricky problem of where to seat them:

> After the pope had made his entry into the Sistine Chapel, three ambassadors of the King of France arrived ... all three were laymen.

LEFT **Men raising a cannon onto a gun carriage.** *This study, by Leonardo da Vinci, shows the artist less interested – for a change – in the human torso, but rather more concerned with analysing the mechanics involved in this massive and complex task of hauling cannons. The lighter, more mobile cannon that the French brought to Italy, with their more rapid firing, instilled fear in the Italians.*

I placed the marshal of France [Pierre de Rohan] on the steps of the papal throne and the other two I intended to seat on the benches of the lay ambassadors, but there were two envoys of the King of Naples there who, not wishing to argue with the three Frenchmen, announced that they did not recognize their diplomatic status and left their places. However, on the order of the pope, I told them that the Frenchmen were ambassadors of the King of France whereupon they reassumed their seats. Then many more Frenchmen arrived, sitting without hesitation next to the prelates. I tried to move them to more appropriate seats, but the pope beckoned me to him and said irritably that I was upsetting all his plans and that I must let the French sit where they wanted.[18]

Early in the morning of 31 December, Alexander VI sent his secretary Bartolomeo Florès, together with four leading Roman citizens and Johannes Burchard, to the French camp to discuss the royal entry into the city, which was to take place that evening. It appeared that a battle for Rome had been avoided.

1495

THE ARRIVAL OF THE FRENCH army brought chaos to Rome. On 3 January:

> ... the French pillaged the palaces of the bishop of Cosenza, the nephew of Cardinal Oliviero Carafa, the son of Giacomo Conti and of Bartolomeo Lunati, the pope's chamberlain. To find lodgings the French generally forced their way into houses, driving out the inhabitants and their horses, then burning their firewood, eating and drinking all they could find without paying for anything. This led to violent protestations and the King of France was forced to issue an order forbidding this.[19]

Thus, many houses were requisitioned by French courtiers, including that of the master-of-ceremonies himself. When Burchard returned home he found a French nobleman

Fear of the French artillery

The new pestilence of artillery had been developed by the Germans many years before ... the cannon were made of iron or bronze but they were so heavy that they could only be moved slowly ... and, once in place, there was such a long time between shots that the defending troops had time to retrench. Nevertheless, the explosive force of the gunpowder mixed with saltpetre was so great that cannonballs flew through the air with astonishing speed and with such a noise that they made all other weapons look ridiculous. But the French had made their cannon of bronze and they were much easier to move around, and they used iron cannonballs not stone ones and these were much larger and heavier. Moreover, they were on carts drawn by horses, not by oxen as is usual in Italy, and could be moved and positioned very quickly; and there was little space between the shots so the attack was so violent that it took them only a few hours to do the damage that used to take several days.

FRANCESCO GUICCIARDINI, *Storia d'Italia*, I, 11.

197

ensconced in his rooms; French soldiers also broke into the house of the pope's former mistress, Vanozza de' Cataneis. The streets were filled with armed men, who looted and pillaged at will, despite the edict issued by Charles VIII.

On 7 January Alexander VI took refuge in Castel Sant'Angelo, along with cardinals Cesare and Juan Borgia, Carafa, Orsini and several others, fearful for their safety amid the chaos. The same day, as the Mantuan ambassador recorded, 'a quarrel broke out between some of the French and the Swiss [mercenaries], and the whole king's camp took up arms and it was astonishing to see so many armed men on the streets'. In his view, it was 'impossible for such a large army to stay longer in Rome where supplies are running out, even for those with money'.[20] On 12 January, in an attempt to quell the violence, Charles VIII and his courtiers rode around Rome with one of the French cardinals, escorted by a guard of armed foot soldiers.

Three days later, on 15 January, Alexander VI and Charles VIII reached an accord. The king agreed to perform a public ceremony of obedience to the pope who, in turn, promised to give

RIGHT **Entry of Charles VIII into Florence,** *painted by Francesco Granacci (1477–1543). As with all the cities that Charles VIII entered, the arrival of this huge foreign army was viewed with trepidation by the inhabitants – witness these Florentines with their backs to the walls of their houses, in real fear for their lives and of the famine that would inevitably occur as soldiers looted the stores of foodstuffs and fodder for their horses.*

The king kissed neither the pope's foot nor his hand.

red hats to two French bishops. Alexander VI also named Cardinal Cesare Borgia as legate to the French court for the following four months – a cloak to disguise the fact that Cesare was in fact a hostage for the pope's good behaviour – and gave the French the right of passage through the Papal States. But Alexander VI remained evasive about when he would invest the French king with the throne of Naples.

The following day, with order restored, Charles VIII moved into the guest apartments that had been prepared for him in the Vatican. The pope and the king finally met later that afternoon, and the pope acquiesced to the king's demand to create his councillor Guillaume Briçonnet – Bishop of St-Malo – a cardinal; a red hat was found and Cardinal Cesare Borgia loaned his cape, so that the ceremony could take place immediately.

In a public consistory on 19 January, held in the main hall of the Vatican, Charles VIII declared his obedience to the pope, genuflecting and kissing Alexander VI's foot. The next day Cesare Borgia resigned his bishopric of Castres, which the pope now gave to one of Charles VIII's courtiers, and both the king and the pope attended pontifical mass at St Peter's. In a further conciliatory gesture, at a secret consistory on 21 January Alexander VI gave a red hat to the king's cousin Philippe of Luxembourg, Bishop of Le Mans.

Four days later, on 25 January – the Feast of the Conversion of St Paul – the two rulers made a public statement of their new friendship with a state procession from St Peter's to San Paolo fuori le mura.

Charles VIII and his entourage left Rome

Games of status

When the king *[Charles VIII] heard that the pope had arrived [at the Vatican], he went to the meet him at the end of the second of the private gardens, where he climbed onto the walkway, followed by the cardinals who were also waiting. When the pope arrived at the entrance to the garden, he descended from his chair and walked on foot into the middle of the garden to where the cardinals now led the king. Charles VIII spotted the pope and, while Alexander VI was still some twelve feet away, made two genuflections which the pope pretended not to see. Then, just as the king was about to genuflect for the third time, Alexander VI removed his biretta and motioned him to stop, and then kissed him. Both men had their heads uncovered and the king kissed neither the pope's foot nor his hand; and Alexander VI refused to replace his biretta before the king replaced his own cap but eventually both did so at the same time.*

Johannes Burchard, *Liber notarum*, pp. 165–6.

200

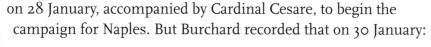

on 28 January, accompanied by Cardinal Cesare, to begin the
campaign for Naples. But Burchard recorded that on 30 January:

> the pope was informed that Cardinal Cesare had escaped
> from the French at Velletri disguised as a royal groom. It
> was true. On returning to Rome, the cardinal had gone
> to the house of Antonio Florès, the auditor of the rota,
> where he spent the night. When the cardinal had left
> Rome with Charles VIII he had taken with him 19 mules,
> richly caparisoned and, he claimed, laden with objects of
> value, though in fact only two were thus laden. On the first
> day, while His Majesty and Cardinal Cesare were riding to
> Marino, these two mules were left behind and that evening
> they returned to Rome. Cesare's servants made it known at
> the royal court that the animals had been seized and their
> goods ransacked. After Cesare's escape, the chests on the
> other 17 beasts were opened and found to contain nothing.
> That's what is being said, but I don't believe it.[21]

The next morning the pope sent his private secretary Bartolomeo
Florès to the French camp to apologize to the king on his behalf.

Two days previously, on 29 January, Alexander VI was informed
that Alfonso II of Naples had abdicated on hearing of the pope's
agreement with Charles VIII, and he had left his throne to his son
Ferrante, who was aged twenty-six.

Reports of the progress of the French soldiers arrived daily in Rome,
including their brutal sacking of the
border fortress of Monte San Giovanni, where the
soldiers murdered all the inhabitants. The violence
of this attack persuaded the rest of the towns and
cities on Charles VIII's route to surrender without
opposition.

On 22 February the new Neapolitan king,

Reports of the progress of the French soldiers arrived daily in Rome.

ABOVE **Italian dagger, or *cinquedea*, and sheath.** *In
Renaissance Europe the making of weapons and their
accoutrements involved the skills of several different craftsmen.
The best steel blades came from Toledo, but their hilts –
bronze or, more expensively, silver-gilt – were added by local
armourers, while sheaths and scabbards were usually made by
leatherworkers and lined with fabric by a tailor. Daggers were
highly effective in a brawl.*

A fracas in Rome

In the evening *of 22 January there was
a violent quarrel between the Swiss and the
Catalans guarding Castel Sant'Angelo, which
was soon joined by some hooligans. Two
Swiss were stabbed and thrown into the Tiber,
though more of the Catalans and hooligans
were killed by the Swiss. The next morning
two of the Swiss were beheaded, one at the
Capitol and the other on Ponte Sant'Angelo.*
JOHANNES BURCHARD, *Liber notarum*, P. 181.

201

Ferrante II, fled for Ischia with his court, including the pope's son Jofrè with his wife Sancia, and later the same day Charles VIII entered Naples in triumph. However, Alexander VI continued to delay his recognition of Charles as the legitimate King of Naples, despite the king's very tempting offer of 150,000 ducats in cash and an annual tribute of 40,000 ducats.[22]

Having reached an expedient agreement with King Charles when Rome was threatened, the pope now commenced moves to retilt the political balance. On 29 March Alexander VI announced his intention of giving the papal award of the Golden Rose this year to the Doge of Venice. Two days later, the pope announced the formation of a Holy League against the Turks, signed by Alexander VI, the Holy Roman Emperor Maximilian I and the rulers of Spain, Venice and Milan. The subtext, as Charles VIII knew well, was that this league had been formed against the French. As a Ferrarese chronicler observed, 'the King of France was left out of the league, something which displeased our duke because of his friendship with France'.[23] But the truth was that even Milan, normally a French ally, was now alarmed by the power the French forces were wielding in Italy.

On 12 May Charles VIII was finally crowned 'King of Naples, Sicily and Jerusalem' in the cathedral at Naples, and a week later he hastily left the city he had so recently conquered before his enemies had time to gather their forces. As for Rome, the city prepared itself once again for the arrival of a hostile French army: the Milanese ambassador reported that 'more silver and valuables have been removed from the city than at any time these last hundred years; none of the cardinals has enough silverware to serve six guests'.[24] Alexander VI absented himself from Rome – and another encounter with King Charles – on 27 May, heading for Orvieto and taking with him 20 cardinals, including Cesare and Juan Borgia, and a strong bodyguard of Venetian and Milanese soldiers.

Charles VIII arrived in Rome on 1 June, where he was greeted by Cardinal John Morton, the Archbishop of Canterbury, who had been left by the pope to govern the city in his absence. The French king declined the offer of hospitality at the Vatican, but stayed two nights at the palace of Cardinal Domenico della Rovere and, to underline his spiritual allegiance to the pope, forbade his soldiers from sacking Rome; the Swiss mercenaries were not even allowed to enter the city. On

The city prepared itself once again for the arrival of a hostile French army.

PREVIOUS PAGE, LEFT **Ludovico Sforza, Duke of Milan,** *in a detail from an anonymous painting. Ludovico was an impressive patron, undertaking a major campaign of urban renewal in Milan, commissioning repairs and embellishments to the city's churches and similar projects in the other centres of the duchy. In this way he provided visual proof of his authority, and he compensated for the lack of legitimacy of his position.*

PREVIOUS PAGE, RIGHT **Beatrice d'Este, Duchess of Milan,** *in a detail from the same painting. The daughter of Ercole d'Este, Duke of Ferrara, Beatrice had been betrothed to Ludovico Sforza in 1480 when she was just five years old. They finally married in 1491, and she introduced the cultured tastes of the Ferrarese court to Milan. Tragically, she died in childbirth in 1497.*

The murder of Rome's law enforcer

On the morning of *Saturday 4 April Alfonso Sardinas, once one of his Holiness's couriers and now the chief of Rome's civic guard, was on his way to the fish market with his men when he was assaulted by Saba Staglia, a Roman who had planned this attack and was armed. They both inflicted grave wounds on each other and one of the guards sliced into Saba's neck and he fell to the ground. Sardinas tried to get away but he also fell and when his men tried to carry him away to safety they were prevented by a Roman who held them back by their feet until he was joined by others who killed Sardinas and carried Saba away. Soon afterwards Sardinas's corpse was taken without light or torches to the hospital at the Spanish hospice, where it was buried.*

JOHANNES BURCHARD, *Liber notarum*, P. 202.

27 June, having successfully evaded a meeting with Charles VIII, Alexander VI returned to the city.

Charles VIII's army saw action on 6 July when it was intercepted at Fornovo, midway between Milan and Bologna, by the troops of the recently convened Holy League, led by the Marquis of Mantua, Francesco Gonzaga. It was a French victory, but the Italians, who seized the great chests filled with jewels, gold, silver and other booty that the French had plundered over the past year, as well as the king's sword and his great seal, claimed it as their own.

In July Ferrante II began his campaign to reconquer his kingdom, and by the end of the month, with the help of the Spanish commander Don Gonsalvo de Cordoba, who had been sent to his aid by Ferdinand and Isabella of Spain, most of Naples had been retaken, though the French remained securely in the royal fortress of Castel Nuovo. On 27 November Ferrante II's troops finally reconquered the castle, thanks to the ingenious use of exploding

RIGHT **Francesco Gonzaga, Marquis of Mantua.** *This handsome portrait bust by Giancristoforo Romano (1465–1512), which was based on the style of Ancient Imperial Rome, displays Francesco Gonzaga's military prowess. He was a distinguished soldier, commanding the armies of Venice, France and Pope Julius II, and a highly successful breeder of race horses, though his reputation is often overshadowed by that of his famously cultured wife, Isabella d'Este.*

The Battle of Fornovo

*... **it was impossible** to use the artillery because of the heavy rain, and they fought on the banks of the river Taro where the horses got stuck in the mud as did the infantry. But the French fought with great vigour and force, and they had plenty of archers and crossbowmen, but they fought more with fixed weapons, like swords and daggers, with great cruelty, slaughtering for a full two hours. Around 4,000 Italians were killed and not more than 600 French, though many were wounded on both sides. It was a French victory because the Italians had disagreed about their orders. With the French there were many Swiss and Breton infantrymen who all fought very bravely. And so, because of the heavy rain, they stopped fighting; they had started in the early morning and it only lasted two hours or less.*

BERNARDINO ZAMBOTTI, *Diario Ferrarese*, PP. 252–3.

This year Rome was hit by another disaster.

mines laid by the Italian engineer, Francesco di Giorgio, in a tunnel dug into the foundations.

Meanwhile, further north there had been alarming reports of the fanatical sermons being preached in Florence by the Dominican Fra Girolamo Savonarola. On 8 September Alexander VI banned him from public speaking, and when the friar had continued to ignore the order the pope was forced to issue another brief on 16 October.

This year Rome was hit by another disaster, on 4 December, when the Tiber flooded. The weather had been unseasonably cold in late November but had warmed up on 1 December when it started to rain heavily, continuing thus for the best part of three days. The cardinals, on their way home from a consistory, were lucky to get across the Ponte Sant'Angelo before the streets around the castle were inundated. By daybreak on 6 December, the floodwaters had begun to subside, but the destruction was enormous. Thousands drowned, and many of those who

RIGHT **Madonna della Vittoria.** *This votive altarpiece, showing the Virgin and Child enthroned with St George and St Michael, was commissioned in 1495 from the painter Andrea Mantegna by Francesco Gonzaga, Marquis of Mantua, to commemorate his victory at the Battle of Fornovo – Francesco is portrayed as the donor receiving the blessing of the Virgin. The following year the finished altarpiece formed the centrepiece of the celebrations held on 6 July to mark the first anniversary of the battle. Mounted on a dais, and accompanied by Mantuans acting the roles of God and saints, with a choir of young singing angels, the altarpiece was carried in procession through the streets of the city with much rejoicing.*

survived had lost their possessions; the damage was estimated at 300,000 ducats. A Venetian witness described the devastation:

> By yesterday morning the floods had subsided but the courtyards and cellars are full of dead animals and rubbish, which will take months to clear. The damage to Rome is terrible and will take decades to repair. The boats on the Tiber, the mills and the houses on the banks are gone, and all the horses have drowned in their stables. With the mills gone there will be no bread. Thank God that all our people are alright. Many of the prisoners in the Tor di Nona have drowned, and the moats around Castel

209

LEFT **A castle under siege.** *This drawing by Francesco di Giorgio (1439–1502) is from his treatises on military architecture. One of the foremost engineers of the period, he had learned his trade working on the complex system that supplied water to the hill-top city of Siena, his home town, before designing a series of innovative fortresses for Federigo da Montefeltro, Duke of Urbino, and accompanying the army of Ferrante I of Naples as its military expert.*

ABOVE **The Ripa Grande.** *This drawing (c.1560) by Pieter Breughel of the port of Rome illustrates the importance of the river in the life of the city. In addition to providing access for galleys provisioning the city, the Tiber also drove the wheels of the flour mills that were constructed on pontoons midstream, supplied freshwater fish and eels for the inhabitants, and was even used as a source for drinking water (Pope Paul III used to carry Tiber water with him whenever he travelled away from Rome).*

The pope summoned his son Juan, Duke of Gandia, from Spain, with the intention of using his military skills in the Papal States.

Sant'Angelo are still brimful of water. The men working in the vineyards have died as have most of the cattle in the fields that were flooded. On Friday evening they found a poor man by the wharves clinging to a tree trunk and almost dead with exhaustion. He had been swept into the waters at Monterotondo, 11 miles outside the city, and carried down here. The monks of San Paolo fuori le mura came to see our ambassador late yesterday and said that the water had reached the high altar in their church. You know how high up that basilica is, so you can imagine how awful the flood must have been elsewhere.[25]

1496

IN JANUARY ALEXANDER VI reportedly spent 80,000 ducats on repairs to Castel Sant'Angelo following the depredations of the previous year.

With the French threat over for the present, Alexander VI now turned his attention to restoring his authority in the Papal States, especially against those who had sided with the French in the recent conflict. On 6 February he 'announced in consistory that Virginio Orsini and the others were declared rebels and confiscated their estates because they had disobeyed him by taking pay from the French'.[26] One month later, on 5 March, the pope summoned his son Juan, Duke of Gandia, from Spain, with the intention of using his military skills in the Papal States.

Meanwhile, on 19 February Alexander VI created four new cardinals, all of them Spanish, including his great-nephew Juan Borgia, aged 26: he would be known as 'Cardinal Borgia' to distinguish him from his older namesake Juan Borgia, Cardinal of Monreale.

Lucrezia Borgia, now 15 years old, arrived back in Rome from Pesaro on 16 April, along with her husband Giovanni Sforza; he obtained a *condotta* – a contract for raising troops to fight for the pope – and left on 28 April to join his troops. The 14-year-old Jofrè Borgia also arrived in the city, on 20 May,

PREVIOUS PAGE **Virginio Orsini accompanied by his nobles.** *This scene, which once decorated the entrance to the imposing Orsini Castle at Bracciano, is part of a larger painting commissioned by Virginio Orsini in 1491 to celebrate his appointment as captain-general of the army of Ferrante I of Naples. Striking for its detailed depiction of sartorial and military fashions of late 15th- century Italy, the fresco shows Virginio and his nobles at the head of a vast army of lances that stretches back into the hilly landscape. Virginio himself, mounted on a superb charger, is dressed in armour, holding his baton of command and wearing the chain of the prestigious royal Neapolitan Order of the Ermine, bestowed on him by the king.*

accompanied by his wife Sancia of Aragon: the couple made an exceptionally grand entry into the city. Met at the gates of Rome by all the cardinals and ambassadors, as well as by Lucrezia, they rode past San Giovanni in Laterano and the ruins of the Colosseum to Campo dei Fiori and over the Ponte Sant'Angelo to the Vatican, where Alexander VI was waiting to greet them. Lucrezia brought with her 'some twenty ladies-in-waiting, preceded by two pages on horseback dressed in robes. One of their horses was covered with a magnificent caparison of gold brocade while the other wore crimson velvet. Lucrezia gave her brother and his bride an affectionate welcome.' [27]

On 1 June Alexander VI extended his punitive actions against the Orsini clan by excommunicating them on the grounds of treason against the pope during the previous year. Furthermore, he confiscated their possessions and ordered Ferrante II to arrest Virginio Orsini and his son Giangiordano in Naples and to imprison them.

Lucrezia at the Feast of Pentecost

On the feast of Pentecost the pope went in his mitre, without the canopy, to the basilica of St Peter's to hear mass … the Spanish cardinal gave a sermon which was much too long and boring, which annoyed His Holiness … from the beginning of the mass up to the moment when the pope was carried out of the church, Sancia and Lucrezia, the daughter of the pope, sat on the marble bench where the canons of the basilica usually chant the epistle and the gospel. Many other ladies were seated around the pulpit. This indignity was disgraceful and scandalized us.

JOHANNES BURCHARD, *Liber notarum*, PP. 214–15.

The 20-year-old Juan Borgia, Duke of Gandia, arrived in Rome on 10 August after an absence of three years, leaving his pregnant wife and their two-year-old son Juan in Spain, under the protection of the monarchs Ferdinand and Isabella. The following month, on 15 September, Alexander VI appointed his son as Governor of Viterbo.

In a magnificent ceremony at St Peter's on 26 October, the pope named the Duke of Gandia as Captain-General of the Church. The next day the duke took his place at the head of the papal army and, accompanied by the Duke of Urbino, Guidobaldo da Montefeltro, set out from Rome to capture the Orsini castles. Initially they met little resistance – Sacrofano, Galeria, Formello, Campagnano and Anguillara all fell without trouble. They now faced the more daunting prospect of Bracciano and its fortress, the ancestral home of the Orsini family perched above the lake, which was deliberately flaunting the French flag. In one sortie Guidobaldo was wounded, leaving the duke in charge. In late November artillery pieces arrived from Naples, but the weather was appallingly wet and the campaign stalled.

Meanwhile, Alexander VI was reminding the Doge of Venice of his duty to the Holy League, in particular reiterating that the French remained a threat to peace in Italy. He wrote to him on 4 September:

> Even though we are not at war with the French, it is important not to forget the threat they pose. While they refuse to evacuate Naples and Ostia ... and continue to send soldiers and ammunition into Italy, to send warships to Gaeta and to cut the traditional diplomatic ties in Rome, they do everything as if they were at war, and we must continue to look on them as the enemy. They do not lack the desire to fight, only the manpower. We see just the signs of war; we see none of peace, and must defend ourselves.[28]

Ferrante II's brief tenure of the crown of Naples ended with his death on 7 October. He had no children to inherit his title and was succeeded by his uncle, Federigo, aged forty-four.

On 16 October, Alexander VI wrote yet another letter to the Florentine firebrand Savonarola banning him from preaching.

1497

In the middle of January, despite reinforcements sent by the pope, two assaults on the castle at Bracciano failed. The Orsini were now saved by the timely arrival of Vitellozzo Vitelli, ruler of Città di Castello, with two Orsini cousins who, with the help of French gold, had raised troops to relieve Bracciano. The Duke of Gandia was forced to retreat with the heavy artillery to Anguillara.

On 24 January the two armies fought a battle at Soriano and the Orsini won a narrow victory – though Alexander VI's enemies claimed that the papal troops had been routed. The dead numbered over 500; the Duke of Gandia was slightly wounded and Guidobaldo da Montefeltro was taken prisoner by

The two armies fought a battle at Soriano and the Orsini won a narrow victory.

PREVIOUS PAGE **Procession in Piazza San Marco, Venice.** *Painted in 1496 by Gentile Bellini in the detailed pictorial style for which Venetian painters were famous, this panel depicts the grandeur and solemnity of public ceremonial in Venice staged in the great square in front of San Marco, its facade decorated with statues and columns looted from Constantinople during the Fourth Crusade (1204).*

RIGHT **Designs for machinery.** *These war machines, designed for moving and raising heavy objects, are also from the treatises of Francesco di Giorgio (see page 208); in the bottom drawing he has removed some of the boards to show the workings of the heavy screws used to move the trolley.*

Failure against the Orsini

On Sunday 15 January [1497] the soldiers of the Church, who were stationed outside Bracciano, entered the town and scaled the walls, which served as a sort of ladder. However, they sustained serious losses, without gaining any advantage. Among the cavalry alone there were about forty dead and sixty wounded. Another hundred men were killed and many more wounded. Following the intervention of Carlo Orsini, the illegitimate son of Virginio Orsini, and of Vitellozzo Vitelli, Lord of Città di Castello, who arrived to reinforce Bracciano with some two hundred cavalry and infantry, there was such confusion that our men were obliged to stop the attack and retreat from the town.

JOHANNES BURCHARD, *Liber notarum*, P. 228.

He began to make plans to dissolve Lucrezia's marriage.

the Orsini. Under pressure from Spain and Venice to make peace, Alexander VI restored the castles to the Orsini in return for 50,000 florins; the Orsini preferred to pay this huge sum to avoid the very real threat from the troops of Gonsalvo de Cordoba, who was now marching north from Naples to join the Duke of Gandia in a campaign to remove the French from the fortress at Ostia.

Savonarola's sermons in the cathedral at Florence during Lent, which publicly attacked and insulted Alexander VI, were angering many in Rome, as was the preacher's refusal to obey the pope. Even Cardinal Carafa, the protector of the Dominican Order, now withdrew his support for the angry friar.

In a private audience with the Florentine ambassador on 13 March, Alexander VI told him to inform his government that it must abandon both its policy of support for Savonarola and its alliance with France: 'be loyal to Italy,' he urged, 'let the French stay in France'.[29] Alexander VI's anti-French policy was also bringing him into conflict with Milan, which had reverted to its pro-French stance. During the spring, he began to make plans to dissolve Lucrezia's marriage with Giovanni Sforza, and when rumours of this plan began to circulate, Giovanni fled Rome for Pesaro.

On 15 March the pope's son Juan, Duke of Gandia, and Gonsalvo de Cordoba returned to Rome in triumph after capturing of Ostia, and both were received by Alexander VI at the Vatican. On Palm Sunday, 19 March, the two commanders were present at mass in the Sistine Chapel, where it was clear that the Spanish captain resented the precedence granted to the Borgia duke. For the Easter mass, the master-of-ceremonies, Johannes Burchard, was careful to include Gonsalvo de

Savonarola lambasts the Church

O bawdy Church ... *The Lord said 'I gave you wondrous vestments but you have made them into deities. You have dedicated the holy vessels to vanity and the sacraments to simony. You have become a wanton prostitute with your lust. You are lower than the beasts, a monster of depravity. Once upon a time you felt shame when you sinned but now you are unrepentant. Once the sons of ordained priests were called nephews but now there is no more talk of nephews, only and everywhere of sons. Wherever you have built a public square you have built a brothel. And what does the prostitute do? She sits on Solomon's throne and solicits all the world. Those that are rich are made welcome and may do as they please but those who would do good are driven out. You O harlot Church have shown your filthiness to all and your stench can be smelled in Heaven.*

FRA GIROLAMO SAVONAROLA
(L. VON PASTOR, *History of the Popes*,
VOL. VI, P. 17).

219

ABOVE **Alexander VI as the Devil.** *This woodcut belongs to an imaginative genre of anti-papal imagery printed in northern Europe by Protestant reformers. When closed, the card was an inoffensive image of the pope dressed in his formal vestments, tiara on his head and slippers embroidered with a cross on his feet. By lifting a flap, the upper portion of the image was transformed into a grotesque caricature of the Devil, headed by the words* Ego sum Papa, *'I am the Pope'.*

Cordoba in the rituals. Several weeks later, on 6 May, Alexander VI left Rome with his cardinals to visit the recaptured Ostia.

On 12 May the pope finally excommunicated Savonarola for his continued disobedience and in the hope of forcing Florence to abandon her alliance with France. By the terms of the excommunication, 'all are prohibited from giving him aid, under pain of the same punishment, to converse with him, or to endorse his views by either word or deed, for he is an excommunicate and suspected of heretical beliefs'.[30]

During May Cardinal Ascanio Sforza wrote to his brother Ludovico, Duke of Milan, to inform him that the pope intended to dissolve the marriage of Lucrezia Borgia and Giovanni Sforza. When Giovanni heard the news in early June, he set off immediately from Pesaro to ride to Milan for discussions with his cousin. On 4 June Lucrezia left her palace by the Vatican, where she was 'said to have felt unwelcome', to take refuge with the Dominican nuns of San Sisto; the Ferrarese ambassador reported that 'some are saying here that she wants to become a nun, though others have explanations which are not credible'.[31]

At a secret consistory on 7 June Alexander VI created a new papal duchy of the fief of Benevento, which he planned to bestow on his son Juan, Duke of Gandia. The following day he appointed his son Cesare as legate to Naples, for the purpose of crowning the new King Federigo; this was a special honour for such a young and inexperienced member of the College of Cardinals.

On 14 June, a Wednesday, Cardinal Cesare and the Duke of Gandia went to dine with their mother Vanozza de' Cataneis at her villa near San Pietro in

Crime and punishment

On Sunday 16 April *Pietro Palozzi, a Roman citizen, whose servants had been robbed by brigands, sent a company of his friends, all armed, to the place where it had happened. Of twenty-four they found nine and sent them bound to Rome. That day four were hung from the loggias of the Capitol and the Palazzo dei Conservatori. A fifth, who had also been hung, was taken down and sent to the pope who pardoned him, but he died that night in prison.*

JOHANNES BURCHARD, *Liber notarum*, PP. 229-30.

Lucrezia … She wants to become a nun.

220

HIERONYMI·FERRARIENSIS·A·DEO·

Vincola. The two brothers, accompanied by a few servants, rode home late in the evening. On the way back, Juan parted from Cesare, saying he wanted to make a private visit. He had still not returned to the Vatican the following morning when his servants went to his rooms. According to Burchard:

> The pope also became uneasy. However, he persuaded himself that the duke had been delayed at a party at the house of some girl, and that he would not leave this house until later in the day and that he would return without doubt before nightfall. The duke did not come back. The pope, who was growing increasingly worried and troubled to his guts, desired to have information at any cost and ordered men used to this business to find it by any means they could.[32]

Alexander VI's distress increased as Friday wore on. During the day civic guards found the Duke of Gandia's groom, badly wounded and unable to talk; they also found the duke's horse, which showed signs of a struggle. The following morning a timber merchant reported seeing a body thrown into the Tiber late on Wednesday night. By midday the guards had found a body not far from Santa Maria del Popolo: it was the duke. He had been wounded nine times and his throat was cut.

On 17 June Alexander VI ordered the Governor of Rome to search all houses along the Tiber, but nothing was found. Two days later the pope held a public consistory attended by all the cardinals in Rome, with the exception of Ascanio Sforza. After hearing the cardinals offer their condolences, the pope gave a speech on his grief at the tragic death of his son, which he felt was a punishment for his sins, and promised to do all he could to reform the Church. Furthermore, he was appointing a reform commission to start work immediately. He also announced

ABOVE **A view of old Rome.** *One of the distinctive features of large Renaissance cities was the marked contrast between the huge piazzas that opened up, as in front of Rome's major churches or the large open market squares of the Campo dei Fiori and Piazza Navona, and the narrow streets of the city. Most of Rome was a warren of narrow dark alleys. Even during the day, sunlight rarely penetrated here, blocked by the upper storeys of buildings that jutted out over the streets. At night it was deathly dark and notoriously dangerous – robbers and cutpurses prowled in search of the solitary homegoer, while murderers lay in wait for their prey.*

Evidence and hearsay on the death of Juan Borgia

Amongst others they interrogated a certain Giorgio Schiavo who regularly unloaded his cargoes of wood on the banks of the Tiber and, in order to protect his merchandise from thieves, regularly spent the night on his barge in the Tiber. When he was asked if he had seen anything being thrown into the Tiber on Wednesday night, he replied, so it is said, that he was on his barge that night guarding his wood and, after midnight, had seen two men on foot come down the alley to the left of the Ospedale degli Schiavoni at San Girolamo. They had walked along the road by the river, looking carefully to the right and left to see if anyone was about but, finding no one, they had returned to the alley. Shortly afterwards, two other men came out of the same alley and made the same inspection. Not seeing anything, they signalled to their companions. A rider on a white horse appeared, with a corpse slung over behind him, heads and arms on one side, feet on the other. The first two men were were walking beside the rider in order to keep the corpse from slipping. The horse was ridden further along to the place where the sewer emptied into the river ... the two men on foot then lifted the body, one taking the arms and the other the legs and threw it into the Tiber with as much force as they were capable. The man on the horse asked if the operation had worked and they answered, 'Yes, Lord'. Then, watching the river intently, and seeing something on the surface, the man on the horse asked the others what was the black thing floating in the river; they replied that it was the coat, so one of them had thrown stones to make it sink. Once that was done all five men left.

JOHANNES BURCHARD, *Liber notarum*, PP. 234-5

Two days ago it was being openly said that the brother of the Lord of Pesaro [Galeazzo Sforza] was guilty of the murder, but nobody now believes that. There are so many different rumours but as every conversation about this matter is dangerous, I would leave it to those to whom it concerns. The pope understandably is most distressed and plans to change his life and become quite a different man ... yesterday in consistory he said he intended to reform the Church and has appointed cardinals to oversee this ... Moreover he also announced at the said consistory that he wanted to equip 40 squadrons of soldiers and won't include a single Roman baron. It is thought he wants Gonsalvo de Cordoba as Captain-General of the Church who is a brave and noble man, and he promises to do other praiseworthy and virtuous things; we shall see whether he is lying or really inspired.

AN ANONYMOUS CORRESPONDENT TO GIOVANNI BENTIVOGLIO, 20 JUNE 1497 (L. VON PASTOR, *History of the Popes*, VOL. V, P. 554, DOC. 38).

with ostensible sadness that he had to dissolve the marriage of his daughter and Giovanni Sforza, explaining that it had never been consummated. After the pope had resumed his seat, the Spanish ambassador apologized for Vice-Chancellor Ascanio's absence, which, he said, was due to his fear of the Spaniards: the pope replied that he did not suspect Cardinal Ascanio of any involvement in Juan's

Who killed the Duke of Gandia?

Juan Borgia, Duke of Gandia, was not much liked, either in Spain – where he struck one contemporary as 'an avaricious youth, self-important, proud, vicious and irrational'[33] – or in Rome, where he had made many enemies, not least among the husbands of his many mistresses.

One of his conquests was reputed to be his sister-in-law Sancia of Aragon. A letter was found in his apartments warning him that a Roman friend was actually his enemy. One of the most obvious suspects in his murder was Giovanni Sforza, whose fury at the pope's decision to annul his marriage to Lucrezia Borgia was widely known; but he was fortunately in Milan at the time, and his brother Galeazzo – another suspect – could prove he had never left Pesaro. Cardinal Ascanio Sforza, who had had a violent argument with the duke a few days before his death, was also suspected, but Alexander VI insisted 'God forbid that I should have such terrible suspicions of someone I have always loved as a brother'[34] and continued to behave in a friendly manner towards his old

ally. Another man with a grudge against the duke was Guidobaldo della Rovere, whom the pope had refused to ransom after the Battle of Soriano.

Despite the lack of hard evidence, popular history has ascribed the murder to Cesare, the duke's brother, though he was not among the immediate suspects. The rumour seems to have emerged somewhat later in the circle around Giovanni Sforza, after he had been forced by Alexander VI to state publicly that he was impotent – a patent falsehood in order to enable the dissolution of the marriage with Lucrezia. The Duke of Gandia's widow, Maria, certainly thought Cesare guilty, and she even commissioned an altarpiece to record this terrible fratricide.

RIGHT **The Virgen de los Caballeros.** *Maria Enriquez, the widow of Juan Borgia, took the highly unusual step of commissioning this altarpiece, from the Spanish painter Pablo de San Leocadio, in order to give visual expression to her belief that her husband had been cruelly murdered by his own brother, Cesare, who is seen here on the far right of* the picture in the act of stabbing the Duke of Gandia. *In the years following her husband's assassination, she worked hard on behalf of her son, the new duke who had been just three years old when his father died, increasing his wealth and his prestige at court, before retiring to a convent after he had married and secured the succession.*

death: 'I have always considered him my brother, and I will welcome him when he chooses to come to me.' [35]

On 20 June Alexander VI went to St Peter's, where he planned to erect a new tribune, 'which will cost 50,000 ducats; and there will be another new tribune for the papal benediction which will be built in Santa Maria Maggiore'.[36]

On 22 June it was reported that the new reform commission, which consisted of cardinals Oliviero Carafa, Jorge da Costa, Antoniotto Pallavicini, Giovanni Antonio Sangiorgio, Francesco Piccolomini and Raffaello Riario, assembled in the Vatican every morning. Alexander VI now appointed them to deal with the case of Savonarola, who had declared his excommunication invalid.

One month later, on 22 July, Cardinal Cesare Borgia left Rome with a large retinue, and 3,000 ducats for his expenses, to fulfil his role as legate to Naples.[37] On 11 August he crowned King Federigo in Capua. Meanwhile, Alexander VI was worrying about the safety of his other children remaining in Rome, and during July he made arrangements for all of them to leave the city: Jofrè and Sancia were sent to their ducal residence at Squillace, and there were rumours that Lucrezia was to be sent to her Borgia relatives in Spain. Her husband Giovanni Sforza, meanwhile, was refusing to contemplate agreeing to divorce on the grounds of non-consummation of the marriage – especially given the contrary evidence that his first wife had died in childbirth.

During August, Ascanio Sforza, in Rome for the funeral of his Milanese ally Cardinal Bernardino Lunati, had a long audience with Alexander VI, which was reported by the Venetian ambassador to be very friendly. [38]

On 5 September Cardinal Cesare arrived back from Naples and that same

A forger in the Vatican

Late in the evening of Thursday 14 September [1497] the pope sent for his private secretary, Bartolomeo Florès, and had him arrested ... and taken to Castel Sant'Angelo where he was locked up under guard. Alexander VI had the said secretary arrested for fraudulently issuing papal briefs of a deceitful nature. Some of the briefs had been requested by members of Florès's staff. One authorized a Portuguese nun, a member of the royal family, to leave her Order, despite the vows she had taken, and marry the illegitimate son of the last king, while another was a papal dispensation allowing a subdeacon to marry ... they are speaking of around 3,000 fraudulent briefs.

JOHANNES BURCHARD, *Liber notarum*, PP. 240.

evening went to the Vatican for a private conversation with Alexander VI. At his formal reception by the pope in consistory the next day, it was noted by many that the two men did not speak, and rumours were soon rife in Rome that Cesare had told his father that he wanted to resign his cardinalate.

At the end of October a series of misfortunes befell Castel Sant'Angelo. On 26 October its governor, Bartolomeo Lunati, died of syphilis.[39] Three days later a powder magazine exploded in the castle after being struck by lightning, destroying the upper part of the fortress. 'The pontificate of Alexander VI has seen many astonishing and strange events,' wrote a Venetian chronicler; 'the Tiber flooded all the city, his son was brutally murdered and now Castel Sant'Angelo is destroyed'.[40]

Having started formal proceedings to dissolve the marriage of his daughter Lucrezia and Giovanni Sforza in September, a resolution was reached in December. On 20 December Lucrezia's divorce was made public, after Giovanni had been persuaded by his family to agree to declare, in writing, that the marriage had never been consummated. The unfortunate husband was also obliged to return the 31,000 ducats he had received as Lucrezia's dowry.

On 24 December Alexander VI gave an audience to Vice-Chancellor Ascanio Sforza and the ambassadors of Milan and Naples, at which they discussed the annulment but also – more importantly – the issue of Cesare's red hat: 'we talked about how anxious Cesare is to resign his place in the College of Cardinals,' the cardinal informed his brother Ludovico, in code, 'and the pope wants to manage this so as to create as little scandal as possible'.[41]

LEFT **Pen case with lid.** *Designed to be attached to a belt, pen cases were often made of tooled leather, like this elegant example of the genre. They were used to hold a selection of quill pens, and sometimes contained compartments for ink and paper as well.*

ABOVE **Alexander VI.** *This portrait of the Borgia pope is a posthumous work by the 17th-century painter Juan Ribalta, who has depicted Alexander VI in all his pontifical splendour. Rodrigo Borgia's reputation in his home country of Spain, a state that benefitted politically and economically from his policies, was far greater than in Italy where he was widely viewed with suspicion as a foreigner.*

In Florence, on Christmas Day, Savonarola celebrated three masses and gave out communion to many, in express contravention of the terms of his excommunication. In Rome the following day, mass in the Sistine Chapel was notable for the absence of some of the cardinal-bishops. According to the master-of-ceremonies:

> His Holiness ordered me to inform cardinals Giovanni Michiel, Jorge da Costa and Girolamo Basso della Rovere that it was an insult to the apostolic throne that these cardinal-bishops had been absent from a solemn public mass in the presence of the pope in the chapel. If they claimed they were tired after the long services for Christmas, I was to tell them that His Holiness himself, despite the weight of his years, had celebrated the same Christmas offices and still managed to attend the next day ... after lunch I did what His Holiness asked and today all the cardinal-bishops attended. [42]

By the close of 1497, Alexander VI had shown that he could play the political game with consummate skill, exploiting the rivalries between Milan and Naples, and between France and Spain, not only to maintain the independence of the papacy but also to boost the status and wealth of the younger members of the Borgia family. Siding first with Milan against Naples, he had reversed this policy when Milan entered into alliance with an ambitious young King of France determined to enforce his claim to the Neapolitan throne. When the king invaded Italy, Alexander VI stayed on the fence long enough to keep all sides guessing.

Alexander VI's family proved useful pawns in the game: he had appointed his son Juan as Captain-General of the Church, given a red hat to Cesare, had his daughter Lucrezia married to a cousin of the ruler of Milan and his son Jofrè espoused to the daughter of the King of Naples; he had also distributed bishoprics and other benefices and favours to his nephews in Spain. But by the end of 1497 Juan was dead, the victim of a brutal – possibly fratricidal – murder; Cesare was planning to set aside his cardinal's hat and return to secular life, an unusual though not unprecedented move; and Lucrezia was being recycled in the marriage stakes yet again. The Borgia clan was suffering setbacks and uncertainties, as well as enjoying the fruits of Pope Alexander's position.

The Borgia clan was suffering setbacks and uncertainties, as well as enjoying the fruits of Pope Alexander's position.

228

RIGHT **Alexander VI's coat of arms, Borgia Apartments, the Vatican.** *Extravagant expenditure was the traditional vehicle for the display of power and prestige in Renaissance Europe – and the use of costly gold and lapiz-lazuli here testifies to the tastes of this famously ostentatious pope; but the embellishment of the Borgia Apartments also provided evidence of cultural innovation. One of the features of the friezes surrounding the panels is the appearance of elaborate and imaginative details, known as grotesques, inspired by the rediscovery of the Golden House of Nero by the Colosseum. During the 1490s artists crawled in the dark, and in extreme discomfort, down the narrow passages excavated under the vaults of this legendary palace to see authentic imperial Roman decoration at first hand. Their astonishment was understandable, and this event was to have a dramatic impact on the development of Renaissance art.*

ALEXANDER VI, CESARE AND LUCREZIA

A POPE, A WARRIOR AND A WIDOW

1498–1500

Alexander VI's son Cesare Borgia was chafing at the restrictions of his ecclesiastical career, reluctant even to compromise with the worldly interpretation of the role that his father had pursued. Persuading his father to allow him to resign his cardinal's hat – an unusual act, but one not without precedent – was proving difficult. But the real question was: what would this ambitious 22-year-old do next? He was eminently unsuited to a Church career, but he was also equally unfitted for a life in the shadows. The pope and his son found the answer through deft political manoeuvring, audacious fund-raising and a new alliance with one of Europe's superpowers.

1498

Savonarola ... was unrelenting in his virulent criticism of the Church and its servants in Rome.

ON 30 JANUARY Alexander VI gave permission for the opening of the coffin of his predecessor, Pope Innocent VIII, who had died in 1492. The corpse was discovered to be perfectly preserved, except for an injury to one foot, and it was now solemnly buried in the grandiose bronze tomb commissioned by Innocent's nephews.

In Florence, the excommunicated preacher Savonarola remained stubbornly active. On 11 February he gave a sermon at the Dominican convent of San Marco: 'Anyone who still believes that the excommunication is valid and that I should not be allowed to preach,' he ranted, 'supports the kingdom of the Devil and is a heretic.'[1] He was unrelenting in his virulent criticism of the Church and its servants in Rome:

PREVIOUS PAGE **Madonna of the Raccomandati.** *Painted c.1500 by Cola da Roma for the confraternity of the Raccomandati in Orte, north of Rome, this altarpiece shows Alexander VI among the members, who are grouped in traditional style under the protective cloak of the Virgin. (See also page 235.)*

RIGHT **The Visitation,** *painted by Domenic Ghirlandaio for a fresco cycle (1485–90) in Santa Maria Novelle, Florence. Savonarola was particularly critical of scenes like this, in which religious figures – in this case, the Virgin Mary and her cousin, Elizabeth, the mother of St John the Baptist – were portrayed in modern dress.*

Competing claims to Milan

Louis XII and Ludovico Sforza were both great-grandsons of Giangaleazzo Visconti, Duke of Milan. Ludovico's father, the great *condottiere* Francesco Sforza, had married Bianca Maria, the illegitimate daughter of the last Visconti duke, Filippo Maria, and had taken Milan by force in 1450. He established the legitimacy of his regime by forging a document that proclaimed him as his father-in-law's rightful heir, and he adopted the Visconti viper as his emblem. Louis XII's claim to Milan had no taint of illegitimacy: his grandmother, Valentina, was the legitimate daughter of Giangaleazzo Visconti and had married the Duke of Orléans, making his claim superior to that of Ludovico Sforza, and legal.

All the clergy in Rome have acquired their benefices through simony. They buy preferments and give them to their brothers and their children, who then use violence and other sinful methods to enforce their rights. They are greedy beyond belief and will do anything for cash. They ring their bells for coins and candles, and only go to vespers and other services when they can gain thereby. They sell their benefices, sell the sacraments and make merchandise of masses. Money is their only motivation, and they fear excommunication for this reason. At nightfall one goes out gambling, another visits his mistress. At funerals they host banquets so that they are eating and drinking and talking instead of praying for the soul of the departed. They are riddled with sin and vice but go around in fine clothes looking clean and well-dressed. Many have no idea of the rules they should follow, or how to find them; they are ignorant of penance and of the care of souls. In the past sinners were careful to be discreet but now nobody bothers to pretend. Living modestly is considered a disgrace: if a priest or cleric lives in an orderly fashion he is ridiculed and called a hypocrite.[2]

On 14 February the body of one of Alexander VI's valets, Pedro Calderon, was found on the banks of the Tiber: 'various things are being said about this in the city,' recorded Johannes Burchard.[3] Many believed Cardinal Cesare had murdered the valet, who was a favourite of Lucrezia and by whom she was rumoured to be pregnant. A week later Cardinal Cesare and his cousin, the younger Cardinal Juan Borgia, were seen in Ostia, dressed in hunting outfits 'in the French fashion'.[4]

Alexander VI gave an audience to the Florentine ambassador on 25 February, at which he threatened to place Florence under an interdict if Savonarola continued to defy the papal ban. On 9 March the pope wrote directly to the Florentine government, inquiring: 'Does the friar really believe that he alone was exempt when Christ gave our predecessor St Peter' supreme authority over the Church?[5] The Florentine ambassador was in a difficult position. 'Think what you yourselves would do,' he wrote to his masters, 'if one of your subjects not only deliberately disobeyed your orders but treated you with contempt as well.'[6]

On 14 April startling news arrived of the death of the 28-year-old French king, Charles VIII, a week earlier, after he had knocked his head on a lintel. His heir was his cousin Louis XII, the 16-year-old Duke of Orléans, who had inherited not only Charles VIII's claim to Naples but also, in his own right, a claim to the Duchy of Milan.

It was said that:

> Eight days before his death, in what was either a marvel or an omen, he [Charles] saw a great dragon or serpent in the sky and, fearful of this vision, sent immediately for his astrologers to ask them what it meant. They replied that it signified his triumphant return to Italy, that he was the serpent devouring everything in his path. But after he had died, the astrologers changed their verdict, saying that the serpent signified the succession of the Duke of Orléans, which has happened, who carries this emblem on his coat-of-arms and the reason why it is on the coat-of-arms of the new king is that he is descended from the Visconti [of Milan], whose device was a viper.[7]

ABOVE **Alexander VI,** *detail from* Madonna of the Raccomandanti *(see page 231). This profile of the second Borgia pope shows him in the company of a bishop, a cardinal and a king, readily identifiable by their head gear, among the ordinary members of the confraternity of the Raccomandati in Orte. Situated some 20 miles east of Viterbo in the Upper*

Tiber Valley, the small hilltop city of Orte had been a centre of Etruscan culture and a Roman municipality before being sacked by the Goths, Byzantines and Lombards as the Roman Empire collapsed in the 5th and 6th centuries. Raised to a bishopric in the Middle Ages, it was an important strategic stronghold that guarded the northern approaches to Rome.

In April the Florentine authorities finally took action against Savonarola. The friar was arrested on 8 April, Palm Sunday, and committed to trial in Florence, the government ignoring Alexander VI's request to try him at the ecclesiastical court in Rome. On 19 April the preacher admitted, under torture, that he was not the prophet he had claimed to be. The apothecary Luca Landucci attended his trial and was stunned by Savonarola's confession:

> On 19 April 1498 in the Great Council Hall the deposition of Fra Girolamo, whom we believed was a prophet, was read out. He had written it in his own hand and confessed that he was not a prophet and that God had not told him what to say ... I was there and, when I heard this, I was amazed and stupefied. And I felt pain in my soul when I saw the structure on which I had built my faith now tumbling down because it had poor foundations. I was waiting for Florence to become the new Jerusalem from which would flow the laws and the splendour of Christian life and to see the renovation of the Church, the conversion of the infidels and the consolation of the good.[8]

On 23 May Savonarola was hanged and his body burned in the Piazza della Signoria in Florence before a huge crowd of men and boys; women and girls had been barred from the spectacle.[9]

A month earlier, on 21 April, Alexander VI's head of household had been arrested on a charge of heresy: Pedro de Aranda was a Spanish Jew who had converted to Christianity and was currently the Bishop of Calahorra.

On 18 June Alexander VI, now almost 70 years old, became a father again.

ABOVE **Bianca Maria Visconti,** *painted in 1462 by Bonifacio Bembo. As the wife of Francesco Sforza, Duke of Milan, Bianca Maria played a major role in establishing the Sforza dynasty in Milan: she was the mother of Duke Galeazzo Maria and of his formidable brothers Duke Ludovico and Cardinal Ascanio; moreover, she played a major role in commissioning artistic projects that testified to the family's legitimate authority in the city.*

RIGHT **The Execution of Savonarola.** *This depiction of the burning of Savonarola and two of his fellow Dominicans shows the last moments of the friars as they were led along the specially constructed walkway to the gallows. In marked contrast to his precise detailing of the buildings that surrounded the Piazza della Signoria, the anonymous artist chose not to record the large crowds that witnessed this grisly event.*

An unnamed mistress, perhaps Giulia Farnese, gave birth to a son, whom the pope named Juan, probably in memory of his murdered son. However, he would become better known by the Italian version of his name, 'Giovanni'. The boy's birth was legitimized in 1501.

In June Alexander VI announced the fourth betrothal of his daughter Lucrezia, this time to Alfonso of Aragon, Duke of Bisceglie, with a dowry of 41,000 ducats. He was the illegitimate son of Alfonso II of Naples (who had died in 1495) and the brother of Sancia of Aragon.[10]

King Federigo of Naples, however, baulked at the pope's request to consider another marriage to cement the alliance – between Cesare and the king's daughter Carlotta of Aragon. Alexander VI now tried another route to bring Cesare and Carlotta together. He decided to listen favourably to Louis XII's desire for a divorce from his wife so that he could marry the wealthy widow of Charles VIII, Anne of Brittany, at whose court Carlotta was currently living.

Louis XII's ambassadors arrived in Rome in late June, conveying the king's oath that he had never consummated his first marriage, and Alexander VI duly set up a commission to examine the case. With Louis XII poised to assert his claims over both Milan and Naples, the pope now considered it opportune to pursue an alliance with the French king. In July, while publicly insisting that Louis XII must abandon his claim to Milan, Alexander VI sent envoys to the French court with formal instructions to get the king's support for a crusade. Their secret instructions were to persuade the king to arrange the marriage of Cesare and Carlotta, and to provide military assistance for Cesare to take control of the Papal States in the Romagna. In return, Alexander offered Louis XII the divorce, a cardinal's hat for his chief adviser Georges d'Amboise, and a promise that Cesare would fight for the French during the campaign the king was planning against Milan.

Meanwhile, Alfonso of Aragon had arrived in Rome, where he was received without ceremony, and a few days later, on 21 July, the 17-year-old prince was married to Lucrezia Borgia. During one of the theatrical performances for the occasion, Cardinal Cesare played the role of a unicorn, the symbol of chastity – contrary to his reputation.

Alexander VI now tried another route to bring Cesare and Carlotta together.

239

LEFT **Louis XII of France,** *painted by Jean Perréal. A mature 36 years old when he inherited the French throne from his cousin, Charles VIII, Louis XII is best known for the political and military skill with which he pursued his dynastic ambitions in Italy. At home, however, he did much to consolidate royal authority across the realm. He vastly improved the efficiency of his government, reorganized the administration of justice and refilled the royal coffers that had been almost emptied by his predecessor. His own popularity was considerably enhanced by his policy of cutting the costs of his own court and keeping taxes as low as possible – he was named 'father of the people' in gratitude and, in the political chaos of the 16th century, his reign was remembered as an 'Age of Gold'.*

A Borgia wedding feast

Don Alfonso and Donna Lucrezia consummated their marriage privately and the following day it was announced and celebrated with many festivities, banquets and dances to which no ambassador or other public dignitary was invited. Cardinal Cesare's courtiers and those of the princess his sister-in-law [Sancia] behaved very badly, unsheathing their swords in the presence of the pope in one of the rooms by the chapel where they were serving refreshments before dinner last Sunday and two bishops were wounded ... later they had dinner, which lasted three hours and ended after daybreak. There was a theatrical entertainment in which Cardinal Cesare appeared as a unicorn, which will take too long to describe ... but it does not seem to have been particularly brilliant. What you need to know is that Donna Lucrezia seems very happy with her new husband.

GIOVANNI LUCIDO CATANEO TO FRANCESCO GONZAGA, 8 AUGUST 1498 (L. VON PASTOR, *History of the Popes*, VOL. VI, P. 612, DOC. 3).

On 23 July, Alexander VI's erstwhile secretary Bartolomeo Florès died in Castel Sant'Angelo, where he had been imprisoned for forgery during his papal service.

A week later, on 29 July, a group of 24 Spanish Jews were converted to Christianity in front of St Peter's.

Cesare Borgia finally renounced his cardinal's hat on 17 August, during a secret consistory. He was giving up the security of ecclesiastical prestige and wealth for the far more risky world of secular power. That evening, Louis de Villeneuve, Baron de Trans, arrived in Rome with letters from Louis XII investing Cesare as Duke of Valence and orders to escort the new duke back to the French court. Thus, the Cardinal of Valencia had become the Duke of Valence, though the Romans still called him by his nickname, 'Il Valentino'.

On 13 September Alexander VI signed the documents allowing Louis XII to contract a marriage with Anne of Brittany – though the annulment of Louis's first marriage would have to wait until its authorization by the commission examining it. Four days later, in a secret consistory, the pope announced that Georges d'Amboise would indeed be created a cardinal. On 1 October Cesare left Rome with his entourage, carrying both documents in his luggage; according to Johannes Burchard, 'he also took much money' and 'many, or rather most of his horses had silver harnesses'.[11] Three days later Duke Cesare and Baron de Trans, with their retinues, boarded two French galleys at Civitavecchia and set sail for France.

Cesare landed at Marseilles on 19 October and set out for the French court. He stopped briefly at Avignon, where he was received with all honours by Cardinal Giuliano della Rovere, who then joined him on his long ride north to Chinon in the Loire Valley, where the court was currently stationed.

Two months later, on 19 December, Cesare made his formal entry into Chinon, where, on 21 December, Cardinal Giuliano performed the ceremonies making

ABOVE **Banquet scene from the Villa Caldogno, near Vicenza.**
Accounts of villa life in Ancient Roman literature described a cultured elite indulging in leisurely feasts and conversation or flirtation with friends in their rural residences built on the hills of Rome, in the countryside around or by the sea. These lyrical descriptions inspired Renaissance patrons, who began to build their own rural retreats where they could enjoy pleasurable idleness as an antidote to the hectic political or commercial business of the city. At a practical level, these villas were *smallholdings that produced oil, wine, fruit, vegetables and herbs to be used in the town kitchens of their owners; but they were also designed as purpose-built dining-rooms, where the heavy summer heat of the urban streets could be lightened by gentle breezes, cascading fountains, shaded loggias and pavilions, and beautiful gardens. Innocent VIII built the Villa Belvedere on the hill behind the Vatican palace; Cardinal Oliviero Carafa built a sumptuous villa on the Quirinal Hill, while cardinals Giovanni Michiel and Jorge da Costa both owned properties on the Pincian Hill.*

Georges d'Amboise a cardinal. 'On the journey from the royal camp to the church, Cesare, Duke of Valence, once a cardinal, rode after the other princes, immediately in front of the king, carrying the said red hat for all to see.'[12]

In Rome on the following day, Alexander VI gave an audience to the envoys of Ferdinand and Isabella of Spain, who were furious at the pope's new alliance with France. The envoys began by accusing the pope of effectively purchasing his election, and Alexander VI retorted that at least he had been elected unanimously, which was more than could be said for the Spanish monarchs, whom he accused of usurping their thrones.

1499

AT THE BEGINNING OF the year Rome witnessed terrible winter weather. According to the papal master-of-ceremonies, 'on Thursday 10 January before daybreak it started to snow heavily and continued all day. That evening the wind turned northerly bringing freezing weather which lasted for many days. This wind and a great freeze returned again in February, lasting for many days.'[13]

On 6 January Louis XII married Anne of Brittany at Nantes. A fortnight later the Venetian ambassador reported that letters had arrived in Rome with news from the French court announcing that attempts to persuade Carlotta into

A diplomatic tiff

The magnificent ambassadors of the King and Queen of Spain arrived in Rome during December ... and His Holiness agreed to give them an audience, in the presence of six cardinals, on Wednesday 23 January [1499]. They were received in the late afternoon, after lunch, in the room adjoining the Sala del Pappagallo. In the room were cardinals Jorge da Costa, Giovanni Antonio Sangiorgio, Bernardino Carvajal, Ascanio Sforza and Juan Borgia the Younger. After a long speech from the ambassadors a violent and abusive argument developed between them and the pope. The envoys said that, by order of their king and queen, they wanted a notary and other witnesses present while they spoke and for the audience to be written up and authenticated. So they demanded that a notary be summoned. The pope replied that they could write up the minutes among themselves later, but they could not do this in his presence. It is said that the ambassadors were demanding that the pope must recall his son, the Cardinal of Valencia, from France and to restore him to his dignity as cardinal.

JOHANNES BURCHARD, *Liber notarum*, PP. 278–9.

LEFT **Ships in harbour unloading cargo,** *detail from the Tavola Strozzi panel (see pages 24–5). Swift merchant galleys, which used both sail and oars, were expensive to run, but the profits that could be earned trading in luxury goods made them commercially viable – both Florence and Venice had fleets of state-owned galleys which were auctioned off for each voyage. These ships traded across the Mediterranean, east to Beirut, Alexandria and Constantinople, west to Pisa, Genoa, Marseilles, Aigues Mortes, Barcelona and Valencia; there were also ships sailing regularly up the Atlantic coast to Southampton, London, Antwerp and Bruges. The accommodation provided for passengers on these merchant vessels was notoriously uncomfortable, even for the rich and powerful, though the dishes on the captain's table included fresh meat and white bread, thanks to the regular stops they needed to make in order to take on food and water for the large numbers of sailors and oarsmen on board.*

a marriage with Duke Cesare had so far failed. Alexander VI was also unsuccessful when he tried to put pressure on Carlotta's father, King Federigo.

Alexander VI had another stormy audience with the Spanish ambassadors on 23 January; they were rumoured to have demanded that the pope recall Cesare and restore his cardinal's hat.

By early February, Carnival was in full swing in Rome. On Sunday 3 February Jewish inhabitants ran their usual race from Campo dei Fiori to Castel Sant'Angelo, but the prize for the winner, a bolt of red cloth, was not awarded because of a false start. The race was rescheduled for the next day, before the youths were to have their race from Castel Sant'Angelo to St Peter's. A few days later the masked Bishop of Toul nearly ran foul of an angry crowd: 'On Tuesday 7 February there were celebrations in the Piazza Navona, very well organized according to Roman tradition. Jean Maradès, the Bishop of Toul was there disguised in a mask. His horse accidentally barged into a group of Romans, who did not recognize him and he narrowly avoided being injured because he was protected by the people around him. Following this episode, the next day it was ordered that the wearing of masks was forbidden, on pain of a heavy fine, but no one took any notice.'[14]

The festivities continued with daily entertainments until Ash Wednesday, 13 February.

In the early part of the year, Lucrezia, who had been married now for seven months to Alfonso of Aragon, suffered a miscarriage after a fall in the orchard in which she was taking a walk.

ABOVE **Medals of Louis XII and Anne of Brittany.** *Louis XII had married his first wife, Jeanne of France, in 1476 at the age of 14 but this daughter of Louis XI had tragically proved deformed and unable to bear children. Alexander VI, keen for the king's help for Cesare, agreed to annul the marriage, subject to the conclusions of a commission set up in France to examine the case. Much to everybody's surprise, Jeanne insisted on defending herself in person at the tribunal and conducted herself with dignity through the long cross-examination, at which she insisted the* marriage had been consummated while the king insisted that it had not: the verdict, inevitably, was in favour of Louis XII. But Louis was generous to his ex-wife, giving her money and lands to enable her to retain the lifestyle of a royal princess; she became a nun and was canonized in 1950. His marriage to Anne of Brittany proved fruitful – she bore him two daughters: Claude, who married Francis I, and Renée, who married the Duke of Ferrara. After Anne died in 1514, Louis XII married Mary Tudor, the sister of Henry VIII, but died the following year.*

Cesare Borgia joins the Order of St Michael

Another courier arrived at Pentecost, the 19th of the same month [May 1499], to say that the king [Louis XII] had admitted the duke to the Order of St Michael, which is a most honourable royal order. Following this news, His Holiness announced that there would be fireworks and bonfires on the evening of 23 May as a sign of his joy, and they would be lit in front of the palaces of Cardinal Giovanni Battista Orsini, Cardinal Jean Bilhères, his daughter Lucrezia and several Spaniards.

JOHANNES BURCHARD, *LIBER NOTARUM*, PP. 288.

Late in the evening of 23 February a courier arrived in Rome with urgent letters from France, bringing news that the alliance between France, Venice and Rome had been signed at Blois; there was also news that the marriage between Cesare Borgia and Carlotta would soon be arranged. Furthermore, in early March Louis XII announced his intention of sending an army of 25,000 men into Lombardy to capture Milan.

On the fourth Sunday in Lent, 10 March, Alexander VI performed the customary blessing of the Golden Rose in the Sala del Pappagallo, and carried it in to the Sistine Chapel – he hoped this year to use the papal award to celebrate the marriage of Cesare and Carlotta.

In April, by the pope's order, work began on demolishing houses to create a new ceremonial route between Castel Sant'Angelo and St Peter's in preparation for the anticipated crowds of pilgrims who would arrive for next year's Jubilee.

On 20 April Alexander VI received more letters from Louis

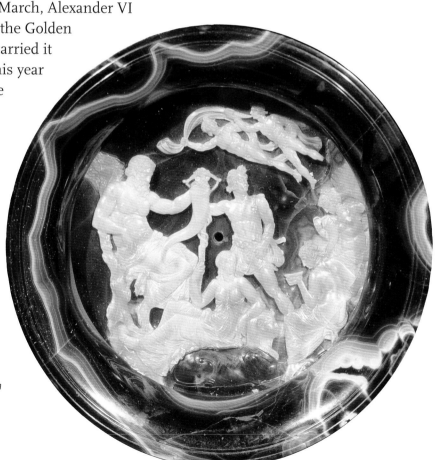

RIGHT **Tazza Farnese,** *a priceless late Hellenistic sardonyx cameo from Egypt, carved with an allegory of Cleopatra I and dated to around 200 BC. It was one of the treasures amassed by Pope Paul II and then sold by his austere successor, Sixtus IV, to the wealthy banker, Lorenzo de' Medici. The inventory made after Lorenzo's death valued it at 10,000 florins.*

245

XII, this time with the news that a bride had been found for Cesare. It was not, however, Carlotta of Aragon, but rather Charlotte d'Albret, the sister of the King of Navarre and a niece of Louis XII. There were conditions: the pope himself had to provide the dowry of 200,000 ducats and give a red hat to the bride's brother. The couple had been married at the royal château of Blois on 10 May and had consummated their union – whereby Cesare had, according to Johannes Burchard, 'managed to give her eight proofs of his virility'. The news was a welcome relief for the pope: this direct alliance with the King of France would prove advantageous.

On 29 May, to appease the anger of Ferdinand and Isabella when the details of his alliance with France were made public, the pope granted the 'Catholic Kings' an extension of their control over the Church in Spain; they responded in kind, by sending an ambassador to Rome with the offer of the Archbishopric of Valencia, vacant since Cesare has resigned his ecclesiastical posts, for another member of the Borgia family. The pope bestowed it on his great-nephew, Cardinal Juan the younger.

During July, in preparation for Cesare's plans to take over the Romagna region of the Papal States, Alexander VI declared that the rights of the rulers of Camerino, Faenza, Forlì, Imola, Pesaro, Rimini and Urbino were to be forfeited, using the justification that they had not paid their annual census.

With news that Louis XII's armies were crossing the Alps, Cardinal Ascanio Sforza fled Rome on 14 July, on the pretext of going out of the city on a hunting expedition, and joined his brother Ludovico in Milan. The alliance between the pope and France was also causing considerable problems for Alexander VI's own family, two of whom were married to relatives of King Federigo of Naples, whose position, as with that of the Sforzas in Milan, was now under threat. On 2 August Alfonso of Aragon, Lucrezia's husband, left Rome to ride to Naples 'without authorization from the pope'.[15] Six days later Lucrezia and her brother Jofrè left Rome for Spoleto, where Lucrezia was installed as governor.

On 14 August it was reported that Giulia Farnese was reinstalled as Alexander VI's mistress. Just over a week later, on 22 August, the body of a Spanish groom from the household of Cardinal Juan Borgia the younger was found in the Tiber: he had been murdered.[16]

The couple had been married at the royal château of Blois on 10 May.

RIGHT **St Dominic presiding at an *auto-da fé*.** This image of the ritual burning at the stake of a heretic by Pedro Berruguete (c.1450–1504) shows the tribunal under a golden canopy with the saint seated between six judges and twelve inquisitors. The first inquisitions were organized by the Church in France to root out the heretical beliefs of the Waldensians and Cathars during the 13th century. The format was adopted by Ferdinand and Isabella for the Spanish Inquisition ,which prosecuted Jews, Muslims and others in their realm who refused to adopt the Catholic religion – the sign the 'Catholic Kings' required as a demonstration of loyalty from all their subjects. The Spanish Inquisition should not be confused with the Roman Inquisition, set up in the middle of the 16th century as part of papal policy during the Counter Reformation.

**Leonardo da Vinci's
*The Last Supper.***
*Commissioned in 1496
by Ludovico Sforza
for the refectory of the
convent of Santa Maria
delle Grazie, the scene of
Christ eating the Passover
feast with his Apostles
was the traditional choice
for refectories throughout
Christendom. Leonardo's
approach, however, was
far from traditional.
Instead of the usual
focus on the institution
of the Eucharist, this
fresco depicts the earlier
moment when Christ
predicted that one of
those present would
betray him. Moreover,
he also decided to
experiment here with a
new technique, using oil
rather than egg white
as the paint medium
– the experiment was
not a success and the
painting quickly began to
deteriorate.*

Michelangelo's Pietà and French symbolism

Michelangelo's celebrated *Pietà* was commissioned in 1497 by Cardinal Jean Bilhères for his tomb in the chapel of the King of France in St Peter's (the chapel was dedicated to St Petronilla, the legendary daughter of the first pope). The image of the *Pietà* was a favourite with French monarchs, and its appearance in Rome at precisely the time when France was struggling to assert her political presence in the peninsula is symbolic.

This exquisite and poignant image of the Virgin Mary, with the body of her dead son lying on her lap, is prosaically described in the contract with Michelangelo as 'a marble statue to be made at his expense, that is a Virgin Mary dressed with the dead Christ in her arms, as large as if this were a real man'.[17] The price paid, 450 ducats, was to include the cost of the marble and all the Florentine sculptor's labour and expenses for the following 12 months, by which time the statue was to have been completed. Cardinal Jean Bilhères died in 1499.

Meanwhile, letters were arriving daily with news of the progress of Louis XII's armies through Savoy and across the border into the Duchy of Milan. On 1 September Ludovico and Ascanio Sforza fled for the Tyrol, where they would be protected by the Holy Roman Emperor, Maximilian, and five days later the first French troops entered Milan. On 6 October Louis XII made his formal entry into the city at the head of a splendid procession, which included the dukes of Valence (Cesare Borgia), Ferrara and Savoy; cardinals Giuliano della Rovere and Georges d'Amboise; the marquises of Mantua, Monferrato and Saluzzo; and the ambassadors of Genoa, Florence, Siena, Lucca, Pisa and – in place of honour – Venice.

By 1 October, Alexander VI was back in Rome having left for Nepi a week before, where he had held talks with Lucrezia and Jofrè. With the fall of Milan, it was now time for Louis XII to honour his part of the bargain he had made with the pope. Duke Cesare was supplied with 1,800 cavalry and 4,000 infantry under the command of Yves d'Alègre to start his campaign in the Papal States, as well as a loan of 45,000 ducats from Milan to raise more troops. On 7 November, his objective ostensibly achieved, Louis XII left the city to return to France.

On 14 October Lucrezia – now heavily pregnant, following her earlier miscarriage – returned to Rome with her husband Alfonso and brother Jofrè. Alexander VI attended mass in the Sistine Chapel to celebrate Halloween, the eve of the Feast of All Saints, and early the next morning Lucrezia gave birth to a baby boy. He was named Rodrigo in honour of his grandfather.

In early November Alexander VI sent invitations to Europe's rulers to attend a conference in Rome to discuss a crusade against the Turks. On 26 August a sharp reminder had come of the Turkish threat in the form of reports from Venice that 10,000 Turkish horsemen had raided the Venetian mainland, burning villages and killing their inhabitants.

Lucrezia Borgia leaves Rome

On Thursday 8 August [1499] Lucrezia Borgia of Aragon, much-loved daughter of His Holiness, left Rome by the Porta del Popolo to travel to the castle of Spoleto where His Holiness has installed her as governor. She was accompanied on her left by her brother, Jofrè, Prince of Squillace, and preceded by many pack mules. The pope watched the cavalcade from his loggia in the palace. Lucrezia and her brother mounted their horses at the bottom of the steps of St Peter's, then they bowed their heads to the pope with great humility and, after the pope had blessed them three times, they left. The palace guard and the governor of Rome with all his men rode in front of them. There was also a mule laden with a litter, a mattress and a crimson silk cover decorated with flowers, with two white damask cushions and a magnificent canopy. The litter was for Lucrezia to rest on when she was tired of riding, and there were also men with her to carry it.

JOHANNES BURCHARD, *Liber notarum*, PP. 290–1.

251

The christening of Rodrigo of Aragon

The procession began with the papal squires, the papal valets dressed in red, as for the feast of Corpus Christi, followed by musicians, pipers and other musical instruments. Then came two papal squires, the one on the right carrying a golden dish and ewer, a golden salt cellar and a bowl containing soap, and the other on the left carrying a great white beeswax candle, gilded and elegantly worked, that weighed about three pounds. Then came Don Juan Cervillon, a Catalan who had been the captain of the papal guard, carrying the infant on his right arm, covered, as is the tradition, with a piece of gold brocade ornamented with the emblem of the [royal Neapolitan] Order of the Ermine. On his right walked the Governor of Rome with the imperial ambassador on his left. After them, walking in pairs, came the papal priests on the right with the other ambassadors on the left.

JOHANNES BURCHARD, *Liber notarum*, PP. 300–1.

On 6 November, Alexander VI nominated his treasurer-general Francisco Borgia to the see of Cosenza after the death of its bishop three days earlier: in Johannes Burchard's record, the previous incumbent had suddenly 'died of the plague' after being apparently well the day before, on which he had 'stopped at Viterbo, the city of which he was governor and legate, to attend to business. May his soul rest in peace!'[18]

Lucrezia's baby son Rodrigo was baptized a week later, on 11 November, in the chapel of Sixtus IV at St Peter's. It was a very grand ceremony for this first official grandson of the pope. The following day Lucrezia received a valuable present of 'two silver sweetmeat dishes from the College of Cardinals, laden with 200 ducats which were disguised as bonbons'.[19]

On 18 November Duke Cesare returned quietly to Rome and spent three nights at the Vatican in discussion with his father. He left on 21 November to ride to Imola to begin his military campaign. That evening a papal musician was arrested in Rome on a charge of bringing poisoned letters that he had intended to give to the pope. He came from Forlì, another of the targets of Cesare's imminent offensive in the Romagna.

At the end of the month, on 29 November, Lucrezia left the residence where she had been confined for the birth of her baby and went to hear mass at St Peter's, before spending the evening at the Vatican with her father.

Alexander VI attended mass in the Sistine Chapel on 8 December, to celebrate the second Sunday in Advent, accompanied by his nephew the elder Cardinal Juan Borgia, 'who has been suffering from syphilis for two years or more and has not appeared in public for a long time'.[20]

On 17 December Imola surrendered to Cesare's assault and Alexander VI appointed his great-nephew, the younger Cardinal Juan Borgia, as legate to join his son on the campaign. On 19 December the city of Forlì also surrendered, but Caterina Sforza – who had ruled Forlì since the death of her husband Girolamo Riario – remained in possession of the citadel there.

Meanwhile Alexander VI was busy with preparations for the coming year's Jubilee. On 18 December he held a long meeting with the penitentiaries in St Peter's, who would be on duty throughout the year

'The French disease'

It seems to me worth noting that at the same time as the arrival of the French, which marked the beginning of hard times for Italy, there also arrived that illness which the French call 'the Neapolitan pox' and the Italians have named boils, or 'the French disease'. This was because it first appeared among the French when they were in Naples and then they spread it all through Italy as they marched back home. This illness [syphilis], which was unknown here before those times, is so terrible that it must count as another catastrophe that befell us. It manifested itself with hideous boils, which then developed into incurable ulcers, and very bad pains in the joints and nerves. Because the doctors knew little about it they used remedies which often made the patient even worse. It killed men and women of all ages, others becoming deformed and suffering almost continuous pain, and many of those who seemed to be cured often had relapses later, which proved fatal ... but we should absolve the French of any guilt because it is clear that the disease actually came from Spain, and not really from there either because it came from those islands found by Christopher Columbus.

Francesco Guicciardini, *Storia d'Italia*, II, 13.

to hear the confessions of pilgrims. He also appointed clerics to stand by the doors of St Peter, which would be open all day and all night, and commissioned a large chest to be built with three different locks and installed in the basilica to receive the pilgrims' offerings.

On 24 December, Christmas Eve, Alexander VI was carried to St Peter's dressed in his full robes for the ceremony to open the so-called 'golden door'. Johannes Burchard described how the pope:

> Having been given a hammer by ... Tommaso Matarazzo, the master mason in charge of the fabric of the basilica, he hit the wall three times at an opening which had been prepared in the middle of the door, and the bricks fell down. Then he returned to his chair while the workmen demolished the wall, a job that took nearly half an hour, during which time the choir sang continually. [21]

Alexander VI knelt briefly in prayer and then walked through the door into the basilica, carrying his lighted taper while the choir sang the *Te Deum*.

1500

ON 1ST JANUARY Alexander VI went to Castel Sant'Angelo to watch Lucrezia leave her palace to visit San Giovanni in Laterano:

> Her escort comprised around a hundred horses, of which about fifty preceded her. The bishop of Carignola, Pedro Gamboa, rode before here with a noble baron on his right and the one-eyed Orsino Orsini, the husband of Giulia Farnese, on his left. Lucrezia had on her left her husband, Alfonso of Aragon, the Duke of Bisceglie. Behind them came Rodrigo Borgia, the captain of the papal guard and brother to Cardinal Juan Borgia the younger. He had a lady on his right. Then came a number of ladies-in-waiting, each with a noble on their left.[22]

The sacking of Bondeno

His Majesty *King Louis of France left Milan to return to France ... and he sent 6,000 troops down the Po on a barge to attack the state of Forlì ... to aid Duke Cesare Valentino, son of our pope, Alexander VI, who intends to give Imola and Forlì to his son ... when the 6,000 soldiers arrived in Bondeno [near Ferrara], they sacked the outskirts of the town and destroyed a tavern, then they entered the town and pillaged the castle and took anything they could carry out of the houses and killed many people including Battista Bendedio, a doctor of law from Ferrara, and the chaplain of the church, and two other priests; about twelve were killed and many more were wounded.*

BERNARDINO ZAMBOTTI, *Diario Ferrarese*, P. 294.

ABOVE **Preaching of the Antichrist,** *painted by Luca Signorelli. 'For there shall arise false Christs, and false prophets, and [they] shall shew great signs and wonders; insomuch that, if it were possible, they shall deceive the very elect': Signorelli's interpretation of St Matthew's words, commissioned in 1500 for the cathedral at Orvieto, shows soldiers massacring innocent people and stripping the church in the background of its treasures. The Antichrist, with piles of these sacred objects at his feet, is speaking the persuasive words whispered in his ear by the demon at his*

shoulder. In his audience, which consists of people from all walks of life – wealthy merchants, poor labourers, old men, young girls, even monks and nuns – are many portraits that would have been recognized at the time: the young bearded man with fashionably curled hair seen in profile on the far edge of the group on the left is generally thought to be Cesare Borgia.

OVERLEAF **Sword scabbard.** *Constructed of calf's leather, this was made in northern Italy around 1498, probably for Cesare Borgia.*

All of this 'for the glory of the Holy Roman Church!' the master-of-ceremonies added. The following month, on 12 February, Lucrezia bought the fief of Sermoneta, with its castles and villages, for 24,000 ducats, 'which she paid to the Apostolic Chamber in cash'.[23]

On 2 January Alexander VI issued the regulations that would govern the plenary indulgences, which were to be granted to all those who made the pilgrimage to Rome during the Jubilee year, in forgiveness of their sins. Early in the evening on 12 January, after vespers in St Peter's, the precious relic of the Holy Lance was shown to the congregation.

Duke Ercole d'Este of Ferrara felt unable to attend the Jubilee 'because of the danger of the fighting that is taking place in the Romagna where Duke Cesare … is attacking Imola and Forlì, and also because he has heard news that soldiers are on their way from Germany with Duke Ludovico Sforza to reconquer the Duchy of Milan.'[24]

News from Cesare's campaign arrived in Rome on 14 January: that Caterina Sforza had finally surrendered the castle at Forlì; Burchard reported that she was taken prisoner, and that 'all the others have been killed'.[25] The French soldiers demanded a ransom for Caterina, which Cesare paid; he then had her conveyed to Rome. There she was imprisoned first in the Vatican and then, after she had tried to escape, in the more secure but less salubrious prisons at Castel Sant'Angelo.

A few days later another courier arrived with news for Alexander VI that his great-nephew, Cardinal Juan Borgia the younger, had died of a fever at Fossombrone while on his way to Forlì to congratulate his cousin Cesare.

With Forlì secured, Cesare's next objective was Pesaro, the fief belonging to his former brother-in-law Giovanni Sforza. While on the road south, however, Yves d'Alègre and his soldiers were recalled by Louis XII to fight Ludovico Sforza, who was approaching Milan with the Duke of Saxony at the head of a large number of imperial troops. Duke Cesare now informed Alexander VI that he was making his way back to Rome.

On 27 January Alexander VI gave an audience to the ambassador of the King and Queen of Navarre, Jean d'Albret and Catherine de Foix, who addressed the pope as a relative of his masters. Alexander VI agreed that he was related to the royal house of Navarre – the queen could trace her lineage back to the ancient Kings of Aragon, from whom the Borgias also claimed descent – and added, wittily, that a new marriage had made the kinship even closer.

During February, one of the papal grooms killed a pelican on a beach near the port; when they opened its beak they found a fish weighing six pounds inside.[26]

On 2 February the trial took place of Alexander VI's head of household, Pedro de Aranda, the Jewish convert to Christianity who was under arrest for heresy.

A few days later came the news that Milan had rebelled against the French and that Ludovico Sforza had entered the city in triumph.

On 26 February Alexander VI sent orders to all ambassadors in Rome, as well as officials of the government and the curia, to assemble that afternoon at the Porta del Popolo to receive Duke Cesare on his return to Rome. The cardinals were ordered to send their courtiers. The entry of the triumphant duke was impressive: strings of packhorses, all with new black caparisons, 800 soldiers carrying banners emblazoned with Cesare's coat-of-arms and 100 grooms dressed in black velvet proceeded along the streets of Rome; after them rode the duke's brother Jofrè and his brother-in-law Alfonso of Aragon, then Cesare himself, also austerely dressed in black, with the gold chain of the French Order of St Michael hanging round his neck, flanked by cardinals Giovanni Battista Orsini and Alessandro Farnese; and finally came all those officials who had assembled at the gate.

A trial for heresy

The order to interrogate the Bishop of Calahorra [Pedro de Aranda] and to prepare the case against him was given to Pietro da Vicenza, the Bishop of Cesena ... from what I have been able to find out from one of the auditors, Pedro de Aranda called more than a hundred witnesses in his defence, but there was not one who did not speak against him. According to their evidence, Pedro professed to believe, among other things that the law of Moses rested on one prince while the Christian law rested on three – the Father, the Son and the Holy Ghost. Pedro also said that Christ, if he were God, would not suffer the Passion; that indulgences had no value and produced nothing but had been invented by the papacy for its own interests; that neither hell nor purgatory existed, solely paradise. Moreover, when he prayed he said 'Glory to the Father' but omitted to add 'to the Son and to the Holy Ghost'. He also ate his lunch before celebrating mass, ate meat on Fridays and on other days when it was forbidden.

JOHANNES BURCHARD, *Liber notarum*, P. 322.

In commemoration of his victories in the Romagna, Cesare now adopted the motto of Julius Caesar – *Aut Caesar aut nihil*, 'Either emperor or nothing'. The day after the entry into Rome –the Thursday of the last week of Carnival – the traditional display of floats in Piazza Navona this year celebrated the triumph of Julius Caesar, in Cesare's honour.

On 11 March Alexander VI held a secret consistory to which he invited all the ambassadors to remind them that, the previous October, he had asked them to inform their masters of the dangerous threat posed by the Turks, but that so far he had received little response.

For the Feast of the Annunciation, 25 March, Alexander VI missed the traditional papal mass at Santa Maria sopra Minerva and the customary handing out of dowries to poor girls.

On the fourth Sunday in Lent, 29 March, the pope announced to the cardinals assembled in the Sala del Pappagallo that this year he was giving the Golden

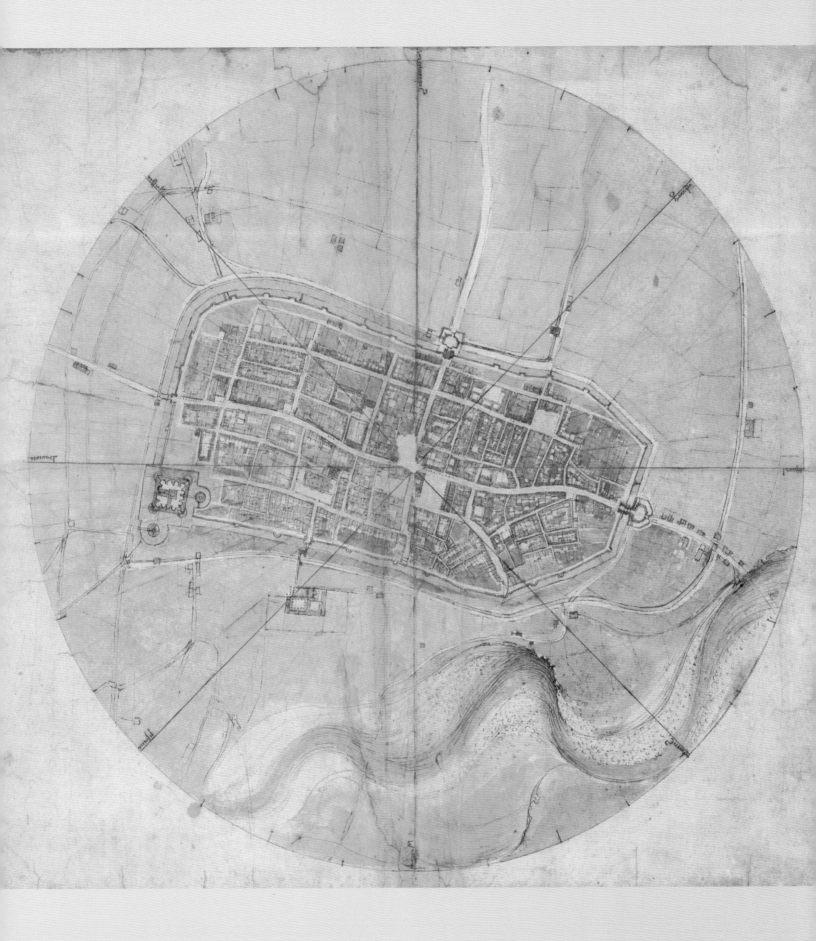

Rose to 'his well-beloved son, Cesare' and furthermore would appoint him Captain-General of the Church. The pope was then carried on his chair to St Peter's, preceded by the duke. They heard mass together in the basilica, where the pope ceremonially draped his son with the mantle of his new office and gave him the Golden Rose. For the ceremony:

> The duke wore a ceremonial brocade robe which came down to his knees; a papal squire walked in front of the valets carrying the insignia of the Captain-General, the mantle and the hat. The hat was made of crimson velvet, 18 inches high and trimmed with ermine; around the edge it had a band of gold brocade decorated with four buttons, which were pearls the size of walnuts; on each of the four corners and on the lower parts was a broad fringe of ermine, which hung down from two of the corners in long flaps; on top there was a dove made of pearls and from it four lines of pearls descended down to the fringe.[27]

On 13 April, the Monday before Easter, Alexander VI visited the four great basilicas of Rome – St Peter's, San Paolo fuori le mura, San Giovanni in Laterano, where he granted Jubilee indulgences to all the attendants of the cardinals present, and Santa Maria Maggiore.

During the following night, of 14 April, a courier arrived with news that Louis XII had achieved a great victory on 8 April at Novara, just west of Milan, helped by the defection of the Swiss mercenaries in Ludovico Sforza's army, and that the Duke of Milan was now a prisoner of the French.

Late on the evening of 16 April, news arrived of Alexander VI's formerly close ally Cardinal Ascanio Sforza. 'An envoy of Carlo Orsini arrived from Lombardy and told His Holiness

LEFT **Plan of Imola,** by Leonardo da Vinci. Commissioned as part of his job as Cesare Borgia's chief engineer and fortifications expert, this detailed bird's-eye plan of Imola shows the layout of this heavily fortified city – its walls, gates, and fortresses. Imola had been an important stronghold in Roman times, and its origins are still visible in the regular pattern of its streets. Built across the Via Emilia, the Ancient Roman road that bisects the city, it guarded this important route linking Milan and the ports in southern Italy.

Carnival festivities

On the Friday of Carnival, 28 February [1500], the Jews ran their race as usual from the sewer by the palace of Cardinal Ascanio Sforza to the Vatican palace. The same day the boys ran their race from the Borgo to the same palace. On the Saturday the bulls were taken to the Capitol hill and on the Sunday they held the bull race at Monte Testaccio; two of the animals broke free from their chains without wounding anybody, and they swam across the Tiber to the opposite bank. They also held the races of the Barbary horses and the mares, but the bolts of cloth were not awarded. On the Monday, 2 March, the old men ran their race to the piazza in front of St Peter's and then the mares ran. On Tuesday 3 March the asses' race was run, then that of the buffalo, both to the piazza of St Peter's. On Tuesday 5 March, the illustrious Duke Cesare began his visits to the reverend cardinals; he took no bishop nor prelate with him, just his servants and courtiers.

JOHANNES BURCHARD, Liber notarum, PP. 326–7.

Italy prostrate

Thanks to foreign troops, *Italy has been conquered by Charles VIII, pillaged by Louis XII, raped by Ferdinand of Spain and ridiculed by the Swiss.*

NICCOLÒ MACHIAVELLI, *The Prince*, CHAPTER 12.

that Cardinal Ascanio [Sforza] had been captured on Palm Sunday in a castle near Piacenza. The cardinal had fled with 600 horsemen and all his goods, worth 200,000 ducats, which were seized as booty. The cardinal himself has been taken with a dozen of his men to Venice, where he is being kept under close guard.' Johannes Burchard added: 'it is said that the pope tipped the courier 100 ducats for this news'.[28]

On Easter Day, 19 April, Alexander VI celebrated high mass in St Peter's and gave his customary Easter blessing to the crowds of pilgrims in the piazza outside where, it was estimated, as many as 200,000 had gathered to witness this special event. Johannes Burchard obtained, from one of the penitentiaries hearing confessions, examples of the 'varied and often strange' sins admitted.

LEFT **Cesare Borgia.** *An engraving by an anonymous artist showing the duke at the height of his powers.*
ABOVE RIGHT **Silver pilgrim's badge.** *Badges like this would have been bought by thousands of pilgrims in Rome for the 1500 Jubilee. Marked with the arms of Alexander VI, it depicts the towel with its miraculous imprint of Christ's features used by St Veronica to wipe his face; holding the towel are St Peter and St Paul, who had preached in Rome.*

On 12 May the French ambassador, on his way to Rome, was attacked on the road near Viterbo by a gang of robbers; he was unharmed but one of his courtiers and a servant were both seriously wounded. On hearing of the crime, the pope sent the head of the civic guard to Viterbo to arrest the brigands, several of whom were brought to Rome. On 24 May Alexander VI issued a proclamation banishing all members of the Corsi family, notorious bandits who were known to have made many attacks on the pilgrims arriving in such numbers for the Jubilee. On 27 May, the eve of the Feast of the Ascension, 18 criminals were hanged on the Ponte Sant'Angelo for crimes against these pilgrims. One of them was:

> ... a doctor, a surgeon at the hospital attached to San Giovanni in Laterano. He used to leave the hospital early each morning, dressed in a short robe and carrying a crossbow, with which he proceeded to murder anyone he could and take their money. It is also said that a confessor at the said hospital, when told by someone in confession that they had money, he informed the said doctor who then killed the man and the two shared the money between them.[29]

Also during May, Charlotte d'Albret, wife of Cesare Borgia, gave birth to a baby girl, whom they named Louise.

Alexander VI formally declared war against the Turks on 1 June, in a papal bull that he ordered to be read, in the local

Confessions during the Holy Year

One man *contracted marriage with a young girl and, having had carnal knowledge of her, he moved in with her. Then he contracted another marriage with another, and again with a third, and a fourth, and he had four wives, all living. There was a similar case of a woman with four living husbands. A Benedictine monk, after taking holy orders, contracted and consummated a marriage with a girl; they lived together for some thirty years and had six children; when his wife died, he married another, whom he knew carnally and lived with her for seven years, but admitted his sin when he came for the Jubilee ... A priest had carnal knowledge of his niece and she became pregnant and gave birth to a child; the priest baptized the baby even though he was the father, then he killed her and buried her in the stables; he continued to say mass for another 18 years.*

JOHANNES BURCHARD, *Liber notarum*, P. 360.

261

language, on a feast day in all dioceses of Christendom. The crusade was to be financed by a levy imposed on all benefices, including those held by the cardinals, and by a tax on Jews.

Three weeks later, on 24 June, a bullfight was held in the piazza in front of St Peter's, to celebrate the Feast of St John the Baptist. As Burchard recorded, 'After lunch five or six bulls were let in to the arena so that they could be cut with swords and then pierced with arrows by the picadors. Duke Cesare was on horseback and cut them many times, and others joined him. The fight lasted until all the bulls were dead.'[30]

While watching another bullfight, four days later, Alexander VI had a lucky escape when an iron lantern fell from the bell-tower of St Peter's, landing at the pope's feet on the balcony where he was seated. On 29 June he survived another mishap, this time in his own apartments. After attending mass in St Peter's to celebrate the Feast of St Peter and St Paul, the pope had returned to the Vatican and was chatting with Cardinal Juan Lopez and a secretary when a violent hailstorm erupted very suddenly, with great gusts of wind. The cardinal and the secretary went to close the windows of the room and, as they were doing so, a chimney collapsed in the room above them, bringing the ceiling crashing down onto Alexander VI. The cry went out: 'The pope is dead!' Amazingly, he emerged from

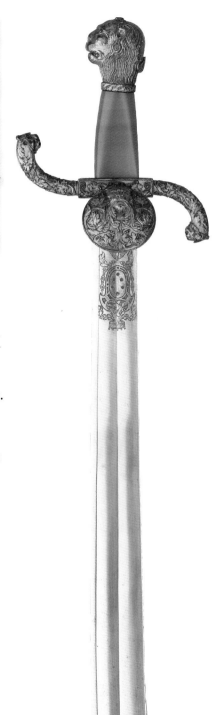

Murder and mutilation

That same day [18 August 1500] a man from Rieti whose wife had become the mistress of Luca Dolce, a valet of Cardinal Domenico della Rovere ... and as Dolce was passing the Palazzo Massimi, the husband stabbed him to death and cut off his penis. He was taken into the Massimi palace, but died three or four hours later.

JOHANNES BURCHARD, *Liber notarum*, PP. 350–1.

the rubble concussed but otherwise unhurt except for a few cuts on his hand and right arm. 'He was lifted out of the chair onto his feet and went to an adjoining room, where his domestic servants applied salves. Then the city and the cardinals were informed that the pope was out of danger.'[31]

Lucrezia Borgia's husband, Alfonso of Aragon, was not so fortunate. During the evening of 15 July he was stabbed by a group of men on the steps of St Peter's and badly wounded. Fighting off the attackers, who rode away, Alfonso's servants dragged him into the Vatican and he was taken to the safety of the papal apartments, where he was nursed back to health by his wife and his sister Sancia. A doctor was sent specially from Naples to treat him and Lucrezia herself supervised his meals. As far as Alfonso was concerned, his brother-in-law Cesare was responsible for organizing the attack; furthermore, while convalescing, Alfonso tried to shoot Cesare, whom he spotted walking unattended in the Vatican gardens. A few days later, on 18 August, Miguel de Corella – one of Cesare's Spanish courtiers – strangled Alfonso in his bed. Alfonso's servants were then arrested on the charge of conspiring against Cesare but soon released from Castel Sant'Angelo,

LEFT **Oak leaves and acorns.** *This exquisitely detailed drawing, done in red chalk by Leonardo da Vinci, reflects his interest in the forms and textures of the natural world. An oak tree was also the emblem of the della Rovere family.*

RIGHT **Ceremonial sword.** *Swords like this, with their steel blades and ornamental gilded grips, were expensive weapons – a good sword cost over 20 ducats. This example has a grip made of agate decorated with a gilded pommel in the shape of a lion, and would have been used for hunting or for display.*

263

and the whole affair was hushed up by Alexander VI. Lucrezia, deeply upset by the murder of her husband and by the role played by her brother, left Rome with 600 horsemen on 31 August and settled in Nepi, with her baby boy.

On the same day as Alfonso's murder, the valet of Cardinal Domenico della Rovere fell victim to brutal crime of passion.

On 10 September news arrived in Rome that the Venetian port of Modon in the Adriatic had been taken by the Turks. Alexander VI levied taxes on all the cardinals to finance a fleet – exempting those whose countries were already under Turkish attack – and on the hospitals of Rome, raising a total of 45,376 ducats.[32]

These taxes might have been destined for the crusade – as were the funds left in the coffers of the churches of Rome by the hoards of pious Jubilee pilgrims – but how much of this money was used for that purpose remained murky. During the autumn Alexander VI's main priority was raising funds for Cesare,

Providing for the papal son

At this time [1500] *the pope did much towards the aim he shared with his son, Duke Cesare. He created 12 [sic] cardinals, choosing not those most suitable for the dignity but those who could pay the most money; he also proclaimed the Holy Year which brought great numbers of pilgrims to Rome, notably from beyond the Alps. He also offered indulgences to those who did not come to Rome but who paid instead. All this, along with the money he removed by other means from the temporal and spiritual funds of the Church, he sent to his son.*

FRANCESCO GUICCIARDINI, *Storia d'Italia*, V, 2.

Alexander VI's price list for red hats

Diego Hurtado de Mendoza, the Archbishop of Seville	*25,000 ducats*
Jaime Serra, Archbishop of Oristano	*5,000 ducats*
Thomas Bakócz, Archbishop of Esztergom	*20,000 ducats*
Pedro Isvalies, Archbishop of Reggio and Governor of Rome	*7,000 ducats*
Francisco Borgia, Archbishop of Cosenza and papal treasurer	*12,000 ducats*
Juan Vera, Archbishop of Salerno	*4,000 ducats*
Ludovico Podocatharo, Bishop of Capaccio and papal secretary	*5,000 ducats*
Antonio Trivulzio, Bishop of Como	*20,000 ducats*
Giambattista Ferreri, Bishop of Modena and datary	*22,000 ducats*
Amanieu d'Albret, brother-in-law of Duke Cesare	*10,000 ducats*
Marco Corner, of Venice	*20,000 ducats*
Pedro Luis Borgia, cousin of Duke Cesare	*10,000 ducats*

JOHANNES BURCHARD, *Liber notarum*, P. 353.

ABOVE **The Healing of the Possessed Man** *by the Patriarch of Grado,*
by Vittore Carpaccio. With the depiction of the miracle relegated to a
private room in the upper far left of the scene, this painting was above
all a celebration of Venetian wealth, set at the heart of the commercial
district at the Rialto. Carpaccio skilfully captured the movements of the
gondoliers as they expertly ferried their passengers through the busy traffic
on the Grand Canal, and the forest of ornamental chimneys that marked
the palaces of rich patrician merchants along its banks. Among the crowds
of onlookers strolling along the waterfront or gathered under the portico
are young elegantly dressed Venetians gossiping idly, older businessmen
wearing plain black outfits, Greek merchants in their black broad-brimmed
hats, turbanned Muslim traders, and government officials in their red robes
of office, who exercised strict control over all aspects of Venetian life; and
the Rialto bridge itself, with the pulleys that enabled the central section
to be raised to allow tall ships to sail through (this old wooden bridge was
replaced by the present solid stone structure in the 16th century).

Virgin and Child with St Jerome and Bernardino da Feltre.
Although not a saint (he was beatified in 1653), Bernardino da Feltre was a Franciscan preacher who made his reputation with forceful sermons against the evils of usury and the outrageous rates of interest charged by commercial bankers. To help the poor and needy, who often needed to borrow money to tide them over to pay day, he worked hard to establish a system of Christian pawnshops, known as the Monte di Pietà, in towns across northern Italy. These 'banks' acquired their capital from charitable donations from the rich and were able to offer small loans at low interest rates. The loans were secured with the pledge of household goods – a piece of jewellery, a nice coat, even a cooking pot or an old mattress, all could be pawned, though the size of the loan would depend on the value of the pledge. The artist was Filippo Mazzola (fl. 1490–1505).

267

who was amassing his own mercenary army to complete his conquests in the Papal States. At a secret consistory on 18 August, and at another a week later, the pope tried in vain to persuade the College of Cardinals to allow him to create cardinals. He did succeed, however, on 28 September, when he nominated 13 men, all of whom paid substantial sums for their prestige, raising over 160,000 ducats. Cesare was careful to show his gratitude by hosting a banquet in his apartments in the Vatican after they had received their red hats. Among the new cardinals were Pedro Luis Borgia, the pope's great-nephew and brother of Cardinal Juan who had died in January, and two of Alexander VI's cousins, Francisco Borgia and Jaime Serra. Two more Spaniards, Pedro Isvalies and Juan Vera, had long been part of Cesare's court. There were also red hats for Cesare's brother-in-law, Aimery d'Albret, and Alexander VI's physician, Ludovico Podocatharo. The new intake also meant that 60 per cent of the college had now been created by Alexander VI.

Turbulence in the Romagna

The lords who ruled the states of the Romagna, before they were extinguished by Pope Alexander VI, were examples of every type of villainy, using the slightest pretext as an excuse for murder and pillage. This was the fault of the lords, not, as they claimed, of the inhabitants. Because the lords were poor but wanted to live like rich nobles, they were obliged to steal, which they did in various dishonest ways.

NICCOLÒ MACHIAVELLI, *Discorsi*, CHAPTER 29.

October [1500]. *Duke Cesare Valentino, son of Pope Alexander VI has arrived with 40 squads of men-at-arms in Romagna and the Marche; they have taken Rimini and the Lord of Rimini has fled, and they have taken Cesena and Pesaro. He has many cavalrymen and infantry including French soldiers, 2,000 Swiss, also Burgundians. And because of this the Bolognese are taking up their arms and Giovanni Bentivoglio has surrounded himself with a large armed guard for fear of being driven out of Bologna.*

BERNARDINO ZAMBOTTI, *Diario Ferrarese*, P. 301.

December [1500]. *Duke Cesare's troops who were camped around Faenza have moved because of the heavy snow and severe frosts, and also because more than 800 of them have been killed in the fighting. The men of Faenza are defending vigorously and there are 2,000 brave soldiers in the city. The town of Brisighella has signed an agreement with the duke, who has retired to the castle at Forlì for his safety and his men have set up their winter camp around Imola.*

BERNARDINO ZAMBOTTI, *Diario Ferrarese*, P. 302.

That autumn, Venice made Cesare Borgia an honorary citizen, effectively voicing the city's support for the next stage of his campaign in northern Italy. On 2 October he marched at the head of an army of 10,000 men, including Spanish and French troops, as well as mercenaries under Italian captains such as Vitellozzo Vitelli (Lord of Città di Castello), Paolo Orsini and Gianpaolo Baglione (Lord of Perugia).

On 5 October Alexander VI appointed legates to send to the rulers of Spain, Portugal, Germany, Hungary, Denmark and Sweden to collect funds promised for the crusade. He also asked the cardinals to pay the taxes they owed, and ordered Gonsalvo de Cordoba, who was in charge of 65 Spanish ships, to join the fleet assembling at Venice.

On 27 October Pesaro surrendered to Cesare after Giovanni Sforza had fled the city. Duke Cesare moved on to take possession of Rimini, which had also capitulated peacefully. His next objective was Faenza, whose ruler, Manfredo Astorre, had no intention of giving up his state and fought off Cesare's first attack. With the weather deteriorating, Cesare retired now to Cesena, where he would spend the winter consolidating his authority in this capital of his new state.

On 3 November in Rome the Tiber flooded, 'to such an extent that it was impossible to reach the Vatican palace even on horseback,' recorded Johannes Burchard. The great river:

ABOVE **The Arch of Augustus, Rimini.** *An important port on the Adriatic Sea in Roman times, Rimini was founded in 268 BC at the meeting point of the Via Flaminia and the Via Emilia. Evidence of her illustrious history is still visible in the magnificent triumphal arch, built by Emperor Augustus in 27 BC to commemorate his restoration of the Via Flaminia, and five stone arches of the great bridge that carries the Via Emilia across the River Marecchia, which was finished by Augustus's successor, Tiberius. In 1295 Rimini came under the rule of the Malatesta family, who extended the city's power in the hinterland and remained in power until the city was captured by the troops of Cesare Borgia.*

... continued to rise until the next day when the wind changed direction. It was still impossible to get to the palace by horse on 6 November, and it was necessary to hire one of the 12 boats at the wharf by the Ponte Sant'Angelo. The water rose to within three metres of the mark made on Castel Sant'Angelo during the great flood of 1495 ... on the island of San Bartolomeo [Isola Tiberina] however, many houses have collapsed as their foundations have been washed away by the flood.[33]

In fact the waters reached to within a metre of the great flood of 1495 but quickly subsided, doing only limited damage.

As the year gradually drew to its close, on 11 November, Louis XII and Ferdinand II signed the Treaty of Granada regarding the long-disputed question of the Kingdom of Naples. It was to be divided between Spain, France and Venice.

𝕴n 1498 the succession to the French throne of Louis XII, a sovereign with a legitimate claim not only to the Kingdom of Naples but also to the Duchy of Milan, had made the political scenario considerably more complicated for Pope Alexander VI. Over the next three years he had successfully exploited the situation by agreeing to recognize Louis XII's claims; in return he had obtained a royal bride for Cesare and French support for his son's post-ecclesiastical ambitions to create a duchy in the Romagna. Alexander VI had also provided financial support for his son's campaign by redirecting funds intended for the crusade, notably the offerings of pious pilgrims in Rome for the Holy Year and the huge sums he had charged for the conferring of cardinals' hats.

As for Alexander VI himself, now 70 years old, not only had he survived two potentially fatal accidents during 1500 but, in the Venetian ambassador's opinion, 'looks younger every day. He never lets his worries keep him from sleep, is continually cheerful, and never does anything unless he wants to; his children are his main concern, other matters do not trouble him.'[34]

270

RIGHT **Louis XII triptych.** *This expensive enamelled altarpiece made in Limoges was commissioned for the royal chapel by the king, probably to celebrate his marriage to Anne of Brittany. The central panel depicts the Annunciation, taking place in a loggia. On the left is King Louis XII accompanied by King Louis IX of France, the king who led the Sixth Crusade in 1248, died of dysentery in Tunis and was canonized in 1297; on the right is the new queen, accompanied by her name-saint, St Anne. In the corners are the couple's coats-of-arms, while the charming border panels depict angels praying and playing musical instruments.*

Cesare and Lucrezia Borgia

Conquests in Battle and in Love

1501–1503

As the new century got underway, Cesare's territorial ambitions continued to prosper, thanks to the substantial financial and political support he received from his father, whose assiduous efforts on behalf of the Borgia family remained undimmed. And Alexander VI now had another instrument he could use to bolster his family's power in the shape of the recently widowed Lucrezia. Aged only 20, she was still eminently capable of bearing children, and of contracting another marriage of strategic advantage to the Borgia dynasty.

1501

ON 6 JANUARY, the Feast of the Epiphany, Alexander VI arrived late for mass in the Sistine Chapel and the sermon was cancelled: it was to have been given by the procurator of the Servite Order, 'who everybody thinks is dull and boring' recorded Johannes Burchard.[1] That evening, after the religious relic of Veronica's Towel had been shown to the congregation, the golden door which Alexander VI had opened to mark the start of the Holy Year was now ceremonially bricked up again.

On 22 January the French military commander Yves d'Alègre and 1,000 soldiers passed through Reggio, where they refused to pay for their food and pillaged the countryside. They were on their way to help Duke Cesare at the siege of Faenza, a favour from Louis XII in return for which Cesare had agreed to fight with the French in the invasion of Naples planned by the king for later that year.

PREVIOUS PAGE **Cesare Borgia.** *One of a series of portraits of famous men commissioned in the 1550s by Cosimo I, Duke of Florence, from the painter Cristofano dell'Altissimo to decorate his study. This profile study shows Cesare as a duke, dressed in secular clothes, including a finely detailed linen shirt.*

ABOVE **Bust of a warrior,** *by Leonardo da Vinci. This famous drawing, which dates from around 1480, shows a soldier dressed in magnificent armour, its details based on an antique relief.*

RIGHT **Elisabetta Gonzaga, Duchess of Urbino,** *painted c.1504 by Raphael. The sister of Francesco Gonzaga, Marquis of Mantua, Elisabetta was betrothed to Guidobaldo da Montefeltro in 1476 at the age of 15 and married two years later. As Duchess of Urbino, she presided over an elegantly cultured court, described in Baldassare Castiglione's* The Courtier.

Target practice during Carnival

During Carnival this year, and almost every day around Candlemas, a stake about five feet high was planted in the ground, some forty feet in front of the image of the Holy Angel on a corner of the steps at the entrance to St Peter's. On the top of the stake was a little wooden statue of a man with an iron shield in front of his chest, which leaned slightly to the left, and in his left hand he held a baton which was about two feet long, with two plaited cords, some three or four feet long, attached to its point, from which hung two large wooden balls. The courtiers used this to practice with their lances. When the mannequin was hit, it moved and the wooden balls hit the jouster rather harder than the jouster hit the little shield.

JOHANNES BURCHARD, *Liber notarum*, PP. 363–4.

In February, Dorotea Caracciolo, a lady-in-waiting to Elisabetta Gonzaga, Duchess of Urbino, was travelling north to Venice where she was to be married, when 'she was abducted by some 20 riders and removed from her companions. The Venetian government asked the duke to have her released but he said that he did not know who had taken her, nor where she was. But the bridegroom, knowing what Duke Cesare was like, threatened reprisals for the injury done to him.'[2]

On 5 April Alexander VI gave an audience to the ambassador of Grand Duke Alexander of Lithuania, who presented the pope with a costly collection of sable, ermine, marten and other furs, as well as two gold cups; the master-of-ceremonies reported that the pope had 'much appreciated the gift'.[3]

Alexander was absent from mass in the Sistine Chapel on 17 April because, it was said, 'of the rumours circulating that many of Duke Cesare's soldiers have been killed at Faenza'.[4] But a courier arrived in Rome early in the evening of 26 April with the news that Cesare had finally taken the city. A few days later came further news, that Cesare had forced Giovanni Bentivoglio, Lord of Bologna, to surrender his border fortress, Castel Bolognese. The pope now summoned his son back to Rome, but Cesare, instead of returning directly, moved on towards Florence, setting up his camp ten miles from the city gates. Dissuaded by Louis XII from a direct attack on Florence, which was a loyal ally of the French, Cesare made an alliance with the government, which agreed to pay him 36,000 florins a year, and he then moved on to menace Piombino. A Florentine coppersmith recorded how 'Duke Valentino ... travelled through our countryside

RIGHT **Vitellozzo Vitelli,** *painted c.1505 by Luca Signorelli. Following in the tradition of his family, who were the lords of Città di Castello and had built up an enviable reputation for bravery and boldness on the battlefield, Vitellozzo became a mercenary soldier fighting for the French and then for Florence. When his brother, Paolo, was charged with treachery by the Florentines and hanged from the Palazzo della Signoria in 1499, Vitellozzo took service in Cesare Borgia's army to seek revenge. Despite the plain black civilian clothes in which Vitellozzo is depicted here, Signorelli has managed to convey the hard eyes and powerful physique that made him such an intimidating opponent.*

A cardinal's hairstyle

When Cardinal Pedro Luis Borgia *arrived at Santa Maria del Popolo … he entered the convent and went to the apartments which had been prepared for him. When I went to see him I suggested calling a barber to cut his hair because it was well below his ears, and also to widen his tonsure which was very small and rather irregular. The cardinal replied that his hair and his tonsure were fine as they were. I decided not to reply and left the room.*

JOHANNES BURCHARD, *Liber notarum*, P. 370.

attacking everyone he found. He stopped near Prato with his troops, which numbered between 7,000 and 8,000 on horses and on foot. They stayed for four to six days, trampling the fields, thieving and doing all sorts of harm, and leaving a huge amount of damage.'[5]

During May Alexander VI issued a papal bull investing Cesare as hereditary ruler of the fiefs he had conquered and crowned his son's achievements by conferring on him the title of Duke of the Romagna.

On 7 May the immensely wealthy Venetian Cardinal Zen died. His will left 25,000 ducats to charity, one half of the rest to the Church and the other half, rumoured to be 100,000 ducats, to Venice for war against the Turks. But Alexander VI annulled the will and appropriated the funds for his own purposes.[6]

Meanwhile, French troops were converging on Rome for Louis XII's campaign to capture Naples, and a camp was set up for them outside the city walls. Food and drink were sent out to the camp, as well as 16 prostitutes for the comfort of the men.

On 17 June Cardinal Pedro Luis Borgia entered Rome with the usual pomp, and the same evening Duke Cesare arrived in secret at the Vatican for talks with his father, having left Vitellozzo Vitelli in charge of the siege of Piombino.

Alexander VI watched from the loggia at Castel Sant'Angelo, with some relief, as 12,000 soldiers, 2,000 cavalry and the 26 gun carriages of the French army left Rome on 28 June. The next day the pope invested Louis XII as King of Naples. On 4 July Cesare left to join the campaign, where he soon received news that Piombino had

The conquest of Capua

Late last night *the pope was informed of the taking of Capua by Duke Cesare … the fall of the city was due to the treason of one inhabitant, named Fabrizio, who secretly opened the gates for the duke's troops. They killed this Fabrizio, and about 3,000 soldiers and 200 cavalrymen. They also killed the priests without mercy, all the monks and nuns whether in churches or monasteries, and also all the women they found. Many young girls were cruelly raped, and the dead numbered over six thousand.*

JOHANNES BURCHARD, *Liber notarum*, PP. 372–3.

278

capitulated to Vitellozzo Vitelli. During the night of 25 July news arrived in Rome that Capua had fallen and that many inhabitants had been massacred – some said Cesare was responsible for the atrocities, but others blamed the French.

On 27 July Alexander VI left Rome for a trip to Sermoneta and other places. He was away until 5 August, leaving his daughter Lucrezia in charge of papal affairs during his absence, with permission to open his correspondence. Although it was common practice among rulers to give their wives such responsibilities, Lucrezia's presence in the papal apartments in the Vatican caused no little surprise to visitors.

In August Louis XII accepted the surrender of King Federigo and occupied Naples. The deposed Federigo would spend the rest of his life in exile, in France.

On 1 September Alexander VI issued a papal bull legitimizing Giovanni Borgia, who had been born in June 1498, as the son of Cesare. A second bull, issued in secret and only to be made public if necessary, legitimized the boy as the son of Alexander VI himself, born during his pontificate. However, the real origins of Giovanni were widely known at the time: Johannes Burchard straightforwardly described him that year as 'the son that the pope had by a Roman woman during his pontificate'.[7]

279

ABOVE **Ercole I d'Este,** *painted by Dosso Dossi. The third brother to succeed their father, Niccolò III, as ruler of Ferrara, Ercole I secured the Este dynasty with his marriage to Eleonora of Aragon, daughter of King Ferrante I of Naples. She proved an excellent duchess, taking charge of Ferrara while her husband was away fighting, and producing six children who lived to adulthood. Ercole I made prestigious alliances for these children: Isabella was married to Francesco Gonzaga, Marquis of Mantua; Beatrice to Ludovico Sforza, Duke of Milan; and his heir, Alfonso, to Ludovico's niece Anna, though she died in childbirth soon afterwards. His second son, Ippolito, was made a cardinal by Alexander VI.*

Meanwhile, during the summer Alexander VI had been busy negotiating a new husband for Lucrezia to strengthen his alliance with France. His choice of Alfonso d'Este, heir to the Duchy of Ferrara, would also offer some protection for Cesare's duchy in the Romagna. The betrothal was announced on 4 September, and the dowry set at 100,000 ducats. It was clear that Duke Ercole d'Este had driven a hard bargain before being persuaded to accept a girl about whom rumours of lovers, illegitimate children, even incest, were widely believed, as a suitable mother for his descendants. In Rome salvoes were fired from Castel Sant'Angelo 'without ceasing, from vespers to nightfall'; in Ferrara 'the betrothal was published with church bells ringing out across the city'.[8]

On 5 September Lucrezia, escorted by 300 horsemen, including four bishops, rode across Rome to the church of Santa Maria del Popolo. On the following Monday, 6 September:

> Two clowns or buffoons were seen around the city. Lucrezia had given one of them the gold brocade dress, which she had worn for the first, and last, time the day before and was worth 300 ducats or thereabouts. He rode up and down the streets and piazzas loudly shouting: 'Long live the illustrious Duchess of Ferrara! Long live Pope Alexander!' The other one, to whom Lucrezia had also given one of her robes, followed him on foot, shouting the same words.[9]

A grimmer sight was on display four days later, when a woman was hanged because 'the night before she had stabbed her husband with a knife'.[10]

In a secret consistory on 17 September Alexander VI announced a cut in the census due from the Duchy of Ferrara from 4,000 ducats to 100 ducats, negotiated as part of the marriage settlement with Duke Ercole d'Este. The elderly Portuguese Cardinal Jorge da Costa, aged 95,

Lucrezia enjoys a double-entendre

Before leaving Rome on his trip, His Holiness entrusted his rooms, all the palace and his affairs to his daughter Lucrezia who, during the absence of her father, moved into the papal apartments. The pope authorized her to open his letters and told her that, if she had any problems, she was to seek the advice of Cardinal Jorge da Costa and the other cardinals, whom she had the power to assemble if necessary. I don't know what the problem was but Lucrezia did seek out Cardinal Costa, telling him what the pope had said and explaining the issue with which she needed his help. Deciding that the problem was not serious, the cardinal said, 'when the pope discusses an issue in consistory, the vice-chancellor or, if he is absent, the cardinal who has been appointed in his place, takes the minutes of the meeting and records the votes; we just need someone to make a note of our conversation'. Lucrezia replied that she was fully capable of writing and the cardinal asked her: 'But where is your pen?' [Italian 'penna' meaning 'pen', but also slang for 'penis']. Lucrezia understood the witty double-entendre and she smiled.

JOHANNES BURCHARD, *Liber notarum*, P. 374.

280

voted in favour of the cut 'out of regard for the illustrious Lady Lucrezia'.[11] The College of Cardinals also agreed on the redistribution of Lucrezia's fiefs that she would relinquish on becoming Duchess of Ferrara: the pope's son, Giovanni, now four years old, was made Duke of Nepi, while Lucrezia's son Rodrigo of Aragon, now nearly two years old, became Duke of Sermoneta. Rodrigo would also remain in Rome – by tradition children of a previous marriage did not stay with their mother if she remarried.

On 25 September Alexander VI left Rome for Nepi and Civita Castellana. This was a family trip: with the 70-year-old pope were his cousins – much the same age as him – Cardinal Jaime Serra and Cardinal Francisco Borgia and two much younger relatives, his great-nephew Cardinal Pedro Luis Borgia and his son Cesare, both in their late twenties. As before, Lucrezia moved into the papal apartments in the Vatican to take care of his affairs until he returned on 2 October, and again for the week of 10–17 October when Alexander VI and his relatives were also absent from Rome.

After the pope's return, in a secret consistory held on 27 October, Alexander VI granted the rights of the abbey of Subiaco, which he had received as a gift after the election of Sixtus IV in 1471, to the Borgia family 'in perpetuity'.[12]

On 31 October Duke Cesare hosted a banquet in his apartments in the Vatican. His guests included both the pope and Lucrezia, and the entertainment afterwards was provided by 50 nude courtesans. The term 'courtesan' was a new one; until recently prostitutes had been referred to as *peccatrice*, 'sinners'.

The party may have taken its toll on the elderly pontiff. The next morning Alexander VI failed to attend mass in St Peter's to celebrate the Feast of All Saints; nor was he present in the Sistine Chapel on the following day for the mass of the Faithful Departed.

On 11 November one of Alexander VI's personal valets, Pedro Caranza, died, leaving 8,000 ducats and other goods which the pope expropriated; according to Johannes Burchard, 'Lucrezia asked him for the estate, which he gave her; however she never actually received it.'[13]

A man was arrested on 5 December for insulting Duke Cesare and thrown into jail. The following night 'one of his hands was cut off as was the tip of his

Rumours of Borgia depravity

It was also widely believed, if it is possible to believe such terrible depravity, that not only her two brothers but also her father himself, all competed for the love of Madonna Lucrezia. This is because, as soon as he had been elected pope, he had separated her from her first husband as he was of lesser social status and married her to Giovanni Sforza, Lord of Pesaro. He then found that he could not bear having this husband as a rival so he dissolved their marriage, which had already been consummated, though the pope chose judges and witnesses, who were false, to prove that Giovanni was naturally frigid and impotent as well.

FRANCESCO GUICCIARDINI, *Storia d'Italia*, III, 14.

The party of the naked courtesans

On Sunday, the last day in October and the eve of All Saints [1501] ... Duke Cesare held a banquet in his rooms in the Vatican palace. Fifty girls of the type called courtesans, not the lowest sort, took part. After the meal they danced with the servants and others who were there. At first they were dressed but then they took off all their clothes and were quite nude. The candlesticks were moved from the table to the floor, that was now strewn with chestnuts which the courtesans, walking about on the hands and knees, then picked up. The pope, with Duke Cesare and Lucrezia were present and watched the fun. Finally a display of silk robes, shoes, hats and other objects was promised to those who gave the courtesans the greatest number of proofs of their virility. This was done in public in the room. The servants, who took up the role of judges, gave the prizes to those they thought had done best.

JOHANNES BURCHARD, *Liber notarum*, P. 379.

LEFT **Battle of Love and Chastity**, *painted by Perugino. Commissioned by Isabella d'Este in 1505 for her study, this detailed picture charts the amorous adventures of several of the gods of classical antiquity. It was based on an esoteric programme drawn up by one of the humanists at her court in Mantua, which has yet to be convincingly deciphered.*

Dowry negotiations

Two ambassadors have arrived here from Ferrara and the pope has lodged them in the palace of his daughter, where there has been much feasting and dancing. She danced so much one night that the following day she was ill with a fever, but she is fine now. The ambassadors are here to negotiate the dowry on behalf of Ferrara, and first we must see what is being offered. Ferrara needs money and wants the pope to pay the expenses of her journey as far as the borders of the Romagna. The pope is preparing to send her with a most lavish escort with many Roman ladies.

GIOVANNI LUCIDO CATANEO TO FRANCESCO GONZAGA, 24 SEPTEMBER 1501 (L. VON PASTOR, *History of the Popes*, VOL. VI, P. 614, DOC. 7).

tongue which was stuck onto the little finger of the severed hand and the hand was hung out of the prison window where it remained for two days'.[14]

About this time Cesare's mistress, perhaps Dorotea Caracciolo, gave birth to his daughter, who was named Camilla; the duke also had an illegitimate son, Girolamo, born either in this year or in the subsequent one.

On 17 December Alexander VI announced that the usual celebrations for the last week of Carnival would start directly after Christmas this year, to provide entertainment for the large party of Este princes and Ferrarese courtiers who were on their way to Rome to escort Lucrezia back to the duchy for her wedding.

Five days later orders were sent out to all cardinals, ambassadors and the entire papal court that they were to assemble the following afternoon to receive the bridal party, led by Cardinal Ippolito d'Este, the groom's brother, at the Porta del Popolo. When asked by the one of the officials in charge of organizing the event to confirm that the cardinals were to wear their purple robes, the appropriate colour for this penitential season of Advent, 'the pope replied that this was a silly question, and that the cardinals should wear red'.[15]

The bridal party was exceptionally large – six Este princes, forty Ferrarese courtiers, musicians and servants, making over six hundred people in all, and almost as many horses and mules[16] – and was received with unusual honour as it rode through Rome, led by Duke Cesare and Cardinal Ippolito, to the Vatican, where the visitors were received by the pope. Duke Ercole's ambassador was relieved to be able to send a favourable report back to his master on Lucrezia's beauty, her cheerful disposition and her piety:

> She is exceptionally elegant in demeanour and her behaviour is modest, ladylike and polite, She is pious, and intends to go to confession at

RIGHT **Arch of Septimius Severus,** *drawn by G.A. Dosio. Situated in the Forum Romanum, beside the orator's platform (Rostra) and the House of the Senators (Curia), this arch is one of the best-preserved monuments of Ancient Rome, thanks to its incorporation into other buildings during the Middle Ages. Before the excavation of the Forum began in the 19th century, all but the largest monuments were buried beneath the* layers of detritus that had built up over the centuries since the collapse of the Roman Empire. Nevertheless, as interest in the culture of classical antiquity blossomed during the decades around 1500, artists travelled in their hundreds to Rome, where they could see the ruins and make drawings of the ancient methods of construction and the style of their decoration, to provide inspiration for their own work back home.

Christmas, and take communion. She is pretty and her cheerful manner and gracefulness make her appear even lovelier. I would say that we have nothing to fear, indeed on the contrary, there is much to feel positive about in every way.[17]

The pope decided to billet the Ferrarese attendants who would accompany Lucrezia to the duchy on his curia officials, such that 'the chamber clerks each had to take 12 people and their horses, as did the clerks of the college, and other officials likewise. Each had to provide food for their guests without receiving any money from either the pope or the Apostolic Chamber.'[18]

On Christmas Day Alexander VI celebrated mass as usual in St Peter's, and the following afternoon after lunch the Carnival races began with that of the

A display of equine virility

On Thursday 11 November [1501] a countryman came into Rome with two mares laden with wood and, when the animals arrived at the piazza in front of St Peter's, some of the papal staff ran out and cut their harness, removed their saddles and took the mares into the small courtyard inside the gate of the Vatican. The men then let loose four of the papal stallions, without bridles or halters, and the stallions ran towards the mares. After biting and kicking each other with loud neighs, they mounted the mares and covered them, stamping all over them and wounding them badly. The pope was at the window of his room, which is above the palace gate, and he had Madonna Lucrezia with him. They both watched and laughed loudly, showing how much they enjoyed the spectacle.

JOHANNES BURCHARD, *Liber notarum*, P. 381.

Cheating during Carnival

On Tuesday 30 December [1501] they held the races of the barbary horses, the genets [light horses for riding] and the mares, which ran, one after the other, from the Campo dei Fiori to St Peter's, for the traditional bolt of cloth. There was much violence and cheating. The barbary belonging to Francesco Gonzaga, Marquis of Mantua, came first but he did not receive the bolt of cloth because the horse lost its rider, who had fallen off at the start of the race, so the prize went to the barbary belonging to Duke Cesare. The prize for the genets' race was given to one of Duke Cesare's household, though his horse did not begin with the others at Campo dei Fiori but was seen leaving the vice-chancellor's palace before the pack arrived, which was how he managed to come first. During the mares' race one of Duke Cesare's grooms crossed the course on the Ponte Sant'Angelo, causing the leading mare to lose her jockey.

JOHANNES BURCHARD, *Liber notarum*, PP. 386–7.

young men and then the boys. On 27 December, after a query about Lucrezia's marriage contract was discussed in consistory, the traditional races held by Jewish inhabitants and old men were run.

After the last race was run on 30 December, the trumpeters announced the arrival of the bride Lucrezia in the piazza in front of St Peter's:

> She was dressed in a robe of gold brocade, designed in the Spanish style, with a long train behind, which was carried by a young girl. She was escorted by the brothers of her husband: Ferrante on the right and Sigismondo on the left. Fifty magnificently dressed Roman ladies came next, followed by Lucrezia's household, walking in pairs. The procession climbed the stairs up to the great hall inside the Vatican, where the pope was waiting in the company of 13 cardinals … and Duke Cesare. Cardinal Pedro Luis Borgia left immediately but the other cardinals remained.[19]

286

Inside the Vatican the guests listened to a sermon given by Niccolò Maria d'Este, the Bishop of Adria, which Alexander VI thought too long, interrupting the bishop 'on several occasions' to tell him to finish.[20] After the sermon Lucrezia was presented with rings and a casket of precious jewels by the Este princes on behalf of their brother Alfonso.

Jewels for Lucrezia

After giving the order for the casket to be opened, Cardinal Ippolito d'Este took out a tiara set with fifteen diamonds, also with rubies and about forty pearls, eight brooches of various designs ornamented with precious stones and pearls, to be used either at the neck or on a hat, then more brooches of diverse sorts and four more of great value. There were also four large pearl collars and four superb crosses, one in the form of the cross of St Andrew and the other three like the cross of Christ, all covered with diamonds and other precious gems. Finally he brought out another tiara, almost as valuable as the other one. The jewellery was estimated to be worth 8,000 ducats.

JOHANNES BURCHARD, *Liber notarum*, P. 388.

1502

THE PROCESSION OF FLOATS which, by tradition, normally took place in Piazza Navona on Shrove Tuesday, was held this year on 1 January in the piazza at St Peter's. That evening Alexander VI hosted theatrical entertainments and a display of dancing at the Vatican. On 2 January, a Sunday, the piazza in front of the basilica was fenced off with grandstands for a bullfight where 'eight bulls and a buffalo were killed,' recorded Burchard, 'which was, as ever, a great fête in Rome'.[21]

During the evening of 5 January Alexander VI gave an audience to Alfonso d'Este's brothers, Ferrante and Sigismondo, and handed over to them his daughter's dowry of 100,000 ducats in cash. The following day Lucrezia, now Duchess of Ferrara, left Rome with the

FAR LEFT **Cloth of gold.** *Hand-made silk textiles, often woven with complex designs, were expensive and wearing clothes made from these materials formed the key component in the display of wealth and status across Renaissance Europe – the equivalent of modern designer labels.*

LEFT **Woven silk.** *Expensive clothes were never thrown away – on the contrary, they were carefully unstitched and the pieces recycled to make covers for horses and mules, altar frontals, covers for commodes and cushions, or given away as alms.*

287

escort provided by her father-in-law and her own entourage of ladies-in-waiting, her household, as well as a body of courtiers belonging to Alexander VI and Duke Cesare. The pope had ordered the cardinals 'each to supply two horses or two mules and over twenty bishops received orders to furnish one horse or one mule for those accompanying Lucrezia to Ferrara,' explained Burchard, adding that 'none of these animals was ever returned'.[22]

Lucrezia's cavalcade made slow progress and by 13 January had only reached Foligno. Duke Ercole was advised by the envoys travelling with the bride to delay the date of her formal entry into Ferrara, because 'we will not arrive in Ferrara before the end of the month'.[23] On 18 January the party received a lavish welcome at Urbino, where they stayed two nights – it cost Duke Guidobaldo da Montefeltro over a month's revenues on accommodating and entertaining such a large throng of guests.[24]

In Rome on 30 January a Venetian, who had translated some scurrilous letters insulting Duke Cesare, was strangled and his corpse thrown into the Tiber. After an audience with Alexander VI the next day, the Ferrarese ambassador reported to Duke Ercole that the pope had said his son could not stand being insulted, even though he had 'frequently explained' to Cesare 'that everyone has the right to free speech in Rome; much is said about me and I just ignore it'.[25]

That evening Lucrezia arrived at the gates of Ferrara, where she was met by her new father-in-law, the 70-year-old Duke Ercole. He escorted her to a family palace outside the walls where she spent the night in preparation for her formal entry into the city. In Ferrara, by special dispensation of Alexander VI, the usual ban on eating meat during Lent had been lifted 'for the festivities, to celebrate the arrival of Lucrezia'.[26]

A cavalcade to Ferrara

Today during the afternoon the pope's daughter Lucrezia left the Vatican palace to start her journey to Ferrara to join her husband. Riding over the Ponte Sant'Angelo, she turned left towards the Porta del Popolo. With her were about 500 horses and, because it was snowing, she was not wearing expensive clothes. The procession took the usual form as far as the men-at-arms, after which came Cardinal Francisco Borgia who had been appointed by His Holiness as legate to accompany Lucrezia through the Papal States. The two brothers of the groom rode with him, Ferrante in the right and Sigismondo on the left. After them came Lucrezia who had Cardinal Ippolito d'Este on her right and Duke Cesare on her left and they were followed by their households. There was no bishop, nor protonotary nor abbot with them. The squires of the pope and of the Roman barons had been appointed to accompany Lucrezia at their own expense, though each had been given a new outfit in gold brocade or silk.

JOHANNES BURCHARD, *Liber notarum*, PP. 396–7.

288

RIGHT **Guidobaldo da Montefeltro, Duke of Urbino,** *painted by Raphael. The only son of the famous one-eyed condottiere Federigo da Montefeltro, Guidobaldo inherited his title at the age of ten after Federigo died of malaria while fighting in Ferrara. His own career as a mercenary soldier included leading the armies of Venice and of Alexander VI; he was made a Knight of the Garter by Henry VII of England.*

The city of Ferrara

Ferrara was the capital city of a wealthy state that stretched from the Apennines in the west, with their mines of precious metals, across the lush farmland of the Po plain to the Adriatic in the east. With a population of around 40,000 the city was only slightly smaller than Rome and was surrounded by a massive circuit of walls built by Duke Ercole, who had enlarged the town in the 1490s, building spacious new streets, all paved, and an impressively large hunting park with its own racecourse.

The Ferrarese were prosperous. There were over 50 churches in the city, attached to monasteries and convents of the large number of religious orders that existed before the Counter-Reformation. Many families had vegetable gardens and orchards inside the walls, while even modest carpenters and painters could afford to keep a pig in their backyards. Their lives were dominated by the ducal court, which gave employment to ten per cent of the population, and provided a lucrative income for merchants dealing in silks and velvets, for apothecaries, grocers, butchers and for the men employed in the building trades.

ABOVE **The city of Ferrara.** *This woodcut shows the principal features of Ferrara: at the bottom are the wharves along the River Po; in the centre is the main square flanked by the cathedral with its elaborate campanile on the right, and the imposing towers of the ducal palace on the left. Behind is the large area of land enclosed within the new circuit of walls built by Ercole I.*

A 16th-century gourmet enthused about the culinary delights Ferrara had to offer:

What can I tell you about the wonderful city of Ferrara, the true master of the art of making salamis and of candying fruits and roots? here in summer you will taste little sweet wines called Albarelle and you will not enjoy a more welcome drink; here you will eat good river fish, sturgeon and little eels; and they make the best cakes in all the world; I wish I could be there on Thursdays and Sundays at the market to fill my stomach with them.

ORTENSIO LANDI, *Commentario*, in E. FACCIOLI (ED.), *L'arte della cucina in Italia*, P. 279.

ABOVE **A fruit and vegetable market.** *This scene shows men and women shopping in a crowded Italian market square, filled with stalls selling melons, marrows, cabbages, figs, garlic, pears and other fresh produce. The busyness of a market provided tangible evidence of a city's prosperity – a quiet and empty market was a worrying sign, an indication that food supplies had been interrupted by war or famine.*

Lucrezia entered Ferrara, crossing the bridge at Castel Tedaldo, on 2 February, to the sound of trumpeters, church bells and cannon:

After a short distance, just when the bride had reached the church of San Giovanni di Castel Tedaldo, where there was a very elaborate stage on which they were celebrating by firing a small cannon, the bride fell off her horse but she was not harmed. Our duke [Ercole] immediately found her a very beautiful mule and she proceeded past the church of Santa Maria dei Servi, along the road of San Domenico, with Don Alfonso [the groom] riding at the front, dressed in lordly robes, accompanied by three squads of crossbowmen, all wearing red and white, his colours, and white French-style hats with large feathers in them. There were more than 100 trumpeters and pipers and all our courtiers followed, each one accompanying one of the guests, according to their status ... on the Via Grande they passed performers and people reciting verses in praise of the bridal couple and of the pope. There were also 20 court carriages in the procession, all covered with gold brocade and drawn by white horses.[27]

A 'most beautiful bride'

The bride is about 24 years old and she is most beautiful, with smiling eyes. She is upright in form and personality, prudent, wise, happy, vivacious and kind. The Ferrarese like her very much and all are extremely thankful, expecting great things from her for this city, and from the pope who is said to love his daughter dearly, as he has shown by the dowry and the castles he has given to Don Alfonso.

BERNARDINO ZAMBOTTI, *Diario Ferrarese*, PP. 314–15.

Lucrezia rode in state through the city to the main piazza and into the ducal palace, where she was received on the grand ceremonial staircase by her new sister-in-law, Isabella d'Este, wife of the Marquis of Mantua and daughter of Duke Ercole, and his illegitimate daughter, also named Lucrezia, who was married to Annibale Bentivoglio, one of the ruling family of Bologna. 'After the bride had been greeted by most of the ladies of the court at the top of the stairs, she was escorted by the ambassadors and gentlemen into the Great Hall which had been hung with gold, silver and silk curtains, of tremendous value.'[28] At the end of the evening the couple were escorted to their bed.

The next day, 3 February, a thief was hanged in the piazza: he was a Roman youth who had hidden under the bed of one of Duke Cesare's Spanish courtiers and had been apprehended during the night when he tried to steal a gold collar.[29] That afternoon Duke Ercole hosted a banquet in the palace, which was followed by dancing. The secretary to the French ambassador recounted how 'the bride performed many dances, in both the Roman and Spanish styles, to the music of her own tambourines'.[30] In the evening the guests watched a performance of Plautus's *Epidicus*, a comedy about the gullibility

of an elderly man duped by his slave: 'there were so many tapers and candles that everyone could see it all in detail'.[31] The festivities continued for the following week, with daily banquets and dancing followed by the performance of a comedy by Plautus. On Sunday 6 February the guests attended mass in Ferrara cathedral, where Alfonso d'Este was invested, in the name of the pope, as ducal heir, kneeling in front of the altar wearing a ducal cap embroidered with pearls and trimmed with ermine, and a magnificent gilded sword, both presents from his new father-in-law.

On Ash Wednesday, 9 February, the bridal couple received presents from the ambassadors and Duke Ercole escorted his daughter-in-law to watch the performance of a tightrope artist, who 'did many things on two ropes which were stretched across the piazza, including walking across in full armour and dancing *a la moresca* and many other marvellous things'.[32]

In Rome meanwhile, on 17 February, Alexander VI left the city with a party that consisted of Duke Cesare, cardinals Francisco Borgia, Pedro Luis Borgia, Juan Castellar, Ippolito d'Este, Giovanni Battista Orsini, Federigo Sanseverino and Antoniotto Pallavicini, seven bishops and over a hundred of his household, including the papal choir. They headed for Civitavecchia, where:

> Three boats were prepared for the pope's journey to Piombino and oarsmen were needed. They used all those prisoners in jail for petty crimes, and they also found many men in the inns of Rome, or on the piazzas, who they persuaded by violence or deception, whatever was necessary. Finally they requisitioned all barge owners, many fishermen and woodcutters. All of them and others, were forced into service on the galleys and were kept there under guard.[33]

The papal party spent four nights in Piombino, a key stronghold in Duke Cesare's plans for Tuscany, then sailed to Elba for a night, returning to Piombino on 26 February. 'I heard from a reliable witness that in Piombino the pope had all the beautiful women and young girls dancing for many hours in the public square in front of his palace and that

295

throughout the course of their journey, many of those who accompanied the pope ate meat', even though it was Lent, recorded a shocked Johannes Burchard.[34]

On 1 March the party decided to take two boats out from Piombino for a day at sea, but a storm brewed up suddenly and they were unable to re-enter the harbour. They were still on board the galleys on 4 March when the sailors tried to dock at Porto Ercole, without success. The next day:

> ... the tempest continued unabated and the sea was very rough. The two galleys sailed towards Corneto, which they could see in front of them. After the hour of lunch, Duke Cesare, dreading a greater danger, left the galley on a small boat and landed ashore and sent to Corneto for horses. But the pope, who had stayed on the galley, was unable to put into the port. His companions, paralysed with fear, lay down on the deck. Only the pope, sitting on the poop, retained a positive and strong manner ... On several occasions he told the sailors to make lunch but they replied that the waves and the wind made it impossible to light the fire ... to fry the fish for his meal. [35]

The pope and his entourage eventually landed safely at Porto Ercole that evening.

On 23 April in Ferrara the court celebrated the Feast of St George, the patron saint of the city, with horse races. This year the race was won by Isabella d'Este, who got the traditional prize of 'gold brocade fringed with fur, and the suckling pig and the cock'.[36]

On 2 May Duke Ercole and his courtiers left Ferrara to go fishing for sturgeon at Volano in the marshes of the Po delta, and Alfonso d'Este departed on his father's orders to meet Louis XII in Milan; Lucrezia and her ladies retired to the ducal villa at Belriguardo.

In Rome Duke Cesare was making his final plans for military action in Tuscany: in May he withdrew 54,000 ducats from the papal treasury to pay his troops, and between May and July the treasury spent 3,320 ducats on gunpowder alone.[37]

In June the body of Manfredo Astorre, Lord of Faenza – one of the papal fiefs conquered by Duke Cesare – who had been imprisoned in Castel Sant'Angelo,

In Rome Duke Cesare was making his final plans for military action in Tuscany.

RIGHT **St George Slaying the Dragon,** *painted c.1505 by Raphael. St George was the patron saint of Ferrara, and his feast day, 23 April, was celebrated with particular magnificence in the city, starting the evening before when the duke and his court would attend a service in the cathedral. On the day itself, horses, asses, men and young girls ran races along the Via Grande, in a similar manner to the races held during Carnival in Rome. The prize for the winner of the horse race was a length of cloth of gold lined with fur, and there were bolts of cloth for the victors in the other three races: this tradition still survives in the Palio, which is run every year in Siena (the Italian word* palio *means a length of cloth).*

was found floating in the Tiber: he had been strangled.

On 5 June Alexander VI excommunicated Giulio Cesare Varano, the ruler of Camerino, who had been accused of giving help to enemies of the Church. The following day news arrived in Rome that Arezzo had been occupied by Cesare's captain, Vitellozzo Vitelli, and the pope ordered Guidobaldo da Montefeltro, Duke of Urbino, to send troops to help Vitelli. On 13 June Duke Cesare left Rome with an army of 8,000 troops, and cannons he had bought from Naples for 50,000 ducats, asking the duke for permission to pass through Urbino on his way north. On 24 June news arrived in Rome that Duke Cesare, far from passing through Urbino, had actually seized the duchy itself, and that Guidobaldo da Montefeltro had fled.

On 8 July Vitellozzo Vitelli captured the Florentine border fortress of Borgo San Sepolcro for Duke Cesare. On 20 July Cesare captured Camerino and took Giulio Cesare Varano prisoner. When the news arrived in Rome late in the afternoon of 23 July, Alexander VI was with the Venetian ambassador, who reported that the pope 'was so excited' that he interrupted the audience, 'left his chair and moved over to the window, where he

LEFT **Isabella d'Este,** *painted c.1534–6 by Titian. The eldest daughter of Duke Ercole, Isabella assiduously cultivated an image of taste and elegance. An important patron of the arts, she avidly collected antique sculpture and medals and ornamented her study with works by some of the greatest artists of the period. This portrait, which shows her as a lovely young girl, was in fact painted when she was 60 years old.*

The dispossessed Duke of Urbino

Duke Cesare, *son of Pope Alexander VI, pretending to set up his camp at Camerino with his troops, asked Guidobaldo da Montefeltro, Duke of Urbino, for the loan of his infantry and artillery, which he was given. So Duke Cesare, escorted by some of his cavalry, went immediately to the fortress and the contract was signed. One of the Duke of Urbino's secretaries then advised his master to flee, and Duke Cesare seized the fortress and the rest of the state of Urbino. And when Duke Guidobaldo saw that he would not be safe anywhere in his state, he left with five horses, and reached Monisterolo, where he was met by our Duke Ercole, and they dined together talking for two hours; it is said that our duke has given him 500 ducats so he can travel to Mantua, where his wife is staying with her brother. This has shown the other lords hereabouts that they should consider carefully before lending weapons, artillery and men to someone fighting a war.*

BERNARDINO ZAMBOTTI, *Diario Ferrarese*, PP. 339–40.

ABOVE **Inlaid panel from Urbino.** *This panel, from the study of Federigo da Montefeltro in the ducal palace at Urbino, is exquisitely inlaid to show a squirrel eating a nut and a bowl of fruit set in a tiled loggia against the backdrop of the landscape of the Marche.*

had [Cesare's] letter read out'.[38] Alexander's young son Giovanni was now made Duke of Camerino.

Louis XII arrived in Milan on 28 July and was immediately petitioned by Guidobaldo da Montefeltro and the Orsini, as well as by envoys from the Florentine government, for his help in recovering territories lost in Duke Cesare's recent military manoeuvres. But on 5 August Duke Cesare left Urbino, disguised as a Knight of St John, and arrived in Milan where he succeeded in renewing his friendship with the king, offering Louis XII his support for the forthcoming campaign in Naples in return for French support against his next target, Bologna.

On 18 August Duke Cesare appointed Leonardo da Vinci as his architect and military engineer with orders 'to inspect the strongholds and fortresses of our state'.[39]

Five days later, the joint fleets of Venice, Spain and Rome captured the island of Leucadia from the Turks.

Leonardo da Vinci

Leonardo da Vinci, one of the geniuses of European art, is best known as the painter of such works as the *Mona Lisa* and *The Last Supper*; but it was his imaginative skills as a designer of military machines that appealed most to his Renaissance patrons.

In a letter he wrote to Ludovico Sforza seeking employment at the Milanese court, Leonardo laid much stress on these abilities, offering such items as portable bridges, cannons, explosives and transport. His scientific approach to the world about him also led him to dissect corpses and make anatomical studies of the structure of the human body.

Leonardo's military thinking encouraged a radically new approach to the problems faced by armies fighting the new type of artillery. Among his drawings, many of which have survived, are sketches of inventions that include prototypes for machines resembling the modern helicopter and the tank.

RIGHT **Self-portrait** *by Leonardo da Vinci. Leonardo left behind huge quantities of drawings and notes recording his ideas and opinions on a broad range of topics. This portrait, drawn around 1512 when the artist was 60 years old, shows this towering figure of Renaissance art sage-like, in old age.*

In Ferrara Lucrezia gave birth to a stillborn daughter on 5 September and succumbed to the dangerous puerperal fever; she was seriously ill when Cesare arrived on 7 September on his way back from Milan. Cesare then travelled on to meet Alexander VI, who was in Camerino to invest his son Giovanni as the new duke. By the beginning of October, Lucrezia was out of danger. 'The illustrious Lady Lucrezia,' recorded a chronicler, 'left her residence in the Old Castle and went to the monastery of Corpus Domini with several ladies-in-waiting for a few days after the illness she suffered following the birth of a daughter of eight months some weeks ago; a few days later her husband, Alfonso d'Este, left Ferrara to visit the shrine of the Santa Casa at Loreto, to give thanks in fulfilment of a vow he had made while his wife was ill'.[40]

On 7 October Niccolò Machiavelli arrived in Imola, where he had been sent by the Florentine government as envoy to Duke Cesare.

Two days later, a group of Duke Cesare's captains met at La Magione, near Lake Trasimeno. Fearful that Cesare's ambitions knew no bounds, they worried that their own states were now under threat from him, and they turned to conspire against him. The conspirators included several members of the Orsini family, Hermes Bentivoglio from Bologna, Oliverotto Euffreducci (Lord of Fermo), Vitellozzo Vitelli (Lord of Città di Castello) and Gianpaolo Baglione (Lord of Perugia). On 15 October, with the help of Vitelli and the Orsini, Guidobaldo da Montefeltro retook Urbino, where he was welcomed, according to a Ferrarese chronicler, 'with the love that all the people had for the said duke, who was their ancient and rightful lord'.[41]

Duke Cesare's response was to retrench and concentrate on holding his Romagna territories. By the end of October, it was clear that he would survive, not least thanks to the French troops and the papal funds he had at his disposal. As Machiavelli wrote on 23 October:

The conspirators included several members of the Orsini family.

RIGHT **Bust of Niccolò Machiavelli.** *Working as a secretary in the republican government of Florence, Machiavelli had an extensive knowledge of the devious and vicious machinery of Italian Renaissance politics, and this formed the basis for his most famous work,* The Prince. *Among his other writings are histories and some entertaining comedies.*

301

It would be superfluous to describe the whole story of the poisonous hostility of the Orsini.

A conspiracy takes shape

Duke Cesare had decided not to rely any more on the fortunes and arms of others and his first step was to weaken the Orsini and Colonna factions in Rome. This he did by bringing all their noble supporters to his side making them his nobles, giving them large salaries, and giving them military commanders or governors, as befitted their status. In this way in just a few months, he extinguished their affection for the factions and turned them to himself ... When the Orsini realized that the grandeur of Duke Cesare and of the Church spelled their ruin, they held a meeting at Magione, near Perugia.

NICCOLÒ MACHIAVELLI, *The Prince*, CHAPTER 7.

... the territory of this lord [Duke Cesare] has held together by fortunate circumstances, of which the main one is, an opinion widely held here, that the King of France will supply the men and the pope will send the money. And another thing which has played no small role is the delay of his enemies to tighten their noose. In my opinion it is far too late now to do him any harm because he has sent soldiers to all the important cities and provisioned the fortresses. [42]

The conspiracy against Cesare now quickly unravelled as, one by one, the plotters made separate agreements with him. On 24 October, Machiavelli informed the Florentine government from Imola that 'Paolo Orsini is at Cesena this evening and is expected here tomorrow morning to speak with the duke'. The captains appeared to have been forgiven, though each was required to leave his son with Cesare's men as a hostage for his future loyalty. Machiavelli sent a copy of the peace agreement to the government of Florence, highly sceptical that it would work: 'knowing this lord [Cesare] to be bold, fortunate and optimistic, and the favourite of a pope and of a ring, and to have been injured by them,' he wrote, 'I cannot see how he can forgive their treachery'. He added: 'It is difficult to believe in this new alliance.' [43]

Meanwhile, the pope used the death of the Bishop of Cortona as a means to replenish his coffers. According to Johannes Burchard, the bishop:

... left a will in which he appointed cardinals Oliviero Carafa, Lorenzo Cibò and Antoniotto Pallavicini as executors. But the pope put the execution of the will in the hands of the Governor of Rome, in order that he himself might inherit. He seized all the bishop's goods, even selling the wheat that was found in Cortona; he also sold the diocese to a Florentine for 2,000 ducats. [44]

During this time Alexander VI was watching the deterioration of relations between France and Spain, a major cause for concern not solely because it was clear that another war was inevitable in Naples but also because the pope needed to support the winner of the coming conflict. He appealed to Venice for aid: 'it would be bad for both of us if Spain were to conquer Naples, but even worse for us if it became French,' Alexander told the Venetian ambassador in desperation.[45]

On 3 December the papal treasury sent two sacks of coins worth 15,000 ducats to Duke Cesare. His expenses were enormous – the upkeep of his army was costing 2,000 ducats each day.[46] Nevertheless, the effort seemed to be reaping rewards. Late in the evening of 9 December news arrived in Rome that Duke Cesare had recaptured Urbino and signed an agreement with Guidobaldo da Montefeltro; later that month Cesare retook Camerino and on 30 December Senigallia surrendered to his troops.

On 31 December Cesare arrived at Senigallia and warmly greeted the former conspirators Vitellozzo Vitelli, Paolo and Francesco Orsini and Oliverotto Euffreducci at the gates, and they entered the city together. Once inside Cesare's men promptly arrested all four captains. Later that night Vitelli and Euffreducci were garrotted. According to Machiavelli, they pleaded with their murderer to ask Pope Alexander VI to grant them absolution for their sins.[47] The duke justified his actions to the people of Pesaro:

> It would be superfluous to describe the whole story of the poisonous hostility of the Orsini and their collaborators towards His Holiness and ourselves, as this is already known and detested by the whole world ... they wanted to join our undertaking against Senigallia, making us believe that they had only a few men with them, and with the help of the castle at Senigallia they conspired against

303

RIGHT **Helmet and cuirass.** *The manufacture of steel armour was a thriving industry in Renaissance Europe, where it was used not only in battle but also in jousting. Battle armour of the period, plainer than the elaborately decorated suits worn by jousters, was usually custom-made. While it offered a cavalryman protection from swords and arrows, the limited visibility through the slit in the helmet and the massive weight of the breastplate and other protective pieces must have proved a hindrance. This cuirass belonged to Federico Gonzaga, Marquis of Mantua.*

PA
CV
F

Carnival frolics

After lunch on Christmas day [1502] 30 masked men arrived in the piazza in front of St Peter's, all wearing fat long noses that looked like phalluses. It was led by a man purporting to lead a procession of cardinals, who carried a shield with three dice. He was followed by the squires and the mace-bearers and then a man on horseback wearing a long robe and an old cardinal's hat and finally several chaplains. The mace-bearers were mounted on donkeys some of which were so small that the riders' feet touched the ground and they walked with the beasts. They stopped at the small area by the gate to the Vatican and gave audiences, then they showed themselves to the pope who was at the window above, then the procession rode all around Rome.

JOHANNES BURCHARD, *Liber notarum*, P. 415.

our person which, when we fully understood it, we had to prevent ... so in the same moment we not only took the city of Senigallia but also the Duke of Gravina (Francesco Orsini), Paolo Orsini, Giulio Orsini, Vitellozzo Vitelli and Oliverotto Euffreducci of Fermo and all their men.[48]

1503

ON 1 JANUARY DUKE CESARE left Senigallia with his troops and a few days later occupied Vitellozzo Vitelli's fief of Città di Castello, where Vitelli's possessions were pillaged by the soldiers: Cesare, it was said, 'has the state under his control more through fear than love'.[49] He then moved on to Perugia, which he took after its ruler Gianpaolo Baglione fled.

Two days later Alexander VI, acting on Cesare's request, arrested Cardinal Giovanni Battista Orsini, and confiscated his palace and its contents. The cardinal had arrived at the Vatican to congratulate the pope on the capture of Senigallia, but 'as he entered the Sala del Pappagallo he was surrounded by armed guards and thrown into prison', while the horses he had brought with him were taken to the papal stables.[50] On 5 January Alexander VI sent his son Jofrè, Prince of Squillace, with troops 'to take possession of Orsini fortresses in the name of the pope'.[51] That evening Alexander VI failed to attend vespers in the Sistine Chapel, and after the service 'all the cardinals went to the pope to plead on behalf of Cardinal Orsini,' reported Burchard, but Alexander VI 'reminded them that Vitellozzo Vitelli, the Orsini, the Baglione and their allies had intended to kill Duke Cesare'.[52]

PREVIOUS PAGE **The Disputation of St Catherine of Alexandria,** *painted by Pinturicchio. The centrepiece of the Sala dei Santi, the most impressive room of Alexander VI's apartments, this fresco exploits the legend of St Catherine of Alexandria outwitting the pagan Emperor Maxentius to commemorate the Conquest of Granada, which happened on her feast day, with figures in Muslim dress among the imperial retinue. At the centre, surmounted by the Borgia bull, stands a triumphal arch, based on the Arch of Constantine, whose victory over Maxentius at the Battle of the Milvian Bridge established Christianity as the religion of the Roman*

Empire. The story is also a vehicle for the display of the pope's court, notably the recognizable portraits of his children and other members of the papal entourage: Lucrezia Borgia (centre) as St Catherine, the more diminutive Sancia of Aragon and Jofrè Borgia (centre right; see page 308) and Juan Borgia (right, mounted; see page 186).

RIGHT **Protection in war.** *Another of Francesco di Giorgio's precise and careful instructive drawings, illustrating how soldiers – here rather elegantly attired – might use this mobile protective shield.*

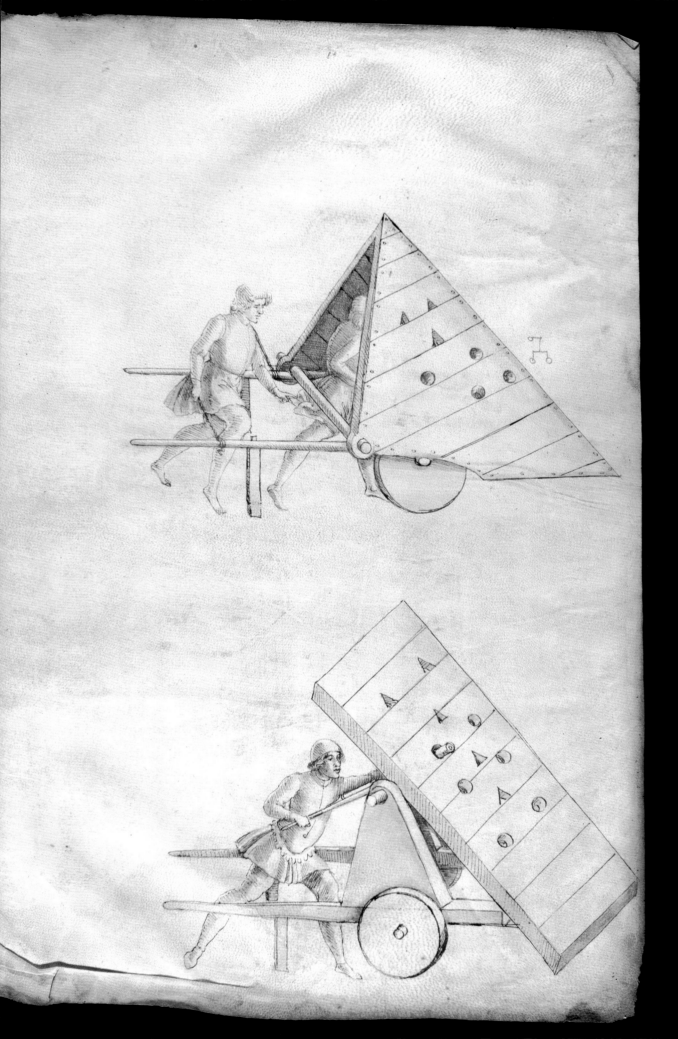

The retribution against the Orsini was not over. On 18 January Cesare's courtier Miguel de Corella, acting on his master's orders, strangled Francesco and Paolo Orsini in the fortress near Siena where they were being held.

On 20 January the duke signed an alliance with the Bentivoglio of Bologna. Three days later news arrived in Rome that Cesare's soldiers had taken Chiusi, Pienza, Sarteano and San Quirico Val d'Orcia, where they hung 'two old men and nine elderly women by their arms and lit a fire under their feet to force them to reveal the place where they had hidden their valuables'.[53]

Meanwhile, Cardinal Giovanni Battista Orsini remained incarcerated, while his mother negotiated with Alexander VI to try and ensure his welfare:

> ... it is said ... that the pope had demanded 2,000 ducats which the cardinal had received from one of his brothers for the sale of a property. It is also said that the pope had demanded a large pearl, worth 2,000 ducats, bought by Cardinal Orsini from Virginio Orsini or one of his heirs. At this news the cardinal's mother supplied the pope with the 2,000 ducats, and the cardinal's mistress, who possessed the pearl in question, put on men's clothes

LEFT **Jofrè Borgia and Sancia of Aragon.** *This portrait of Alexander VI's fourth son and his wife is a detail from the Disputation of St Catherine of Alexandria (see pages 304–5) in the pope's Vatican apartments. Sancia was widely reported to be dissatisfied with her husband, who was four years her junior, and she was reputed to have enjoyed affairs with her two brothers-in-law, Cesare and Juan, as well as with Lucrezia's brother-in-law, Cardinal Ippolito d'Este.*

and took it to the pope. Having got what he wanted, Alexander VI gave permission to allow the ... men to bring food and drink to the cardinal.[54]

But on 15 February the Venetian ambassador reported that Cardinal Orsini had become delirious.

That same day, after attending consistory, Cardinal Ippolito d'Este, Lucrezia's new brother-in-law, left Rome to return to Ferrara 'to avoid the anger of Duke Cesare', reported Burchard, explaining that 'the cardinal was having an affair with the princess [Sancia of Aragon] who was married to Cesare's brother, and that the duke himself was also having an affair with this woman'.[55]

In Ferrara Duke Ercole celebrated Carnival on 19 February with one of his usual comedies, attended by Alfonso d'Este and Lucrezia Borgia, who was 'most beautifully dressed and wearing large jewels'.[56]

On 22 February, while the Carnival festivities in Rome were also in full swing, Cardinal Orsini died in Castel Sant'Angelo. Within two months, after the capture of their fortresses, the Orsini were forced to negotiate peace with Alexander VI and Duke Cesare.

On 29 March Alexander VI held a consistory at which he announced the creation of 80 new posts in the curia, which were to be sold at 760 ducats each.[57] Money-raising continued by other means too. The sudden death of the Venetian Cardinal Giovanni Michiel was announced on 10 April. 'His nephew has told me that his stomach had been badly upset for the last two days and a little diarrhoea; it is greatly feared that he has been poisoned,' wrote the Venetian ambassador.[58] His estate, like so many others, went into the papal coffers.

On 13 April in Ferrara the annual Maundy Thursday ceremony was performed, in which 'Duke Ercole gave dinner to 160 poor men most splendidly in the great hall of the palace, with himself and his sons, with all the courtiers, serving at table ... then he knelt before each one and washed their feet and dried them, and gave each bread and money for clothes'.[59] On Good Friday Lucrezia was present for the performance of the Passion of Christ in Ferrara cathedral.

The value of fortresses

It is the habit *of princes to keep a secure hold on their states by building fortresses that can act as bridle and bit restraining those who might plot against them and provide them with secure places of refuge in case of an attack. I praise this belief, because it was used in ancient times, nevertheless Niccolò Vitelli in our times is known to have destroyed two fortresses in Città di Castello in order to keep that state ... Some fortresses, therefore, are useful and some are not, depending on the circumstances; and if they are helpful in one way, they can damage you in another. It is possible to conclude this: those princes who are more afraid of their subjects than they are of foreigners should build fortresses, while those who fear foreigners more than their people should not.*

NICCOLÒ MACHIAVELLI, *The Prince*, CHAPTER 20.

309

The Passion of Christ in Ferrara cathedral

Once mass was over the performance of *Christ's Passion took place on the stage constructed in front of the high altar by the large baptismal font. There were banks of seats on the other side of the church on which sat all the ladies-in-waiting with Madonna Lucrezia Borgia, wife of the illustrious Don Alfonso, and the duke was also present. Above, just under the roof a ceiling had been constructed of planks which opened in a brilliant way to let the angel come down from heaven and present the chalice to Christ while he prayed in the garden. Above the stage there was a great serpent's head, as large and as wide as a standing man, which was the mouth of Hell, from where the holy fathers came out of Limbo to the singing of hymns by the ducal choir, who were all there. In front of the high altar was the mount of Calvary where Christ was crucified, and everything was done really well. It lasted five hours.*

BERNARDINO ZAMBOTTI, *Diario Ferrarese*, P. 348.

On 28 April King Ferdinand II of Spain's armies, under Gonsalvo de Cordoba, defeated Louis XII at Cerignola, and on 16 May the victorious captain entered Naples in triumph.

When Alexander VI created nine new cardinals on 31 May, giving him seventy per cent of the college, there were five for Spain, including his treasurer Francisco Loriz and another relation, but none for France. The Venetian ambassador queried their qualifications, and added that 'all paid generously for their titles', which produced '120,000 to 130,000 ducats; and if we add the 64,000 ducats raised from the sale of posts in the curia, and the legacy of Cardinal Michiel, we have a large sum,' he calculated. He concluded: 'Pope Alexander shows us all that a pope's income can be as high as he wants.' [60]

The weather in Italy that summer was unusually hot. In Ferrara there was an outbreak of the plague and 'everyone is leaving the city because people are falling down dead in the streets'.[61] In Rome an outbreak of malaria caused many deaths, and on 5 August Alexander VI's nephew Cardinal Juan Borgia the elder, already sick with syphilis, died: 'he was fifty years old and fat, and died very suddenly,' reported the Mantuan ambassador, 'and many are ill though it is not the plague but a fever which kills very quickly'.[62] Watching the funeral cortège pass by his window, the pope, himself quite plump, remarked to the Venetian envoy that August 'is a bad month for fat people'.[63]

On 6 August Alexander VI and Duke Cesare were guests for an evening party at the villa of Cardinal Adriano Castellesi, Bishop of Hereford and one of the cardinals the pope had created on 31 May. On 9 August Alexander VI gave the archbishopric of Monreale, which had belonged to the late Cardinal Juan Borgia, to Juan Castellar, another of the cardinals created in May. The following day the Ferrarese ambassador informed Duke Ercole that Alexander VI was busy negotiating with Emperor Maximilian to have Cesare confirmed as ruler of Siena, Lucca and Pisa.

Two days later, on 12 August, Alexander VI started to feel unwell during the afternoon and spent the night vomiting; Cesare, who had planned to leave that day to join his armies, was also suddenly taken ill. On 13 August the Venetian ambassador reported that Cardinal Adriano Castellesi too was sick and assumed they had all caught the same fever – it was unlikely to have been poison. The pope seemed to recover over the next few days, and was reported to have been playing cards; by 16 August, however, Cesare was gravely ill, and the doctors attempted to reduce his temperature with an ice bath. He was better on 18 August, though still very weak, but Alexander VI had a serious relapse and his condition worsened as the day wore on.

Rodrigo Borgia, Pope Alexander VI, died on the evening of 18 August. 'The duke never came to visit the pope, neither before or after his death,' recorded Johannes Burchard, 'and the pope made not a single mention of either the duke or Lucrezia while he was ill.'[64] It was now the master-of-ceremonies' role to dress the papal corpse 'in red brocade garments, a short amice [a white linen vestment worn at mass] and a clean surplice'. Then he:

> ... attended to his shoes: because the ones he was wearing had no cross on them, I put on his ordinary slippers, which were of crimson velvet embroidered with a gold cross, which I attached to his heels with laces. He did not have his ring and I could not find it. When everything was ready, we carried him to the Sala del Pappagallo ... where we prepared a nice bier, covering a table with crimson cloth and a piece of tapestry, with four cushions, two of brocade, one of crimson satin and an old one of crimson velvet.[65]

In Ferrara, where the pope was widely believed to have been poisoned, Lucrezia was in a difficult position: Louis XII strongly advised Duke Ercole II to dissolve her marriage to his son Alfonso,

ABOVE **Medal of Lucrezia Borgia.** *This bronze medal of Lucrezia was made in Mantua, probably by the renowned artist, Giancristoforo Romano, who was court sculptor to Francesco Gonzaga, Marquis of Mantua, and Isabella d'Este, Lucrezia's new sister-in-law. The inscription, in elegant classical lettering, records her Borgia surname and illustrates the Renaissance practice whereby women did not change their names after marriage. The medal was cast after 1505, when she was 30 years old. Carefully detailed in profile, with her long blond hair loosely held in a braid, it captures the essence of the attractive, high-spirited girl who had arrived at the Ferrarese court in 1502, having said goodbye to Rome, and to her father, for the last time.*

but the prospect of repaying her huge dowry was daunting. The poet Pietro Bembo, enamoured of Lucrezia, wrote to offer his sympathy at losing 'your very great father' and to remind her 'that Time soothes and lessens grief'.[66]

The death of his powerful father now threatened to undermine Cesare's ambitions and achievements. The duke had 'imagined every possibility that might occur when his father died, but not that he himself would be so very ill when it happened'.[67] He had, however, been alert enough to send Miguel de Corella with an escort to the papal apartments where they 'threatened to stab Cardinal Casanova and throw him out of the window if he refused to hand over the keys of the papal treasury, which the terrified cardinal did'.[68]

The funeral of the second Borgia pope began on Monday 4 September. As Johannes Burchard recorded:

> ... the catafalque was positioned by the three stones which mark the centre of the basilica [of St Peter's] towards the entrance door. After the funeral oration the prayers for the dead pope were given by cardinals Oliviero Carafa, Giovanni Antonio Sangiorgio, Bernardino Carvajal and Domenico Grimani. On the catafalque were nine torches and twelve hundred candles, each weighing half a pound. Around it were some fifty torches, two on the candelabra and the others placed at the head and feet. This first mass was followed by eight more, one each day for the next eight days.[69]

Death by poison?

As pleases Almighty God, on 18 August Pope Alexander VI died; he was Spanish and been pope for eleven years. They say he was poisoned and also that Duke Cesare, his son, was the cause of his death. The said duke had held a great feast to which he had invited several cardinals he wished to poison and he ordered two flasks of a special wine, which he secretly poisoned, telling no one, and gave them to a trusted servant telling him not to serve them to anyone ... because he wanted them for himself. When the pope arrived he asked for the best wine ... and the servant brought one of the flasks which the pope tasted.

BARTOLOMEO MASI, *Ricordanze*, PP. 59–60.

Friday 18 August. Pope Alexander VI has died in Rome and it is said he was poisoned. His son, Cesare, Duke of the Romagna, has also been poisoned but has been cured thanks to various remedies, especially after he was put inside the bodies of two mules which were still warm. All Rome is in uproar.

BERNARDINO ZAMBOTTI, *Diario Ferrarese*, P. 351.

LEFT **Playing cards.** *Card games were a hugely popular pastime for both men and women at the courts of Renaissance Europe, and they often involved gambling for high stakes. Condemned by hardline Church reformers as the work of the Devil, this form of entertainment provided courtiers and ladies-in-waiting with a forum for gossip and flirtation, a more leisurely alternative to the rigours of hunting and jousting, and a useful way to occupy those long hot days of summer when all physical activity was unpleasant.*

Studies of Cesare Borgia, *drawn by Leonardo da Vinci. Leonardo had been one of the court artists of Ludovico Sforza of Milan, who had commissioned a wide range of projects from the Florentine, including not only portraits and frescoes but also temporary decorations for court celebrations, a massive equestrian monument of his father, Francesco Sforza, and military and hydraulic projects. When Milan was conquered by Louis XII of France in 1499, Leonardo was left without a patron until he took service in 1502 with Cesare, who was in his late twenties when these drawings were made.*

Lucrezia and Pietro – a love story

Lucrezia Borgia's ardent flirtation with the poet Pietro Bembo, ten years her senior, was said by many to have gone further than it should have done.

The son of a Venetian nobleman, Bembo had good friends at the Ferrarese court, where he met Lucrezia sometime in late 1502. By the summer of 1503 they were exchanging passionate love letters. Bembo, who would become one of the greatest literary figures of his generation, dedicated his first major work, a dialogue on love entitled *Gli Asolani,* to Lucrezia, and kept many of her letters and her charming poems, written in Spanish, until he died.

Their correspondence tells us little about Lucrezia's daily life in Ferrara; on the contrary, the writers were delightfully obsessed with their love for each other, which they disguised beneath the cloak of the courtly language of the period. She sent him a lock of her blonde hair, 'those shining tresses that I love so much'. Bembo wrote: 'My heart has flown straight into that golden softness as a bird flies into the green laurel.' 7º

ABOVE **Pietro Bembo,** *painted c.1506 by his friend Raphael. Bembo's growing literary reputation brought him to the attention of Elisabetta Gonzaga, who invited him to join the ducal court at Urbino, where he stayed from 1506 to 1512, before becoming a secretary at the papal court in Rome under Leo X.*

By that time, Duke Cesare was not even in Rome. On 22 August, with his soldiers still in the city, he had sworn fealty to the College of Cardinals in his role as Captain-General of the Church. The college, however, was threatened not only by Cesare's troops but also by a French army to the north, near Viterbo, and Gonsalvo de Cordoba approaching from the south with the Spanish forces. The cardinals insisted that all soldiers must leave Rome before the conclave could start. On 2 September Cesare reluctantly agreed to go, and he rode north to join the French. Gonsalvo de Cordoba immediately ordered all the Spaniards in Cesare's army to desert.

The abrupt loss of the power and resources of the papacy following the death of his father was inevitably a challenge for Cesare. The astute observer Niccolò Machiavelli assessed the duke's options at this moment of transformation in the political landscape:

> As for the future, [the duke] had to consider that the next pope might not be a friend, and might try to remove all that Alexander VI had given him. He had tried to guard against this possibility in four ways. Firstly he had got rid of all those blood relations of the lords he had ousted to stop them siding with the new pope. Secondly he had bought all the noble barons of Rome so that their power would act as a curb on the pope's actions. Thirdly he had made the College of Cardinals as much in favour of him as he could. And fourthly, by acquiring as much land as he could before Alexander VI died, he had hoped to resist any attack. He had achieved the first three of these things when Alexander VI died, and the fourth was almost secure ... but when Alexander VI died only the Duchy of the Romagna was consolidated; the other states were in the air, confined between two very powerful enemy armies and he himself was gravely ill.[71]

The treasure of Alexander VI

On 19 August ... *after lunch the said cardinals, accompanied by the clerks of the chamber and the notaries, made an inventory of the silver, jewels and other precious objects. They found the tiara and two valuable mitres, all the rings which the pope wore at mass, all the sacred vessels the pope used when he officiated at mass, which filled eight large chests. They also found the silver ewers which had been in the room next to that of the pope which Miguel de Corella had not seen, as well as a box of cypress wood covered in green tapestry, which contained precious gems, rings worth 25,000 ducats and a number of documents, including the cardinals' oaths, the bull investing the King of Naples and other similar items.*

JOHANNES BURCHARD, *Liber notarum*, P. 433.

317

Cesare and Lucrezia Borgia

The Duke and the Duchess

1503–1519

When Pope Alexander VI died in August 1503 he left a College of Cardinals dominated by his appointees: over seventy per cent of the cardinals had been created by him. They included five of his relatives and another ten cardinals who owed their allegiance to Spain. By this means Alexander VI had done as much as he could to assure the election of a pope who would be well-disposed to the Borgia family, and especially of one who would support Cesare's duchy in the Romagna. But no papal election could be guaranteed, and the uncertainty was exacerbated by a college that remained riven by factionalism.

1503

THE CONCLAVE TO ELECT Alexander VI's successor opened on 16 September, bitterly divided between its French and Spanish factions. In the end the cardinals opted for a compromise candidate, and on 22 September the elderly Cardinal Francesco Piccolomini – not too old, at 64, but frail and suffering badly from gout – was elected. He chose the name Pius III in memory of his uncle Pius II, Enea Silvio Piccolomini, from whom he had received his cardinal's hat. 'It is said that he comes from a good background and has lived a good life. He is 72 [sic] years old and they say he has 12 children, sons and daughters.' ¹

PREVIOUS PAGE **Lucrezia Borgia,** *painted (early 16th century) by Bartolomeo Veneto. This beguiling portrait of Lucrezia, with her golden hair and a posy of daisies, a symbol of innocence, in her hand, conforms to all that we know about her. It displays the loveliness that so impressed the citizens of Ferrara when she arrived as Alfonso's bride in February 1502, and silenced many of those who suspected she was guilty of adultery and incest.*

ABOVE **Embossed copper brazier** *(late 15th century). Portable and convenient, braziers were part of the furnishing of a cardinal's conclave cubicle, where they were filled with charcoal and used to heat dishes of food brought to the Vatican.*

RIGHT **Cesare Borgia.** *The best-known portrait of Cesare, attributed to Altobello Meloni (fl.1497–1517), it portrays an elegant modish man, wearing expensive leather gloves, which were usually perfumed with musk.*

The news of Pius's election was late in reaching Ferrara – not until 26 September – 'and the reason for this delay is that Duke Ercole and all his sons and his daughter-in-law [Lucrezia] are at Comacchio, Codigoro or Marina, with all the court, because of the plague in Ferrara. Over two-thirds of the population have left the city for fear of the plague, though only six to ten are dying each day.' [2]

Cesare Borgia's political mistake

I can only criticize [Cesare Borgia] for the election of Julius II, which was a bad choice ... he should never have supported one of those cardinals he had offended, or one who feared him. For men do injury out of fear or hatred, and among those he had wronged was Cardinal Giuliano ... His principal aim should have been to engineer the election of one of the Spanish cardinals or, failing that, Cardinal Georges d'Amboise, but never Cardinal Giuliano.

NICCOLÒ MACHIAVELLI, *The Prince*, CHAPTER 7.

At his first consistory on 25 September, the new pope announced that his primary aim would be the reform of the Church and that he intended to call a council for this purpose. The next day he informed the Venetian ambassador that he had been asked by some of the Spanish cardinals to do certain favours for Cesare, 'but I will not do anything more for him,' he said, 'though I do not wish him ill'.[3] However, with his army depleted, Cesare persuaded Pius III that he was gravely ill and 'wanted to die in Rome',[4] where he returned on 3 October – very far from his death bed. On 7 October Pius III told the Venetian ambassador: 'I am not a saint or an angel, just a man who can make mistakes and I have been deceived.' [5]

Pius III's coronation took place the next day, 8 October, and he confirmed Duke Cesare in his post of Captain-General of the Church. But before the month was out, events took a radically different course for Cesare. The exertions of the pontificate were already proving too much for the new pope, who now fell seriously ill. With Pius III on his deathbed, and the Colonna and Orsini families joining forces against Cesare, the duke tried to leave Rome; but his escape was blocked by his enemies, and he fled instead to the safety of Castel Sant'Angelo, taking with him his soldiers and the young Borgia dukes, Giovanni and Rodrigo.

Pius III died on 18 October, after a pontificate that had lasted less than one month, leaving Rome once again in chaos.

During the following fortnight it became clear that Cesare's authority in the Romagna was beginning to unravel, as news arrived in Rome that first Forlì and then Faenza, Rimini and Pesaro had fallen, the latter retaken by its former lord and former husband of Lucrezia, Giovanni Sforza.

On 29 October Cesare and the Spanish cardinals held a meeting with Cardinal Giuliano della Rovere to discuss tactics for the forthcoming conclave. Thanks to Alexander VI, these Spanish cardinals formed a powerful faction in the college

The duke tried to leave Rome; but his escape was blocked.

ABOVE **Tempietto, Rome.** *A major landmark of Renaissance architecture, this tiny votive chapel was commissioned from Donato Bramante by Ferdinand and Isabella of Spain for the Franciscan convent of San Pietro in Montorio, to commemorate the presumed site of St Peter's martyrdom and finished in 1502. Bramante, who had worked for Ludovico Sforza on many ducal projects in Milan, chose a circular format for the building which followed the traditional design for a martyrium, but he broke new ground when he adapted the classical language of architecture in order to communicate a Christian message. In antiquity the Doric order had been used to represent strong, male deities, making this an entirely appropriate choice for St Peter, and Bramante's Doric columns supporting the elegant peristyle of the Tempietto are correctly proportioned, as is the surmounting frieze. However, Bramante was careful to temper the pagan overtones by tailoring the classical details in the frieze with the addition of the crossed keys – the symbol of St Peter, and the pope.*

and they agreed to offer Cardinal Giuliano their votes in return for the promise that, if he were elected, he would allow Cesare to keep his duchy and his post as Captain-General of the Church. The deliberations opened on 31 October, and the following morning – after the shortest conclave in history – it was announced that Cardinal Giuliano had been elected, as Pope Julius II.

Cesare now surrendered Castel Sant'Angelo and moved back into the Vatican, sending the young Borgia dukes Giovanni and Rodrigo to Naples, to the care of his sister-in-law Sancia of Aragon. But Julius II was not about to be constrained by former promises. On 18 November Cesare left Rome for Ostia, from where he hoped to reach the Romagna; but before he could set sail, two cardinals arrived with orders to arrest him if he did not reveal the passwords he had given to the men in charge of his fortresses. On 29 November, Cesare was brought back to Rome and imprisoned.

By now, Cesare's Duchy of Romagna was collapsing. In November, a Ferrarese chronicler recorded that:

Other Borgias now began to take precautions for their own safety.

> Faenza has come to an agreement with the Signoria of Venice, although the Venetians have sent their army and have occupied the territory and taken castles. The Lord of Rimini has sold his state to the Venetians, taking Cittadella in exchange and 24,000 ducats for the value of his possessions and immovable goods, and the promise of a hundred soldiers during his lifetime ... and so the states of Duke Cesare's duchy have rebelled against him and returned to their earlier lords. Also the state of Urbino has been taken by Duke Guidobaldo da Montefeltro, who is now in great favour with the new pope after having made Julius II's nephew his heir, because he has no sons of his own.[6]

Other Borgias now began to take precautions for their own safety. On 20 December Cardinal Pedro Luis Borgia left Rome for the security of Naples, where, on 27 December, the Spanish military commander Gonsalvo de Cordoba finally defeated the French armies at the Battle of Garigliano. Naples had been added to the vast Spanish Empire.

324

1504

EARLY IN JANUARY several cartloads of goods arrived at the customs house in Bologna purporting to belong to Cardinal Ippolito d'Este. When the officials opened the packs they discovered items stolen from the papal apartments by Cesare's courtier Miguel de Corella, which the duke had sent to Lucrezia for safekeeping.

On 29 January Cesare negotiated an arrangement with Julius II, whereby the duke would gain his freedom in return for the surrender, within 40 days, of the castles of Cesena and Forlì, which he was still holding; until then he would be imprisoned, under the careful eye of Cardinal Bernardino Carvajal, in the fortress at Ostia, where he was taken on 16 February.[7]

Cesare finally did surrender his castles, and on 19 April Cardinal Carvajal allowed him to leave Ostia for Naples, where he joined the Borgia cardinals and his younger brother Jofrè – and where he continued to plan a way of recovering his states. Julius II took further action against Borgia interests. He issued papal bulls disinvesting Rodrigo (the son of Lucrezia and Alfonso of Aragon) of the Duchy of Sermoneta, and Giovanni (the son of Alexander VI) of the Duchy of Camerino; he also reinstated Giovanni Sforza as Lord of Pesaro.

On 27 May King Ferdinand of Spain, alarmed that Cesare's plans might jeopardize his relationship with Julius II, ordered Gonsalvo de Cordoba – now the king's viceroy in Naples – to arrest Cesare. After three months in prison, Cesare was sent to Spain on 20 August, to the greater security of the stronghold of Chinchilla, in the mountains near Valencia.

In July Duke Ercole of Ferrara fell seriously ill. His heir, Alfonso, had left in April on a trip to France and England; Lucrezia Borgia had good grounds to worry that, if her father-in-law died while her husband were absent, then one of Alfonso's brothers would seize the title of duke. Alfonso hurried home, arriving on 8 August 'safe and well but very worn out by the worry and sorrow he had experienced at the thought of the danger he had been in, if his father had died'.[8]

This year, a terrible harvest in Ferrara was followed by unseasonably warm autumn weather, which continued into December such that:

Cesare's stolen goods

On 2 January *several carts of goods belonging to Duke Cesare arrived at the customs in Bologna under the name of the Cardinal of Ferrara. When they opened the chests and bales they found great riches stolen from the Church: the cross of St Peter embellished with jewels of infinite price, the mantle of St Peter with many jewels and gold ornaments, an image of Our Lady worth 10,000 ducats, a large camauro to wear with the pontifical mantle, the pope's gold and jewelled breastplate lined with velvet and a gold cat with two diamonds for eyes ... worth over 300,000 ducats.*

BERNARDINO ZAMBOTTI, *Diario Ferrarese*, P. 356, N. 5.

At this feast of Christmas plenty of violets have been brought in from the countryside, and also dishes of fresh broad beans and peas. It is said that our duke was told of someone who had a vine which had put out tendrils and made three grapes ... the Governor of San Felice has written to the duke to say that the cuckoo has been heard singing there this December. These things have happened because it is so warm and there has been plenty of

Plan of Ferrara. *This bird's-eye view of Ferrara shows the city much as it was in the 16th century, although it does include several late additions, notably the heavily fortified bastions (1598) that reinforced the circuit of walls built by Ercole I and the massive fortress on the left (1608). A comparison with the earlier woodcut of the city (page 290) shows how the area enclosed by Ercole I's walls in 1492 developed over the following century. The new walls brought several churches into the city for the first time, many of which were embellished or rebuilt by the duke himself. He also built several palaces and encouraged his wealthy courtiers to do likewise: the area soon became popular as they built large comfortable residences, which they embellished with gardens. Finally, more densely populated areas developed along the major roads, lined with more modest housing and shops. The old centre of Ferrara is in the lower half of the picture, and the line of the original set of walls is marked by the street that crosses the city from the right to meet the castle in the complex of buildings that formed the ducal palace. The reduced remnants of Ercole's hunting park and race course can be seen in the upper right of the picture – this is now a municipal park.*

ABOVE **Sisters playing chess,** *painted by Sofonisba Anguissola. This charming picture illustrates the popularity of board games during the Renaissance, of which chess was just one type, though considered more respectable than many others because of the skill needed to play the game well. The board, with its precisely detailed set of chessmen, rests on a table covered with a carpet, a distinctive feature of the furnishings of a wealthy household. The*

sisters too are depicted with care, providing clear evidence of the materials and styles of the dresses worn in a prosperous 16th-century home. The necklace worn by the youngest sister is made of coral, widely believed to protect children from harm. This intimate family portrait, which depicts Sofonisba Anguissola's own sisters and one of their servants, was painted by one of the few female artists to gain fame in the Renaissance.

rain. There have also been powerful thunderstorms with much lightning, so that on the first day of the month the Po broke its banks and flooded all of Bondeno.[9]

Lucrezia Borgia celebrated Christmas and New Year in Ferrara, where the ducal court usually also celebrated Carnival; she also discovered that she was pregnant for a third time since her marriage to Alfonso d'Este.

1505

ON 1 JANUARY Alexander VI's cousin Cardinal Juan Castellar died of kidney disease, at the age of 63. He was in Valencia, where he was negotiating with Ferdinand of Spain.

Towards the end of the month, on 25 January, Duke Ercole died. He was succeeded by his son, who became Alfonso I of Ferrara, and thus Lucrezia was now Duchess of Ferrara. Nevertheless, she needed to bear Alfonso sons and heirs to make her position properly secure.

By now Lucrezia also had the care of several Borgia children in Ferrara: Cesare's illegitimate children, Girolamo and Camilla, had probably been sent to her two years earlier, and this year they were joined by the seven-year-old Giovanni Borgia – Alexander VI's son and thus Lucrezia's half-brother. In June Lucrezia appointed Alberto Pio, the lord of nearby Carpi, as guardian to Giovanni.

Ferrara's Palazzo Ducale

The ducal palace was in the centre of Ferrara, next to the cathedral and the main market square. The massive 14th-century Castello Vecchio was one of the largest and most impressive defensive structures in Italy, and it provided a fitting symbol of ducal power. Attached to the castle was the Palazzo del Corte, which provided a setting for the display of cultural prestige.

The palace had been remodelled by Duke Ercole with new courtyards and gardens, a chapel, apartments for himself and his wife, an imposing ceremonial staircase for the reception of important guests and the Sala delle Commedie – the first purpose-built theatre since Antiquity. The reception rooms inside the palace were superb: they were known as the *Camere Dorate* (golden rooms) from their ornate gilded stucco decoration. Their walls were hung with costly tapestries and the floors ornamented with tiles painted with the Este arms and devices. Duke Ercole even installed flaps in the doors of the rooms for his beloved cats.[10]

329

A heavily pregnant Lucrezia moved first to Modena.

Early that summer in Spain, the captive Cesare Borgia made a dramatic bid to escape from his prison of Chinchilla. Some reports had him trying to strangle the governor of the castle, while others said that he knotted together his sheets but fell when the 'rope' broke; whatever the truth was, the result was that he was transferred in July to the fortress of Medina del Campo in Castile.

In Ferrara this year, the inhabitants suffered severe food shortages. A chronicler recorded that on 17 May 'there is no wheat nor fodder of any sort in the market, except for rice which is selling for 42 soldi a staro [a Ferrarese measure of volume], and there has been no bread for sale for the last two days ... all over the city the poor are crying for mercy, begging for a slice of bread, eating herbs and garlic shoots ... the famine is worse even than that during the wars of 1482'.[11]

In July, with the plague now exacerbating the famine in Ferrara, a heavily pregnant Lucrezia moved first to Modena, the second city of the Este duchy, and then, when the plague threatened there, to Reggio on 14 August. While in Reggio, on 19 September, she gave birth to a son who was named Alessandro in honour of his papal grandfather. But the child was sickly and died on 16 October.

The Duchess Lucrezia consoled herself for her misfortune with a trip to Mantua, where she began an affair with its marquis, Francesco Gonzaga, who was the husband of her sister-in-law Isabella d'Este.

Lucrezia and the Venetian ambassadors

On 14 February [1505] the ambassadors of Venice arrived in Ferrara to congratulate the Lord Duke Alfonso on his accession ... The duke sent his courtiers to meet them at Francolino and he himself went as far as Barco. They stayed in Ferrara for four days and on the fifth day His Excellency the duke took them out early in the morning, together with his courtiers, his falconers and the leopards, into the hunting park where they hunted with the falcons and leopards before leaving to return to Venice. The evening before they left Ferrara our illustrious duchess, Signora Lucrezia Borgia, went to visit them in their lodgings at the house of Count Uguzone Contrari with three court coaches carrying her ladies-in-waiting ... when the ambassadors heard of her arrival, they raced down, when she dismounted with all her ladies and invited the said ambassadors to take a tour of the city of Ferrara. They accepted the invitation and were about to mount their horses but she insisted, with much laughter, they ride in the coach, which they both did, Tommaso Mocenigo with the duchess, and Niccolò Michiel with Madonna Angela Borgia, a relative of the duchess, with all the ladies-in-waiting in the third, and thus they enjoyed their trip around the city. At the end, the ambassadors refused to let the duchess accompany them home, indeed, they insisted on accompanying her to the palace, and walked back to their lodgings on foot.

GIOVANNI MARIA ZERBINATI, *Croniche di Ferrara*, P. 55.

In November the bitter rivalry between Duke Alfonso's brother, Cardinal Ippolito, and his half-brother, Giulio, came to a head. Both men were courting the favours of Angela Borgia, the sister of Cardinal Pedro Luis Borgia and Lucrezia's cousin as well as her lady-in-waiting. While returning from a hunting expedition on 3 November, Giulio d'Este ran into the cardinal, whom Angela had just spurned in favour of Giulio's beautiful eyes. Cardinal Ippolito's grooms, acting on the orders of their insanely jealous master, proceeded to stab those eyes with their daggers.

As the year drew to a close, Lucrezia returned to Ferrara to celebrate Christmas, New Year and Carnival. By now, the city was recovering from the pestilence: 'at the beginning of December the illustrious lord our duke with his courtiers, the duchess with her ladies, and his brothers returned ... and for the whole month no one died of the plague'.[12]

ABOVE **Drawing of a cheetah** (15th century), by Pisanello. Duke Ercole I's hunting park was a famous attraction for honoured guests at the Este court. With the assistance not only of dogs and falcons but also cheetahs and leopards, a particular Italian fashion, huntsmen could chase a wide range of prey here, including stags, bucks, boars, hares, bears and porcupines. Hunting was immensely popular among the nobility and all aristocratic courts had their own hunting parks built, however modestly, in imitation of the great parks of the royal rulers of France and Burgundy. Good hunting dogs – greyhounds, boar hounds, harriers, mastiffs – were exchanged as valuable presents. The passion for the hunt was also reflected in the subject-matter of many tapestries that survive from the period.

Parnassus, *painted by Andrea Mantegna. Commissioned as part of the decorations for Isabella d'Este's study and completed in 1497, this panel shows Venus standing with Mars, who is not depicted as the god of war but as her lover, gazing into her eyes as they preside over the dancing figures of the nine Muses below. In a cave on the left, dressed in an angry red cloak, is the figure of Vulcan, Venus's cuckolded husband and the blacksmith of the gods, who rages and gesticulates beside his forge. This picture also reflects the importance of music at Isabella's court, a passion she developed during her childhood in Ferrara.*

333

1506

The pope himself led his troops into battle, and on 11 November he made his triumphal entry into Bologna.

DURING THIS YEAR Sancia of Aragon, wife of Cesare's brother Jofrè, died in Naples. Rodrigo, the son of Lucrezia and her previous husband Alfonso of Aragon, who had been in the care of Sancia, was now sent to Bari and the court of Isabella of Aragon, Dowager Duchess of Milan. The widowed Jofrè soon married again, choosing Maria de Milà, another member of the Borgia clan, and the couple would go on to have four children.

On 22 July Cardinal Francisco Loriz, Alexander VI's great-nephew, died in Rome at the age of 36, after having led an 'immoral life'. Nevertheless, Julius II ordered him to be buried in St Peter's.

In late July two of Duke Alfonso's brothers, Don Ferrante and Giulio, were discovered plotting to assassinate the duke. At the trial, which opened on 3 August, the two men and their fellow conspirators were found guilty and sentenced to death. The duke, however, pardoned his brothers though he imprisoned them for life. 'Don Ferrante threw himself onto his knees at the duke's feet and begged his forgiveness,' recorded the chronicler Zerbinati, 'but he was put in a room in the tower with several guards and four days later the duke bricked up the windows so that he could not see out of the room; he was about 28 years old.'[13]

In Spain, on 25 October, Cesare Borgia managed successfully to escape from the fortress at Medina del Campo and, although injured in a fall, was able to ride off and make good his escape. Lucrezia was again pregnant when the joyful news of Cesare's escape arrived in Ferrara, on 20 November. By 3 December, Cesare had made his way to the safety of Pamplona, capital of the kingdom of his brother-in-law Jean d'Albret, King of Navarre.

Meanwhile, Julius II had embarked on a military campaign to restore his authority in the Papal States, where the Venetians had taken advantage of the power vacuum left by the collapse of Cesare's duchy to expand their influence on the mainland. The pope himself led his troops into battle, and on 11 November he made his triumphal entry into Bologna.

RIGHT **Pope Julius II,** *painted by Raphael. One of the scenes decorating the pope's new apartments in the Vatican, this detail from the* Mass at Bolsena *(1512), shows the pope kneeling in prayer. He is as witness to a 13th-century miracle that saw blood seep out of a communion wafer as proof of the Catholic doctrine of transubstantiation, a controversial issue that was soon to take centre stage in the Protestant Reformation and divide both Europe and the Church. Raphael's portrait captures the character of this fierce and stubborn pope who before his pontificate, as Cardinal Giuliano della Rovere, had been one of Alexander VI's most vexing rivals and who, after Alexander's death, would not only effectively end the Borgia pope's ambitions for his son, Cesare, but also threaten the future of Lucrezia.*

1507

IN JANUARY LUCREZIA SUFFERED another miscarriage, owing, it was said, to too much dancing and revelry over Christmas.

On 12 March, Lucrezia lost her much-loved older brother. Cesare Borgia died in battle, killed in a skirmish while fighting for the King of Navarre. His wife, Charlotte d'Albret, went into deep mourning. She wore black for the rest of her life, even hanging her rooms with black cloth, using black sheets and decorating her dinner-plates with black patterns; she did, however, take good care of her daughter's inheritance, to which she added several titles, including the French county of Châlus.[14] Lucrezia was told the news of her brother's death on 22 April: 'she did not cry but displayed great sadness and great fortitude'.[15] As for Cesare's own attitudes to death, 'better to die in the saddle than in bed' was his view according to one chronicler.[16]

In a further sign of the changing times, Julius II announced on 26 November that he was moving out of the papal apartments in the Vatican, which had been decorated by Alexander VI with many portraits of his family, because he could not abide being reminded of these 'marrani'.[17] He moved into the rooms above, which had once been occupied by Cesare, commissioning Raphael's frescoes – the so-called *Stanze di Raffaello*.

By the end of the year Lucrezia was pregnant again.

1508

ON 4 APRIL Lucrezia gave birth to another son, named Ercole in honour of his paternal grandfather. The event was celebrated in grand style, though not without mishap on the first days, when fireworks caused fires to start.

On 5 June the Spanish priest who had helped Cesare to escape from Medina del Campo the previous year, and who had been given shelter in Lucrezia's

Lucrezia gave birth to another son, named Ercole in honour of his paternal grandfather.

LEFT **Horseman Falling.** *This masterful sketch by the Venetian artist Titian captures, with consummate skill, the dramatic moment when a bareback rider loses control just before falling off his mount. It conveys vividly the alarm in the horse's eyes as it loses its footing in a charge. In the violence that was endemic in Renaissance society, many cavalrymen lost their lives in battle, trampled to death under the feet of their horses, felled by cuts from a sword or blown apart by cannon fire. As Cesare Borgia said, it was 'better to die in battle than in bed'.*

Music at the Ferrarese court

Secular music played an important role at the court of Ferrara, which had a long-established tradition of employing musicians from France and Burgundy, particularly boy sopranos (Alfonso I returned from France in 1504 with a young French singer, who unfortunately became mixed up in the conspiracy to assassinate the duke). These musicians were employed at court, where they devoted their time to the composition and singing of madrigals and other types of songs, accompanied by lutes, rebecs (three-stringed instruments, played with a bow), spinets, pipes and other wind instruments.

It was not just the professionals who performed: the ladies and gentlemen of the court were expected to be proficient musicians too. Duke Alfonso was an accomplished viol player, while Lucrezia and her sister-in-law Isabella d'Este were important patrons of the new vogue, the *frottola*, a song sung by one voice accompanied by a string or keyboard instrument. Lucrezia managed to poach Bartolomeo Tromboncino from Mantua, and this composer and lute player wrote *frottole* with Spanish texts for his new patron.

household, was found brutally murdered in Ferrara.

At the end of the same month Lucrezia left Ferrara for Modena and Reggio, where she stayed until September in the company of the former Queen of Naples, Isabella del Balzo, who had joined the court in Ferrara.

On 10 December Louis XII of France and Emperor Maximilian signed the treaty of the League of Cambrai. Its purpose was ostensibly a crusade against the Turks, but everyone knew that it was, in reality, directed at curbing the power of Venice, whose growing influence on the Italian mainland was causing widespread alarm.

The birth of a Borgia-Este heir

Late in the afternoon of 4 April Madama Lucrezia Borgia the duchess gave birth to a baby boy in Ferrara, though the duke was in Venice. It was celebrated with great joy with church bells, salvoes of artillery and fireworks. All the screens and the cloth in the windows in the piazza caught fire; in the court house the benches of the notaries, the judge's stand, the windows and doors all burnt down, as well as the pews of the ladies in the cathedral and other churches, and all the seats, tables and footstools in the public schools ... and the festivities continued for three days. He was not christened publicly, and it is not known who held him for the baptism but the wet nurse who will look after him is the daughter of Guagraio di Maso and the wife of the carpenter Jacomo Savanuzo.

GIOVANNI MARIA ZERBINATI, *Croniche di Ferrara*, P. 76.

LEFT **A concert,** *painted (c.1485–95) by Lorenzo Costa. Depicting a performance by a lute player and two voices, one male and one female, this picture reflects the popularity of music-making at Italian Renaissance courts. Musicians like these were regularly employed at the Este court in Ferrara to entertain guests at the ducal dining table, where music and dancing provided pleasurable interludes between the numerous courses of a grand feast.*

ABOVE **Inlaid wood showing musical instruments.** *This cupboard with its door open to reveal the viols stored within was one of several musical images depicted with great skill in the intarsia decoration on the walls of the study of Duke Federigo da Montefeltro in his palace at Urbino.*

1509

EARLY IN 1509 THE LEAGUE of Cambrai was joined by those Italian powers most at threat from an expansionist Venice: Mantua, Ferrara and Rome. And Spain joined on behalf of Naples.

On 26 April 'there were fireworks, the firing of salvoes and the ringing of church bells to celebrate'[18] the news in Ferrara that, on 20 April, Pope Julius II had appointed Alfonso I as the Captain-General of the Church for the forthcoming war against Venice. With the duke absent from Ferrara, it was Lucrezia who took over the reins of power, much as she had done earlier for her father in Rome.

At the Battle of Agnadello on 14 May, the armies of the league inflicted a heavy defeat on the Venetian forces. 'On the same day triplets were baptized in the cathedral at Ferrara, the daughters of Cornelio, one of the duke's singers.'[19]

On 21 June, 'around midnight', part of the ducal palace in Ferrara burned down, causing damage estimated at 10,000 ducats. The losses included 'the Sala dei Paladini by the clock tower and 33 pavilions, all the beds, pillows, mattresses, bedcovers, all the lures for the falcons and the falcons themselves, which were in the mews underneath for their annual moult'.[20]

On 8 August Cesare Borgia's illegitimate daughter Camilla, who was about seven years old, was legitimized. Two weeks later, on 25 August, Lucrezia gave birth, this time producing a son for Alfonso; he was named Ippolito and was, like his uncle the Cardinal Ippolito, destined for a career in the Church.

During the year, Juan Borgia, 3rd Duke of Gandia, who was now 15 years old, was married to Joanna of Aragon, the illegitimate granddaughter of Ferdinand of Spain, thereby strengthening the Borgia family ties to the royal Spanish court.

341

LEFT **The Worship of Venus,** *painted by Titian. Alfonso I d'Este commissioned this painting in 1518 to form part of a series of eight mythological scenes to decorate the so-called 'Camerino', his study in the ducal palace where he displayed his collection of antiquities and medals. When Pope Clement VIII arrived in Ferrara in 1598, together with his nephew the great art collector Cardinal Pietro Aldobrandini, they stripped the Camerino of its treasures, taking the paintings to Rome. There the artefacts were proudly displayed at the Aldobrandini family palace before being acquired in the 17th century by the agent of the King of Spain.*

1510

ON 15 FEBRUARY Cesare's daughter Camilla entered the convent of San Bernardino, a new foundation which had been endowed by Lucrezia and staffed with 20 nuns from the convent of Corpus Domini. It was located 'on the street called Giovecha where the fur traders have their shops'.[21] Camilla chose to be known as Sister Lucrezia, out of affection for her aunt.

The happy arrival of another healthy son for the Duke and Duchess of Ferrara was undercut by a worsening political situation. In the months following the League of Cambrai's victory at Agnadello, Julius II had not only made peace with Venice but also formed an alliance with that city against the French. When Alfonso I refused to abandon his traditional loyalty to France, the pope dismissed him as Captain-General of the Church, replacing him with the Marquis of Mantua, Francesco Gonzaga. The pope now started to plan his campaign for the conquest of Ferrara.

In May the Venetian ambassador reported that worry about the French had given Julius II insomnia; the pope's hope was 'if God wills, the Duke of Ferrara will be punished and Italy will be liberated from the French'.[22] On 9 August the pope excommunicated Alfonso I, deprived him of his title as Duke of Ferrara and placed the city under an interdict. Some days later, on 18 August, papal forces captured Modena and two days after that the Venetians captured Rovigo. By 22 September Julius II had arrived in Bologna, but he soon fell seriously ill, halting the campaign.

Given the new political situation, in early October Cardinal Francisco Borgia left the papal court, in the company of cardinals Carvajal, Briçonnet, de Prie and Sanseverino, to join the French camp at Milan and to support Louis XII's plans to call a council whereby he hoped to depose Julius II.

On 28 October an heir was born to Juan Borgia, 3rd Duke of Gandia. The boy – whose ancestry made him great-grandson to both Pope Alexander VI and King Ferdinand of Spain – was named Francisco.

Fortifying the city of Ferrara

Early in the morning of Monday 2 December the ducal trumpeters went around Ferrara announcing to all and sundry that the duke asked courtiers, citizens, merchants, artisans and everyone who could to start working on the bastions and earthworks, for the love of him and there was not a single courtier or citizen, young or old, who declined to go; and I sent my sons, Giovanni Maria and Pietro Maria, and then went myself, taking my servant Girolamo Girondo as well. We worked on the bastion at the Porta di Sotto, where there were courtiers and citizens working, more than I can say, some carrying earth, others loading carts or pounding the ground over the bastions and earthworks with rammers ... the duke himself was working too, along with people of every social class, and there were lots of young boys.

GIOVANNI MARIA ZERBINATI, *Croniche di Ferrara,* P. 104.

With the birth of an heir, the duke's mother, Maria Enriquez, retired to the convent of Santa Clara in Gandia.[23]

On 28 November a large body of French troops arrived in Ferrara to help defend the city against the threat posed by Julius II. A ducal edict was published on Sunday 1 December ordering shops and businesses to close for a week, so that the citizens of Ferrara could help build the fortifications that would be needed. And the Duchess Lucrezia pawned many of her jewels and silver to raise money for the defence of the city.

During the year the 80-year-old Cardinal Luis Juan de Milà, who had been given his red hat at the same time as his cousin Rodrigo Borgia, died in Bélgida, after spending most of his life in Spain. Giovanni Sforza, who had been forced to divorce Lucrezia on the fabricated grounds of impotence, also died, leaving Pesaro to Costanzo, the son born to his third wife.

ABOVE **Courtyard of the ducal palace, Gandia.** *The grand palaces of Spanish aristocrats followed a similar pattern to those in the rest of Europe, with great reception halls on the first floor, reached by means of a monumental staircase, separate sets of apartments for the duke and duchess, nurseries for the children, and courtyards and gardens, often ornamented with fountains. Unlike Italy, however, where the fashion for the rounded arches of Ancient Rome had largely replaced the Gothic pointed arch of the Middle Ages, in Spain the architectural language of classical antiquity took much longer to establish itself.*

1511

ON 20 JANUARY THE CITY of Mirandola fell to the besieging papal forces, with the pope taking an active if unconventional role:

> Julius II had no notion of how undignified it was for someone as powerful as the Roman pontiff to lead his armies in person ... When he arrived at the camp he lodged in a farm-worker's hovel that was in range of the guns ... riding about all the time ordering the positioning of the artillery, which had not been done before because of the freezing weather and heavy snow.[24]

According to the Venetian ambassador, Julius II was now 'burning with impatience to take Ferrara', though he was dissuaded from leading his troops in person and retired to Bologna.[25]

Ferrara prepared for siege, and Carnival celebrations were cancelled. With Duke Alfonso preoccupied with war preparations, it was Lucrezia who entertained the steady stream of French aristocrats who arrived in Ferrara that winter; one visitor was full of praise for her 'marvellous parties and banquets in the Italian manner,' adding that she was 'beautiful and kind, gentle and friendly to all'.[26]

As with the siege of Ferrara , the terrible winter weather would last into the spring. Ferrarese chronicler Zerbinati recorded that 'this past winter has been one of the greatest cold, the greatest ice and the greatest snows that I have ever seen, and also it has been a very long one so that now, on the last day of April, we still light the fires and wear our fox-lined coats.'[27]

On Good Friday, 18 April, the Lenten sermon could not be given in Ferrara's cathedral – forbidden by the pope's interdict – but instead, at the request of Duchess Lucrezia, the friar preached in the courtyard of the palace; he preached there again on Easter Day.

On 22 May Louis XII of France and Emperor Maximilian called a council to depose the pope, which was to meet in October in Pisa. One of the nine cardinals who signed the document of convocation was Cardinal Francisco Borgia, and another was Cardinal Ippolito d'Este. At nightfall that same day, news arrived in Ferrara that Bologna, with the assistance of French troops, had rebelled against Julius II and the papal armies had been defeated. 'The bells rang out in Ferrara, there were fireworks, salvoes of artillery, and singing, boys and girls with boughs of blossom in their hands celebrating the defeat of the pope, who has been here the whole winter.'[28]

Two Borgia cardinals died this year. On 4 October Cardinal Pedro Luis Borgia, aged 39, had a fatal accident, falling from his horse. Three weeks later, on 24

Julius II and the papal armies had been defeated.

344

October, Julius II held a public consistory at which he excommunicated those cardinals who had supported Louis XII's call for a council to be held at Pisa; one of them was Francisco Borgia, but the 70-year-old cardinal failed to attend the proceedings, dying on 4 November while on his way to Pisa.

1512

DESPITE THE COUNCIL OF PISA, the threat posed by Julius II had not dissipated. The pope now negotiated a new alliance with the armies of Ferdinand of Spain against Louis XII and his allies, notably the Duke of Ferrara. On 11 April the two armies clashed at the Battle of Ravenna, where the French achieved a resounding victory but were forced to flee after news arrived that a large body of Swiss troops had entered Lombardy. Among the 10,000 men who died was the French commander Yves d'Alègre, who had done so much to establish Cesare Borgia's duchy in the Romagna.

Alfonso I and Lucrezia gave thanks for the victory to St Maurelio, patron saint of Ferrara, with a set of three silver plaques commissioned that year to mark the Battle of Ravenna: they depicted the duke in armour, Lucrezia presenting her eldest son Ercole to the saint, and the prior of the Olivetan monastery dedicated to the cult of the saint, set against the background of the city itself.

The Battle of Ravenna

On Easter Day *the famous Battle of Ravenna was fought between the army of the King of France, led by Gaston de Foix, and the troops of the pope and the King of Spain. The French were the victors thanks to our duke who, seeing that the French were losing ground, pretended to retreat towards Ravenna with the vanguard, of which he was captain, crossing the river with his artillery, with which he attacked the enemy's flank, slaughtering many lords and capturing many prisoners.*

GIOVANNI MARIA ZERBINATI, *Croniche di Ferrara*, P. 124.

On 23 June Alfonso I left Ferrara to travel to Rome, where he hoped to persuade Julius II not only to lift his excommunication and the interdict but also

OVERLEAF **Two details from *The Month of April,*** *by Francesco Cossa. Painted for Borso d'Este in the Palazzo Schifanoia in Ferrara, the backgrounds to these mythological scenes of the months show the ducal court at leisure. Fashionable courtiers and elegantly dressed ladies-in-waiting, many of whom are carrying musical instruments, are depicted indulging in those hardy staples of court life, gossip and flirtation. Among the groups of youths and girls chatting in the garden, conversing more intimately on a bench, embracing, even kissing amorously, Cossa has included quantities of rabbits to provide a lighthearted undercurrent of lust to the scene.*

to obtain the return of his cities of Modena and Reggio. Arriving in Rome on 4 July, he found the pope happy to lift the ecclesiastical measures but only in return for Ferrara itself, offering him the tiny state of Asti in its place. The duke refused this indignity and fled the city on 19 July, returning to Ferrara by a circuitous route to avoid capture.

In August Lucrezia received the sad news that her son by Alfonso of Aragon, Rodrigo, had died: he was only 12 years old and she had not seen him since he was a baby, when she had left him behind in Rome upon her remarriage and move to Ferrara.

ABOVE **Lucrezia Borgia presents her son to St Maurelius.** *This silver plaque shows the duchess presenting the young Ercole d'Este, heir to the duchy, to St Maurelius, the first Bishop of Ferrara who was martyred for his faith and shared the patronage of Ferrara with St George. It was one of three plaques commissioned in 1512, after the victory at the Battle of Ravenna, from the court goldsmith and master of the Mint, Giovanni Antonio Leli da Foligno, and placed in the cathedral. Behind Lucrezia are her ladies-in-waiting, wearing stylish dresses, though they are deliberately plainer versions of that worn by their mistress.*

1513

ON 21 FEBRUARY POPE JULIUS II, who had done so much to vex the Borgias, died. He was succeeded by Cardinal Giovanni de' Medici, who chose the name Leo X and claimed: 'God has given us the papacy, let us enjoy it!' One of his first acts was to lift Julius II's excommunication of Alfonso I and the interdict on Ferrara. This news was celebrated with a mass in the duchy's cathedral:

> Friday 18 March, the Friday before Palm Sunday, the mass of the Holy Ghost was sung in the cathedral of Ferrara ... and afterwards all the clergy and the monks and the people went in procession along the Via Saraceno past San Francesco and through the new town, into the market place and then to the cathedral, thanking God for the absolution; the duke and duchess had mass said in their chapel. [29]

On 11 April Alfonso I was in Rome to take part in the coronation of the new pope, returning to Ferrara by the end of the month. By the end of the summer the Duchess Lucrezia was pregnant again.

1514

ON 11 MARCH CESARE BORGIA'S widow, Charlotte d'Albret, died; their daughter Louise, now 14 years old, was sent to join the household of Louise of Savoy, the Duchess of Angoulême.

Late in the afternoon of 1 April Lucrezia gave birth to another son, in her rooms in the ducal palace. The boy was named Alessandro, in memory of her father, and on 5 November he was christened. 'His godfathers were the Viceroy of Spain and His Holiness the pope, who gave him two gold sleeves ornamented with jewels.'[30] Alfonso and Lucrezia's eldest son, Ercole, was also confirmed that day and Leo X, his patron, sent a collar ornamented with jewels and a fine horse.[31]

'A horrible year'

1514 has been a horrible year and troublesome because it began to rain during March and it continued wet all through the summer with not a single week when it did not rain. This lasted until Martinmas [11 November] and since then to the end of the year it has also rained, something that has never been recorded before. And although so much water and storms have devastated much of the land, the harvest has not been very bad.

GIOVANNI MARIA ZERBINATI, Croniche di Ferrara, PP. 136–7.

349

1515

A happier event unfolded for the duke.

ON 1 JANUARY France acquired a new king, when Louis XII died. He was succeeded by his cousin, Francis I, the son of the Duchess of Angoulême who had care of Cesare Borgia's now-orphaned daughter.

The Duchess Lucrezia gave birth to a daughter on 3 July, 'in her rooms in the ducal palace and she was baptized immediately because it seemed unlikely she would live, and she was given the name Eleonora', after Alfonso's mother.[32]

In the more peaceful years that followed the siege of Ferrara, Alfonso had time to devote to his hobbies. He 'would retire frequently to the private chamber he had built, more a workshop, where he would spend his leisure hours working on his lathe with pleasure and delight to produce flutes, tables and chess pieces, little boxes and other similar things.'[33]

A poet's paean to Lucrezia

And what can I say of Alfonso's second wife, Lucrezia; her honour, name and loveliness increase every hour. Favoured by fortune and by wealth, she flourishes like a plant in the best soil. She is as silver is to tin, gold to brass, the garden rose to the field poppy, the luscious bay to the withered willow, a jewel to coloured glass ... and she will be praised for the nobility of her sons: Ercole and his brothers will be crowned with shining laurels.

LUDOVICO ARIOSTO, *Orlando Furioso*, XIII, 69–71.

1516

ON 11 FEBRUARY KING FERDINAND of Spain died; he was succeeded by his grandson Charles V, who was also heir to Emperor Maximilian.

Exactly five months later, on 11 July, Lucrezia's son Alessandro – who had been a sickly infant – died, aged just two years old. But later in the year a happier event unfolded for the duke and duchess when, on 1 November, Lucrezia gave birth to another son, Francesco. He was baptized on 16 December with King Francis I as his godfather.

1517

IN EARLY JANUARY Lucrezia suffered further family losses when she heard the news of the death of her brother Jofrè – her last full sibling – whose son Francesco now inherited his title of Prince of Squillace. And on 15 March Cardinal Jaime Serra, the only remaining Borgia cardinal created by Alexander VI, died in Rome during the last session of the current Lateran Council. He was buried in the Spanish church of San Giacomo degli Spagnoli.

There was a Borgia marriage too this year, when Lucrezia's niece – Cesare's daughter Louise – married Louis de la Trémouille, a battle-scarred soldier.

1518

ON 15 NOVEMBER in Ferrara, Duke Alfonso, preparing to travel abroad, summoned all his courtiers to the audience hall in the ducal palace: 'I have sent for you to announce that I am leaving tomorrow for France, and I recommend my wife and my sons to your care.'[34]

Some days later, on 26 November, the Borgia dynasty – and Lucrezia personally – suffered another loss when Vanozza de' Cataneis, the former mistress of Rodrigo Borgia, died in Rome at the age of 76: the inscription on her tomb in Santa Maria del Popolo recorded her as the mother of Cesare, Juan, Lucrezia and Jofrè Borgia.

By the winter of this year Lucrezia was pregnant again.

The epitaph of Vanozza de' Cataneis

To Vanozza de' Cataneis, mother of Cesare, Duke of Valence, Juan, Duke of Gandia, Jofrè, Duke of Squillace and Lucrezia, Duchess of Ferrara, her noble children. Distinguished by her virtue, her exceptional piety, her age and her great prudence, and deserving of merit for her service to the Lateran hospital. Erected by Girolamo Pico, commissioner and executor of her will. She lived 76 years, 4 months and 13 days, and died on 26 November in the year 1518.

1519

ALFONSO I RETURNED HOME from France on 20 February, 'by boat before daybreak'.[35] On Sunday 3 April the nine-year-old Ippolito, Alfonso and Lucrezia's second son, was installed as the Archbishop of Milan, in place of the duke's brother Cardinal Ippolito who had renounced the benefice in favour of his young nephew. Ippolito presented Pope Leo X with an expensive golden vase worth 600 ducats in return for the favour.[36]

Lucrezia gave birth to another daughter, Isabella Maria, on 15 June. She was a weakly baby and was baptized immediately. But this was to be Lucrezia's last pregnancy. She succumbed once again to the dangerous puerperal fever, and this time she did not recover. On 24 June Lucrezia Borgia died, aged just thirty-nine. 'Her funeral took place the next day when she was buried with the nuns at Corpus Domini. All the orders of monks, the priests and the confraternities of Ferrara attended, and she was accompanied by the duke and her sons, the lords and courtiers and the people.'[37]

The 16 years following the death of Alexander VI had proved a turbulent and challenging period for his children, and for the whole Borgia clan. Cesare's decision to support the election of Pope Julius II had been a disastrous error of judgement. His arrest and subsequent imprisonment in Spain had left him impotent, unable to stop the total disintegration of his hard-won territories in Italy. Many of the relations Alexander VI had established in careers in the Church were now dead – and he could not have foreseen that only one of his children by Vanozza de' Cataneis would outlive their mother, and then only by a matter of months.

On Lucrezia's death, the poet Jacopo Sannazaro suggested an insulting epitaph for the duchess, citing Alexander the Great's mistress, the courtesan Thais: 'In this tomb lies Lucrezia by name, Thais by nature, daughter, wife and daughter-in-law of Alexander.' [38] But she was much mourned by the people of Ferrara. Despite her lascivious reputation, she had been an excellent duchess, governing the city with admirable skill during the many absences of her husband. She played an important role defending Ferrara from the armies of Julius II, during the siege lasting several months. Above all, Lucrezia ensured the future of the Borgia-Este dynasty: although some of her many children had died young, she had provided Alfonso I with an heir to the duchy in the shape of Ercole, and another son for the Church in the shape of Ippolito.

352

RIGHT **Alfonso I d'Este,** *painted by Dosso Dossi (fl.1512–42). In this powerful image of the military duke, Dossi has portrayed him in armour wielding his baton of command, with his troops lined up in the background. Alfonso I was fascinated by the apparatus of modern warfare, building his own foundry to cast cannon. When Julius II was ousted from Bologna, he bought Michelangelo's immense bronze statue of the pope and, reserving the head, melted the rest down and made it into a cannon which he named 'La Giulia'. His military interests, however, did not prevent him from becoming a major patron of the arts: he embellished the ducal palace with gilded ceilings, marble floors and painted decoration, and built a villa on the edge of the city set in magnificent gardens. Ferrara flourished as an important centre of literature, drama, music and art during his reign.*

THE BORGIA DESCENDANTS

DUKES, CARDINALS AND SAINTS

1520 and after

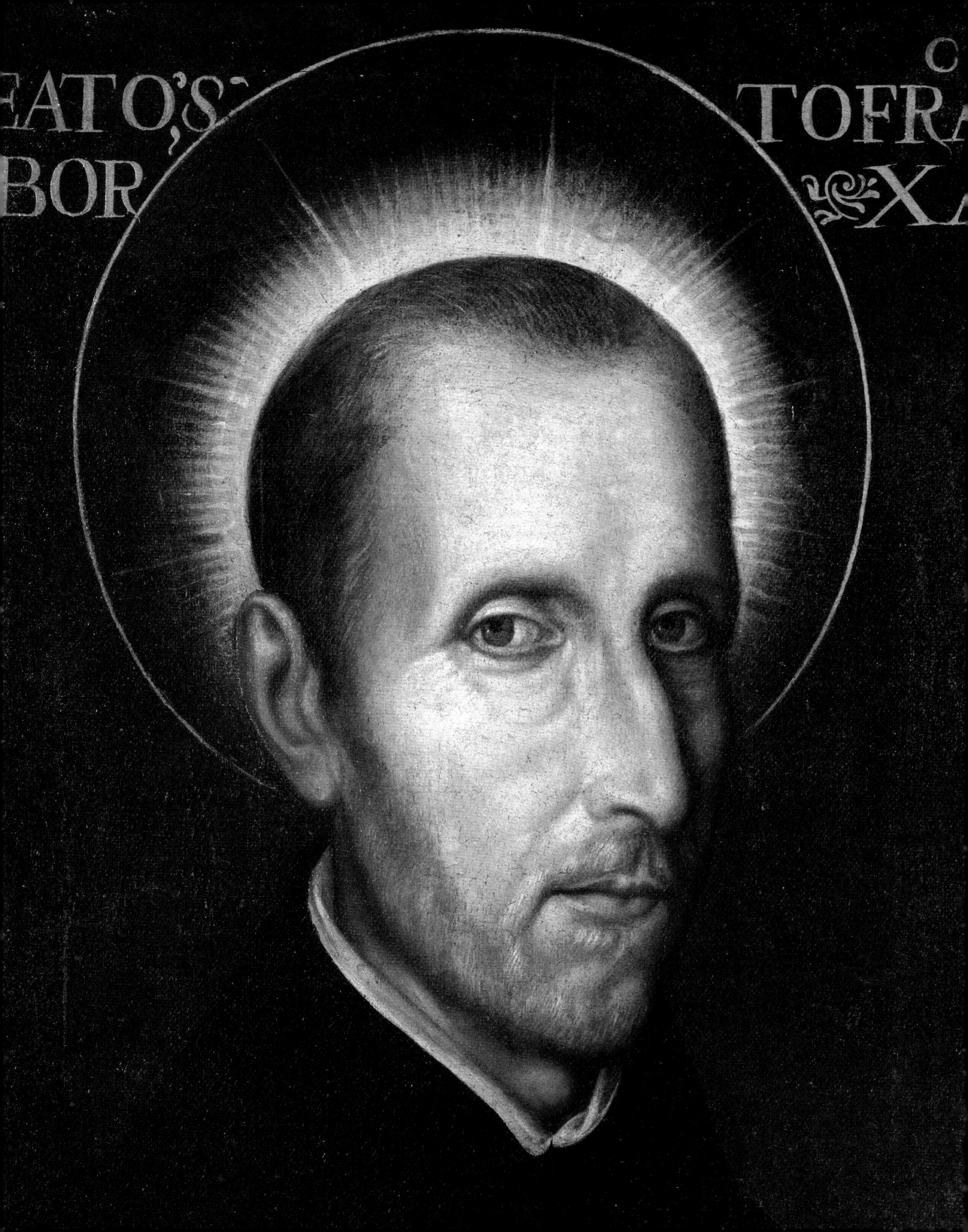

EATO S
BOR

O
TOFRA
XA

The Borgia blood line had considerably extended its power and influence in Europe over the century since Alonso de Borja had been appointed as secretary to the King of Aragon. The family may have lost its influence at the papal court in Rome by 1520 but, thanks to the machinations of Alexander VI, these once modest aristocrats, living on their estates at Játiva, were now dukes of Gandia, premier nobles at the Spanish court, princes of Squillace and heirs to the Duchy of Ferrara.

Even the loss of influence in Rome would prove only temporary, for when Lucrezia's son Ippolito received his cardinal's hat in 1539, another member of the family could be seen operating at the papal court very much in the mould of his grandfather, Alexander VI. Although he would never be elected pope, the magnificent and worldly Cardinal Ippolito would play an important role in the political, religious and cultural history of the 16th century. Moreover, in the devout and austere atmosphere of Counter-Reformation Rome, another descendant of Alexander VI – Francisco Borgia – would emerge into prominence leading the new Jesuit Order; and, in the century to come, he would be canonized.

1520–1524

IN 1520, THE GERMAN Augustinian friar Martin Luther published three pamphlets calling for the reform of the Church. In the realm of culinary tastes, the New World continued to introduce novelties, and in 1520 chocolate was first imported into Europe, from Mexico.

356

PREVIOUS PAGE **St Francis Borgia.** *This posthumous portrait successfully illustrates the severe and ascetic character of the saint, who was inspired to live a perfect Christian life after listening to the sermon preached at the funeral of Empress Isabella, wife of Charles V in 1538. A powerful figure in Counter-Reformation Rome, he would play a significant role in the reform of those abuses in the Catholic Church that his own papal great-grandfather had introduced.*

ABOVE **Mirror frame.** *Exquisitely carved in walnut and partly gilded, this luxury object was made for Alfonso I d'Este, and it has long been associated with Lucrezia Borgia.*

RIGHT **Four Evangelists Stoning the Pope,** *painted c.1538–44 by Girolamo da Treviso. An energetic depiction of the fury felt by Protestants at the behaviour of the pope, this painting shows the pope thrown to the ground along with personifications of Hypocrisy and Greed.*

On 7 March 1521, Isabella Maria d'Este, Lucrezia Borgia's last daughter – whose birth had led to Lucrezia's death – herself died. Pope Leo X also died this year, on 1 December; Duke Alfonso I commissioned a medal engraved with the motto 'out of the Lion's paw', and he hoped that the new pope would be more accommodating about returning the territories that had been seized from him by Julius II. The conclave elected Cardinal Adrian von Utrecht on 9 January 1522, and he adopted the name Adrian VI.

On 22 September 1522, Alfonso I sent his son Ercole to Rome to negotiate the formal reconciliation between Rome and Ferrara. 'On the last day of [October] the lord Don Ercole arrived in Ferrara on his return from Rome with the said absolution, which was published on 1 November on the order of our lord duke.'[1]

Adrian VI's papacy did not last long: on 14 September 1523 he died and Cardinal Giulio de' Medici was elected as Clement VII, the second Medici pope, on 19 November. In that year too, the eight-year-old Eleonora d'Este, Lucrezia Borgia's eldest daughter, entered the convent of Corpus Domini in Ferrara.

On 20 February 1524 Cardinal Campeggio arrived in Ferrara on his way to Germany to meet Martin Luther in order to 'root out the errors he preaches against the Church'.[2] It was also during 1524 that Duke Alfonso made known his liaison with his mistress Laura Dianti, the daughter of a bonnet-maker, when

It was also during 1524 that Duke Alfonso made known his liaison with his mistress.

358

he installed her in the Palazzo della Rosa: they would go on to have two children – known as Alfonso and Alfonsino – who were legitimized by the duke. The couple never married.

1525–1529

ON 24 FEBRUARY 1525 THE FRENCH were decisively defeated by the armies of Emperor Charles V at the Battle of Pavia. One casualty of the conflict was Louis de la Trémouille, husband of Cesare Borgia's daughter Louise, who died fighting for the French king.

The following year, Francisco Borgia, heir to Duchy of Gandia, married Eleonora de Castro, a lady-in-waiting to the empress, Isabella of Portugal. In November 1526, Duke Alfonso I decided to ally Ferrara with Charles V against the French; and on 1 December it was announced in Ferrara that the Emperor had promised to return Modena to Alfonso's dominion and to give his illegitimate daughter, the seven-year-old Margaret of Austria, as a bride for Alfonso's heir Ercole.

After Rome was sacked by Charles V's troops on 6 May 1527, Pope Clement VII was forced into an alliance with the Emperor; it would take another two years for Charles V to establish the imperial hegemony in Italy when, in the summer of 1529, he signed treaties at Barcelona with the pope and at Cambrai with Francis I.

Meanwhile, with the promise of the restitution of Modena assured, Alfonso I could return to his traditional alliance with France and, in 1528, arranged another prestigious marriage for Ercole with Renée of France: she was the daughter of Louis XII of France and Anne of Brittany, whose own marriage had proved such a useful tool for Pope Alexander VI in gaining French support for his dynastic policies. Moreover, Renée's sister Claude was married to Francis I.

The betrothal of Ercole and Renée took place in France on 28 June 1528 and, on 1 December the 18-year-old bride made her official entry into Ferrara. The grandiose scale of the wedding celebrations, which were her due as a royal princess, contrasted sharply with crowds of beggars 'wailing throughout the city that they were dying of hunger and cold and everyday they found the dead lying in the church porches'.[3]

LEFT **Young Woman at Her Toilet.** *Titian's skill as a portrait painter gained him fame across Europe. Official painter to the Venetian government, he was appointed court painter to Charles V and knighted by the Emperor in 1533; Alfonso I commissioned Titian to paint portraits of the duke and his mistress Laura Dianti, with whom he lived after Lucrezia's death. This painting of a lovely young girl arranging her hair in a mirror is probably not a portrait of her, but belongs to the genre of sensual images of beautiful young women, many by Titian, painted for wealthy Italians, who hung them in their bedrooms.*

1530–1534

Ercole succeeded to the duchy as Ercole II.

IN 1530 CESARE BORGIA'S DAUGHTER Louise, widowed in 1525, married Philippe de Bourbon by whom she would go on to have six children. In the same year Charles V invested Alfonso I with the fiefs of Modena and Reggio Emilia, which had been part of the Papal States since 1510 when Julius II had captured them from the Duchy of Ferrara.

On 16 November of the following year, the Duchess Renée gave birth to a daughter, Anna; she was the first of five babies who could claim to be the grandchildren of Louis XII of France and the great-grandchildren of Pope Alexander VI. The next child was born on 22 November 1533, when Renée produced an heir for Ercole, who was named Alfonso after Ercole's father. Less than a year later, on 31 October 1534, Duke Alfonso I died; now Lucrezia Borgia's son Ercole succeeded to the duchy as Ercole II.

Around 1532 another child of Alfonso I and Lucrezia, the 17-year-old Eleonora, was appointed abbess of the convent of Corpus Domini in Ferrara; Cesare Borgia's illegitimate daughter, who had taken the name Sister Lucrezia, would also become abbess of the convent of San Bernardino.

On 25 September 1534 Pope Clement VII died; Cardinal Alessandro Farnese, brother of Alexander VI's beautiful mistress Giulia, was elected Paul III on 13 October.

1535–1539

ON 16 DECEMBER 1535 RENÉE OF FRANCE gave birth to her second daughter, who was named Lucrezia after Duke Ercole's mother.

360

ABOVE **Medal of Ercole II d'Este,** *Duke of Ferrara. Ercole II, Lucrezia's eldest son, inherited the duchy at the age of 26 and continued the pattern of cultural patronage established by his predecessors, persuading many northern musicians to move to Ferrara and establishing a tapestry workshop in the city. He was particularly fond of imagery associated with Hercules and staged a banquet for his aunt, Isabella d'Este, decorating the table with huge sculptures depicting the labours of his hero made out of sugar.*

RIGHT **Francis I,** *commissioned from Titian in 1537. This magnificent portrait of the French king shows him in profile, and Titian probably based the features on a medal. Francis I tried to persuade the artist to come to France, without success. Despite never meeting the king, Titian managed to capture the jovial spirit of this powerful and majestic ruler, who thoroughly enjoyed hunting and gambling as well as many other pleasures of life.*

Lucrezia's second son with Alfonso, Ippolito, left Ferrara on 13 March 1536 for France at the invitation of Francis I: he would spend most of the next 13 years as a guest at the French court. One of his closest friends there was to be Henry II d'Albret, King of Navarre, and first cousin to his own cousin Louise Borgia. In October 1536 King Francis gave Ippolito the Archbishopric of Lyon, one of the premier sees of France.

In April 1536 the Protestant reformer John Calvin spent several weeks in Ferrara as a guest of Duchess Renée, who was very sympathetic to the Protestant cause. On 22 December of the same year Pope Paul III gave a cardinal's hat to the 12-year-old Rodrigo Luis Borgia, the first son of Juan, 3rd Duke of Gandia, by his second wife. But on 6 August 1537 the young cardinal died, just as the papal legate arrived in Gandia to bestow the red hat on him.

During 1537 Cesare Borgia's illegitimate son Girolamo was married to a daughter of the Lord of Carpi; and Renée of France gave birth to another daughter, named Eleonora.

On 20 December 1538 Pope Paul III created Ippolito d'Este a cardinal, but the promotion remained secret; the other cardinal whose name was kept back from the official list that day was Pietro Bembo, the former lover of Ippolito's mother, Lucrezia Borgia. The next day, the Duchess

LEFT **Cardinal Pietro Bembo,** *painted by Titian. A close friend of Titian, Bembo was 70 years old when this portrait was painted in 1540, marking his recent creation as cardinal by Pope Paul III. The poet who had once been Lucrezia's lover was now in old age, with a long and successful career behind him, which included serving as secretary to the two Medici popes Leo X and Clement VII.*

Protestantism in Italy

When the Augustinian monk Martin Luther nailed his 95 theses against indulgences on the door of the castle in Wittenberg, on 31 October 1517, he had no idea that he was starting a revolution that would dramatically and conclusively change the religious map of Europe.

Despite papal attempts to silence Luther, his ideas were rapidly disseminated in cheap pamphlets printed in private presses across Europe. 'Man is justified by faith alone' he argued, and his study of the Bible led him to challenge many of the basic tenets of the Church, including the miracle of transubstantiation that Catholics believed took place at the consecration of the host, clerical celibacy and the supreme power of the pope in Rome.

Luther's ideas found many followers in Italy, especially among those keen to eradicate corruption in the Church. The head of the Augustinians, Girolamo Seripando, was accused of being a Lutheran, while the head of the Capuchin Order, Bernardino Ochino, announced his conversion to Protestantism in 1540, as did Cardinal Odet de Châtillon in 1561. When Pietro Vermigli, an Augustinian, became a Protestant, he was forced to leave Italy; he moved to England, where he was appointed Professor of Divinity at the University of Oxford. Others were less fortunate, and many were denounced as heretics and executed for their beliefs by the Roman Inquisition, set up in 1542.

363

Renée gave birth to another son, Luigi; he was destined, with the assistance of his Uncle Ippolito, for a career in the Church.

Paul III published the creation of Ippolito as cardinal on 5 March 1539, and Ippolito travelled from France to Rome during the summer. On 27 October he was received in consistory by Pope Paul, who gave him the red hat and the titular church of Santa Maria in Aquiro, commenting: 'It is not one of the best titles, but nothing else is vacant at the moment, and they do say it is one of the oldest.' [4]

On 26 June 1539 Francisco Borgia, the heir to the Duchy of Gandia, was appointed at the age of 29 as Governor of Catalonia by Emperor Charles V. On 19 December Paul III gave a cardinal's hat to Enrique Borgia, aged 21, the younger brother of Francisco, to replace that given to his now-deceased half-brother Rodrigo Luis.

Cardinal Ippolito's tailor was busy making a lavish red damask outfit as a present.

1540–1544

IN APRIL 1540 CARDINAL IPPOLITO'S tailor was busy making a lavish red damask outfit as a present for Ippolito's cousin, the newly-created Cardinal Enrique.[5] During August Cardinal Ippolito was appointed to Francis I's privy council. But Cardinal Enrique did not have long to savour his new position, for he died on 16 September 1540.

That same month Pope Paul III issued a papal bull, *Regimini militantis ecclesiae*, giving his approval to the formation of the Society of Jesus – the Jesuits. The next year, in response to the challenge of Protestantism, the pope announced that a council to reform the Church was to take place at Trent, in Italy.

In Rome on 31 October 1541, Michelangelo's *Last Judgement*, created for the altar wall of the Sistine Chapel, was uncovered for the first time. In Spain, Juan Borgia, 3rd Duke of Gandia, died on 9 January 1543; he had fathered seventeen children – eight sons and nine daughters – and was now succeeded by the eldest of them, Francisco Borgia.

RIGHT **St Francis Borgia,** *painted by Alonso Cano. This portrait, which dates from 1624, shows the saint contemplating a crown that was a symbol of the secular power and prestige he had chosen to abandon in 1548 in order to pursue a life of charity, fasting and prayer as a member of the ascetic Jesuit Order. In 1607, 35 years after his death, a young girl was miraculously cured after prayers were made to him to intercede by her grieving family: the girl was one of his descendants, the granddaughter of his grandson Francisco, the Duke of Lerma. As the chief minister at the court of King Philip III of Spain, it was the duke's influence that enabled the process of Francisco Borgia's canonization to begin.*

1545–1549

Cardinal Ippolito left France for Rome.

IN 1545, THE NEW DUKE FRANCISCO founded a Jesuit College in Gandia. The next year saw the death of his wife, the Duchess Eleonora de Castro, and Francisco now decided to renounce his title and name his son, Carlos, the 5th Duke of Gandia; and on 1 February 1548, Francisco Borgia joined the Jesuits.

Alexander VI's eldest daughter, Isabella Borgia, died at the age of 80 in 1547; she had lived most of her life in Rome, in the house provided for her by her father. And the following year Alexander VI's youngest child Giovanni Borgia, born to him during his papacy, died in Genoa.

During 1547, Giovanni Battista Borgia, Prince of Squillace and grandson of Alexander's son Jofrè, built a new town near Catanzaro, which he named Borgia; it replaced a village that had been decimated by malaria and Turkish pirates.

The Jesuits

The Society of Jesus was founded in 1534 by the Spaniard Ignatius Loyola and a group of companions in Paris. They moved to Rome in 1538, where the society was recognized by Pope Paul III in 1540: Loyola was elected as the society's first general the following year.

The Jesuits were not a monastic order, though they took vows of poverty, chastity and obedience, especially to the pope, and demanded strict conformity to their rules. Above all, they followed Loyola's *Spiritual Exercises*, a programme for prayer that urged his followers to meditate on the life of Christ and re-enact the scenes of the Passion, the torments of Hell and the bliss of Paradise in their minds. The Jesuits lived in society, and dedicated their lives to education and missionary work, converting heretics and non-believers.

The order grew dramatically under the generalships of Loyola and his successor Diego Laynez, one of Loyola's original companions. During the 1540s Jesuit colleges were founded across Spain and Italy, while another of Loyola's original followers, Francis Xavier, travelled as far as Goa to begin his missionary work in the Far East.

Jesuit churches in Rome were decorated with horrifying scenes of the brutal murders of Christian saints to encourage young novitiates to emulate these martyrs in their often dangerous missions on behalf of the Order. The mother church of the Jesuits, the Gesù, which was begun in 1568 in Rome, was built with funds supplied by Cardinal Farnese, the grandson of Paul III.

On 16 December 1548 Anna d'Este, daughter of Duke Ercole II and Renée of France, was married at St-Germain-en-Laye to Francis of Lorraine, heir to the powerful Catholic nobleman, the Duke of Guise. In May the following year, Ercole's brother Cardinal Ippolito left France for Rome, where he was to take up the prestigious post of Cardinal-Protector of France.

Pope Paul III died on 10 November, heralding another conclave in Rome.

1550–1554

ON 8 FEBRUARY 1550 CARDINAL GIOVANNI MARIA DEL MONTE was elected as Pope Julius III. Cardinal Ippolito d'Este was rewarded for his part in the conclave with the governorship of Tivoli.

After the death of his father, Francis of Lorraine inherited the Duchy of Guise on 12 April 1550, and thus his wife Anna d'Este became duchess.

Pope Julius III reconvened the Council of Trent in 1551: it had been forced to close in 1548 because of the wars between France and the Empire.

In 1552 King Henry II of France appointed Cardinal Ippolito d'Este as Governor of Siena. On 1 October 1553 the cardinal's daughter Renata married Luigi Pico, the Lord of Mirandola. Also in 1553, Louise Borgia – Cesare's daughter by Charlotte d'Albret – died in France.

Meanwhile Francisco Borgia, having given up the Duchy of Gandia, was progressing up the hierarchy of the Society of Jesus. On 10 June 1554 Ignatius Loyola appointed him as Commissioner-General of the Jesuits in Spain.

In Ferrara during 1554, Duke Ercole II started official proceedings against his wife, Renée of France, for heresy. She was arrested but recanted her Protestant faith on 23 September, after being threatened with losing all her possessions.

1555–1559

ON 23 MARCH 1555 POPE JULIUS III died; he was succeeded by Cardinal Marcello Cervini on 9 April, but the new pope died less than a month later, on 1 May. The second conclave of the year saw the election of the reformist founder of the Theatine Order, Giampietro Carafa, who took the name Paul IV. One of his first actions was to accuse Cardinal Ippolito d'Este of trying to buy votes during the recent conclave: the cardinal was punished by being deprived of all his posts

Duke Ercole II started official proceedings against his wife, Renée of France, for heresy.

367

Alfonso II arrives in Ferrara

All the streets along which the duke rode were filled with people of all backgrounds and condition, both men and women. The palaces and houses on the said streets were hung with tapestries and decorated with festoons of greenery and the ducal arms. Outside the windows hung costly carpets with beautiful ladies leaning out, married women and girls, which was a delightful sight.

PAOLO DA LIGNAGO, *Cronaca*, PP. 784–5 (IN *Storia di Ferrara*, ED. LUCIA CHIAPPINI, VI, P. 25)

and exiled to Ferrara. The following year, Paul IV issued the Index of Forbidden Books, and several works in Cardinal Ippolito's library were confiscated by the Inquisition in Rome.[6]

In January 1556 Charles V renounced his Spanish kingdom (which included the Spanish Netherlands and his American possessions, as well as Milan and Naples) in favour of his son, who became Philip II of Spain. In September of the same year he also renounced the imperial crown in favour of his brother, Ferdinand I, and retired to the monastery of Yuste in western Spain. Charles died on 21 September 1558, and the oration at his funeral in Valladolid was given by Francisco Borgia.

Also in 1558, Lucrezia Borgia's grandson and heir to Ferrara, Alfonso d'Este, married Lucrezia de' Medici, the daughter of Cosimo I, Duke of Florence. Alfonso left his 13-year-old bride in Florence while he returned to the enjoyment of life at the French court.

Pope Paul IV died on 18 August 1559, but it was not until Christmas Day, after one of the longest conclaves in history, that Cardinal Giovanni Angelo Medici was elected, taking the name Pius IV. Cardinal Ippolito d'Este, who again played a key role in this election, was now reinstated in all his posts in Rome. On 3 October the cardinal's brother Duke Ercole II died unexpectedly, while Ippolito was

RIGHT **Medal of Cardinal Ippolito d'Este the younger.**
Lucrezia's second son, Ippolito, pursued an illustrious career in Church politics. Immensely rich, thanks to the benefices heaped on him by the French kings Francis I and Henry II, he built two superb villas, both set in magnificent gardens: the Palazzo Monte Cavallo, his suburban villa on the Quirinal Hill in Rome, and the famous Villa d'Este, his summer retreat in Tivoli.

in the conclave. His son, now Duke Alfonso II, left France immediately and arrived in Ferrara on 20 November, just seven days before his twenty-sixth birthday. He soon summoned his young bride from Florence.

1560–1564

WITH HER SON INSTALLED as Duke of Ferrara, the Duchess Renée left the city and returned to France, where her estate at Montargis, south of Paris, soon became a notable haven for French Protestants. The following year, on 21 April, Alfonso II's young wife died of a lung infection, without having produced an heir.

Early in 1561, the Jesuit General Diego Laynez summoned Francisco Borgia to Rome. On 2 June that year, Pius IV named Cardinal Ippolito d'Este as papal legate to France. He left Rome on 27 June with Diego Laynez to attend the Colloquy of Poissy, an attempt by the French crown to negotiate peace between the Catholics and Protestants in France. In November that year Cardinal Ippolito attended a Protestant sermon, and his action was severely condemned by hard-line Catholic reformists in Rome.

In 1562 Pope Pius IV, as a favour to Cardinal Ippolito d'Este, gave a red hat to Luigi d'Este, the younger brother of Duke Alfonso II.

In February 1563, Francis, Duke of Guise, was assassinated by a Protestant fanatic; his widow Anna d'Este continued to work hard for the Catholic faction at the French court.

In the following year the Council of Trent finally completed its work; Pius IV issued the papal bull *Professio fidei*, setting out the premises of the Roman Catholic faith.

Alfonso II's extravagance

Hearing that some imperial ambassadors were passing through Ferrara, he [Duke Alfonso II] arranged to meet them invited them to stay, doing them great honour, and invited them to a banquet in the Hall of Mirrors ... having fixed a large net used for hunting boar in the moat outside the hall the night before ... they ate off silver plates and dishes and after every course the table was cleared and the silverware was thrown out of the windows, where it was caught in the net in the moat below. The guests were unhappy because they had no time to eat more than a few morsels before the table was cleared, but more and more courses arrived on new silver platters, in such abundance that it is impossible to describe. The guests were utterly astonished, and could only marvel at the grandeur of this prince.

J. BENTINI ET AL. (EDS), *A tavola con il principe* (1988), PP. 399–400.

369

1565–1569

ON 2 JULY 1565 Francisco Borgia's high standing among his fellow Jesuits was recognized when he was elected to succeed Diego Laynez as the third Superior General of the Order.

Also in 1565 the widowed Duke Alfonso II of Ferrara married for the second time. His bride was Barbara of Austria, the sister of Maximilian II, who had succeeded his father Ferdinand I as Holy Roman Emperor in 1564. She made her entry into Ferrara on 2 December.

On 9 December 1565 Pope Pius IV died, and on 7 January 1566 his successor, Cardinal Michele Ghislieri – a close friend of Francisco Borgia – was elected Pope Pius V. As the former inquisitor-general, Pius V now instituted rigorous reforms in the Church.

Now allied with the Emperor by marriage, in 1567 Duke Alfonso II joined the Imperial army fighting the Turks in Hungary and Austria; he appointed his uncle Cardinal Ippolito to assist Barbara of Austria in the government of the duchy in his absence. But there was still no sign of an heir to the duchy, and in 1568–9 Cardinal Ippolito considered making Cardinal Luigi, the duke's younger brother, resign his red hat in order to marry. He also opened negotiations for the marriage of his granddaughter Ippolita to Marzio Colonna.

Francisco accepted the invitation of his cousin Alfonso II to recover at the Este court in Ferrara.

370

1570–1572

IN 1570 ANNA D'ESTE and the rest of the Guise family left the French court after the signing of the Treaty of St-Germain on 8 August, which appeared to promise peace and an end to the religious strife between the Catholics and Protestants in the country. The dowager French Queen Catherine de' Medici now planned a marriage between her daughter Marguerite de Valois and the Protestant Henry of Navarre.

But the pope had other ideas. On 7 June 1571 Pius V asked the Jesuit General Francisco Borgia to accompany his legate Cardinal Michele Bonelli to Spain where, among other tasks, they were charged with arranging a marriage between King Sebastian of Portugal and Marguerite de Valois. At the request of Pius V, Francisco and the legate also travelled to France to negotiate with Catherine de'

Medici, who proved intractable. They left the French court on 25 February 1572 to return to Italy: the journey was long and arduous, and Francisco fell seriously ill with pneumonia. Leaving the cardinal to continue the journey to Rome alone, Francisco accepted the invitation of his cousin Alfonso II to recover at the Este court in Ferrara.

On 1 May 1572 Pope Pius V died; he was succeeded by Cardinal Ugo Boncompagni, who was elected Pope Gregory XIII on 14 May.

Three months later, in France, the uneasy peace between Catholics and Protestants dissolved. On 22 August, during the celebrations for the marriage of Henry of Navarre and Marguerite de Valois, an attempt was made by the Guise faction to assassinate the Protestant leader Gaspar de Coligny, who was shot; many blamed Anna d'Este for this action, which sparked off the massacre of Protestants on St Bartholomew's Eve, 23–24 August, during which some 10,000 Protestants (including Coligny, attacked again) were killed in Paris.

In 1572 the Borgia clan lost its two most prominent figures in Church affairs. On 3 September, Francisco Borgia left Ferrara and travelled via Loreto to Rome, where he died on 30 September. Two months later, on 2 December, Cardinal Ippolito d'Este died in Rome.

RIGHT **Alfonso II d'Este,** *painted by Sante Peranda. A major patron of music in the Este tradition, Alfonso II was also famous for encouraging the development of soft-paste porcelain in Ferrara. After a major earthquake hit Ferrara in 1570, which destroyed much of the ducal palace, the duke was fully occupied in its rebuilding; he also commissioned a series of paintings in the courtyard, promoting the antiquity of his family in over 200 portraits.*

The years afterwards

Two descendants of Pope Alexander VI would marry into the royal Stuart house and become queens of England, Scotland and Ireland.

IN 1597 DUKE ALFONSO II of Ferrara died, still without an heir. He left the duchy to his illegitimate nephew Cesare d'Este, the grandson of Alfonso I and his mistress Laura Dianti – and it thus passed from the Borgia family, though not without problems. Pope Clement VIII refused to recognize the succession and reclaimed the Duchy of Ferrara as a lapsed papal fief. The following year the pope's nephew, Cardinal Pietro Aldobrandini, arrived in Ferrara, removing paintings and sculptures for his own collection. Duke Cesare set up the Este court instead at Modena, where it survived until 1796 when the duchy became part of the Napoleonic Empire.

In 1602 the Principality of Squillace, once the possession of Jofrè Borgia, was united with the Duchy of Gandia by a marriage between these two branches of the Borgia family. The last Borgia Duke of Gandia died in 1740, without an heir.

Alexander VI was not the last Borgia pope. A century and a half later, in 1644, Alexander VI's great-great-great-grandson Giambattista Pamphili was elected Pope Innocent X.

On 20 June 1671, Francisco Borgia – who had been elected Jesuit General in 1565 – was canonized by Pope Clement X.

Two descendants of Pope Alexander VI would marry into the royal Stuart house and become queens of England, Scotland and Ireland: Catherine of Braganza, descended from the dukes of Gandia, married Charles II in 1662; and Mary of Modena, a descendant via the Este line, married James II in 1673; neither of them had any children.

A Borgia aristocracy does, however, exist to this day, in the form of the descendants of Cesare Borgia's daughter Louise – the counts of Busset and Châlus.

RIGHT **Pope Innocent X,** *painted c.1650 by Diego Velázquez. Court painter to Philip IV of Spain, Velázquez visited Rome to study Italian art and was commissioned to paint this portrait of Innocent X. One of the greatest papal portraits of all time, it skilfully captures the contrasting textures of the pope's shiny red satin cape, his fine white linen vestments that billow out beneath and the heavy velvet upholstery of the chair on which he is seated. This masterly study of power shows the last Borgia pope as a timid old man, neither a majestic figure nor a great communicator as his ancestor Alexander VI had been, and one who relied heavily, both politically and socially, on his domineering sister – though the rumours that their relationship was incestuous were undoubtedly false.*

HOLY ROMAN EMPIRE

SWISS
CONFEDERATION

MARUISATE
OF MANTUA

Lausanne

Geneva

Trent

HUNGARY

Aosta

DUCHY
OF
SAVOY

Milan

Turin

Brescia

Pavia

Verona

Vicenza

R. Piave

Padua

Venice

Belgrade

FRANCE

DUCHY
OF
MILAN

R. Po

Parma

OTTOMAN
EMPIRE

MARQUISATE
OF MONFERRATO

Modena

Genoa

Ferrara

Imola

DUCHY
OF
FERRARA

REPUBLIC
OF
GENOA

Bologna

Forli

Cesena

ROMAGNA

Rimini

DALMATIA

Florence

Pisa

REPUBLIC
OF
FLORENCE

Pesaro

Senigallia

Urbino

Ancona

REPUBLIC
OF
LUCCA

Siena

Arezzo

Perugia

REPUBLIC
OF
SIENA

Assisi

Piombino

Elba

Orvieto

R. Tiber

Viterbo

CORSICA

PAPAL
STATES

Chieti

Ajaccio

Ostia

Rome

N

Gaeta

Capua

Benevento

Bari

Naples

KINGDOM
OF
NAPLES

Brindisi

SARDINIA

Salerno

Amalfi

Otranto

TYRRHENIAN
SEA

Cosenza

Catanzaro

MEDITERRANEAN SEA

ADRIATIC SEA

REPUBLIC OF VENICE

Lipari
Islands

Reggio

IONIAN
SEA

Renaissance Italy
at the end of the 15th century.

Messina

SICILY

—— Boundary of Cesare Borgia's
duchy at its greatest extent

0   200 km

0   200 miles

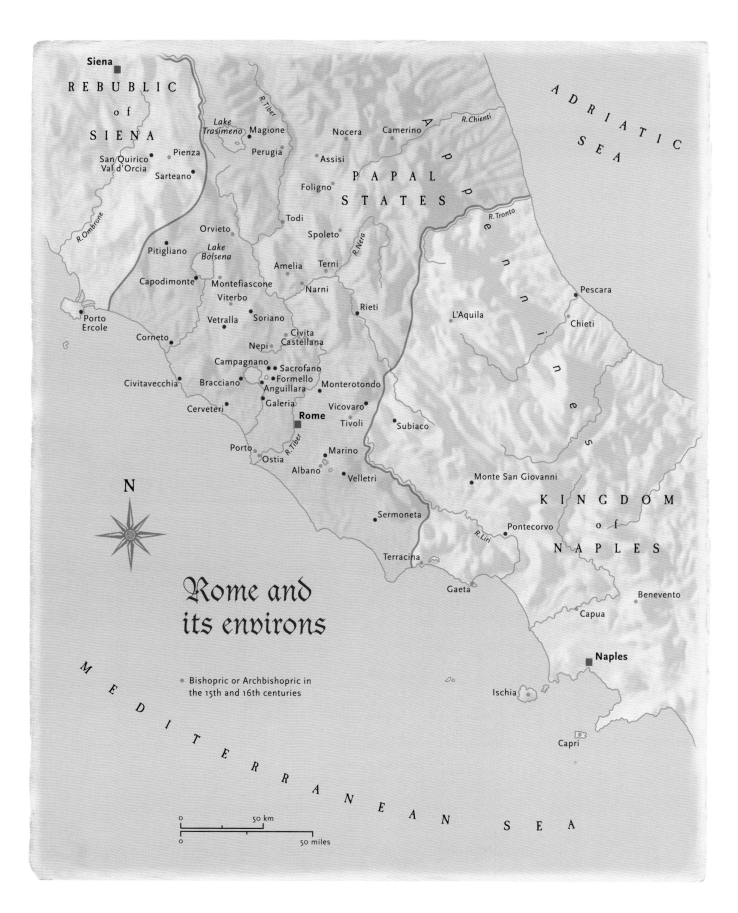

Siena

REBUBLIC
of
SIENA

R. Tiber

ADRIATIC
SEA

Lake
Trasimeno

Magione
Nocera
Camerino
R. Chienti

San Quirico
Val d'Orcia
Pienza
Perugia
Assisi
PAPAL
STATES

Sarteano
Foligno

R. Ombrone
Todi
Spoleto
R. Tronto

Orvieto
Amelia
Terni
R. Nera
Pescara

Pitigliano
Lake
Bolsena

Capodimonte
Montefiascone
Narni
L'Aquila
Chieti

Viterbo
Rieti

Porto
Ercole
Vetralla
Soriano

Corneto
Civita
Castellana

Nepi

Campagnano
Sacrofano
Monterotondo

Civitavecchia
Bracciano
Formello
Vicovaro
Subiaco

Anguillara
Galeria
Rome

Cerveteri
Tivoli

Porto
Marino

Ostia
Monte San Giovanni

Albano
Velletri

N
Sermoneta
KINGDOM
of
NAPLES

Pontecorvo
R. Liri

Terracina

Benevento

Gaeta

Capua

Rome and
its environs

Naples

• Bishopric or Archbishopric in
the 15th and 16th centuries

Ischia

Capri

MEDITERRANEAN SEA

APPENNINES

R. Tiber

0   50 km
0   50 miles

Borgia family tree

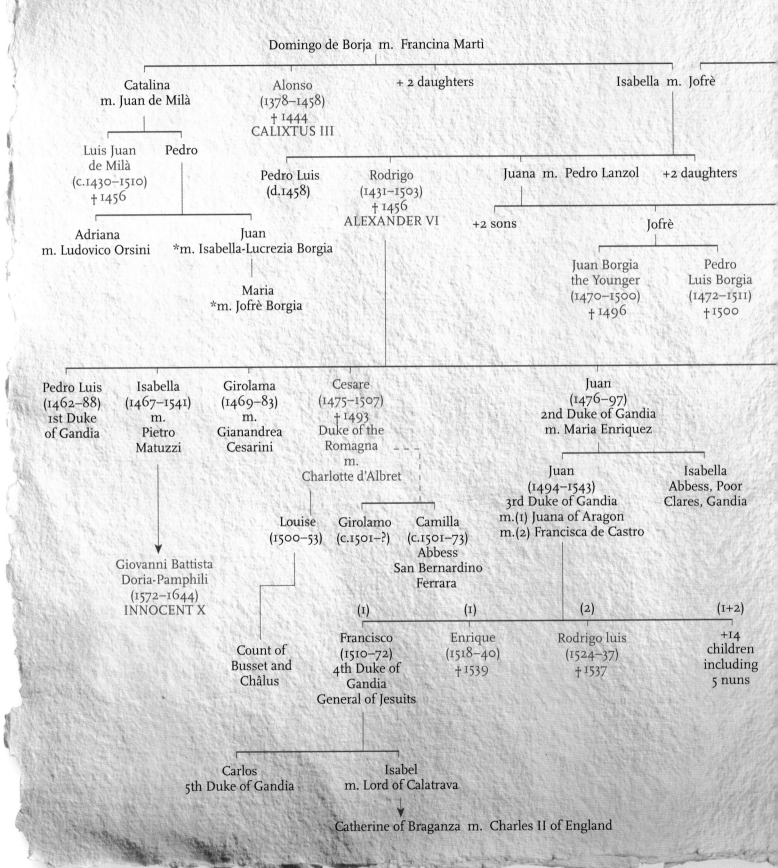

Domingo de Borja m. Francina Martì

Catalina
m. Juan de Milà

Alonso
(1378–1458)
† 1444
CALIXTUS III

+ 2 daughters

Isabella m. Jofrè

Luis Juan
de Milà
(c.1430–1510)
† 1456

Pedro

Pedro Luis
(d.1458)

Rodrigo
(1431–1503)
† 1456
ALEXANDER VI

Juana m. Pedro Lanzol

+2 daughters

Adriana
m. Ludovico Orsini

Juan
*m. Isabella-Lucrezia Borgia

+2 sons

Jofrè

Juan Borgia
the Younger
(1470–1500)
† 1496

Pedro
Luis Borgia
(1472–1511)
† 1500

Maria
*m. Jofrè Borgia

Pedro Luis
(1462–88)
1st Duke
of Gandia

Isabella
(1467–1541)
m.
Pietro
Matuzzi

Girolama
(1469–83)
m.
Gianandrea
Cesarini

Cesare
(1475–1507)
† 1493
Duke of the
Romagna
m.
Charlotte d'Albret

Juan
(1476–97)
2nd Duke of Gandia
m. Maria Enriquez

Juan
(1494–1543)
3rd Duke of Gandia
m.(1) Juana of Aragon
m.(2) Francisca de Castro

Isabella
Abbess, Poor
Clares, Gandia

Louise
(1500–53)

Girolamo
(c.1501–?)

Camilla
(c.1501–73)
Abbess
San Bernardino
Ferrara

Giovanni Battista
Doria-Pamphili
(1572–1644)
INNOCENT X

Count of
Busset and
Châlus

(1)

Francisco
(1510–72)
4th Duke of
Gandia
General of Jesuits

(1)

Enrique
(1518–40)
† 1539

(2)

Rodrigo luis
(1524–37)
† 1537

(1+2)

+14
children
including
5 nuns

Carlos
5th Duke of Gandia

Isabel
m. Lord of Calatrava

Catherine of Braganza m. Charles II of England

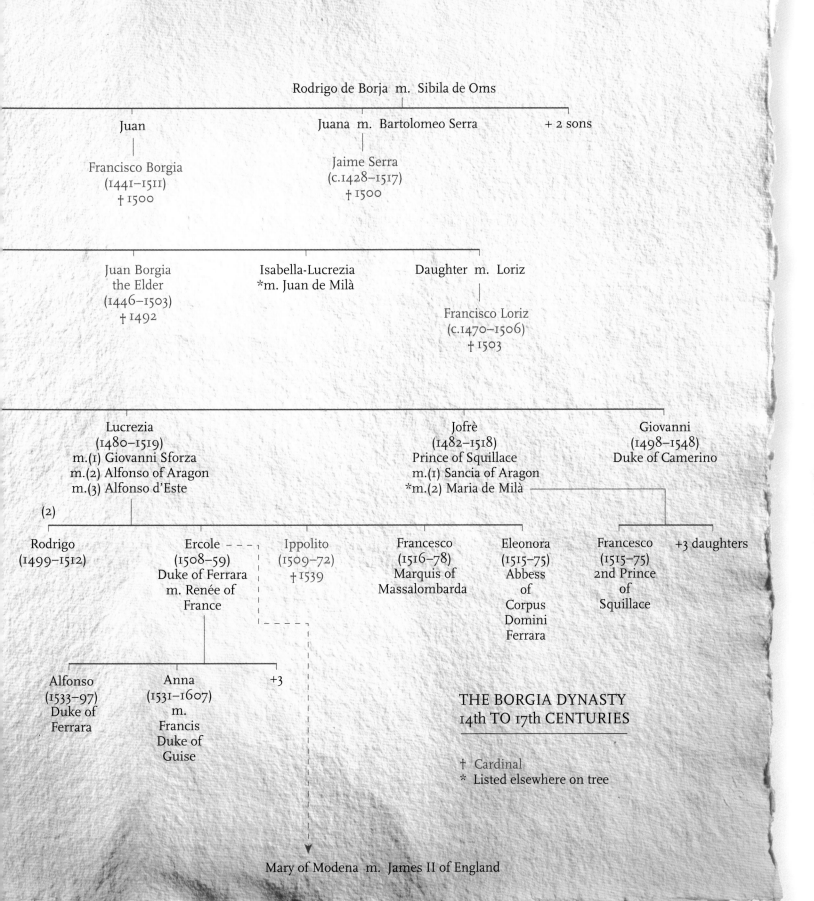

Rodrigo de Borja m. Sibila de Oms

Juan

Juana m. Bartolomeo Serra   + 2 sons

Francisco Borgia
(1441–1511)
† 1500

Jaime Serra
(c.1428–1517)
† 1500

Juan Borgia
the Elder
(1446–1503)
† 1492

Isabella-Lucrezia
*m. Juan de Milà

Daughter m. Loriz

Francisco Loriz
(c.1470–1506)
† 1503

Lucrezia
(1480–1519)
m.(1) Giovanni Sforza
m.(2) Alfonso of Aragon
m.(3) Alfonso d'Este

Jofrè
(1482–1518)
Prince of Squillace
m.(1) Sancia of Aragon
*m.(2) Maria de Milà

Giovanni
(1498–1548)
Duke of Camerino

(2)

Rodrigo
(1499–1512)

Ercole - - -
(1508–59)
Duke of Ferrara
m. Renée of
France

Ippolito
(1509–72)
† 1539

Francesco
(1516–78)
Marquis of
Massalombarda

Eleonora
(1515–75)
Abbess
of
Corpus
Domini
Ferrara

Francesco
(1515–75)
2nd Prince
of
Squillace

+3 daughters

Alfonso
(1533–97)
Duke of
Ferrara

Anna
(1531–1607)
m.
Francis
Duke of
Guise

+3

THE BORGIA DYNASTY
14th TO 17th CENTURIES

† Cardinal
* Listed elsewhere on tree

Mary of Modena m. James II of England

BIBLIOGRAPHY AND SOURCES

Ariosto, Ludovico, *Orlando Furioso*, 2 vols, Harmondsworth, 1975.

Bentini, Jadranka, *et al.* (eds), *A tavola con il principe*, Ferrara, 1988.

Berengan, Giuliana, *Le dame della corte estense*, Ferrara, 2000.

Bernardi, Andrea, *Cronache forlivesi dal 1476 al 1517*, Bologna, 1895.

Bradford, Sarah, *Cesare Borgia*, London, 1976.

Bradford, Sarah, *Lucrezia Borgia*, London, 2004.

Burchard, Johannes, *Liber notarum*, abridged in *Dans le Secret des Borgia*, Paris, 2003.

Chambers, David, 'The Economic Predicament of Renaissance Cardinals', *Studies in Medieval and Renaissance History*, Vol. 3 (1966), pp. 289–313.

Chambers, David, 'The Housing Problems of Cardinal Francesco Gonzaga', *Journal of the Warburg and Courtauld Institutes*, Vol. 39 (1976), pp. 21–58.

Chambers, David, 'Giovanni Pietro Arrivabene (1439–1504): Humanistic Secretary and Bishop', *Aevum*, 58 (1984), pp. 397–438.

Commines, Philippe de, *Mémoires*, Paris, 1843.

Conti, Sigismondo de', *Le storie de suoi tempi dal 1475 al 1510*, Rome, 1883.

Diario Ferrarese, in *Rerum Italicarum Scriptores*, new series, Vol. 24 Pt 7, Bologna, 1928–37.

Eubel, Konrad, *Hierarchia Catholica Medii Aevii*, 6 vols, Monasterii, 1913–24.

Faccioli, Emilio (ed.), *L'arte della cucina in Italia*, Turin, 1992.

Filangieri, R., 'Rassegna critica delle fonti per la storia di Castel Nuovo', *Archivio storico per le provincie napoletane*, Vol. 63 (1938), pp. 75–77.

Gaspare da Verona, *Vita Pauli II*, in *Rerum Italicarum Scriptores*, new series, Vol. 3 Pt 16, Città di Castello, 1904.

Gherardi, Jacopo, *Diarium Romanum*, in *Rerum Italicarum Scriptores*, new series, Vol. 23 Pt 3, Città di Castello, 1904.

Giovio, Paolo, *La vita di Alfonso da Este Duca di Ferrara*, in G.C. Giraldi, *Commentario delle cose di Ferrara*, Venice, 1597.

Gorris, Rosanna, 'La corte di Renata di Francia a Ferrara', in *Il Palazzo di Renata di Francia*, edited by Loredana Olivato, Ferrara, 1997, pp. 139–73.

Guicciardini, Francesco, *Le cose fiorentine*, Florence, 1945.

Guicciardini, Francesco, *Storia d'Italia*, 6 vols, Rome, 1967.

Hollingsworth, Mary, *The Cardinal's Hat*, London, 2004.

Hollingsworth, Mary, 'Coins, Cloaks and Candlesticks', in *The Material Renaissance*, edited by Michelle O'Malley and Evelyn Welch, Manchester, 2007, pp. 260–87.

Hollingsworth, Mary, 'A Taste for Conspicuous Consumption: Cardinal Ippolito d'Este and His Wardrobe, 1555–1566', in *The Possessions of a Cardinal*, edited by Mary Hollingsworth and Carol M. Richardson, University Park, PA, 2010, pp. 132–52.

Krautheimer, Richard, *Rome: Profile of a City, 312–1308*, Princeton, NJ, 1980.

Landucci, Luca, *Diario fiorentino dal 1450 al 1516*, Florence, 1985.

La Torre, Ferdinando, *Del conclave di Alessandro VI papa Borgia*, Rome, 1933.

Machiavelli, Niccolò, *Tutte l'opere di Niccolò Machiavelli*, 3 vols, London 1772; *The Prince* in Vol. I, pp. 323–85.

Mallett, Michael, *The Borgias*, London, 1969.

Martines, Lauro, *Fire in the City*, Oxford, 2006.

Masi, Bartolomeo, *Ricordanze*, edited by G. Odoardo Corazzini, Florence, 1906.

Newbiggin, Nerida, 'Piety and Politics in the *feste* of Lorenzo's Florence' in *Lorenzo il Magnifico e il suo mondo*, edited by G.C. Garfagnini, Florence, 1994, pp. 17–41.

Parks, N. Randolph, 'On the Meaning of Pinturicchio's *Sala dei Santi*', *Art History*, Vol. 2 (1979), pp. 291–317.

Pastor, Ludwig von, *The History of the Popes from the Close of the Middle Ages*, 29 vols, London 1894–1951.

Pedretti, Carlo, *Leonardo architetto*, Milan, 1978.

Piccolomini, Aeneas Silvius, *The Secret Memoirs of a Renaissance Pope*, edited by F.A. Gragg and L.C. Gabel, London, 1988.

Platina (Bartolomeo Sacchi), *Vitae pontificum*, in *Rerum Italicarum Scriptores*, new series, Vol. 3, Pt 1, Città di Castello, 1923–4.

Roover, Raymond de, *The Rise and Decline of the Medici Bank*, Cambridge, MA, 1963.

Rucelli, Giovanni, *Zibaldone*, in *Giovanni Rucellai ed il suo zibaldone*, edited by A. Perosa, 2 vols, London, 1981.

Ryder, Alan, *The Kingdom of Naples under Alfonso the Magnanimous: The Making of a Modern State*, Oxford, 1976.

Sanudo, Marin, *I Diarii*, excerpts edited by Paolo Margaroli, Vicenza, 1997.

Savonarola, Michele, *Libretto de tutte le cose che se manzano comunamente*, Venice, 1515 (reprinted Padua, 1991).

Shankland, Hugh, *The Prettiest Love Letters in the World*, London, 1987.

Shaw, Christine, *Julius II*, Oxford, 1996.

Shearman, John, 'The Chapel of Sixtus IV', in *The Sistine Chapel: Michelangelo Rediscovered*, edited by M. Giacometti, New York, 1986, pp. 22–91.

Stinger, Charles L., *The Renaissance in Rome*, Bloomington, IN, 1985.

Tuohy, Thomas, *Herculean Ferrara*, Cambridge, 1996.

Urban, Günther, 'Die Kirchenbaukunst des Quattrocentos in Rom', *Römisches Jahrbuch für Kunstgeschichte*, Vols 9–10 (1961–2), pp. 72–287.

Vespasiano da Bisticci, *The Vespasiano Memoirs*, edited by W. G. and Emily Waters, London, 1926.

Weil-Garris Brandt, Katherine, 'Michelangelo's Pietà for the Cappella del re di Francia', in *Il se rendit en Italie: études offertes à André Chastel*, Paris, 1987, pp. 77–119.

Zambotti, Bernardino, *Diario Ferrarese dal anno 1476 sino al 1504*, in *Rerum Italicarum Scriptores*, new series, Vol. 24 Pt 7, Bologna, 1928.

Zerbinati, Giovanni Maria, *Croniche di Ferrara*, Ferrara, 1989.

NOTES ON THE TEXT

Details of all works cited below appear in the Bibliography and Sources.

Alonso de Borja 1414–1455

1. Mallett, pp. 60–1.
2. Ryder, p. 28 n. 8.
3. Filangieri, p. 76 doc.1.
4. Krautheimer, p. 267.
5. Piccolomini, p. 45.
6. Mallett, p. 84.
7. Gaspare da Verona, p. 39.
8. Pastor II, p. 81.
9. Pastor II, pp. 83–4.
10. Pastor II, pp. 501–2 doc. 5
11. Pastor II, p. 87 n.
12. Pastor II, p. 274 n.
13. Pastor II, pp. 288–9 n.
14. Pastor II, p. 479 n.
15. Pastor II, p. 330.

Calixtus III 1455–1458

1. Pastor II, pp. 536–7 doc 31.
2. Piccolomini, p. 64.
3. Pastor II, p. 537 doc. 31.
4. Pastor II, pp. 331–2.
5. Pastor II, p. 346.
6. Roover, p. 198.
7. Mallett, p. 80; Pastor II, pp. 334–5.
8. Pastor II, p. 387.
9. Pastor II, p. 387.
10. Pastor II, pp. 348–9.
11. Pastor, II, pp. 539–40 doc. 35.
12. Pastor II, p. 362.
13. Pastor II, pp. 373–4.
14. Pastor II, p. 371.
15. Mallett, p. 71.
16. Pastor II, pp. 548–50.
17. Pastor II, p. 348 n.
18. Pastor II, p. 457.
19. Piccolomini, p. 72.
20. Pastor II, p. 386.
21. Chambers (1966), p. 299.
22. Mallett, p. 89.
23. Burchard, pp. 333–4.
24. Pastor II, pp. 552–3 doc. 46.
25. Pastor II, p. 466.
26. Pastor II, p. 466 n.
27. Pastor II, p. 469 n.
28. Pastor II, pp. 556–7 doc. 50.
29. Pastor V, p. 537–8.
30. Pastor II, pp. 557–9 doc. 51.
31. Piccolomini, p. 89.
32. Pastor II, p. 473 n.
33. Pastor II, p. 473 n.
34. Pastor II, pp. 561–3 doc. 53.
35. Pastor II, p. 563 doc. 54.

The Borgia nephews 1458–1471

1. Piccolomini, p. 75.
2. Piccolomini, p. 76.
3. Piccolomini, p. 76.
4. Newbiggin, p. 31 n. 45.
5. Piccolomini, p. 114.
6. Pastor III, p. 62 n.
7. Piccolomini, p. 144.
8. La Torre, pp. 7–8.
9. La Torre, p. 17.
10. Pastor III, pp. 397–403 doc. 42.
11. Chambers (1976), p. 43 doc. 3.
12. Piccolomini, pp. 242–3.
13. Chambers, 1976, p. 26 n. 38.
14. Piccolomini, p. 251.

15. Piccolomini, p. 260.
16. Piccolomini, p. 265.
17. Chambers (1976), p. 49 doc. 13.
18. Piccolomini, p. 80.
19. Machiavelli I, p. 247.
20. Parks, p. 303 & n.
21. Pastor III, 355 n.
22. Pastor III, p. 357.
23. Pastor II, p. 455 n.
24. Chambers (1984), p. 433 n. 206.
25. Pastor IV, pp. 30–1 n.
26. Pastor IV, p. 447, doc. 5
27. Platina, p. 368.
28. Pastor IV, p. 126.
29. Pastor IV, p. 479 doc. 11.
30. Pastor IV, p. 47.
31. Pastor V, pp. 488–92 doc. 21.
32. Pastor IV, p. 62 n.
33. Pastor IV, p. 190 n.
34. Pastor IV, pp. 494–6 doc. 26.
35. Pastor IV, pp. 131–2.
36. Pastor IV, p. 186 n.
37. Pastor IV, p. 185 n.
38. Pastor IV, p. 185.
39. Pastor IV, pp. 504–5 doc. 42.
40. Pastor IV, p. 190 n.
41. Pastor IV p. 191 n.

Rodrigo Borgia 1471–1484

1. Eubel II, p. 37 n. 313.
2. Eubel II, p. 37 n. 311.
3. Pastor IV, p. 222 n.
4. Eubel II, p. 38 n. 318.
5. Eubel II, p. 38 n. 318.
6. Mallett, p. 94.
7. Pastor IV, p. 254.
8. See Platina.
9. Pastor IV, p. 279.
10. Pastor IV, p. 281 n.
11. Pastor IV, p. 288.
12. Eubel II, p. 39 n. 352.
13. Pastor IV, p. 290.
14. Shearman, p. 27.
15. Pastor IV, p. 334.
16. Pastor IV, pp. 335–6.
17. Pastor IV, p. 340.
18. Pastor IV, p. 343.
19. Pastor IV, pp. 384–5 n.
20. Mallett, p. 103.
21. Pastor IV, p. 379.
22. Pastor IV, p. 380.

Rodrigo Borgia 1484–1492

1. La Torre, p. 81.
2. Pastor V, pp. 236–7.
3. La Torre, p. 40.
4. Pastor V, p. 242.
5. Commines, pp. 381–2.
6. Pastor V, p. 271 n.
7. Pastor V, p. 369.
8. Pastor V, p. 253 n.
9. Mallett, p. 102.
10. Pastor V, pp. 351–2 & n.
11. Urban, p. 280.
12. Bradford (1976), p. 23.
13. Pastor V, p. 403.
14. Parks, p. 310 n 33.
15. Pastor V, p. 315 n.
16. Guicciardini (1945), ch. 9.
17. Guicciardini (1967) I, 2.
18. Pastor V, p. 318 n.
19. Pastor V, pp. 319–20.

20. Pastor V, p. 375 n.
21. Pastor V, p. 378.
22. La Torre, p. 85.
23. Pastor V, p. 536, doc. 11.
24. La Torre, p. 79, n. 1.
25. Pastor V, 390 n.
26. Stinger, p. 304.
27. Pastor V, p. 537, doc. 13.
28. Burchard, p. 44.
29. Burchard, p. 48.
30. Burchard, p. 50.
31. Burchard, p. 45.
32. Mallett, p. 233.
33. See Parks.

Alexander VI 1493–1497

1. Pastor V, p. 407 n.
2. Pastor V, pp. 409–10.
3. Burchard, pp. 66–7.
4. Burchard, p. 71.
5. Burchard, pp. 79–80.
6. Pastor V, p. 414.
7. Pastor V, p. 542 doc. 20.
8. Burchard, pp. 90–2.
9. Burchard, p. 99.
10. Zambotti, p. 231.
11. Burchard, p. 106.
12. Pastor V, p. 424.
13. Guicciardini (1967), I, 9.
14. Pastor V, p. 432 n.
15. Pastor V, p. 438.
16. Pastor V, pp. 547–8 doc. 28.
17. Burchard, p. 136.
18. Burchard, pp. 154–5.
19. Burchard, pp. 160–1.
20. Pastor V, p. 549 doc. 31.
21. Burchard, pp. 187–8.
22. Mallett, p. 140.
23. Zambotti, p. 251.
24. Pastor V, pp. 469–70.
25. Pastor V, pp. 479–80.
26. Guicciardini (1967), III, 11.
27. Burchard, pp. 210–11.
28. Pastor V, p. 485.
29. Pastor VI, p. 16.
30. Pastor VI, pp. 20–1.
31. Pastor V, p. 505 n.
32. Burchard, p. 234.
33. Mallett, p. 145.
34. Pastor V, p. 501.
35. Pastor V, p. 501.
36. Pastor V, p. 554 doc. 38.
37. Pastor V, p. 519 n.
38. Pastor V, p. 503.
39. Burchard, p. 243.
40. Pastor V, p. 523.
41. Pastor V, p. 520.
42. Burchard, pp. 246–7.

Alexander VI, Cesare and Lucrezia 1498–1500

1. Pastor VI, p. 25.
2. Pastor VI, p. 27.
3. Burchard, p. 250.
4. Burchard, p. 250.
5. Pastor VI, p. 32.
6. Pastor VI, p. 33.
7. Sanudo, p. 66.
8. Landucci, p. 173.
9. Martines, p. 3.
10. Mallett, p. 164.
11. Burchard, p. 275.
12. Burchard, p. 284.
13. Burchard, p. 278.
14. Burchard, p. 280.

15. Burchard, p. 290.
16. Burchard, p. 293.
17. Weil–Garris Brandt.
18. Burchard, p. 296.
19. Burchard, p. 301.
20. Burchard, p. 304.
21. Burchard, p. 313.
22. Burchard, pp. 317–18.
23. Burchard, p. 323.
24. Zambotti, p. 295.
25. Burchard, p. 321.
26. Burchard, p. 324.
27. Burchard, p. 329.
28. Burchard, pp. 337–8.
29. Burchard, pp. 342–3.
30. Burchard, p. 346.
31. Burchard, pp. 347–8.
32. Pastor VI, pp. 191–2.
33. Burchard, p. 354.
34. Pastor VI, p. 80.

Cesare and Lucrezia Borgia 1501–1503

1. Burchard, p. 358.
2. Zambotti, p. 303.
3. Burchard, p. 365.
4. Burchard, p. 365.
5. Masi, pp. 46–7.
6. Burchard, p. 368.
7. Burchard, p. 382.
8. Burchard, p. 375; Zambotti, p. 273.
9. Burchard, p. 376.
10. Burchard, p. 376.
11. Burchard, p. 377.
12. Burchard, p. 378.
13. Burchard, p. 381.
14. Burchard, p. 383.
15. Burchard, p. 384.
16. Zambotti, pp. 308–10.
17. Pastor VI, p. 109.
18. Burchard, pp. 397–8.
19. Burchard, p. 387.
20. Burchard, p. 387.
21. Burchard, p. 396.
22. Burchard, p. 397.
23. Bradford (2004), p. 140.
24. Mallett, p. 191.
25. Pastor VI, pp. 112–13.
26. Burchard, p. 398.
27. Zambotti, pp. 312–15.
28. Zambotti, p. 314.
29. Zambotti, p. 315.
30. Zambotti, p. 324.
31. Zambotti, p. 315.
32. Zambotti, pp. 331–2.
33. Burchard, p. 399.
34. Burchard, p. 404.
35. Burchard, pp. 402–3.
36. Zambotti, p. 287.
37. Pastor VI, pp. 119–20.
38. Pastor VI, p. 121.
39. Pedretti, p. 29.
40. Zambotti, p. 342.
41. Zambotti, p. 342.
42. Machiavelli III, pp. 30–2.
43. Machiavelli III, pp. 33–4.
44. Burchard, p. 414.
45. Mallett, pp. 201–2.
46. Mallett, p. 224; Machiavelli III, p. 71.
47. Machiavelli II, p. 6.
48. Zambotti, pp. 344–5.
49. Zambotti, p. 345.
50. Burchard, p. 418.
51. Burchard, p. 421.
52. Burchard, p. 421.

53. Burchard, p. 422.
54. Burchard, pp. 424–5.
55. Burchard, p. 426.
56. Zambotti, p. 346.
57. Pastor VI, p. 127.
58. Pastor VI, p. 128 n.
59. Zambotti, p. 348.
60. Pastor VI, pp. 128–9.
61. Zambotti, p. 351.
62. Pastor VI, p. 131 n.
63. Pastor VI, p. 131.
64. Burchard, p. 428.
65. Burchard, p. 429.
66. Shankland, doc. 14.
67. Machiavelli I, *The Prince*, ch. 7.
68. Burchard, p. 428.
69. Burchard, p. 437.
70. Shankland , doc. 1.
71. Machiavelli I, *The Prince*, ch. 7.

Cesare and Lucrezia Borgia 1503–1519

1. Zerbinati, p. 46.
2. Zerbinati, p. 46.
3. Pastor VI, p. 202.
4. Pastor VI, p. 203.
5. Pastor VI, p. 203.
6. Zambotti, pp. 353–4.
7. Mallett, p. 261.
8. Zambotti, pp. 358–9.
9. Zerbinati, p. 50.
10. Tuohy, pp. 257–63.
11. Zerbinati, p. 57.
12. Zerbinati, p. 60.
13. Zerbinati, p. 62.
14. Mallett, p. 261.
15. Bradford (2004), p. 270.
16. Bernardi, p. 55.
17. Pastor VI, pp. 217–18.
18. Zerbinati, p. 79.
19. Zerbinati, p. 79.
20. Zerbinati, p. 82.
21. Zerbinati, p. 91.
22. Shaw, p. 259.
23. Mallett, p. 274.
24. Guicciardini (1967), pp. 212–13.
25. Pastor VI, p. 342.
26. Bradford (2004), p. 307.
27. Zerbinati, p. 113
28. Zerbinati, p. 116.
29. Zerbinati, p. 132.
30. Zerbinati, p. 134.
31. Zerbinati, p. 76.
32. Zerbinati, p. 137.
33. Giovio, p. 18.
34. Zerbinati, p. 145.
35. Zerbinati, p. 146.
36. Hollingsworth (2007), p. 273 n. 2.
37. Zerbinati, p. 147.
38. Berengan, p. 21.

The Borgia descendants 1520 and after

1. Zerbinati, p. 156.
2. Zerbinati, p. 160.
3. Gorris, p. 142
4. Hollingsworth (2004), p. 233
5. Hollingsworth (2007), p. 271.
6. Hollingsworth (2010), p. 136

INDEX

Page numbers in **bold** denote illustrations.

Major popes are listed under both their personal and papal names, to represent their careers before and after election.

Adimari, Alamanno, Cardinal 16
Adrian VI, Pope (Adrian von Utrecht) 358
Agnadello, Battle of (1509) 341, 342
Alagno, Lucrezia d' 62
Albano 114, 116
Albert II, Emperor 26, 29
Albret, Aimery d', Cardinal 268
Albret, Charlotte d', Duchess of Valence 246, 261, 337, 349
Albret, Henri d', King of Navarre 363, 370, 371
Albret, Jean d', King of Navarre 256, 334
Aldobrandini, Pietro, Cardinal 341, 372
Alègre, Yves d' 251, 256, 274, 345
Alexander V, Antipope 14
Alexander VI, Pope (Rodrigo Borgia) **164**, 174–229, **175**, **227**; actions taken against Orsini clan 212, 213, 216; apartments at the Vatican **171**, 172, **173**, 173, 228, **229**, **304–5**; attributes 165; boosting status and wealth of family 167, 170, 172, 176, 178, 228; coat of arms **229**; coronation 166–7; creation of new cardinals 187, 212, 264, 268, 310; crusade against the Turks 251, 261–2, 264, 269; death and funeral (1503) 311, 313, 320; election 161, 165; financial support for son's military campaign 264, 268, 270, 274; and formation of Holy League 179; and French invasion of Italy (1494) 190, 192, 195–6; mistresses and birth of children 236, 239; money-raising 302, 309; and murder of son (Juan) 222, 224; opinions of 165; papal bulls issued 179, 189, 278, 279; political acumen 187, 228; political alliances 185–7, 198, 200, 204, 239, 240, 243, 245, 246, 270; reorganization of government of Rome 168; and Savonarola 218, 220, 234; survival of mishaps 262–3, 270; treasure of 317; *see also* Borgia, Rodrigo *for career before election.*
Alfonso I, Duke of Ferrara *see* Este, Alfonso I d', Duke of Ferrara
Alfonso I, King of Naples *see* Alfonso V, King of Aragon
Alfonso II, Duke of Ferrara *see* Este, Alfonso II, d', Duke of Ferrara
Alfonso II, King of Naples 128, 132, 141, 143, 146, 147, 189, 190, 190, 201, 239
Alfonso V, King of Aragon (= Alfonso I of Naples) 14–15, **15**, 16, 18, 19, 22, 51, 68, **68**; attack on Genoa 53; conquest of Naples 22, **23**, **28**, 29, 68; death 68–9; reign of 68; relationship with Calixtus III 53, 58, 59, 62, 66
Ambiose, Georges d', Cardinal 239, 240, 243
Amelia 61, 123
Ammanati, Jacopo, Cardinal 95
Ancona 64, 95, 97
Angelico, Fra 35
Anguillara 178, 185, 213
Anguissola, Sofonisba: *Sisters Playing chess* **328**
Anne of Brittany, Queen of France 239, 240, 243, **244**, 359
Aragon, Alfonso, Duke of Bisceglie 239, 263–4
Aragon, Alfonso, Duke of Calabria *see* Alfonso II, King of Naples

Aragon, Carlotta of 239
Aragon, Eleanora of, Duchess of Ferrara 279
Aragon, Federigo of *see* Federigo I, King of Naples
Aragon, Giovanni of, Cardinal 127, 140, 141, 144
Aragon, Isabella of, Duchess of Milan 147
Aragon, Joanna of (daughter of Ferdinand of Aragon) 341
Aragon, Joanna of (sister of Ferdinand of Aragon) 124, 127
Aragon, Juan of, Prince of Asturias 127
Aragon, Luigi of, Cardinal 190
Aragon, Rodrigo of, Duke of Bisceglie 251, 252, 281, 325, 334, 348
Aragon, Sancia of, Princess of Squillace 187, 190, **191**, 192, 213, 224, **308**, 309, 324, 334
Aranda, Pedro de, Bishop of Calahorra 170, 236, 256, 257
Arezzo 298
Ariosto, Ludovico 350
armour **303**
Astorre, Manfredo, Lord of Faenza 269, 296, 298
Aubusson, Pierre d' 129, 149
Aversa, Gasparo, Count of Aversa 167

Baglione, Gianpaolo, Lord of Perugia 269, 301, 306
Bakócz, Thomas, Cardinal 264
Balue, Jean, Cardinal 144
Balzo, Isabella del, Queen of Naples 339
banquets and feasts 87, 90, **91**, 141, 143, 154, 184, 185, **185**, **241**, 281, 283, 292
Barbara of Austria, Duchess of Ferrara 370
Barbo, Marco, Cardinal 103, 140
Barbo, Pietro, Cardinal 33, 52, 66, 71, 95 *see also* Paul II, Pope *for career after election.*
Barcelona 35, 186, 359
Baroncelli, Bandini **128**
Bartolomeo, Fra 220
Basle, Council of (1438) 26
Bazajet, Sultan 149, 183
Beccadelli, Antonio 15
Bélgida 343
Bellini, Gentile 43, 56, 216
Bellini, Giovanni: *The Polyptych of St Vincent Ferrer* **17**
Belriguardo, Villa d'Este 296
Bembo, Pietro, Cardinal 313, 316, **316**, **362**, 363
Bendedio, Battista 254
Benedict XIII, Antipope (Pedro de Luna) 10, 14, 16
Benevento 70, 220
Beninbene, Camilla 184
Bentivoglio, Annibale 292
Bentivoglio, Giovanni, Lord of Bologna 276
Bentivoglio, Hermes 301
Bernardino of Siena, St 36
Bessarion, Cardinal 26, **46**, 49, 52, 97, 112
Bilhères, Jean, Cardinal 250
Bologna 299, 334, 344
Bolsena, Lake 92
Boncompagni, Ugo, Cardinal *see* Gregory XIII, Pope
Boniface VIII, Pope 35
Borgia, Alonso, Cardinal 8–43; as Alfonso V's private secretary and representative

16, 18, 19, 22, 26, 29; appointed Bishop of Majorca 16; attributes 14, 43, 49; birth and education 10; as cardinal 32, **32**, 35, 36, 43; church career 19; university and cathedral posts 14, 16; *see also* Calixtus III *for career after election.*
Borgia, Angela 331
Borgia, Camilla 284, 329, 342, 360
Borgia, Carlos, 5th Duke of Gandia 366
Borgia, Catalina 10
Borgia, Cesare, Cardinal and Duke of Romagna 123, 130, 132, 150, **151**, 152, 167, 170, 178, 187, 200, 201, **260**, **273**, **321**; arrest of and imprisonment 324, 325, 330, 352; collapse of Duchy of Romagna 322, 323, 325, 352; conspiracy against and punishment of conspirators (1502) 301, 302, 303, 306–7; da Vinci's studies of **314–15**; death (1507) 337; and death of father 313, 317; escape from prison (1506) 334; given the Golden Rose 259; ill-health 311; joins the Order of St Michael 245; and Julius II 324, 325, 352; as legate to Naples 220, 226; marriage to Charlotte d'Albret 246; military campaigns in Papal States 251, 252, 254, 256, 268, 269, 274, 276, 278, 296, 298–9, 301, 303, 306, 308; mistress and birth of illegitimate children 284; and murder of Alfonso of Aragon 263, 264; and Pius III 322; relations with father 226–7; resigning of cardinalate 227, 228, 232, 240; stolen goods from the Vatican 324, 325; suspected of murder of brother (Juan) 224
Borgia, Domingo 10
Borgia, Enrique, Cardinal 364
Borgia, Esteban 10
Borgia, Francesco, Prince of Squillace 351
Borgia, Francisca 10
Borgia, Francisco, Cardinal 252
Borgia, Francisco, St (4th Duke of Gandia) 342, **355**, 356, 359, 364, **365**, 366, 367, 369, 370, 371, 372
Borgia, Giovanni (Juan) (son of Alexander VI) 239, 279, 281, 299, 301, 324, 325, 329, 366
Borgia, Giovanni Battista, Prince of Squillace 366
Borgia, Girolama 106, 133, 170
Borgia, Girolamo 284, 329, 363
Borgia, Isabella (daughter of Rodrigo B) 103, 133
Borgia, Isabella (mother of Rodrigo B) 10, 32, 118, 366
Borgia, Jofrè (father of Rodrigo B) 10
Borgia, Jofrè, Prince of Squillace 132, 167, 170, 178, 186, 187, 190, **191**, 192, 212–13, 216, 220, 306, **308**, 334, 351
Borgia, Juan, 2nd Duke of Gandia 124, 170, 183, 186, **186**, 212, 213, 216, 220; murder of 222–4, 228
Borgia, Juan, 3rd Duke of Gandia 341, 342, 363, 364
Borgia, Juan, Cardinal, the elder (nephew of Alexander VI) 129, 133, 167, 170, 178, 190, 192, 196, 198, 204, 212, 252, 310
Borgia, Juan, Cardinal, the younger (great-nephew of Alexander VI) 212, 246, 252, 256

Borgia, Juana 10, 129
Borgia, Louise 261, 349, 351, 360, 367
Borgia, Lucrezia, Duchess of Ferrara 128, 150, 167–8, **168**, 212, 213, 254, 256, **319**, **348**, **350**; affairs 316, 330, 363; appearance and character 168, 320, 350; betrothal to Ludovico Sforza 176; birth of children 251, 330, 337, 339, 341, 349, 350, 351; death and funeral 352; dissolution of marriage to Giovanni Sforza 224, 226, 227; as Duchess of Ferrara 329, 330, 341, 344, 352; family losses 311, 313, 337, 348, 351; governor in Spoleto 246, 251; left in charge of papal affairs during father's absence 279, 280, 281; marriage to Alfonso of Aragon 239; marriage to Alfonso d'Este and arrival in Ferrara 280, 284–5, 286, 287–8, 288, 292, 295; marriage to Giovanni Sforza 179, 183–5; medal of **311**; mirror frame of **356**; miscarriages 244, 337; and murder of husband (Alfonso) 264; puerperal fever contracted after birth of stillborn daughter 301; rumours over depravity 280, 281
Borgia, Pedro Luis, 1st Duke of Gandia 43, 92, 118, 130, 144, 146–7, 170
Borgia, Pedro Luis, Captain-General 56, 61, 66, 67, 70, 71, 74, 77
Borgia, Pedro Luis, Cardinal 268, 324, 344
Borgia, Rodrigo (nephew of Alonso B) 32, 35, 67, 68, 69, 70, 110–72, **111**, **137**; appearance 149; benefices accumulated 132, 134, 140, 150, 160, 172; as Cardinal 56, 64, 67; character and attributes 35, 90, 140; church career and promotions 35, 52, 62, 64, 115, 116, 124, 158; and death of son (Pedro Luis) 146–7; furthering of family's interests 133, 134, 150; illness due to the plague 100; made papal legate to Naples 124, 127; mistresses and birth of children 92, 103, 106, 112, 120, 121, 123, 128, 132, **148**; palace of 87, 143; and Paul II 97, 100; and Pius II 75, 77, 85, 87, 94; relations with Ferdinand of Aragon 118; sent as legate to Spain 116–18, 120, 134; and Sixtus IV 112, 115, 123, 134; survival of storms 93, 94, 118; wealth of 140; *see also* Alexander VI *for career after election.*
Borgia, Rodrigo (great-nephew of Alexander VI) 170
Borgia, Rodrigo Luis, Cardinal 363
Borja, de *see* Borgia
Botticelli, Sandro 126
Bourbon-Busset, Philippe de 360
Bracciano 127, 196, 213, 216, 218
Bregno, Andrea 187
Breughel, Pieter: *The Ripa Grande* **209**
Briçonnet, Guillaume, Cardinal 200
Brisighella 268
bull (Borgia family emblem) 166, **166**, 167, 172, 173, **173**
bullfighting 262, 287
Burchard, Johannes 141, 167, 168, 178, 183, 189, 196–7, 198, 200, 201, 218, 222, 223, 226, 234, 243, 245, 251, 252, 254, 257, **260**, 261, 262, 264, 269–70, 276, 280, 283, 285, 286, 287, 288, 302, 306, 311, 313, 317

Calandrini, Filippo, Cardinal 75
Calchi, Bartolomeo 161
Calderon, Pedro 234
Calixtus III, Pope (Alonso Borgia) 44–71, **45**, 74, 79; and canonization of St Vincent Ferrer 52; coronation 52; creation of new cardinals 53, 56, 61, 62, **63**; crusade against Mehmet II 50, 51, 52–3, 56, 58–9, 64, 68, 71; cuts to papal expenditure 50, 51; deterioration in health and death 69–71, 74; election of as pope (1455) 49; ill-health and gout 61, 69; papal bulls issued 52, 56, 59, 69, 71; as patron of Siena **65**; plain and austere lifestyle 51; promotion of Borgia relatives 56, 61, 62, 71; relationship with Alfonso of Naples 62, 66, 67, 68–9; restoration of authority in the Papal States 61; woodcut of **71**; *see* Borgia, Alonso *for career before election*
Calvin, John 363
Camerino 298, 303
Campagnano 213
Campeggio, Lorenzo, Cardinal 358
Canale, Carlo del 144
cannons 196, **196**, 197
Cantino, Albert **180–1**
Capodimonte 92
Capranica, Angelo, Cardinal 106
Capranica, Domenico, Cardinal 32, 52, 61, 75
Capua 279
Caracciolo, Dorotea 276, 284
Carafa, Giampietro, Cardinal *see* Paul IV, Pope
Carafa, Oliviero, Cardinal 103, 117, 160, 218, 241
Caranza, Pedro 281
Carillo, Alonso, Archbishop of Toledo 106
Carpaccio, Vittore 183; *The Healing of the Possessed Man by the Patriarch of Grado* **265**
Carpi 329, 363
Cartagena, bishopric of 132, 140
Carvajal, Bernardino, Cardinal 325
Carvajal, Juan, Cardinal 52, 90, 106, 116
Casanova, Cardinal Jaime de 313
Castel Bolognese 276
Castel Nuovo (Naples) **24–5**, **28**, 205–6
Castel Sant'Angelo *see under* Rome (buildings)
Castellar, Juan, Cardinal 170, 329
Castellesi, Adriano, Cardinal 310, 311
Castile, Isabella of *see* Isabella of Castile
Castile, Maria of, Queen of Aragon 15, 68
Castro, Eleonora de, Duchess of Gandia 359, 366
Catanzaro 366
Cataneis, Vanozza de' 120, 128, 132, 144, 170, 351
Catherine of Alexandria, St 172, **304–5**, 306
Catherine of Braganza, Queen of England 372
Catherine of Siena, St 10, **12–13**
Centelles, Juan de 150, 167
Cerignola 310
Cerveteri 168, 178, 185
Cervillon, Juan, Captain of the Church 252
Cesarini, Gianandrea 133
Cesarini, Giuliano, Cardinal (1398–1444) 19
Cesarini, Giuliano, Cardinal (1466–1510) 184
Cesena 257, 302, 325
Charles I, Duke of Anjou 24
Charles II, King of England 372
Charles V, Emperor 351, 359, 360, 368
Charles VII, King of France 64, **66**, 189
Charles VIII, King of France 133, 144, 155, **155**, 186, 189–95, **193**, 198, **199**, 200, 235

Châtillon, Odet de, Cardinal 363
Chierigato, Leonello, Bishop of Concordia 189
Chinchilla, fortress of 325, 330
churches *see under city names (buildings)*
Cibò, Franceschetto 146, 149–50, 168
Cibò, Giovanni Battista, Cardinal *see* Innocent VIII, Pope
Cibò, Lorenzo, Cardinal 147
Cibò, Teodorina 184
Cibò, (Usodimare), Battistina 184
Città di Castello 306, 309
Civita Castellana 61, 160, 167, 281
Civitavecchia 71, 77, 240, 295
Claude of France, Queen of France 359
Clement VII, Antipope 10, 14
Clement VII, Pope (Giulio de' Medici) 358, 359, 360
Clement VIII, Antipope 16, 18, 19
Clement VIII, Pope 341, 372
Clement X, Pope 372
Codigoro 322
Coëtivy, Alain, Cardinal 52, 64, 90
Coligny, Gaspar de 371
College of Abbreviators 100, 104
College of Cardinals 33, **33**, 62, 103, 116, 187, 317; ceremonies surrounding appointment of cardinals 62, **63**; conclaves 32, 46, 48, 75, 77, 97, 108, 112, 139, 140, 160–1, 320, 322, 324; creation of new cardinals by popes 53, 62, 85, 103, 116, 147, 187; criticism of by Pius II and reforms 85, 87, 94
Colonna (family) 46, 66, 134, 132, 176, 302, 322
Colonna, Giovanni, Cardinal 167
Colonna, Lorenzo 132
Colonna, Oddo, Cardinal *see* Martin V, Pope
Colonna, Prospero, Cardinal 52
Columbus, Christopher 158, 159, **159**, 168, **169**, 172, 178, 179
Comacchio 322
Condulmer, Gabriel, Cardinal *see* Eugenius IV, Pope
Constance, Council of (1414) 14, 15–16
Constantine, Emperor 30, **31**, 39, **60**, 61, 101, 161
Constantinople 16, 41, **41**, 43, 50, 56, 61
Constantinople, Treaty of (1481) 130
Conti, Giacomo de' 197
Conti, Sigismondo de' 129, 165
Contrari, Uguzone 330
Cordoba, Gonsalvo de, Viceroy of Naples 205, 218, 269, 310, 317, 324, 325
Corella, Miguel de 263, 308, 313, 324
Corner, Marco, Cardinal 264
Corsi family 261
Cossa, Francesco 107; *The Month of April* **346–7**
Costa, Jorge da, Cardinal 160, 228, 241, 280–1
Council of Pisa 344, 345
Council of Trent 367, 369
Croce, Giorgio de 128
crusades: Alexander VI's 251, 261–2, 264, 269; Calixtus III's 50, 51, 52–3, 56, 58–9, 64, 68, 71; Pius II's 94, 95, **96**, 97 ; Sixtus IV's 116, 117, 129, 130
Cusa, Nicholas of, Cardinal 95, 97

da Vinci, Leonardo *see* Leonardo da Vinci
Dianti, Laura 358–9, 372
Diaz, Bartolomeo 159
diet and cooking 22, 29
Diocletian, Emperor 30
Djem, Prince 147, 149, 179–83
Dolce, Luca 263
Dominican Order 17, 218, 220
Donation of Constantine **60**, 61

ducats and florins 117
Dürer, Albrecht: *The Four Horsemen of the Apocalypse* **194**

Eger, Bishopric 150, 167
Elba 295
Eleanor of Portugal, empress 39, **40**
Enrique IV, King of Castile 118, 121
Enriquez, Maria, Duchess of Gandia 144, 186, 224, 343
Ercole I *see* Este, Ercole I d', Duke of Ferrara
Ercole II *see* Este, Ercole II d', Duke of Ferrara
Eroli, Berardo, Cardinal 95
Este, Alessandro d' (son of Alfonso & Lucrezia) 251, 349
Este, Alessandro d' (stillborn son of Alfonso & Lucrezia) 330
Este, Alfonsino d' 359
Este, Alfonso d' (illegitimate son of Alfonso & Laura Dianti) 359
Este, Alfonso I d', Duke of Ferrara 325, 329, 330, 334, 338, 345, **353**, 358; appointed Captain-General of the Church by Julius II (1509) 341; death 360; dismissal of as Captain-General of the Church (1510) 342; excommunication of by Julius II 342; hobbies 350; lifting of excommunication of by Leo X (1513) 349; marriage to Lucrezia 239, 280, 284–5, 286, 288, 292, 295; military interests 352; mistress after Lucrezia's death 358–9; patron of the arts 352; political manoeuvrings 359
Este, Alfonso II, d', Duke of Ferrara 360, 368–9, 370, **371**, 372
Este, Anna d', Duchess of Guise 367, 369, 371
Este, Beatrice d', Duchess of Milan **203**, 204
Este, Borso d', Duke of Ferrara **106**, 107
Este, Cesare d', Duke of Modena 372
Este, Eleonora d' (daughter of Ercole & Renée) 363
Este, Eleonora d', abbess (daughter of Alfonso & Lucrezia) 350, 358, 360
Este, Ercole I d', Duke of Ferrara 192, 204, 256, **279**, 288, 292, 293, 295, 296, 309, 311, 322, 325, 329
Este, Ercole II d', Duke of Ferrara 337, 339, **348**, 352, 358, 359, **360**, 360, 367, 368
Este, Ferrante d' 334
Este, Francesco d' 351, 356
Este, Giulio d' 331, 334
Este, Ippolito d', the elder, Cardinal 284, 287, 308, 309, 344, 352
Este, Ippolito d', the younger, Cardinal (son of Alfonso and Lucrezia) 331, 341, 352, 356, 363, 364, 367–8, **368**, 369, 371
Este, Isabella d', Marchioness of Mantua 292, 296, **298**, 333, 338
Este, Isabella Maria d' 352, 358
Este, Lucrezia d' (daughter of Ercole II) 360
Este, Lucrezia d' (illegitimate daughter of Ercole I) 292
Este, Luigi d', Cardinal 364, 369, 370
Este, Niccolò d', Marquis of Ferrara 82
Este, Niccolò Maria d', Bishop of Adria 286
Este, Renata d', Countess of Mirandola 367
Este, Sigismondo d' 287
Estouteville, Guillaume d', Cardinal 52, 66, 75, **75**, 77, 85, 90, 93, 112, 117, 133
Euffreducci, Oliverotto, Lord of Fermo 301, 303
Eugenius IV, Pope (Gabriel Condulmer) 19, 22, 26, 29, 30, **76**, 79, 97

Faenza 269, 322, 324; siege of (1501) 274, 276

Farnese, Alessandro *see* Paul III, Pope
Farnese, Giulia **148**, 149, 183, 184, 195, 239, 246
Feasts: of All Saints 187; of the Annunciation 79, 257; of the Conversion of St Paul 200; of Corpus Christi 90, 92, 183; of the Epiphany 274; of Pentecost 213; of the Purification of the Virgin 124; of St George 296; of St John the Baptist 262; of St Peter and St Paul 262
Federigo I, King of Naples 170, 176, 216, 220, 226, 239, 244, 279
Feltre, Bernardino da **266–7**
Ferdinand I, King of Aragon 14
Ferdinand II, King of Aragon and Spain 116–17, 118, 127, 143, 152, 154, 159, 169, 179, 185, 243, 246, 270, 310, 325, 351
Ferrante I, King of Naples 26, 29, 68, 69, 77, 103, 123, 128, 130, 132, 143, **144**, 146, 155, 168, 178, 179, 185–7, 189
Ferrante II, King of Naples 201, 204, 205–6, 213, 216
Ferrara 60, 82, 107, 290–1, **290**, 331; bad harvest (1503) 325; Carnival festivities 309; celebrating Feast of St George 296; development of 326; earthquake (1570) 371; food shortages and famine (1505) 330; formal reconciliation between Rome and (1522) 358; joins League of Cambrai (1509) 341; Julius II's campaign against and fortifying against by city 342–3, 344; Lucrezia's arrival in 291, 292; Maundy Thursday ceremony 309; music at court of 338, **338**; plague in 310, 322, 330; plan of **326–7**; siege of (1511) 344, 352
Ferrara (buildings): Castel Tedaldo 292; Cathedral 295, 309, 310, 341, 349; Corpus Domini 301, 342, 358, 360; Palazzo Ducale **293**, 329, **329**; Palazzo della Rosa 359; San Bernardino 342, 360; San Francesco 349; Santa Maria dei Servi 292
Ferrer, Vincent, St 14, 16, 17, **17**, 46, 52
Fiesole, Mino da 74
Filangieri, R. 28
Florence 22, 26, 79, 127, 128, 130, 132, 146, 195, **199**, 276
Florence (buildings): Palazzo Medici 155; Piazza della Signoria 79, 236; **237**; San Marco 97, 232; Santa Maria Novella 79, 155
Florence, Council of (1438) 26, 27, 46
Florès, Antonio 201
Florès, Bartolomeo 197, 201, 226, 240
Foix, Catherine de, Queen of Navarre 256
Foix, Gaston de 124, 288, 345
Foix, Pierre de, Cardinal 18, 19
Foligno 61
Forlì 252, 256, 322
Formello 213
Fornovo, Battle of (1495) 206
Fossombrone 256
Francis I, King of France 350, 351, 359, **361**, 363
Francolino 330
Frederick III, Emperor **2–3**, 29, 39, **40**, 62, 105, 106
Fregoso, Paolo, Cardinal 167

Gabriele da Verona 111
Gaeta 216
Galeria 213
galleys 120, **242**, 243
Gamboa, Pedro de, Bishop of Carignola 254
Gandia: castle at **145**; ducal palace of **343**
Gariglioano, Battle of (1503) 324
Gaspare da Verona 35
Genoa 53, 251, 366
Gherardi, Jacopo 140
Gherardi, Maffei, Cardinal 167

Ghirlandaio, Domenico 126, 158; *Confirmation of the Rule of St Francis* **156–7**; *The Visitation* **233**
Ghislieri, Michele, Cardinal *see* Pius V, Pope
Giorgio, Francesco di 206, **208**, 209, 216, 306, **307**
Giovanni, Benvenuto 10, **12–13**
Girondo, Girolama 342
Giusto, Ser 79
Golden Rose 64, 107, 204, 245, 257, 259
Gonzaga, Elisabetta, Duchess of Urbino **275**, 276, 316
Gonzaga, Francesco, Cardinal 87, 112
Gonzaga, Francesco, Marquis of Mantua 205, **205**, 342
Gonzaga, Ludovico, Marquis of Mantua **83**, 87
Gozzoli, Benozzo: *The Procession of the Magi* **27**
Granada 152, **153**, 154
Granada, Treaty of (1500) 270
Gregory XI, Pope 10, **12–13**, 14
Gregory XII, Pope 14
Gregory XIII, Pope (Ugo Boncompagni) 371
Grimani, Domenico, Cardinal 313
Guagraio di Maso 339
Guicciardini, Francesco 69, 150, 155, 165, 189, 195, 197, 253, 264, 281

Hadrian, Emperor 53
Henry II, King of France 367
Henry VI, Emperor 24
Henry VII, King of England 170
Hispaniola **169**, 172
Holy League 179, 204, 205, 216
Holy Year 35, 261, 274 *see also* Rome: Jubilee
humanists/humanism 104, 105
hunting 331
Hunyadi, John (János) 30, 35, 39

Imola 252, 256; plan of **258**
Index of Forbidden Books 368
Infessura, Stefano 184
Innocent VIII, Pope (Giovanni Batista Cibò) 140–1, 241; alliance with Florence 146; background 142; creation of new cardinals 147; death 158; declares war on Naples 144; deterioration in relation with Ferrante I 147, 149; election and coronation 58, 143, 154; ill-health 58; portrait of 141; reburial of corpse 232; suffers from stroke 149–50; tomb of **142**
Innocent X, Pope (Giambattista Pamphili) 372, **373**
Inter Caetera papal bull 179,
Isabella of Castile, Queen of Spain 79, 116–17, 118, 121, 127, 147, 152, **153**, 154, 159, 169, 185, 243, 246
Ischia 204
Isidore of Kiev, Cardinal 41, 43
Isvalies, Pedro, Cardinal 268

Jaime I, King of Aragon 10, **11**
Játiva 10
Jesuits 356, 364, 366, 367
Jews 35, 154, 185, 187, 240
Joan of Arc 79
Joanna, Queen of Naples 16, 22
John XXIII, Antipope 14
Juan II, King of Aragon 68, 106, 118, 127, 128
Jubilee *see* Rome: Jubilee
Julius II, Pope (Giuliano della Rovere) 325, 334, **335**, 341; action taken against Borgia interests 324, 325, 334; alliance with Venice against the French 342; Council of Pisa called to depose of 344, 345; death (1513) 349; election 324; Ferrara campaign

342, 344, 345, 348; ill-health 342; Vatican apartments 337; *see also* Rovere, Giuliano della *for career before election.*
Julius III, Pope (Giovanni Maria del Monte) 367

Knights of St John 129, 149
Kosovo, Battle of (1448) 35

Lafréry, Antonio: *Speculum Magnificentiae Romanae* **38**
Landi, Ortensio 293
Landucci, Luca 236
Lawrence, St 34, **51**
Laynez, Diego, General of the Jesuits 366, 369, 370
League of Cambria 339, 341, 342, 359
Leo X, Pope (Giovanni de' Medici) 147, 154, 349, 352, 358
Leonardo da Vinci **196**, 300, **300**; 299, 300, 314; bust of a warrior (drawing) **274**; *The Hanging of Baroncelli* **128**; *The Last Supper* **248–9**; oak leaves and acorns (drawing) **262**; plan of Imola **258**; studies of Cesare Borgia **314–15**
Lérida 10, 14
Lignago, Paola da 368
Lithuania, Alexander of, Grand Duke 276
Lolli, Gregorio 93
Lopez, Juan, Cardinal 262
Loreto 95
Loriz, Francisco, Cardinal 170, 310, 334
Lorraine, Francis of, Duke of Guise 367
Louis III, Duke of Anjou 16
Louis XI, King of France 129, 133
Louis XII, King of France 235, **238**, 240, 256, 342, 359; alliance with Alexander VI 239, 240, 243, 245, 246, 270; calls council to depose Julius II 342, 344; commissioning of altarpiece **271**; death 350; marriage to Anne of Brittany 240, 243, 244, **244**, 270; Milan campaign 234, 235, 239, 246, 251, 259; Naples campaign 274, 278–9, 299; popularity of 239; signs Treaty of Granada with Ferdinand II (1500) 270; signs Treaty of the League of Cambrai (1508) 339
Loyola, Ignatius 366, 367
Lucca 251, 310
Luna, Pedro de *see* Benedict XIII, AntiPope
Lunati, Bartolomeo 226, 227
Lunati, Bernardino, Cardinal 226
Luther, Martin 356, 358, 363
Luxembourg, Philippe de, Cardinal 200

Machiavelli, Niccolò 94, 301–2, 317; bust of **301**; *Discorsi*, 132; *The Prince* 152, 260, 301, 309, 322
Magione 301
Majorca, bishopric of 150, 160
Malatesta, Roberto 132
Malatesta, Sigismondo, Lord of Rimini 132
Mantegna, Andrea 82; *Parnassus* **332–3**
Mantua **84**, 341; Congress at (1459) 78, 82, **84–5**
Maradès, Jean, Bishop of Toul 244
Margaret of Austria 359
Marguerite de Valois, Queen of Navarre 370
Marina 322
Marino 187, 195, 201
Martì, Francina 10
Martin V, Pope (Oddo Colonna) 16, 18; tomb of **19**
Martino da Como 29
Masi, Bartolomeo 313
Matuzzi, Pietro 133
Maximilian I, Emperor 155, 165, 204, 251, 339, 344

Maximilian II, Emperor 370
medals, portrait 50, **178**, 179, **244**, **311**
Medici (family) 127, 195
Medici, Catherine de', Queen of France 370–1
Medici, Cosimo de' 27
Medici, Cosimo I de', Duke of Florence 368
Medici, Giovanni Angelo *see* Pius IV, Pope
Medici, Giovanni de', Cardinal *see* Leo X, Pope
Medici, Giulio de', Cardinal *see* Clement VII, Pope
Medici, Lorenzo de' 116, 127, **127**, 128, 146, 147, 154–5, **154**, **156–7**, 158
Medici, Lucrezia de', Duchess of Ferrara 368, 369
Medici, Maddalena de' 146
Medici, Piero de' 27, 195
Medina del Campo 15, 330
Mehmet II, Sultan 41, **42**, 50, 107, 130
Mendoza, Diego Hurtado de, Cardinal 264
Michelangelo, Buonarotti: *Last Judgement* 364; *Pietà* 250, **250**
Michiel, Giovanni, Cardinal 104, 160, 167, 228, 241, 309
Michiel, Niccolò 330
Milà, Adriana de 128, 195
Milà, Juan de, Baron 10
Milà, Luis Juan de, Cardinal 52, 56, 62, 64, 67, 74, 90, 170, 343
Milà, Maria de 334
Milan 53, 60, 101, 128, 130, 132, 147, 167, 170, 178, 204, 218, 234, 235, 251, 257, **307**
Mirandola 344
Mocenigo, Tommaso 330
Modena 342, 359
money 117, **117**
Monferrato 251
Monreale, archbishopric of 310
Monte di Pietà (pawnshops) 267
Monte, Giovanni Maria del, Cardinal *see* Julius III, Pope
Montefeltro, Federigo da, Duke of Urbino 121, 133, 209, 288
Montefeltro, Giovanna da 120
Montefeltro, Guidobaldo da, Duke of Urbino 133, 213, 216, 218, 288, **289**, 298, 299, 303
Montefiascone 195
Monterotondo 212
Morton, John, Cardinal 204
Murat II, Sultan 30, 35
music/musical instruments **338**, 339, **339**

Naples 16, 22, **24–5**, 61, 69, 77, 155, 189, 270; Alfonso V's conquest of 28, **28**, 29; alliance with Milan 53, 147; conquering of by Charles VIII 204; Louis XII's campaign against 274, 278–9, 299; reconquering of by Ferrante II 205–6; Spanish conquest of (1503) 324; wars with Rome 143, 144
Nardini, Stefano, Cardinal 123
Narni 61, 124
Nepi 61, 160, 167, 251, 264, 281
Nicholas III, Pope 126
Nicholas V, Pope (Tomaso Parentucelli) 32, 34, 35, 39, 41, 43, 50
Nocera 61
Novara 259

Ochino, Bernardino 363
Oliva, Alessandro, Cardinal 90
Olivier, Richard, Cardinal 116
Olomouc, bishopric 178
Order of St Michael 245

Orsini (family) 66, 218, 309; Alexander VI's campaign against 212, 213, 216, 218; conspiracy against Cesare and punishment of after failure 301–2, 303, 306–7; rivalry with Colonna family 46, 66, 132, 134
Orsini, Carlo 218, 259
Orsini, Francesco, Duke of Gravina 303, 308
Orsini, Gianantonio, Prefect of Rome 66
Orsini, Giangordano 213
Orsini, Giovanni Battista, Cardinal 140, 306, 308–9
Orsini, Giulio 306
Orsini, Latino, Cardinal 52, 66
Orsini, Ludovico, Lord of Bassanello 128, 149
Orsini, Niccolò, Count of Pitigliano and Captain-General of the Church 149
Orsini, Orsino 149
Orsini, Paolo 269, 303, 308
Orsini, Virginio 168, 176, 186, **210–11**, 212, 213
Orsini Castle (Bracciano) 212, 213, 216, 218
Orvieto 61, 187, 204
Ostia **70**, 93, 218, 220, 325
Otranto 129, 130

Pallavicini, Antoniotto, Cardinal 183, 226, 295, 302
Palos 158, 159, 178
Palozzi, Pietro 220
Pamphili, Giambattista, Cardinal *see* Innocent X, Pope
papacy: establishment of the Vatican as official residency of 34; and Great Schism 10, 14, 19; opulent lifestyles of popes 165; restoration of to Rome 16, 18; ritual of elections 48; *see also individual popes*
papal coronation and *possesso* 53, 115
Papal States, history of 61
Parentucelli, Tomaso, Cardinal *see* Nicholas V, Pope
Paul II, Pope (Pietro Barbo): creation of new cardinals 103, 104; criticism of humanism 104, 108; death 108; election 97; expensive tastes 100, 101; food tastes 108; plot to assassinate (1468) 104; receives Frederick III 105; reform of College of Abbreviators 100, 104, 108; tomb of **109**; treasure and antiquities collected by 97, 108, 115, **245**; *see also* Barbo, Pietro *for career before election.*
Paul III, Pope (Alessandro Farnese) 187, 257, 360, 363, 364, 366, 367
Paul IV, Pope (Giampietro Carafa) 267–8, 368
Pavia, Battle of (1525) 359
Pazzi Conspiracy (1478) 127, **127**, 128
Peñiscola 16, 19
Perugia 306
Perugino, Pietro 126; *Battle of Love and Chastity* **282–3**; *Christ Giving the Keys of the Church of St Peter* **162–3**
Pesaro 256, 269, 322, 343
Pesaro, Jacopo 176, **177**
Peter III, King of Aragon and Sicily 24
Philip II, King of Spain 368
Piacenza 192, 260
Piazza *see* city names (buildings)
Piccolomini, Enea Silvio, Cardinal 62, **63**, 64, 66, 68, 74, 75, **76**, 141 *see also* Pius II, Pope *for career after election*
Piccolomini, Francesco, Cardinal *see* Pius III, Pope
Pico, Luigi, Lord of Mirandola 367
Pienza 78, 79; Palazzo Piccolomini **78**

Pinturicchio, Bernardo 40, 62, 74, 77, 97, 126, 165, 186; *Disputation of St Catherine of Alexandria* 186, 304–5, 308
Pio, Alberto, Lord of Carpi 329
Piombino 276, 278–9, 295–6
Pisa, Cathedral of 124, **125**
Pisa, Council of (1409) 14
Pisanello 28; drawing of a cheetah **331**
Pitigliano 184, 187
Pius II, Pope (Eneo Silvio Piccolomini) 48, **73**, 77, 320; background of 77, 79; cope of **93**; creation of new cardinals 85, 87; criticism of College of Cardinals and reform of 85, 87, 94; and crusade 94, 95, **96**, 97; death 97; election 75; ill-health and gout 78, 79, 95, 97; literary work 79; and Mantua congress 78–82, 84–5; and restoration of Corsignano (Pienza) 78, 79; *Secret Memoirs (Commentaries)* 50, 53, 62, 77, 82, 85, 92, 94; *see also* Piccolomini, Eneo Silvio *for career before election.*
Pius III, Pope (Francesco Piccolomini) 320–1, 322
Pius IV, Pope (Giovanni Angelo Medici) 368, 369, 370
Pius V, Pope (Michele Ghislieri) 370, 371
plague outbreaks 37, 39, 61, 92, 95, 100, 104, 123, 127, 143, 187, 192
Platina (Bartolomeo Sacchi) 58, 103, 104, 108, 114, 121, **122**, 123
Plautus: *Epidicus* 292, 295
Podocatharo, Ludovico, Cardinal 268
Poggio Imperiale 128
Ponte Sant'Angleo *see under* Rome (buildings)
Porcari, Stefano 39
Porta, Ardicino della, Cardinal 160
Porto 115, 116, 124, 140, 160, 167
Porto Ercole 296
Portugal, Eleanor of *see* Eleanor of Portugal, Empress
Portugal, Prince Jaime of, Cardinal 56
Prie, René, Cardinal 342
Protestantism/Protestants: conflict with Catholics in France 369, 370, 371; in Italy 363, 364
Puglia 195

Raphael 274, 288, 316, 334, **335**; *Girl with a Unicorn* **148**; *St George Slaying the Dragon* **297**
Ravenna, Battle of (1512) 345, 348
Reggio Emilia 360
René, Duke of Anjou 22
Renée of France, Duchess of Ferrara 359, 360, 363, 367, 369
Rhodes, siege of (1480) 129, 149
Riario, Girolamo, Lord of Imola and Forlì 130, 132, 138, 144, 146
Riario, Pietro, Cardinal 116, 120
Riario, Raffaello, Cardinal 123, 127
Rieti 61, 263
Rignano, Domenico da 121
Rimini 269, 322, 324; Arch of Augustus **269**
Rohan, Pierre de, Maréchal of France 197
Roma, Cola da: *Madonna of the Raccomandati* **231**, 232, **235**
Romagna, Duchy of 239, 246, 252, 257, 268, 270, 280, 284, 300, 317, 320, 322
Rome 18; alliance with Milan 167, 170; bad winter (1499) 243; Carnival in 101, 103, 244, 259, 276, 285–6, 306; flooding of Tiber 123, 206, 209, 212, 269–70; French arrival in 197–8, 204; joins League of Cambrai (1509) 341; Jubilee 35, 36–7, **36**, 123, 252, 256; malaria outbreak

(1502) 310; plague outbreaks 37, 39, 61, 68, 100, 104, 123, 127, 143, 187, 192; plan of **20–1**; restoration of city by papacy 18, 19, 22, 34, 114; revolution against papal rule (1434) 22; riots (1484) 134, 138; runaway horses disaster (1450) 37–9; sacking of by Charles V's troops (1527) 359; Seven Churches of (map) 38; state entries into 147; view of old **222**; war with Florence 127, 128; war with Naples (1485-6) 143, 144, 146; war with Naples, Florence and Milan (1482) 132–3
Rome (buildings): Arch of Diocletian 150; Arch of Domitian (= Arch of Marcus Aurelius 101, 103, **103**); Arch of Septimius Severus 284, **285**; Benediction Loggia 49; Campo dei Fiori 52, 140, 147, 213, **222**, 244, 286; Capitol 154, 201, 220; Castel Sant'Angelo 53, 56, 70, **104**, 105, 138, 196, 212, 227; Colosseum 43, 115, 173, 213; Corso 101; Gesù 366; Golden House of Nero 173; Isola Tiberina (Isola San Bartolomeo) 270; Monte Testaccio 103, 259; Ospedale degli Schiavoni 223; Palazzo dei Conservatori 220; Palazzo Massimi 262; Palazzo Montegiordano 52, 128; Palazzo Venezia **95**, 97, 108; Piazza Navona 114, **222**, 244, 287; Piazza Santa Maria del Popolo **88–9**; Ponte Sant'Angelo 53, **54–5**, **131**; Porta San Giovanni 123; St Peter's 34, 35, 36, **36**, 37, **38**, 39, 90, **161**, 259; San Celso 38, 39; San Clemente 115; San Giacomo degli Spagnoli 154, 351; San Giovanni in Laterano 37, **38**, 39, 52, **101**, 259; San Girolamo degli Schiavoni 223; San Lorenzo in Damaso 57; San Lorenzo fuori le mura **38**, 39; San Lorenzo in Lucina 101; San Marco 97, 103; San Nicola in Carcere 62; San Pietro in Vincola 220; San Poalo fuori le mura 37, 38, **39**, 130, 259; San Sebastiano **38**, 39; San Sisto 220; Santa Croce in Gerusalemme **38**, 39; Santa Maria in Aquiro 364; Santa Maria del Popolo 187, **188**; Santa Maria Maggiore 35, 37, **38**, 39, **133**, 178, 226, 259; Santa Maria sopra Minerva 32, 179, 189, 257; Santa Maria in Via Lata 77, 150, 167; Sant'Agostino 74; Sant'Eustachio 53; Santi Quattro Coronati 30, **30**, **31**, 43, 53, 60, 62; Stadium of Domitian 114; Tempietto **323**; Tor di Nona 209; Vatican *see* Vatican; Via Banco di Santo Spirito 115; Via del Governo Vecchio 115; Via Papalis 115
Ronda 143
Rosselli, Cosimo 126
Rovere, Domenico della, Cardinal 183, 204, 263, 264
Rovere, Francesco della, Cardinal *see* Sixtus II, Pope
Rovere, Giovanni della, Lord of Senigallia 121, 141
Rovere, Girolama Basso della, Cardinal 228
Rovere, Giuliano della, Cardinal 116, 120–1, 123, 134, 138, 140–1, 144, 158, 172, 186, 187, 190, 240, 322, 324; *see also* Julius II, Pope *for career after election*
Rucellai, Giovanni 37

Sacrofano 213
St-Germain, Treaty of (1570) 370
Saluzzo, Giorgio di, Bishop of Lausanne 56
San/Santa/Santi *see under* city names (buildings) for churches
San Felice 325
San Quirico Val d'Orcia 308
Sänftl, Sigismund 165

Sangiorgio, Giovanni Antonio, Cardinal 226, 243, 313
Sannazaro, Jacopo 352
Sanseverino, Federigo, Cardinal 243, 295, 342
Sardinas, Alfonso 205
Sarteano 308
Savanuzo, Jacomo 339
Savelli, Giovanni Battista, Cardinal 132, 167
Savona 120
Savonarola, Fra Girolamo 195, 206, 216, 218, 220, **221**, 228, 232, 234, 236, **237**
Savoy 17, 192
Savoy, Bona of, Duchess of Milan 124, 146
Savoy, Louise, Duchess of Angoulême 349, 350
Saxony, Frederick III, Duke of 256
Schiavo, Giorgio 223
Sclafenati, Giangiacomo, Cardinal 143, 167
Sebastian, King of Portugal 370
Senigallia 303, 306
Seripando, Girolamo, Cardinal 363
Sermoneta 256, 279
Serra, Jaime, Cardinal 170, 268, 351
Sforza, Ascanio, Cardinal 134, 140, 141, 144, 155, 158, 160, 161, 167, 189, 195, 224, 226, 246, 251, 259–60
Sforza, Caterina 120, 138, **139**, 146, 252, 256
Sforza, Costanzo, Lord of Pesaro 343
Sforza, Francesco, Duke of Milan 47, 49, 53, 71, 84, 85, 101
Sforza, Galeazzo Maria, Duke of Milan 101, **102**, 120, 124, 146
Sforza, Giangaleazzo, Duke of Milan 124, 128, 146, 147, 192
Sforza, Giovanni, Lord of Pesaro **178**, 183, 212, 218, 224, 228, 256, 269, 322, 325, 343
Sforza, Ippolita, Duchess of Calabria 53
Sforza, Ludovico, Duke of Milan 128, 134, 144, **146**, 176, 189, 192, **202**, 234, 251, 256, 257, 259
Sherwood, John, Bishop of Durham 170
Sicily 22, 24, 53, 204
Siena 64; Calixtus III as patron **65**
Sigismund, Emperor 14, 22, 26
Signorelli, Luca 126, 276; *Preaching of the Antichrist* **255**
Silvester I, Pope 30, **61**
Sistine Chapel *see* Vatican
Sixtus II, Pope **34**, 112
Sixtus IV, Pope (Francesca della Rovere) **113**, **122**; advances own family interests 116, 120, 121, 123, 130; background 114; creation of new cardinals 116, 127, 129, 134; crowning of 115; and crusade against the Turks 116, 117, 129, 130; death 134, 138; ill-health and gout 133; promotion of traditional Christian views 112, 114, 126; tomb of **135**; transformation of Rome 114
Soriano, Battle of (1497) 216
Spanish Inquisition 118, 246
Spoleto 61, 95, 121, 246
Squillace 226, 372
Staglia, Saba 205
Subiaco, abbey 115, 281
swords/daggers **200**, **256**, **263**
syphilis 253

Tavola Strozzi panel **24–5**, **242**
Tazza Farnese (cameo) **245**
Tebaldi, Jacopo, Cardinal 90
Terni 61, 95
Terracina, Treaty of (1442) 29
Tiber 70, 209; flooding of 123, 206, 269–70
Titian 298, 360, **361**, **362**, 363; *The Andrians* **86**; *Horseman Falling* **336**;

Sacred and Profane Love **294**; *The Worship of Venus* **340**; *Young Woman at Her Toilet* **358**
Tivoli 68, 366
Todi 61, 95, 121
Tordesillas, Treaty of (1494) 180
Torquemada, Juan, Cardinal 90, 97
Toscanelli, Paolo 159
tournaments **80–1**, 82
Trajan, Emperor 15
Trasimeno, Lake 92, 301
Trémouille, Louis de la 351, 359
Trevisan, Ludovico, Cardinal 29, 52, 53, 56, 58, 59, 64, 97, 100
Treviso, Girolamo da: *Four Evangelists Stoning the Pope* **357**
Triumph of Death (fresco) **125**
Trivulzio, Antonio, Cardinal 264
Tromboncino, Bartolomeo 338
Troy, War of (tapestry) **98–9**
Turin 192

Urban VI, Pope 14
Urbino 298, **299**, 301, 303, 324
Urrea, Pedro de, Archbishop of Tarragona 52, 53, 56
Utrecht, Adrian von, Cardinal *see* Adrian VI, Pope

Valdigne, abbey 77, 160
Valencia 10, 35, 94, 118, 160, 328
Valladolid 368
Varano, Giulio Cesare, ruler of Camerino 298
Vatican **49**, 114; Borgia Apartments **171**, 172, 173, **173**, 228, **229**, 304–5, 306; establishment of as official residency of 34; Library **114**, 122; Sistine Chapel 114, 124, 126, **126**, 127, 133, **162–3**, 364
Venice 130, 132, **214–15**, 269, 276, 339, 341, 342
Vera, Juan, Cardinal 268
Vermigli, Pietro 363
Vespasiano da Bisticci 34, 51
Villeneuve, Louis, baron de Trans 240
Virgen de los Caballeros, The (altarpiece) **225**
Virgin of the Catholic Kings (altarpiece) **119**
Virgin and Child with St Jerome and Bernardino de Feltre **266–7**
Visconti, Bianca Maria, Duchess of Milan **236**
Visconti, Filippo Maria, Duchess of Milan 22
Visconti, Giangaleazzo, Duke of Milan 124, 128, 234
Visconti, Valentina, Duchess of Orléans 234
Vitelli, Niccolò, Lord of Città di Castello 309
Vitelli, Vitellozzo, Lord of Città di Castello 216, 269, 276, **277**, 278, 279, 298, 301, 303, 306
Viterbo 90, 92

Xavier, Francis 366

Zambotti, Bernardino: *Diario Ferrarese* 206, 254, 268, 292, 299, 310, 313, 325
Zen, Giovanni Battista, Cardinal 104, 183, 278
Zerbinati, Giovanni Maria (and *Croniche di Ferrara*) 334, 339, 342, 344, 345, 349

PICTURE CREDITS

SCALA, FLORENCE © 2011 Photo Scala, Florence 1, 12–13, 19, 31, 34, 51, 60–1, 78, 86, 93, 106, 111, 114, 122, 125, 128, 135, 156–7, 159, 162–3, 166, 168, 171, 173, 186, 207, 208, 210–1, 217, 229, 277, 282–3, 297, 300, 301, 304–5, 307, 308, 326–7, 335, 346–7, 368 ; courtesy of the Ministero Beni e Att. Culturali 24–5, 47, 65, 80–81, 83, 102, 146, 148, 155, 180–1, 182, 194, 198–9, 202, 203, 205, 214–5, 221, 236, 237, 248–9, 265, 275, 285, 289, 294–5, 312, 323, 362, 371; Photo Dietmar Katz, BPK, Bildagentur für Kunst, Kultur und Geschichte, Berlin 38; Photo Opera Metropolitana Siena 40, 73, 76, 96; White Images 41, 193, 247, 332–3, 361; Photo Ann Ronan/ Heritage Images 58; Heritage Images/ Scala 68; Image copyright The Metropolitan Museum of Art/ Art Resource 75; BPK, Bildagentur für Kunst, Kultur und Geschichte, Berlin 101, 319, 350; Photo The Philadelphia Museum of Art/Art Resource 129; Fondo Edifici di Culto – Min. dell'Interno – Dipartimento per le Libertà civili e l'Immigrazione – Direzione Centrale per l'Amministrazione del Fondo Edifici di Culto 161, 188, 233; Photo The Print Collector/ Heritage-Images 169; Luciano Romano 190; Photo Pierpont Morgan Library/ Art Resource 191; Copyright The National Gallery, London 266–7, 338; Photo Austrian Archives 298; The Museum of Fine Arts Budapest 316.

WORCESTER ART MUSEUM, Worcester, Massachusetts, museum purchase 2–3

PHOTO12.COM Oronoz 9, 32, 225.

BRIDGEMAN ART LIBRARY J. Paul Getty Museum, Los Angeles, USA/ Index 11; San Giovanni e Paolo, Venice, Italy 17; Piccolomini Library, Duomo, Siena, Italy/ Ghigo Roli 33; National Gallery, London, UK 42; Louvre, Paris, France/ Giraudon 46, 66, 113, 358; Private Collection/ The Stapleton Collection 95; Palazzo Ducale, Mantua, Italy 84; Fitzwilliam Museum, University of Cambridge, UK 117; Prado, Madrid, Spain/ Index 119; Private Collection/ Elizabeth Harvey-Lee 121; Museo e Gallerie Nazionale di Capodimonte, Naples, Italy/ Giraudon 133; Palazzo Medici-Riccardi, Florence, Italy 154; The Royal Collection © 2011 Her Majesty Queen Elizabeth II 196, 238, 258, 262, 357; © Wallace Collection, London, UK 200–1, 263, 303 (top); © Devonshire Collection, Chatsworth/ Reproduced by permission of Chatsworth Settlement Trustees 209; Private Collection 222, 253; Palazzo Ducale, Urbino, Italy 299; Galleria dell' Accademia Carrara, Bergamo, Italy 321; Louvre, Paris, France 331; Prado, Madrid, Spain/ Giraudon 340; Galleria e Museo Estense, Modena, Italy 360; Galleria Doria Pamphilj, Rome, Italy/ Alinari 373.

PHOTOAISA CAGP/ Iberfoto 15; Electa/ Leemage 175, 227; M.C. Esteban/ Iberfoto 260; BeBa/ Iberfoto 273; J. Bedmar/ Iberfoto 343.

BRITISH LIBRARY, LONDON 20–1, 23.

V&A IMAGES, VICTORIA AND ALBERT MUSEUM 26, 98–9, 127, 149, 226, 244, 256, 270–1, 286, 287, 320, 356.

THE ART ARCHIVE Medici Riccardi Chapel Florence/ Collection Dagli Orti 27; Pinacoteca Nazionale di Siena/ Gianni Dagli Orti 45; Isabella Stewart Gardner Museum Boston/ Superstock 57; Piccolomini Library Siena/ Gianni Dagli Orti 63; Museo Nazionale Palazzo Altemps Rome/ Gianni Dagli Orti 91; Miramare Museum Trieste / Collection Dagli Orti 151; Royal Chapel Granada Spain/ Gianni Dagli Orti 153; Biblioteca Estense Modena/ Collection Dagli Orti 183, 353; Malpaga Castello Bergamo Italy/ Collection Dagli Orti 185; Museo Diocesano Orta/ Gianni Dagli Orti 231, 235; Villa Caldogno Pagello Caldogno Italy/ Gianni Dagli Orti 241; Museo di Capodimonte, Naples/ Collection Dagli Orti 242; Galleria Estense, Modena/ Gianni Dagli Orti 279; The Art Archive 291; Gianni Dagli Orti 339.

AKG–IMAGES Tristan Lafranchis 28; Erich Lessing 30, 137, 144, 164, 177, 303 (bottom); akg–images 36, 49, 54–5, 131, 269; Pirozzi 88–9; André Held 142; Electa 314–5; album / oronoz 355, 365.

TOPFOTO The Granger Collection 50; Topfoto 70; Alinari 109, 126; Print Collector/ HIP 336.

ALAMY Interfoto 71, 348; The Art Archive 245; The Art Gallery Collection 328.

GETTY IMAGES Photo by Herbert Orth/ Time Life Pictures 104; DEA/ A. De Gregorio 290, 329.

MARY EVANS PICTURE LIBRARY Finsiel/ Alinari Archives – reproduced with the permission of Ministerio per I Beni e Att. Culturali 139, Interfoto/ Sammlung Rauch 219.

AGE FOTOSTOCK © Barbara Boensch 145.

BRITISH MUSEUM © The Trustees of the British Museum 178, 261, 274, 311.

CORBIS Laurie Chamberlain 250; Sandro Vannini 255.

SUPERSTOCK © imagebroker.net 293.

METRO BOOKS
New York

An Imprint of Sterling Publishing
387 Park Avenue South
New York, NY 10016

METRO BOOKS and the distinctive Metro Books logo are trademarks of Sterling Publishing Co., Inc.

© 2011 by Mary Hollingsworth

This 2011 edition published by Metro Books by arrangement with Quercus Publishing plc.

PROJECT MANAGER AND EDITOR
Mark Hawkins-Dady
PICTURE RESEARCHER
Caroline Hotblack
DESIGNER
Hugh Adams / AB3 Design
CARTOGRAPHER
William Donohoe
PROOFREADER
Carol Maxwell
INDEXER
Patricia Hymans

AUTHOR'S ACKNOWLEDGEMENTS
Many people have collaborated in the preparation of this book. In particular, I would like to thank Slav Todorov at Quercus for commissioning the text, Caroline Hotblack for her hard work in finding the illustrations, Hugh Adams the designer, cartographer Bill Donohoe (for his skill in deciphering my instructions) and Mark Hawkins-Dady, editor and project manager, for his efficiency, wit and unfailing good humour. Finally, I would like to thank my agent, Andrew Lownie, for his support.

This book is dedicated to WLS

ISBN 978–1–4351–3437–9

For information about custom editions, special sales, and premium and corporate purchases, please contact Sterling Special Sales at 800-805-5489 or specialsales@sterlingpublishing.com

Manufactured in China

10 9 8 7 6 5 4 3 2

www.sterlingpublishing.com